Dún Ailinne

Excavations at an Irish Royal Site, 1968–1975

University Museum Monograph 129

Dún Ailinne

Excavations at an Irish Royal Site, 1968–1975

Susan A. Johnston and Bernard Wailes

with contributions from
Pam J. Crabtree, Douglas V. Campana, Ronald Hicks, Katherine Moreau, Elizabeth Hamilton, and *G. C. Fisher*

UNIVERSITY OF PENNSYLVANIA MUSEUM OF ARCHAEOLOGY AND ANTHROPOLOGY

Philadelphia
Copyright © 2007 University of Pennsylvania Museum of Archaeology and Anthropology
3260 South Street, Philadelphia, PA 19104-6324

All Rights Reserved

First Edition

Permission to publish the material from the National Folklore Collection is acknowledged to Professor Séamas Ó Catháin, Head of the University College Dublin School of Irish, Celtic Studies, Irish Folklore and Linguistics.

Research to prepare this manuscript funded in part by the Heritage Council.

LIBRARY OF CONGRESS CATALOGING-IN-PUBLICATION DATA

Johnston, Susan A. (Susan Ann), 1958-
  Dún Ailinne : excavations at an Irish royal site, 1968-1975 / Susan A. Johnston and Bernard Wailes ; with contributions from Pam J. Crabtree ... [et al.]. — 1st ed.
      p. cm. — (University Museum monograph ; 129)
  Includes bibliographical references and index.
  ISBN 978-1-931707-99-2 (hardcover with cd : alk. paper)
  1. Dún Ailinn Site (Ireland) 2. Iron age—Ireland—Kildare (County) 3. Fortifications, Prehistoric—Ireland—Kildare (County) 4. Excavations (Archaeology)—Ireland—Kildare (County) 5. Kildare (Ireland : County)—Antiquities. I. Wailes, Bernard. II. University of Pennsylvania. Museum of Archaeology and Anthropology. III. Title.
  GN780.22.I73J65 2007
  936.1'5--dc22
                                            2007013793

Printed in the U.S. on acid-free paper.

Contents

Illustrations ix
Tables xv
Preface and Acknowledgments xix
Chronological Chart xxiv
Summary of the Excavation, *Bernard Wailes* xxv

1. Excavation Strategy, *Bernard Wailes* 1
   - The Site 1
   - Aerial Photographs 1
   - Descriptions prior to 1968 1
   - The "Royal Sites" in 1968 3
   - The Initial Exploratory Season, 1968 4
   - The Perimeter Bank and Ditch 4
   - The 1968 Exploratory Season: Conclusion 5
   - Excavation: Methods 5
   - Excavation: Some Interpretative Issues 6

2. Excavation of the Summit Area, *Bernard Wailes* 9
   - Blue Phase (Layer) 11
   - Neolithic and Bronze Age: Tan Phase (Features) 11
   - Neolithic and Bronze Age: Khaki (Features) 12
   - Iron Age Features 13
   - White Phase 13
   - Rose Phase 13
   - Lemon Phase 16
   - Mauve Phase 16
   - Iron Age Layers/Surfaces 19
   - Miscellaneous Features of Unknown Date 21
   - Post-Iron Age Activities 22
   - The Iron Age Summit Sequence: Review and Discussion 22
   - The Summit Area: Summary and Interpretation 24

3. Perimeter Survey and Excavation, *Bernard Wailes* 27
   - Bank and Ditch: Survey 27
   - Bank and Ditch: Excavation 27
   - Entrance Area: Survey and Excavation 28
   - Perimeter: Chronology 29

4. Features and Artifacts Summary, *Susan A. Johnston* 31
   - General Distribution of Features 31
   - General Summary of Features 31
   - Artifact Associations 32
   - Neolithic 34

	Bronze Age	38
	Iron Age	38
	Missing and Discarded Artifacts	41
5.	Lithic Remains, *Susan A. Johnston*	45
	General Context: Flint, Chert, and Quartz	45
	Implements	48
	Unretouched Flakes	63
	Raw Material	66
	Chronology and Context	67
	Parallel Sites	68
	Stone Axes	69
6.	Ceramics, *Susan A. Johnston*	73
	Neolithic Pottery	73
	Linkardstown Vessel	74
	Other Neolithic Pottery	76
	Typological Parallels	80
	Parallel Sites	80
	Food Vessel	81
	Clay Pin	83
7.	Iron, *Susan A. Johnston*	85
	General Context	86
	Description, Iron Objects	88
8.	Non-ferrous Metals	101
	Copper Alloy: Introduction, *Susan A. Johnston*	101
	Report On Copper Alloy Objects, *G. C. Fisher*	102
	Gold, *Susan A. Johnston*	112
	Gold Decorative Strip, *G. C. Fisher*	113
9.	Glass, *Susan A. Johnston*	115
	General Characteristics	115
	Description	117
	Glass Working?	122
	Parallel Sites and Chronology	122
10.	Worked Bone, *Pam J. Crabtree and Douglas V. Campana*	125
	Catalog of Worked Bone Objects	125
	Conclusions	131
11.	Miscellaneous Objects, *Susan A. Johnston*	133
	Cupmarked Stone	133
	Lignite Objects	134
	Rounded Stone and Clay Objects	135
	Stone Beads	137
	Spindle Whorls	141
	Whetstones	142
	Uncertain Objects	143
	Probable Natural Objects	143
12.	Specialist Analyses	145
	Slag, *Susan A. Johnston*	145
	Report on the Slag from Dún Ailinne, *Elizabeth G. Hamilton*	145

	Metallography of Bronze Artifacts, *Katherine Moreau*	147
	Metallography of Iron Artifacts, *Katherine Moreau*	152
	Floral Remains from Dún Ailinne, *Pam J. Crabtree*	155
13.	Biological Remains, *Pam J. Crabtree*	157
	Mammal Remains	157
	Materials and Methods	157
	Composition of the Faunal Sample	158
	Species Ratios	159
	Body Part Distributions	160
	Kill Patterns	161
	Measurement	164
	Butchery	165
	Bone Working	167
	Dairying in the Iron Age: An Alternative Approach	165
	Conclusions	168
14.	Medieval and Modern Objects, *Susan A. Johnston*	171
15.	Chronology, *Susan A. Johnston*	177
	Artifact Dates	177
	Absolute Dates	178
16.	Dún Ailinne's Role in Folklore, Myth, and the Sacred Landscape, *Ronald Hicks*	183
	Folklore	183
	Myth	184
	Assembly Sites	186
	The Larger Ritual Landscape	188
	The Ritual Year	189
	Female Figures at the Assembly Sites and Their Festival Roles	191
	Astronomical Aspects of the Sites and Landscape	191
	Summary and Conclusions	193
17.	The Larger Archaeological Context, *Susan A. Johnston*	195
	The Royal Sites of Ireland	195
	Other Royal Sites?	199
	Other Parallels	199
18.	The Social and Cultural Context of Dún Ailinne, *Susan A. Johnston*	201
	Neolithic	201
	Bronze Age	202
	Iron Age	202
	What Kind of Ritual?	203
	Relations of Power?	206
	Directions for Future Research	209
References Cited		211
Contributors		227
Index		229

Illustrations

FIGURES—THOSE NOTED ARE ON THE ACCOMPANYING CD

I-1	Contour map, Knockaulin Hill	xxvi
I-2	Distribution map, the royal sites of Ireland	xxvii
1-1	Site plan showing excavated areas and major landmarks	2
1-2	John O'Donovan's plan from 1837	3
2-1	Major features on the summit area	CD
2-2	Reference plan, North Sheet	CD
2-3	Reference plan, West Sheet	CD
2-4	Reference plan, Northeast Sheet	CD
2-5	Reference plan, South Sheet	CD
2-6	Section drawing, cutting through the summit area	CD
2-7	Features associated with the Blue phase	CD
2-8	Features associated with the Tan and Khaki phases	CD
2-9	Features associated with the White phase	CD
2-10	Features associated with the Rose phase	CD
2-11	Possible reconstruction of Rose phase viewing platform	14
2-12	Line of stake-holes and post-holes southeast of the Rose phase annex	15
2-13	Possible reconstruction of the Rose phase structures	16
2-14	Features associated with the Mauve and Harry phases	CD
2-15	Section, Feature 30 (post-hole)	CD
2-16	Possible reconstruction of Mauve phase structures	18
2-17	Features associated with the Jade surface	CD
2-18	Features associated with the Niamh surface	CD
2-19	Features associated with the pre-Niamh surface	CD
2-20	Features associated with the Lower Emerald surface	CD
2-21	Features associated with the Upper Emerald surface	CD
2-22	Features associated with the Dun surface	CD
2-23	Flame phase scatter of burned material	CD
3-1	Section of bank and ditch	CD
3-2	Plan of original site entrance	CD
4-1	Distribution, number of artifacts per feature	33
4-2	Number of artifacts in possible Neolithic features	35
4-3	Distribution, Neolithic features	CD
4-4	Distribution, Neolithic artifacts	CD
4-5	Distribution, Neolithic ceramics and lithics	CD
4-6	Distribution, stone axes	CD
4-7	Distribution, Iron age artifacts	CD
4-8	Distribution, Mauve phase artifacts	CD
5-1	Distribution, lithic artifacts by phase	47
5-2	Leaf-shaped projectile points from Dún Ailinne	48
5-3	Leaf-shaped projectile points from Dún Ailinne	50
5-4	Projectile points from Dún Ailinne, other types	51

5-5	Three unusual projectile points from Dún Ailinne	51
5-6	Uncertain projectile points from Dún Ailinne	52
5-7	Round scrapers from Dún Ailinne	53
5-8	Round scrapers from Dún Ailinne	54
5-9	Round scrapers from Dún Ailinne	55
5-10	Round scrapers, length by width	55
5-11	Scrapers from Dún Ailinne, other types	56
5-12	Hollow scrapers from Dún Ailinne	57
5-13	Hollow scrapers from Dún Ailinne	58
5-14	Three unusual scrapers from Dún Ailinne	59
5-15	Borers from Dún Ailinne	60
5-16	Implements from Dún Ailinne, uncertain types	60
5-17	Cores from Dún Ailinne	61
5-18	Cores, length by width	62
5-19	Distribution, lithic groups	CD
5-20	Stone axes from Dún Ailinne	69
6-1	Distribution, Neolithic ceramics by feature type	74
6-2	Distribution, Neolithic ceramics by phase	74
6-3	Distribution, number of sherds per vessel	75
6-4	Linkardstown vessel and associated bead from Pit 293	75
6-5	Undecorated Neolithic pottery from Dún Ailinne	76
6-6	Undecorated Neolithic pottery from Dún Ailinne	77
6-7	Undecorated Neolithic pottery from Dún Ailinne	78
6-8	Numbers, Neolithic sherd types (all and diagnostic sherds only)	78
6-9	Decorated Neolithic pottery from Dún Ailinne	79
6-10	Food vessel from Dún Ailinne	81
7-1	Iron sword from Dún Ailinne	88
7-2	Iron spearhead from Dún Ailinne	90
7-3	Three binding strips from Dún Ailinne	91
7-4	Iron blades from Dún Ailinne	91
7-5	Iron needles from Dún Ailinne	93
7-6	Iron nails and rings from Dún Ailinne	95
7-7	Iron shafts from Dún Ailinne	96
7-8	Iron chisel and possible sickle blade	96
7-9	Uncertain iron objects from Dún Ailinne	98
7-10	Uncertain iron objects from Dún Ailinne	98
8-1	Copper alloy fibulae E.79.743 and E.79.899	103
8-2	Copper alloy bracelet, pins, and studs	105
8-3	Copper alloy spiral rings from Dún Ailinne	106
8-4	Copper alloy rings from Dún Ailinne	108
8-5	Copper alloy tracer, ingots, and casting jets	109
8-6	Selection of copper alloy objects from Dún Ailinne	111
8-7	Gold strip from Dún Ailinne	113
9-1	Glass beads from Dún Ailinne	117
9-2	Distribution, glass bead diameters	117
9-3	Glass ring beads and bracelet fragment from Dún Ailinne	118
9-4	Glass toggles from Dún Ailinne	120
9-5	Glass toggle length by width	121
10-1	Worked bone, Dún Ailinne	126
10-2	Worked bone, Dún Ailinne	126

10-3	Worked bone, Dún Ailinne	127
10-4	Worked bone, Dún Ailinne	129
10-5	Worked bone, Dún Ailinne	130
10-6	Worked bone, Dún Ailinne	131
11-1	Lignite objects from Dún Ailinne	132
11-2	Stone, ivory, and amber beads from Dún Ailinne	135
11-3	Stone spindle whorl from Dún Ailinne	141
11-4	Whetstone from Dún Ailinne	142
12-1	Distribution of slag recovered from Dún Ailinne	CD
14-1	Modern copper alloy objects from Dún Ailinne	175
15-1	Distribution, uncalibrated radiocarbon age-determinations	179
16-1	Dún Ailinne and the henge-like enclosures of the Curragh in relation to Carnalway and the hills on the western edge of the Curragh	192
17-1	Chronology, royal sites in Ireland	196
18-1	Stake-holes and post-holes from Harry and Mauve, and Rose, Jade, and Niamh	CD

PLATES—ALL PLATES ARE ON THE ACCOMPANYING CD

I-1	Dún Ailinne from the southwest.
1-1	Aerial view of Dún Ailinne, pre-1968.
1-2	Aerial view of Dún Ailinne (Leo Swan).
2-1	Dún Ailinne under excavation, aerial view.
2-2	Palisade trenches, aerial view 1.
2-3	Palisade trenches, aerial view 2.
2-4	Aerial view, showing variety of features.
2-5	Southeast edge of the Rose "annex."
2-6	Rose feature 314, showing burned stumps of posts (1975).
2-7	Section of Mauve trench 515, showing post bases (1969).
2-8	Post-hole M2 in Mauve 20m circle.
2-9	Post-hole M3 in Mauve 20m circle.
2-10	Post-hole M4 in Mauve 20m circle.
3-1	Original entrance, showing roadway (1975).
5-1	Leaf-shaped projectile points.
5-2	Projectile points, various other types.
5-3	Various flint implements.
5-4	Hollow scrapers.
5-5	Borers.
5-6	Cores.
5-7	Stone axes.
5-8	Stone axe (probably E.79.243) *in situ*, 1968.
6-1	Linkardstown vessel and stone bead..
6-2	Undecorated Neolithic rim sherds.
6-3	Decorated Neolithic rim sherds.
6-4	Decorated Neolithic rim sherd E.79.3635 (two views).
6-5	Food vessel (largest sherds).
6-6	Clay pin, E.79.2304, with clay and stone balls.
7-1	Iron sword.
7-2	Iron sword *in situ* (1969).
7-3	Iron sword just after it was found (1969).
7-4	Detail, hilt guard of the iron sword.
7-5	Iron spearhead.

7-6	Three iron binding strips.
7-7	Two iron blades.
7-8	Iron needles.
8-1	Copper alloy fibulae E.79.743 and E.79.899 (side view).
8-2	Copper alloy fibulae E.79.743 and E.79.899 (top view).
8-3	Copper alloy bracelet fragment and milled ring.
8-4	Copper alloy rings.
8-5	Copper alloy objects indicating manufacturing. E.79.911 and E.79.416 are possible ingots, E.79.1061 is a tracer, and E.79.2119 is a casting jet.
8-6	A selection of copper alloy objects.
8-7	Gold fragment (two views).
9-1	A selection of glass beads.
9-2	Decorated glass bead, E.79.449.
9-3	Glass and bronze objects (1968). E.79.134 is shown in the middle strung on the wire.
9-4	Glass ring beads.
9-5	Glass bracelet fragments.
9-6	Glass toggles and possible waste fragments.
10-1	Worked bone, E.79.203.
10-2	Bone needle fragment, E.79.417.
10-3	Bone spindle whorl, E.79.419.
10-4	Worked bone, E.79.421.
10-5	Worked bone, E.79.422.
10-6	Worked bone, E.79.424.
10-7	Worked bone, E.79.458.
10-8	Probable bone pin, E.79.499.
10-9	Worked bone, E.79.647.
10-10	Worked bone, E.79.664.
10-11	Worked bone, E.79.792.
10-12	Worked bone, E.79.903.
10-13	Worked bone, E.79.1248.
10-14	Worked bone, E.79.1288.
10-15	Worked bone, E.79.1601.
10-16	Worked bone, E.79.1672.
10-17	Worked bone, E.79.1864.
10-18	Worked bone, E.79.1872.
10-19	Worked bone, E.79.2117.
10-20	Worked bone, E.79.2267.
10-21	Worked bone, E.79.2307.
10-22	Worked bone, E.79.2650.
10-23	Worked bone, E.79.2706.
10-24	Worked bone, E.79.2810.
10-25	Worked bone, E.79.3088.
10-26	Worked bone, E.79.3657.
11-1	Cupmarked stone E.79.2894 just after discovery (1973).
11-2	Lignite bracelet fragments, pendant.
11-3	Stone beads.
11-4	Amber bead.
11-5	Stone spindle whorls and whetstones.
11-6	Stone "face."
12-1	E.79.3017, Micrograph 1 (200x Etchants: $K_2Cr_2O_7$ + HCL).

12-2	E.79.3017, Micrograph 2 (600x Etchants: $K_2Cr_2O_7$ + HCL).
12-3	E.79.667, Micrograph 1 (400x Etchants: Klemms III, $K_2Cr_2O_7$ + $FeCl_3$).
12-4	E.79.514, Micrograph 1 (100x Etchants: $FeCl_3$ + $K_2Cr_2O_7$).
12-5	E.79.2271, Micrograph 1 (600x Etchant: Klemms III).
12-6	E.79.1951, Micrograph 1 (100x Etchants: Al. $FeCl_3$ + $K_2Cr_2O_7$).
12-7	E.79.1881, Micrograph 1 (100x Etchant: Klemms III).
12-8	E.79.1881, Micrograph 2 (100x unetched).
12-9	E.79.1881, Micrograph 3 (600x Etchants: NH_4OH + H_2O_2).
12-10	E.79.1881, Micrograph 4 (100x Etchants: NH_4OH + H_2O_2).
12-11	E.79.1986, Micrograph 1 (X100 Etchants: : $K_2Cr_2O_7$ + $FeCl_3$).
12-12	E.79.2836, Micrograph 1 (100x Etchant: $FeCl_3$).
12-13	E.79.2836, Micrograph 2 (100x Etchant: $FeCl_3$).
12-14	E.79.2836, Micrograph 3 (400x Etchant: $FeCl_3$).
12-15	E.79.2836, Micrograph 4 (200x Etchant: $FeCl_3$).
12-16	E.79.911, Micrograph 1 (100x Etchant: $FeCl_3$).
12-17	E.79.911, Micrograph 2 (100x Etchants: NH_4OH + H_2O_2).
12-18	E.79.416, Micrograph 1 (100x Etchants: NH_4OH + H_2O_2).
12-19	E.79.902, Micrograph 1 (600x Etchant: Klemms III).
12-20	E.79.2233, Micrograph 1 (100x Etchant: 3% Nital).
12-21	E.79.2233, Micrograph 2 (100x Etchant: 3% Nital).
12-22	E.79.661, Micrograph 1 (100x Etchant: 3% Nital).
12-23	E.79.661, Micrograph 2 (400x Etchant: 3% Nital).
12-24	E.79.2700, Micrograph 1 (100x Etchant: 3% Nital).
12-25	E.79.2700, Micrograph 2 (100x Etchant: 3% Nital).
13-1	Probable human parietal fragment.
14-1	Stone cresset lamp.

Tables

2-1	Dún Ailinne Summit Area: Sequence of Layers and Surfaces	10
2-2	Dún Ailinne Summit: Composite Sequence Chart	12
4-1	Distribution, Features by Phase	32
4-2	Distribution, Types of Feature	32
4-3	Phases with >5 Features	33
4-4	Distribution, Types of Provenience Information	33
4-5	Distribution, Post-holes and Stake-holes by Presence of Artifacts	34
4-6	Distribution, Possible Neolithic Feature Types	34
4-7	Artifacts in Possible Neolithic Features	35
4-8	Distribution, Types of Neolithic Materials	36
4-9	Contexts of Neolithic Artifacts	36
4-10	Distribution, Neolithic Artifacts by Phase	37
4-11	Numbers of Probable Iron Age Artifacts	39
4-12	Distribution, Iron Age Artifacts by Feature Type	39
4-13	Distribution, Iron Age Artifacts by Phase	40
4-14	Types of Artifacts from Mauve Phase Contexts	40
4-15	Objects Noted as Discarded	41
4-16	Distribution, Missing Objects by Likely Period	41
4-17	Numbers of Missing Neolithic Artifacts	42
4-18	Numbers of Missing Iron Age Artifacts	42
5-1	Descriptive Statistics, Natural Stone Collected from Dún Ailinne	46
5-2	Hammerstones, Basic Dimensions	46
5-3	Distribution, Artifacts by Material	46
5-4	Distribution, Lithic Contexts	46
5-5	Distribution, Lithic Materials by Phase	47
5-6	Distribution, Lithic Artifact Types by Material	49
5-7	Dimensions, Projectile Points	49
5-8	Distribution, Scraper Types by Material	52
5-9	Dimensions, Round Scrapers	54
5-10	Dimensions, Straight Scrapers	55
5-11	Dimensions, General Scrapers	57
5-12	Dimensions, Borers	59
5-13	Dimensions, Cores by Size	61
5-14	Small Cores, Dimensions by Material	62
5-15	Dimensions, Retouched Flakes	62
5-16	Dimensions, Retouched Flakes by Material	63
5-17	Distribution, Unretouched Flakes by Material	63
5-18	Distribution, Unretouched Flake Types by Material	63
5-19	Dimensions, Unretouched Flakes	63
5-20	Dimensions, Unretouched Flakes by Material	64
5-21	Correlation, Platform Width and Thickness Versus Flake Width and Thickness	64
5-22	Number of Unretouched Flakes Compared to Implements by Material	64

5-23	Dimensions, Retouched Implements	64
5-24	Cumulative Frequency, Length of Unretouched Flakes Compared to Implements	65
5-25	Dimensions, Complete Stone Axes	69
5-26	Dimensions, Stone Axe Fragments	70
5-27	Descriptive Statistics, Stone Axe Fragments	70
6-1	Dimensions, Neolithic Sherds	74
7-1	Dimensions, Iron Fragments	84
7-2	Types of Iron Artifact	84
7-3	Distribution, Iron Artifacts by Phase	84
7-4	Identifiable Iron Artifacts and Fragments by Feature Type	85
7-5	Iron Fragments Versus Accession Numbers by Context	85
7-6	Dimensions, Iron Needles	92
7-7	Dimensions, Iron Nails	92
7-8	Distribution, Iron Nails by Feature Type and by Phase	93
7-9	Dimensions, Iron Shafts	93
7-10	Dimensions, Possible Iron Pins	94
7-11	Unidentified Iron Artifacts by Feature Type and by Phase	95
7-12	Dimensions, Iron Rings	95
8-1	Distribution, Types of Copper Alloy Artifacts	100
8-2	Copper Alloy Objects by Feature Type	100
8-3	Copper Alloy Artifacts by Phase	100
8-4	Types of Artifacts by Phase	101
8-5	Dimensions, Pinheads and Pin Shafts	104
8-6	Dimensions, Copper Alloy Rings	105
8-7	Dimensions, Unidentifiable Fragments	110
9-1	Distribution, Types of Glass Artifact	113
9-2	Distribution, Glass Artifacts by Phase (Where Known)	114
9-3	Distribution, Glass Artifact Types by Glass Color	114
9-4	Diameter, Glass Beads	115
9-5	Dimensions, Glass Toggles	119
11-1	Dimensions, Round Stone Objects	134
11-2	Dimensions, Stone Balls	134
11-3	Dimensions, Stone Balls (without E.79.1825)	134
11-4	Stone Beads: Material, Phase, and Context	135
11-5	Dimensions, Stone Beads	136
11-6	Fossil Crinoids by Feature Type and by Phase	138
11-7	Dimensions, Fossil Crinoids	138
12-1	Distribution, Slag by Phase and Context	143
12-2	General Characteristics, Slag Finds	144
12-3	Values for Artifacts Subject to PIXE Analysis	145
13-1	Animal Bones Identified from Dún Ailinne	156
13-2	Minimum Numbers of Individuals for the Main Structural and Stratigraphic Phases	157
13-3	Species Ratios Based on NISP	158
13-4	Body Part Frequencies for the Main Domestic Mammals from Flame Phase	158
13-5	Complete Cattle Mandibles from Dún Ailinne	159
13-6	Wear Stages in Isolated Teeth from Flame Phase Deposits at Dún Ailinne	160
13-7	Epiphyseal Fusion Data for Cattle from Flame Phase	160
13-8	Dental Eruption and Wear Data for Complete Pig Mandibles from Dún Ailinne	161
13-9	Epiphyseal Fusion Data for Pigs from Flame Phase	161
13-10	Sheep/Goat Mandibles from Dún Ailinne (Estimated MWS in Brackets)	161

13-11	Epiphyseal Fusion Data for Sheep from Flame Phase	162
13-12	Summary of Measurements Taken on Cattle, Pig, and Sheep Bones from Dún Ailinne	162
13-13	Withers Height Estimates for Cattle and Horses from Dún Ailinne	163
13-14	Distribution of Butchery Traces on Cattle, Sheep, Pig, and Horse Bones from Dún Ailinne	163
14-1	Distribution, Modern Artifacts Recorded as Missing, by Material	169
14-2	Metal Artifacts Considered Modern, Listed as Missing	170
14-3	Types of Modern Artifacts	170
14-4	Distribution, Modern Artifacts by Type of Feature	171
15-1	Radiocarbon Age Determinations	178
17-1	Comparison, Royal Site Sizes	196
18-1	Artifacts Possibly Associated with Manufacturing	203
18-2	Artifacts Possibly Associated with Manufacturing by Phase	203
18-3	Stake-hole and Post-hole Depths	205
18-4	Average Depth of Stake-holes and Post-holes by Phase, with Statistical Comparison	206
18-5	Possible Post Heights as a Function of Post-hole Depth by Phase	206

Preface and Acknowledgments

In 1967 Bernard Wailes (University of Pennsylvania, Philadelphia, Pennsylvania) was asked to undertake a five-year program of excavation at the royal site of Dún Ailinne, Co. Kildare, Ireland, by the National Monuments Branch, Office of Public Works, Republic of Ireland. We do not know why this site was selected by National Monuments for a substantial excavation project or why Wailes was asked to direct it. Anecdotal evidence and informed surmise, however, suggest several reasons.

First, interest in the archaeology of the Irish royal sites, the supposed seats of the ancient kingdoms of Ireland noted in documentary sources, was growing at that time. Sean Ó Riordáin had excavated at Tara, Co. Meath, in the 1950s, and in Northern Ireland, Dudley Waterman was excavating at Navan Fort, Co. Armagh, the traditional royal site of Ulster. Thus, investigation of another royal site seemed timely. Second, most major excavation projects in the Republic of Ireland at that time were on sites from considerably earlier periods (e.g., Newgrange, Knowth). Third, Wailes had participated, with a group of students from the United States, in the 1963 season's work at Navan Fort and so had at least some limited familiarity with excavating a royal site. Fourth, the then Minister of Finance, Charles Haughey, was providing considerably increased state funding for archaeological research in the Republic of Ireland. Fifth, not least because of the increased funds available, most Irish archaeologists were already engaged in substantial projects, so it was necessary to consider outsiders to undertake any additional major research program. Mindful of the Harvard Archaeological Mission to Ireland in the 1930s and 1940s, an institutional partner was sought in the USA.

Wailes visited Dún Ailinne in summer 1967 and proposed an exploratory season of excavation in order to establish preliminary archaeological information about this hitherto unexcavated site and so to determine whether further excavation was warranted. National Monuments agreed, and a protocol was drawn up with the University of Pennsylvania Museum of Archaeology and Anthropology (UPM) whereby National Monuments provided excavation funds and equipment while the UPM funded travel and living expenses for the excavation director and students from the U.S.

The exploratory excavation, in 1968, produced abundant evidence for Neolithic and Iron Age activity on the summit area of the site. Consequently, National Monuments and UPM agreed to continue excavation, which took place each year until 1975, eight seasons in all. When the site was finally closed in 1975, the excavations had uncovered the summit area of a complex and multi-period site, recovered one of the only Irish Iron Age swords from an excavated context, and produced the largest collection of excavated faunal bones from an Iron Age site in Ireland.

Several progress reports were published during the course of the excavation (Wailes 1969, 1970a, 1970b, 1971, 1973, 1974) and, subsequently, two interim reports (Wailes 1976, 1990). Over the years, various analyses were carried out (most in the 1980s), and several were published in preliminary form (Crabtree 1990 on the animal bone; Johnston 1990 on the Neolithic artifacts; others summarized in Wailes 1990). But time and circumstances prevented preparation of the final report until recently.

This volume represents the full description of our work to date on Dún Ailinne and its archaeology. After a detailed description of the excavation, all of the various classes of artifacts are described and discussed in the larger context of Irish prehistory. Some of the artifact analyses (the faunal section and the Neolithic artifacts) have been updated from previous versions while others (the bronze and gold) have been used largely unchanged and their original date so noted. Some artifact counts and totals have changed due to several factors, in particular the inclusion of additional material not seen previously and the reassessment of some artifacts. Where there are such differences, this publication supersedes any earlier publications.

A number of new technical analyses of the artifacts have been included, and there is also a chapter (Chapter 16) setting Dún Ailinne in the context of the larger ritual landscape of Co. Kildare. Final chapters consider the chronological data for Dún Ailinne and where the site fits in terms of other sites of the Irish, British, and European Iron Ages. It concludes with an interpretation of the site as a major ceremonial center of the Irish Iron Age.

All illustrations are carried on the accompanying CD-Rom. A variety of illustrators have provided line drawings of the artifacts over the years, and we have chosen the best to include. Some of the drawings on a single page are at different scales, so we have provided a scale for each page overall and added additional scales for those artifacts of a different size. The artifacts are now in the keeping of the National Museum of Ireland in Dublin. Some of the photos were taken in the late 1960s and 1970s, showing the original excavation. Many of them have faded over time, but their value as original documentation of the excavation outweighs any concerns as to their quality. Site plans provided on the CD avoid the need either to reduce them to a scale beyond visual coherence or include cumbersome foldouts. All original plans and drawings have been donated to the Archives of the University Museum, University of Pennsylvania.

The Cataloguing of Artifacts

This section describes the ways in which artifacts were counted and measured. All artifacts were entered into a database for the purpose of analysis. All artifacts were numbered consecutively, and carry the prefix "E.79." This designation is unique in Ireland to Dún Ailinne. Copies of the database are in the possession of the National Museum of Ireland and the Heritage Council. Specific questions about the database or the artifacts may be addressed to the authors. The artifacts and biological material from Dún Ailinne are now permanently stored in the National Museum of Ireland, Dublin.

Ceramics

We counted ceramics individually, except where they were clearly joined to another fragment, in which case we counted them as a single sherd. This was because some of the fragments had been given letters in addition to numbers (e.g., E.79.1726A) while others had not. We catalogued those with letters individually, while grouping those with no additional letter with the main number. For example, if there were five joined sherds with the number E.79.1596, three with no letter, one with A, and the other with B, we catalogued the last two individually and grouped the first three together as a single sherd and counted as one. However, if these five sherds were not joined, we would still catalogue the ones with A and B individually, but now the other three would be catalogued as three sherds under the number E.79.1596.

Lithics

If these had been given letters in addition to numbers, we also catalogued them individually.

Iron

Iron in some ways was a special case. Preservation of iron at the site was fairly poor, despite some notable exceptions, and deterioration of artifacts subsequent to excavation also occurred. This made counting artifacts an uncertain process. Chapter 7 describes the guidelines we used to count iron objects.

Other Materials

Objects of other materials—glass, stone, or lignite—had not been given letters. If there were fragments that clearly joined, or if it was certain that they originally represented a single artifact (for example, the better part of a glass bead and 3–4 smaller fragments of the same color, all in a single bag) the object was counted as a single artifact; if not, we counted them individually and catalogued them as a group. The only exception to this was a glass bracelet fragment that was composed of two pieces, each of which had been given separate numbers during the excavation and only later realized to be part of a single artifact. We catalogued these separately and noted the join in the comments.

Measurements

We made measurement in millimeters on all pieces where at least one dimension was larger than 10 mm. Where multiple objects were entered under a single number, we made the measurement on the largest piece. Specific locations for measuring length, width, and thickness are noted in the relevant chapters. For rings (glass and metal), length was usually external diameter, where it was possible to measure this.

Provenience

We generally entered provenience information (typically feature type, feature number, and phase) as it appeared in the finds register. If information was unclear, we sometimes used the feature log, though not consistently, and we did not routinely cross check designations like type of feature with the feature log. Thus there may be discrepancies between these two sources in terms of grid references, feature designations, and other details of provenience. In general, the information that appears in this analysis can be assumed to have come from the finds register. We also took feature types from the finds register and entered them accordingly. If it was clear that the object came from a feature but the type was unclear, we entered it as "Uncertain." If the provenience information was missing, we recorded it as "Unknown."

Objects with No Number

At the request of the National Museum of Ireland, we gave new numbers to any objects that no longer had a number. This sometimes happened because, for example, the number had worn off or tags had become separated from bags. These numbers begin with E.79.5001, in order to distinguish them clearly from the original number series (which ended with E.79.4003) given during the excavation. The new series of artifact numbers therefore runs from E.79.5001 through E.79.5016 and represents a total of 31 objects.

A Note about Names

By convention four sites from the later Iron Age are known in the archaeological literature as "royal." While these are typically referred to in ancient literary and historical sources (using variable spellings) as Teamhair, Emain Macha, Cruachain, and Dún Ailinne, the modern names of the sites are typically used in the archaeological literature. This is done to distinguish clearly the literary identities of these places from their modern archaeological status. For Teamhair, Emain Macha, and Cruachain, the modern names are Tara, Navan, and Rathcroghan, respectively, and these are most commonly used in the archaeological literature when referring to the archaeological sites.

This convention would suggest that we should refer to the subject of this report as Knockaulin rather than Dún Ailinne. Knockaulin is the modern name of the townland in which the site is located and is the name for the hill itself. For a number of reasons, however, we have decided to use Dún Ailinne, recognizing that this flouts the current convention. For one thing, we like "Dún Ailinne" better. For another, unlike Tara, Navan, and Rathcroghan, Dún Ailinne has no literary identity even remotely comparable to their ancient counterparts. Using Dún Ailinne does not conjure an image which is contradicted by the archaeological research described here. Finally, it is in some sense the historical image of "Dún Ailinne" that we present here. Unlike Temair, Emain Macha, and Cruachain, which appear as the backdrop for magical cattle raids, miraculous races, and mythical heroes, Dún Ailinne only ever appears in the documents as the cultural, social, and political center of the ancient kingdom of Leinster. While the archaeological evidence presented here indicates that this image is neither complete nor entirely accurate, it is probably closer to the Iron Age function of the site than modern-day "Knockaulin," which today serves as a pasture for cattle.

* * *

In a project which has taken this long to see to completion, there are many, many people to thank. We hope that we mention everyone, but if we have missed someone, we apologize in advance. We are very grateful to everyone who has offered support and help over the years. This project belongs to all of us.

It is appropriate to begin with appreciative thanks for the support given to Irish archaeology by Charles Haughey. As Minister of Finance for Ireland, he increased funding for excavation considerably and so made our excavation possible. Moreover, he took the time to visit us during the first season, in 1968.

During excavation, the National Monuments Branch (NMB) channeled funding for labor, and the Office of Public Works (OPW) provided excavation equipment. We thank all the staff of that time, but in particular Marcus Ó hEochaidh of NMB and Louis Feeley, supervisor of the Kilkenny OPW depot. Marcus not only shepherded us through the necessary paperwork but recruited supervisors and visited the excavation many times. Louis ensured that we were supplied promptly with all our equipment, and he cheerfully coped with additional requests. The budget staff of NMB went out of their way to help us through the requirements of Civil Service accounting.

We also express our warmest thanks to the University of Pennsylvania Museum (UPM), the Bredin Foundation, and the Ford Foundation. These U.S. institutions funded travel and living expenses for the director (BW) and many others from many U.S. universities who came to work at Dún Ailinne.

In Ireland, the Heritage Council, the Royal Irish Academy, and the National Committee for Archaeology provided generous post-excavation grants which have been invaluable with the preparation of this report.

The excavation would have been impossible of course without the ready permission of Jack Thompson, the landowner, to take some of his farmland out of commission for eight years. He and Mrs. Thompson took a continuing interest in the project, and they did us many favors. Their children, Robert and Evelyn, frequently worked with us on the site, and Robert and his wife Adrian have continued to be unfailingly generous and helpful in our more recent visits. We are extremely grateful to all of them for their help and hospitality.

From the original excavation, we would like to thank all of the many people, local and non-local, who participated in the research. Up to 25 local people worked on the site each year, and we thank all of them most warmly. Most of the excavation supervisory staff came from University College Dublin (UCD), and many of them, too, participated in every season's work. Among them we should mention in particular Jennifer Kelly and Tony O'Daly, in charge of surveying; Judith Barden, who took over much of the catering; and Kathleen Ryan, who did all the accounts. Many American students worked on the site, and a few of these, too, became regular fixtures and members of the supervisory staff. Art Smith and Oliver Goodenough were, successively, responsible for photography. Gayle Wever and Virginia Greene both did artifact conservation work on the site, followed by more back in the UPM Conservation Laboratory. Marga Foley, from UCD, took over on-site artifact conservation in the later years.

Successive Directors and curatorial staff of the National Museum of Ireland (NMI) were kind enough to provide us with help and advice both during and after the excavation and, as artifacts have been processed for publication, they have been transferred to the NMI. Many Irish archaeologists visited the excavation to ask questions, give advice, and engage in constructive debate over method and interpretation. We thank them all for many enjoyable and useful discussions, and in particular thank Leo Swan, who also took a number of aerial photographs of the site.

The people of Kilcullen extended us every courtesy and much help, for all of which we are very thankful. In addition to the Thompson family and all those who worked on the site, we should mention in particular the Byrne family, who allowed us to use the Hideout bar and telephone as an ad hoc office when needed and also provided storage for equipment over the winters.

During the more recent push to get the research published, a large number of people have been generous with their time and help. We would like to detail each of their specific contributions, but space does not permit. We have hopefully expressed our thanks to them personally for what they have done, but it is important that their names appear here.

At the University of Pennsylvania Kathleen Ryan, Amy Zoll, Rachel Scott, Anita Fahringer, Elizabeth Hamilton, Monique Timberlake, the staff in the Anthropology Department, and Pat McGovern; at the National Museum of Ireland Andy Halpin, Mary Cahill, Isabella Mulhall, Ivor Harkin, Margaret Lannin, and Raghnall O Floinn; at George Washington University, Julio Mercador, Christian Tryon, and Richard Grinker; Sorena Sorenson of the Museum of Natural History, Smithsonian Institution; at the Museum Applied Science Center for Archaeology, University Museum, Vincent C. Piggot, Helen Schenck, and Samuel Nash; Emer Ní Cheallaigh, archivist of the National Folklore Collection; Terry Barry at Trinity College Dublin; David Geddes; Simon Holdaway at the University of Auckland; Shannon McPherron of the Max Planck Institute; Chris Lynn of the Department of the Environment, Northern Ireland; and Padraig Clancy. At University Museum Publications, Walda Metcalf, Jennifer Quick, and Matt Manieri have contributed significantly to the final appearance of this book.

A number of drawings of artifacts were done over the years, and many of them are included in this volume. Unfortunately, the artist who did them was not always named. Those whom we know are Virginia Greene, Leah Reynolds, and Kimberley Consroe, and we thank you. If there are others, we thank you, too, anonymous though you may be. Thanks also to Brian Hamill, who did some slick computer rescues of some old drawings. Doug Campana photographed the worked bone. Valerie Dowling photographed the artifacts at the National Museum of Ireland in a last-minute rush, and Kim Leaman did some very valuable last-minute work with plans and sections; we appreciate their efforts. Lindsay Shaffer produced the large-scale drawings from the master site plan.

We would also like to thank personally the contributors to the book. We know of many who have had to chase down and plead with contributors to assure they met their deadlines. But all of the contributors to this book sent me their materials on time as requested, and I never had to threaten them or their issue to get it done. We appreciate that!

— *SAJ and BW*

I would also like to thank Bernard Wailes. He did a beautiful excavation and kept tremendous records. It is a testimony to his meticulousness that it was possible, some 35 years later, to do this analysis. His insights and willingness to discuss possibilities have always been intellectually stimulating. He has also been unfailingly kind and generous with his time and patient in answering, sometimes several times over, my endless detailed questions about phases and stratigraphy. I have benefited immensely from having him as an advisor, as a colleague, and as a friend.

I would also like to thank my family. My children, Kate and Nick, never touched "all that old stuff" in the dining room and usually managed to keep themselves entertained while Mommy was working. My husband, John Hawdon, who has gamely tromped through mud, heat, and rain to indulge my desire to see every little site along the way, has always encouraged my passion for archaeology, even when I rarely get paid for it. My parents, Frank and Pat Johnston, have provided so much that I cannot name it all here—child care, courier services, scholarly advice, personal encouragement, and timely enthusiasm. They made me who I am, and I thank them for their love and support. Without you all, it just wouldn't be any fun.

— *SAJ*

Chronological Chart of Irish Archaeological Periods
(approximate dates based on calibrated radiocarbon age determinations)

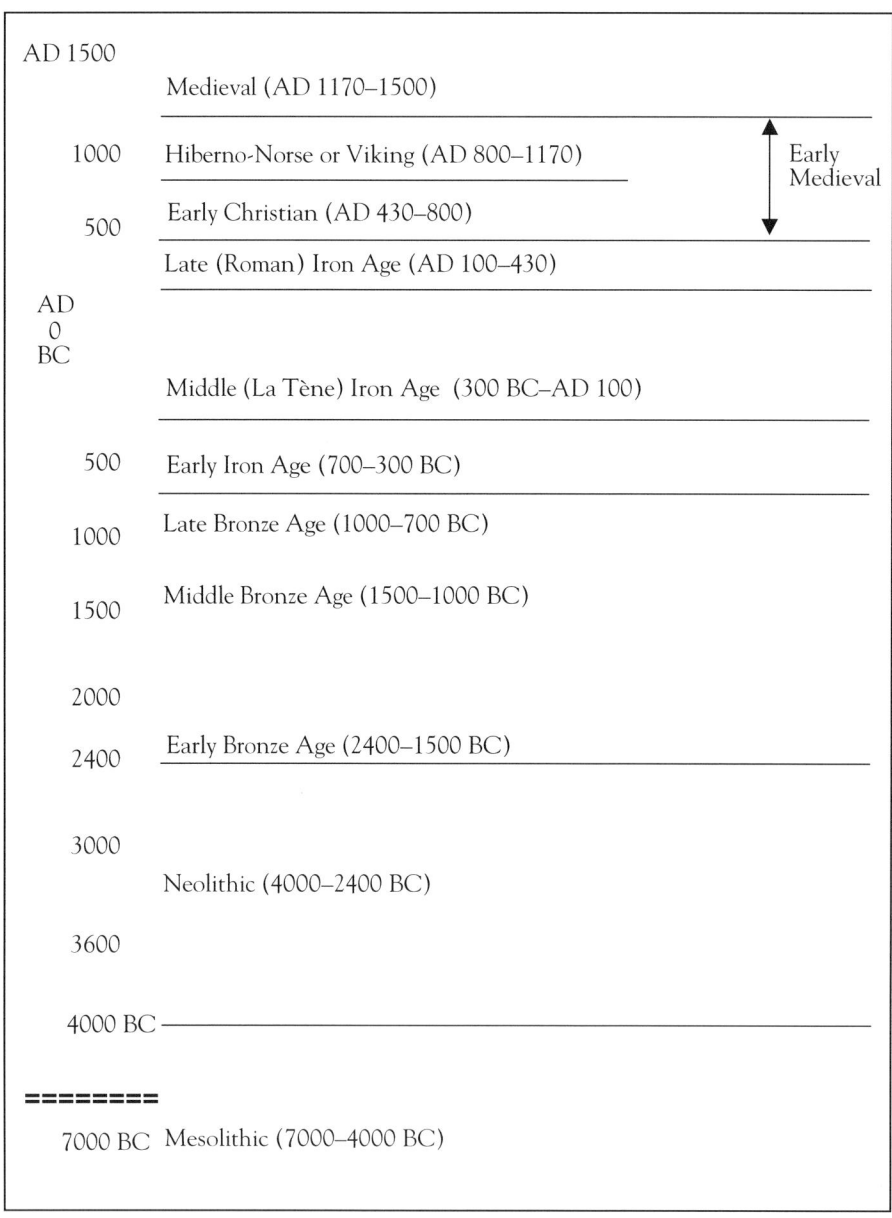

Summary of the Excavation

Bernard Wailes

This Summary introduces the detailed accounts of the excavations that follow in this volume. Dún Ailinne (known locally as Knockaulin Hill) lies in Knockaulin townland, just south of Kilcullen, County Kildare, Ireland. Its Ordnance Survey grid reference for Ireland is N818078. The site crowns the top of a rounded hill of graywacke and slate bedrock (Plate I-1); Figure I-1 shows a contour map of the hilltop. The bedrock, which lies obliquely to the ground surface, is covered with a relatively thin layer of glacial till, and occasionally outcrops in roughly parallel ridges. The hill itself is known locally as Knockaulin, reflecting its (ancient?) connection with the mythological figure of Aillenn, whose name is spelled in a wide variety of ways (see Chapter 16).

In 1837 John O'Donovan identified Knockaulin as Dún Ailinne, and his identification has not been challenged since (O'Donovan 1837:46-53; 119-26; see also Chapter 1). The site is a roughly oval enclosure encompassing the summit of Knockaulin hill. This enclosure was formed by a bank and ditch, the ditch lying inside the bank, and the total area is about 13 hectares in extent. The single original entrance through this bank and ditch is on the eastern side. On the summit of the hill O'Donovan noted a "summit fort," a "little internal rath" (a rath is a circular enclosure) and two large granite boulders.

In the traditional accounts of early Ireland, Dún Ailinne (Ailenn, Alinn, and other variations; see Chapter 16) was the focal site of the Laigin (the historic name for the people of Leinster), and so the equivalent in Leinster of Cruachain for Connacht, Emain Macha (Navan Fort) for Ulster, and Teamhair Breaga (Tara) for Meath (Figure I-2). Each was associated with the ruling dynasty of its territory, and all were perceived as royal residences, inauguration sites, and assembly sites. To medieval Irish historians these four sites were the premier political and ceremonial sites of early Ireland. There is little evidence from the surviving texts that these sites were still operational in the medieval period, and it may be inferred that they fell out of use around the time that Ireland was converted to Christianity in the 5th century AD. Nevertheless, it is clear that they retained a strong symbolic value in medieval Ireland (Grabowski 1990; see also Chapter 17).

In archaeological terms, one would expect that these sites were used during the Iron Age (ca. 7th/6th centuries BC–5th century AD, and that Iron Age construction would be most likely. Earlier construction and use would not be surprising, but construction or use after the 5th century AD would run counter to the chronological inferences drawn from the historical evidence. The variety of uses attributed to these sites by medieval authors and the paucity of information provided about their structures and associated artifacts make it impossible to predict with any accuracy what archaeological evidence to expect. Residences, ceremonial structures, burials, and workshops, together with artifacts appropriate to each of these, would all be possibilities. Since the mid-20th century or so, however, archaeological research at these four royal sites has shown a substantial number of common features between them, even though (as ever) interpretation is not always easy. These matters are discussed further in Chapters 17 and 18.

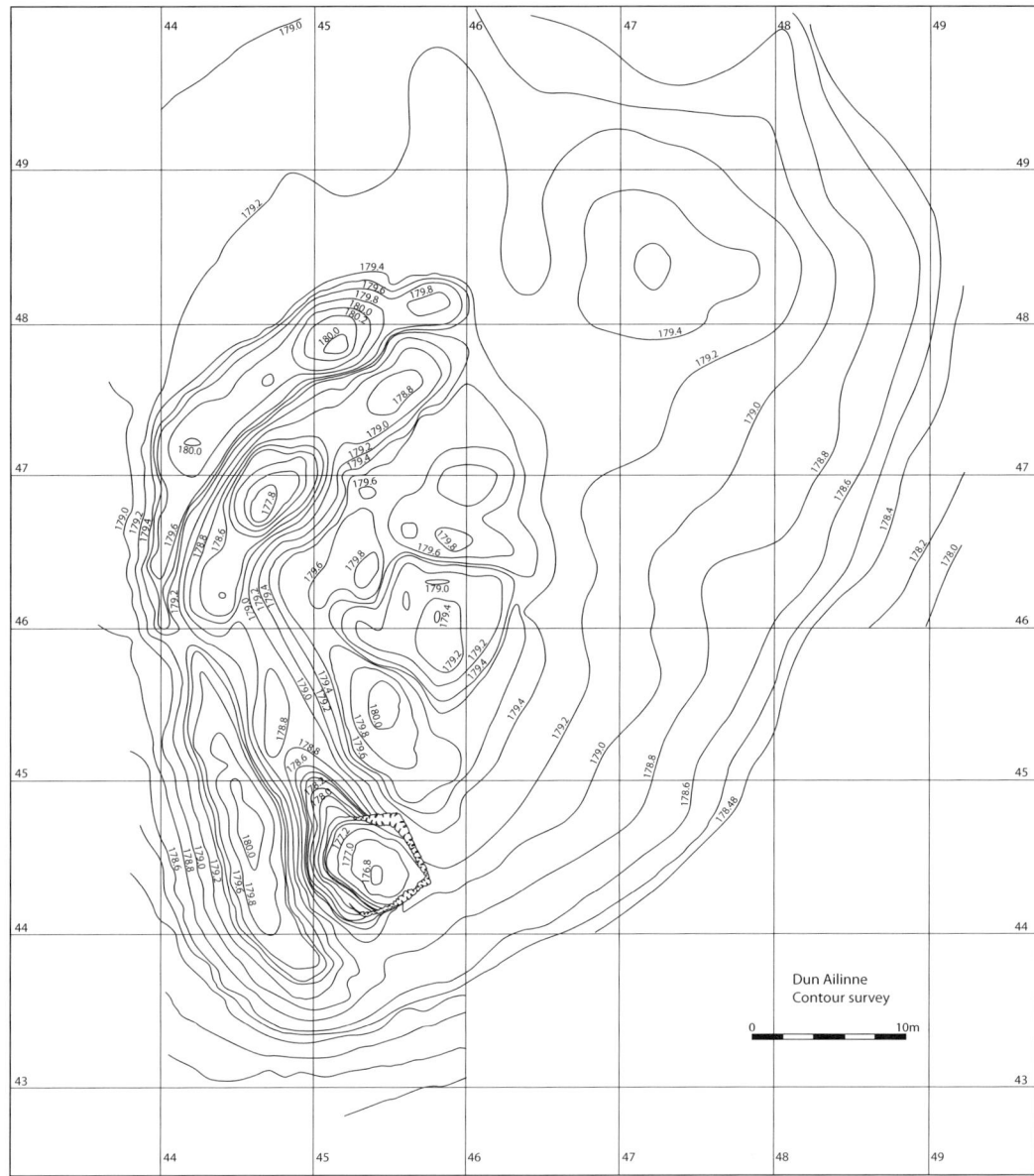

Figure I-1. Contour map, Knockaulin Hill.

In 1967 a team from the University Museum at the University of Pennsylvania, Philadelphia, decided to undertake substantial excavation at Dún Ailinne. This work was funded by the University Museum and other agencies in the U.S. (see Wailes 1976 for other granting agencies) and by what was then the National Monuments Board of the Office of Public Works in Ireland. This work took place from 1968 to 1975. In the first season, a cesium magnetometer survey was conducted over the whole site, revealing a substantial anomaly on the north side, not far inside the ditch, and another on the summit of the hill. More intensive magnetometer survey on the summit, plus resistivity survey, showed strong anomalies that, on subsequent excavation, proved to be the signals of intense burning. An extensive area (roughly 20 m x 80 m) of the summit was stripped of sod to reveal a considerable extent of soil blackened with ash and charcoal, which contained (among other things) small blue glass beads and fragments of heavily oxidized iron. This evidence pointed to activities of some sort during the Iron Age and/or early medieval period, and this summit area remained our primary focus of excavation.

Elsewhere during the first, exploratory, season's work several large test trenches were excavated in order to see if any other traces of prehistoric or early historic occupation might be found. These proved almost entirely sterile in archaeological terms, which reinforced the decision to concentrate on the summit area.

Intensive excavation of the summit area gradually revealed a complex sequence. The earliest activity was Neolithic (the Tan phase), marked by a roughly horseshoe-shaped ditch, about 20 m in diameter, which had been deliberately infilled; the remains of what was probably a "Linkardstown"-type burial pit (mostly cut away by later Iron Age construction); and a small pit containing flint flakes. No radiocarbon samples could be obtained from any of these features, and their Neolithic dating is based on their contents, which were exclusively Neolithic. Neolithic artifacts were found throughout the stratigraphic sequence in the summit area, including the topsoil, and this may be explained primarily by the sequence of extensive later construction in the Iron Age. The Neolithic artifacts mentioned above included characteristic Irish Neolithic worked flint, pottery, and ground stone axes. The nature of Neolithic occupation, however, is unclear.

At a later date, a Bronze Age food vessel was deposited—the only indicator that the summit area was used between the Neolithic and the Iron Age.

The first Iron Age construction was a circular timber palisade (the White phase), ca. 22 m in diameter, with an entrance opening facing approximately east-northeast. This simple structure was dismantled and replaced with a larger and far more complex one (the Rose phase).

The Rose phase structure comprised a larger and a smaller circle arranged in what has come to be known in the literature (see Lynn 1992, 2003) as a "figure-of-eight" structure, with a gap at the junction of the two to permit access between them. The

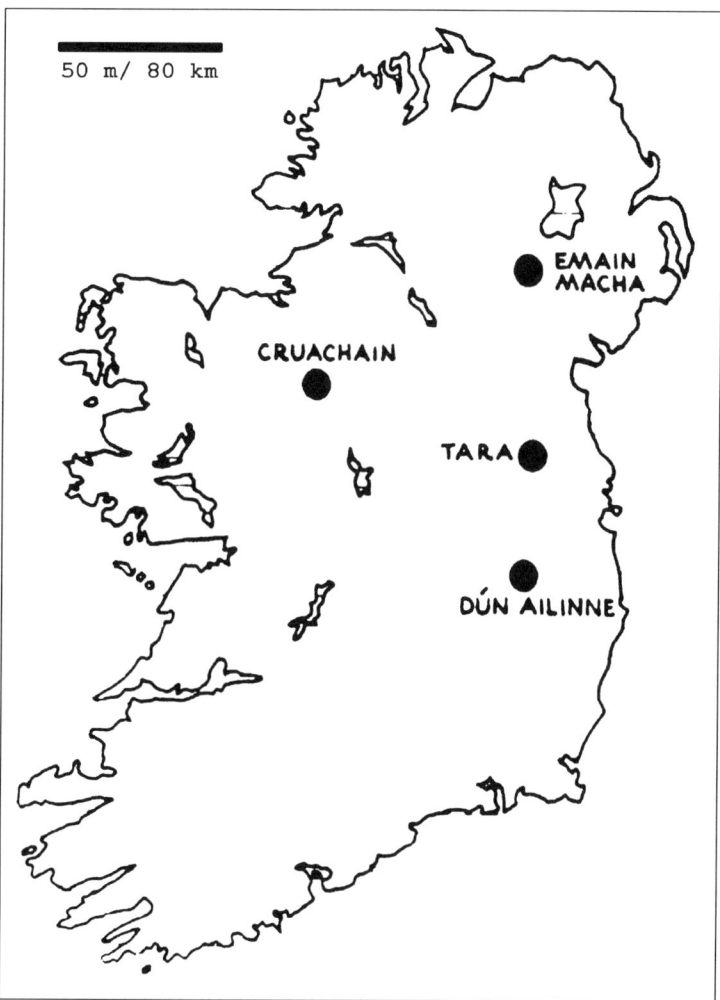

Figure I-2. Distribution map, the royal sites of Ireland.

maximum diameter of the larger circle is about 37 m, and of the smaller about 18 m. Both were configured as three concentric palisades, and each had an entrance facing roughly east-northeast. The entrance to the larger circle was flanked by "antennae" palisades forming a sort of "funnel" from the east-northeast into the interior of the circle. Within this funnel were additional timber works, and the whole entrance approach clearly was designed to impress.

In turn, the Rose phase structures were dismantled, to be replaced by an even larger circular structure (the Mauve phase), with a maximum diameter of about 42 m. This structure had two concentric palisades, and its entrance, like those of the preceding White and Rose structures, faced approximately east-northeast. At the center of the

Mauve phase enclosure stood a circular timber building about 6 m diameter (feature 42). This had *no* ground-level entrance and was surrounded by a series of supporting buttresses. These constructional details imply that feature 42 was not designed as an enclosed space, but rather as a sturdy structure probably designed to support an elevated platform.

Between the outer palisades and the central feature 42 was a concentric circle of very large posts, each about 0.5 m diameter. The distance between the outer palisades and the circle of large posts is about 6 m, and the distance between the latter and feature 42 at the center is about 9 m. These distances are too great to suggest the likelihood of any spans which might have supported any kind of roof without intervening posts, of which there is no sign. The area within the Mauve outer palisades, then, was probably open to the air (with the possible exception of feature 42, as noted).

The Mauve complex was dismantled in stages. The outer palisades were dismantled first, and the circle of large posts left standing until later. Whether the central structure, feature 42, was dismantled in the first or the second stage (or between the two) could not be determined. As the Mauve complex was progressively dismantled, deposits accumulated over a restricted area on the eastern side, between feature 42 and the outer palisade. These deposits (in succession "Lower Emerald," "Crimson," and "Upper Emerald") contained much burnt material and at least one episode of intense burning *in situ*. The large posts in this area survived throughout and were not extracted until after Upper Emerald had been deposited. Above this was placed a layer of redeposited subsoil (glacial till) in which a rough "paving" of stone slabs was set.

The final Iron Age activity of this summit area was marked by the deposit of the "Flame" level. This was composed of loose soil containing much ash, charcoal, and burnt stone. Thin lenses (incomplete soil layers) of archaeologically sterile humic material suggest that the activities leading to the accumulation of this level were intermittent. Flame contained very considerable amounts of animal bone, some of it charred and cracked by heat. This indicates that Flame was the product, at least in part, of periodic feasting when quantities of meat were roasted.

Iron Age artifacts from the summit area included numerous heavily corroded iron objects (among them an Irish-type short La Tène C sword), copper or copper-alloy rings and brooches, and glass beads. Close examination of these artifacts suggests that limited manufacturing of bronze, glass, and bone objects had occurred.

O'Donovan's "summit fort" was not, as he surmised, a surviving arc of a partly destroyed ringfort but an irregular arc-shaped "embankment" with a quarry ditch inside the curve. This bank measures about 40 m end to end. Excavation provided no clue whatsoever as to its date or its function. Stratigraphically, it overlies the western edge of Flame, and since there is a thick and archaeologically sterile layer of humus between the two, it is evident that this embankment was constructed considerably later than the latest Iron Age activities on the summit of Dún Ailinne.

The "little internal rath" that O'Donovan noted inside the arc of the embankment is a small irregular hollow (feature 2432) about 10 m x 7 m, dug into Iron Age and Neolithic features. Neither date nor function can be proposed. Finally, the two substantial granite boulders that lay at the west end of 2432 were examined in order to see if they bore any pictographs or inscriptions and rolled over to examine their stratigraphic relationship to 2432 and neighboring deposits. No markings were discerned on either of these boulders. They lay very close to the surface, and this suggests that they had been moved in the relatively recent past; had they sat in the same place for centuries, let alone millennia, worm action would have removed humus from beneath them and allowed them to "settle" toward the subsoil. Some have suspected that these two boulders were the remnants of some Neolithic or Iron Age construction or monument, but excavation produced no evidence to support this notion, and it may be that they are simply two large glacial erratics that happened to be deposited here (though, as noted, probably moved a little in recent times).

The topsoil of the summit area contained evidence for short-term recent activities. Numerous fragments of 17th or 18th century wine bottles indicate picnicking, while British Army debris (badges of the South Lancashires and many .303 blank cartridge cases) suggest bivouacking and/or maneuvers in the earlier 20th century, perhaps connected with the period 1916–22.

Limited excavations were conducted on the eastern perimeter of Knockaulin. These showed that the bank and ditch that define the site were of simple "dump" construction—that is, the ditch was quarried out and the spoil heaped up on the downhill side to form the bank. There were no traces of internal or external elaborations such as *chevaux-de-frise* or palisades. Excavation of the original site entrance showed what *might* have been the foundations for some type of timber fence or palisade. Inside the entrance a roadway had been constructed by cutting an 8 m-wide strip into the subsoil, with the spoil dumped on its south side. This was visible on the surface running in a straight line up the hillside for some 70 m, directly toward the Iron Age timber structures on the summit. Outside the site entrance there is a shorter (ca. 40 m) line of "roadway." This was perhaps constructed at a different time, since it is sinuous rather than straight, and is not aligned exactly with the "roadway" inside the site entrance.

A number of radiocarbon dates were obtained for the Iron Age. Probably due to the Iron Age construction and consequent redeposition of material, these dates do not fall into a good sequence that correlates with the stratigraphic sequence, and they cover a wide range, from about the 5th century BC to the 4th century AD. Those artifacts to which some dating can be attributed on stylistic grounds indicate mainly 1st century BC through 1st century AD. Only one radiocarbon date could be obtained from the entrance area, but this did at least fall into the range of dates obtained from the summit area, indicating that the bank and ditch enclosing the site had indeed been constructed during the Iron Age, rather than some earlier (or later) period.

The Iron Age remains revealed at Dún Ailinne strongly support an interpretation of the site as ceremonial. None of the structures could be interpreted as having been designed or used for residential or manufacturing purposes (although manufacturing debris was found—see above). Nor were any burials found. Primarily, then, Dún Ailinne was designed and used during the Iron Age for ritual and ceremonial purposes, which could have included assemblies and inaugurations, as well as religious functions. It may be pertinent that the entrances of the three successive circular timber structures on the summit (White, Rose, and Mauve) all have their entrances facing roughly east-northeast, on an axis that correlates very closely with sunrise on or about May 1, the traditional date of the Early Christian holiday known as Beltane. Analysis of the faunal remains indicates that considerable numbers of young animals were slaughtered in the autumn, which might suggest a connection with the traditional Samhain.

Finally, survey and excavation at Dún Ailinne show a number of similarities with the royal sites of Rathcroghan, Tara, and Navan. Most or all of these four sites share a number of features, including Iron Age (pre-Christian) date, large roughly circular enclosures of "henge" type, circular structures (including the figure-of-eight pattern), and avenues or roadways. These archaeological similarities seem to support the traditional belief of medieval historians that these four sites were the preeminent royal sites of pagan Ireland.

1
Excavation Strategy

Bernard Wailes

The Site

Dún Ailinne is a hilltop enclosed by a roughly oval bank and ditch, with an original entrance on the east side. The bank is outside the ditch, and so this enclosure is, morphologically, a henge. The inner edge of the ditch has been quarried in a number of places, presumably for building stone, and probably in relatively recent times. The area enclosed is ca. 13 ha and today is divided radially into three unequal sectors, or "pie slices," by modern field fences (Figure 1-1). In 1968 the western sector, with the steepest slope, was covered by rough grass and bushes, while the other two sectors, which had been cultivated in recent times, were under improved grass and used only for grazing stock.

On the summit of the hill, a little to the south of the center of the site, was an arc-shaped embankment, about 40 m tip to tip, with an irregular internal quarry ditch. Most of this embankment was excavated, and only its southern end remains. Within the arc of this embankment is a small irregular hollow, about 8 m x 10 m, with upcast surrounding it. Two large granite boulders sit nearby. About 20 m east of the northern end of the embankment was the center of a "low mound" (completely excavated and now level ground). The height of this mound was barely 1 m above the surrounding ground, and its diameter was roughly 20 m.

Down the northern slope of the site lies "St. John's Well," a small hollow apparently artificially cut into the hill slope. It was muddy in damp weather and seems likely to have been quarried out, probably in recent times, in the hope of providing a small pond for grazing stock. In more recent times, it has figured in local legend (see Chapter 16).

On the east side of the site, running from the original entrance toward the summit, is a linear hollow about 70 m long. Whether this was an ancient feature or the result of recent farm vehicles wearing a track over time could not be determined prior to excavation. It was tentatively designated as an avenue or roadway of prehistoric date.

Aerial Photographs

Aerial photographs showed surface features, of course, such as the arc-shaped embankment, but no signs of possible subsurface features (Plate 1-1). The earliest (Ó Ríordáin 1953:pl. 20) shows the whole of the site under rough grass and bushes, but does show clear traces of ridge-and-furrow cultivation in the two larger sectors. Two other aerial photos were taken of the site before excavation, one by a commercial firm and the other by Dr. St. Joseph's aerial survey team. By this time the two larger fields had been brought back under cultivation and then seeded as improved pasture. The late Leo Swan took a later series of aerial photographs during the excavation, but these, like the earlier ones, also showed no subsurface features (Plate 1-2).

Descriptions prior to 1968

In the earliest published reference to the site that we could find Camden (1789:543) mentions a "rath, now destroyed" on the summit of the hill, which seems to be the arc-shaped embankment

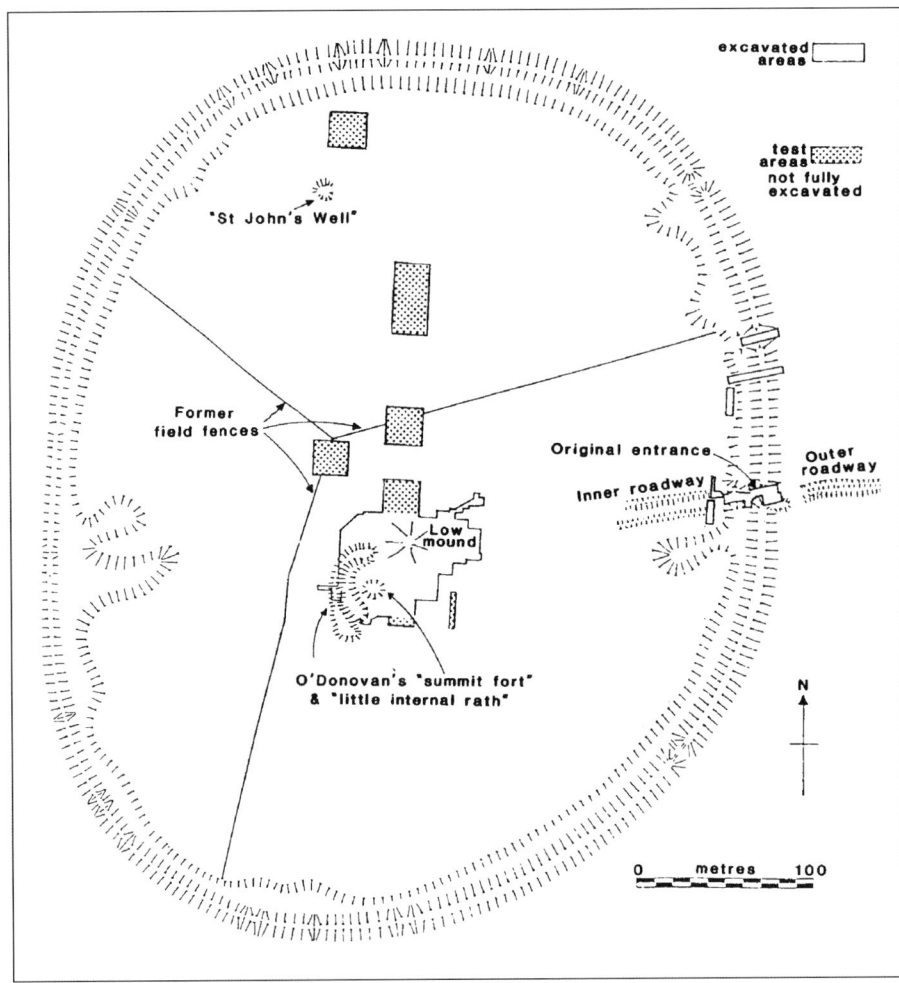

Figure 1-1. Site plan showing excavated areas and major landmarks.

mentioned above. On November 30 and December 4, 1837, John O'Donovan visited Dún Ailinne in the course of his survey of Co. Kildare as a field officer of the Ordnance Survey. His description is characteristically both informative and enthusiastic:

> The rath is prodigious! The very largest in Ireland...perhaps...I viewed it with admiration and paced its diameter and circumference.
>
> It consists of one high fosse and deep ditch, which begirds the entire hill at the middle of its height. It measures in diameter about 1200 feet and in circumference 3772 feet. On the summit of the hill was another fort, now much effaced, but from the segment of its circle remaining, I could calculate it to have been about 100 feet in diameter.
>
> Within this fort is another which is somewhat of square form but of very small dimensions, and in its west mound are two rough mountain boulders of considerable size. One of these might be the Ail mentioned in the Dinnseanchus as placed in the mound by the hero Buirech...
>
> But I think that this little internal rath is the honory (*sic*) monument of Aengus Ossory, placed within the larger one after the Rath had ceased to be a Royal Residence. (O'Donovan 1837:120)

During these visits O'Donovan (1837:46-53; 119-26) made a plan of the site (Figure 1-2) and offered the first identification of Knockaulin as the Dún Ailinne (Aillin, Ailenn, and other variations) of medieval Irish writers.

The site had not attracted much attention by archaeologists until we planned our excavation. It is mentioned in the standard guidebooks and syntheses, but no serious attempt was made to relate it archaeologically to the other historical royal sites, or to evaluate such internal features that it possessed. Estyn Evans, for example, suggested that O'Donovan's "fort...much effaced" and the two granite boulders might perhaps be the remains of a round Neolithic or Bronze Age cairn (Evans 1966:137).

The Royal Sites in 1968

From the above it can be seen that, when excavation commenced at Dún Ailinne in 1968, not much was known archaeologically about the site. The same was broadly true of the other royal sites. Seán P. Ó Ríordáin had excavated at Tara in the 1950s, but had published only the report on the Mound of the Hostages (1955) and the Tara guidebook (Ó Ríordáin 1954) before his untimely death. The Mound of the Hostages was a small passage-grave with Bronze Age secondary burials and so did not throw any light upon the use of Tara as a royal site of the Iron Age. He reopened the Rath of the Synods, so hideously mangled by the careless investigations of the early 20th century (see Macalister 1931 for an account of these; also Carew 2003), and cut a trench south from this across the adjacent north side of the bank and ditch at the north end of the Ráith na Ríg. But he reported these only very briefly in his 1954 Tara guidebook.

Minor and poorly reported excavations had taken place at Rathcroghan, in the 19th century (see Wailes 1982:12-15 for discussion and references), but these had no clear bearing upon Rathcroghan as a royal site.

Excavations at Navan had been under way for several years by 1968, but nothing had been published (the first publication was to be Selkirk and Selkirk 1970). By then the outer sod layer of the Site B mound had been removed to reveal the inner stone layer. Of the complex of successive circular timber structures that lay below, deeper trial trenching had revealed only preliminary glimpses.

At Dún Ailinne, then, the most obvious feature that linked it to Tara and Navan was the enclosure itself. At all three sites an unusually large area of a prominent hilltop or ridge was defined by an external bank and internal ditch. This associated them (at least morphologically) with henges rather than with the hillforts as was typical at that time. Their size placed them among the largest prehistoric (or presumably prehistoric) enclosures in Ireland: the Ráith na Ríg at Tara is about 7ha, Navan about 6ha, and Dún Ailinne about 13ha.

The Ráith na Ríg at Tara enclosed three mounds—the Mound of the Hostages, and the conjoined Forradh and Tech Cormaic. Outside the Ráith na Ríg to the north lay the linear "Banqueting Hall," considered by many to be an "avenue." Navan had the Site B mound, then under excavation, and the Site A ringfort structure, which had been excavated but not published. Rathcroghan *was* a substantial mound (this can now be seen to be enclosed within a large apparently circular structure, but this had

Figure 1-2. John O'Donovan's plan from 1837.

not been identified in 1968), and several avenues. Dún Ailinne showed the following possible parallels: an apparent avenue through what appeared to be the original site entrance and, on the summit, the embankment, the small depression within the arc of the embankment, the two granite boulders, and the low mound. The embankment, depression, and boulders were as O'Donovan had described them and could well have been the remains or partial remains of some prehistoric structure or structures. The low mound just to the east of the embankment had not been noted by previous writers. This was not surprising, for the summit area of Dún Ailinne undulates slightly and, as noted above, the low mound rose barely 1 m above its surroundings: it was simply a rather more marked and apparently fairly symmetrical undulation. Once noticed, however, the low mound appeared likely to be artificial rather than natural, possibly a prehistoric mound that had been severely reduced over time by erosion and—probably most particularly—by plowing.

The Initial Exploratory Season, 1968

Although we planned a five-year excavation project we agreed that future excavation would depend on the results obtained in 1968. The most obvious questions to be asked at the outset of exploration were:

- What were the features on the summit (that is, the embankment and the shallow depression and the low mound)? Given the paucity of information about Tara, Rathcroghan, and Navan in 1968 it was impossible to predict what these various features might be.
- Were there any other traces of prehistoric or early historic activity within the site, apart from the summit area? Given the lack of visible surface or subsurface features this question called for geophysical survey and test excavations.
- What were the constructions of the bank and ditch and where was the original site entrance? This called for careful inspection of the whole perimeter for possible entrances and selection of a suitable location for a cross section of the bank and ditch.

Summit Area

Excavation of this area is described in Chapter 2. In 1968, at the outset of excavation, we anticipated that the depth of soil above the subsoil would be shallow and that there would be little if any undisturbed level (or levels) between the plowsoil and the subsoil. Therefore a substantial area excavation was planned, 20 m east-west and 80 m north-south with an indentation to avoid the embankment. We would investigate the embankment by a 2 m wide east-west cutting extending westward from the main excavation area.

The suspicion that the low mound was artificial was rapidly and amply confirmed, since immediately below the plowsoil an extensive deposit of blackened soil, containing both Neolithic and Iron Age material, was revealed. Sections of palisade trench lay to the north of this.

The cutting across the embankment revealed no useful information. Indeed, the embankment remained an enigma to the end of the excavation: almost total excavation showed only that it overlay Iron Age deposits.

Exploratory Survey And Excavation

The exploratory 1968 season included geophysical survey (Ralph 1968). We conducted a cesium magnetometer survey over the entire interior of the site. On the summit area we conducted a more intensive magnetometer survey, along with resistivity survey. A substantial anomaly was revealed on the summit, under the low mound (later excavation showed this to have been an area of burning). No anomalies showed over the rest of the site interior, with the exception of one on the north side just inside the ditch. We excavated there but found no archaeological evidence.

Five 20 m x 20 m test cuttings were laid out north of the summit, running down the slope of the hill to the perimeter (see Figure 1-1). A further cutting, 20 m x 5 m, was made just to the southeast of the large test area on the summit. These produced no archaeological data apart from the very occasional flint flake.

The Perimeter Bank and Ditch

We excavated a cross section of the bank and ditch on the east side of the site, and conducted test excavations for the presence or absence of an external *chevaux-de-frise* and/or internal palisade. Our examination of the entire perimeter revealed that the apparent original site entrance, on the east side, was the only plausible candidate (see Figure 1-1). This work is described in Chapter 3.

The 1968 Exploratory Season: Conclusion

Since the evidence of the geophysical survey and test cuttings was essentially negative, we decided to abandon further testing of the interior. It was clear that the summit area contained abundant evidence of prehistoric (and/or possibly early historic) activities, so most subsequent excavation was of this area, with subsidiary excavation to clarify the original entrance and its avenue or roadway.

Excavation: Methods

Mechanical Stripping

Since we knew that the whole site (including the summit area) had been plowed except for the steeper western field, there would be no stratified deposits or material in the topsoil. So we decided to speed up the 1968 exploratory area excavations by using mechanical means to strip the topsoil. We were thereby able to expose quickly the summit area and the test cuttings elsewhere, enabling closer examination by traditional manual excavation to proceed sooner and thus for decisions as to the future progress of work to be made more quickly.

This mechanical stripping was done by backhoe. An excavation assistant giving hand signals guided the driver, and we found that, after a very short while, the driver could control the depth of excavation very precisely. Not only was this mechanical stripping rapid, but it was also cost effective. A rough calculation, based on experiment, showed removing sod by hand cost about four times more than mechanical stripping.

Manual Excavation

Apart from mechanical stripping of sod, we conducted excavation by traditional manual methods. We used very gentle pick and shovel work or trowelling as appropriate, and we passed all material through standard 1/4-inch mesh sieves. In areas where the sod had been stripped mechanically, we stopped above the base of the plowsoil and reached the base of the plowsoil by hand excavation.

Recording

Site supervisors recorded information in notebooks on a day-to-day routine basis. The director kept a general site record of progress, including frequent summaries, especially of developing and changing interpretations. In 1968 the relatively recent availability of Polaroid cameras and film proved a major boon in recording: supervisors could photograph any portion of their area, stick the photograph into their site book, and write comments around (or even on) it. As is normal, we took regular photographs frequently, both in black-and-white and color. On the summit area, a scaffolding photographic tower about 10 m high proved invaluable not only for panoramic photographs but also as a viewing tower from which we could survey the progress of the excavation and plan its immediate future progress.

An arbitrary grid of 1 km x 1 km was laid over the site plan, approximating to the cardinal points of the compass. In areas to be excavated, labeled pegs were put down at 10 m or 20 m intervals to act as local reference points. The grid recording system was based on the Ordnance Survey model: the southwest corner of the site grid was zero; any given point could then be recorded to the nearest centimeter by five digits representing distance east, followed by a further five digits representing distance north.

It must be said, however, that it was too easy to transpose digits accidentally when recording in the field. So a very close eye had to be kept on site supervisors' daily records. Even so, some mistakes slipped through and were noticed only later, on analysis. Moreover, site supervisors were clearly sometimes tempted to record the location of a "find" in "round figures" rather than precisely to the nearest centimeter.

We bagged finds daily, assigning each object or group of contiguous objects a number running consecutively 1–∞. We kept a "Finds Register" in which all finds were entered daily. Each entry included the registration number, date, location (the site grid reference number, plus any other location information such as "fill of pit xx"), level, and type of find. We duplicated this information on the slip of paper placed into each finds bag. Objects being individually labeled bore the excavation number plus the finds registration number (for example, E.79.123).

"Features" were also numbered 1–∞. There are, however, breaks in this sequence. As work progressed, supervisors working in different areas were assigned a sequence of numbers for day-to-day use. Consequently, a given sequence of numbers might not be completely used before excavation had finished in that area. Features were entered in the "Features Log," analogous to the "Finds Register." Each feature was entered with its number, grid reference location, dimensions, brief description (sometimes using standard abbreviations) and level.

When the Dún Ailinne excavations began, the "Harris Matrix" system had not come into use, whereby each level, post-hole, lens, etc., was given its own number. At Dún Ailinne, the numbered features were post-holes, stake-holes, trenches, pits, and so forth. Soil levels were not designated by numbers (see below, "Phases").

We recorded all features on plan. In most cases, working field plans were drawn at a scale of 1:50. In some cases, where much detail had to be drawn, the scale was 1:20. Sections were drawn at 1:20 scale. As work progressed, with larger areas planned, 1:100 scale plans were prepared from the 1:50 field plans.

Phases

The complexity of the summit area excavation, with very many features, levels, and lenses, led to the rapid abandonment of the initial scheme of numbered phases (Iron Age phase 1, 2, 4,...). Instead, we introduced nonsense names. Bohumil Soudsky used color names for phases at Bylany, and William Coe III used personal names (Tom, Dick, Harry...) at Tikal. This system still provides an identifying reference but avoids the need to interpolate additional numbers in between existing numbers as the excavation progresses, such as the need to insert 2a between 1 and 2 when an intervening level is identified. These were not needed in the excavation of the site entrance or the bank and ditch, and so refer only to phases of the summit area.

The system described briefly above developed with the recognition of a clear distinction between evidence for *construction* and evidence for *use*. In brief, post-holes, slot trenches, and other features represent relatively short-term *episodes* when structures were being erected and pits dug. Levels, lenses, and surfaces, on the other hand, represent longer-term *periods* of use. Thus, for example, the timber structure dubbed "Mauve" was presumably erected within a fairly short space of time, so is an episode. However, it is likely that this "Mauve" structure stood and was used for some time. During this time, it was demonstrated stratigraphically that a surface named "Harry" was in use. Thus Mauve and Harry were contemporaneous (or at least largely so), but should be distinguished one from the other, not least because an object from a Mauve palisade trench presumably got there during Mauve construction, whereas an object embedded in the Harry surface could have got there at any time while that surface was exposed.

The phases of the summit area excavation, then, are a combination of episodes and periods. The two sequences can be correlated at some points, but not invariably, so it is important to maintain their separation, as shown in the summit area sequence chart (see Chapter 2).

Excavation: Some Interpretive Issues

Soil and Subsoil

The bedrock of Dún Ailinne is slate and graywacke, bedded obliquely from (roughly) south-southeast to north-northwest. The area excavation of the summit thus exposed ridges of bedrock just below the plowsoil, running roughly east-northeast to west-southwest. The bedrock varies very considerably in hardness – in some places it is very hard, indeed, while in others it is quite soft and friable.

Over the bedrock lies a sheet of glacial till, up to 1 m or more deep between the ridges of bedrock, but very thin or even nonexistent where the bedrock ridges occur. As is commonly the case, the glacial till contains fragments of very varied geological origin (including Antrim flint), and varies considerably in texture—in most places rather "gravelly" but in others finer and more "sandy."

These variations in the bedrock and overlying glacial till subsoil provided both a substantial problem in excavation (see below), and—we judge—considerable problems for the Iron Age construction crews (see Conclusion to Chapter 2).

Glacial Till—Natural and Redeposited Natural

In all excavated areas there was the usual endemic problem of distinguishing between undisturbed subsoil ("natural") and disturbed subsoil ("redeposited natural"). On the summit area in particular this problem loomed large because of the many trenches, post-holes, and pits that were found, as well as the sequence of levels that formed the low mound. First, when a hole is dug, the spoil has to go somewhere. In the case of a hole or trench dug to receive an upright post or posts, some of the spoil may be packed in again around the post as primary fill, while the rest may be spread around in a thin layer. Second, the material that forms an archaeological level or lens must come from somewhere; some of this is likely to come from the excavation of post-holes and trenches.

The problem of distinguishing undisturbed natural from redeposited natural, then, is not merely a mechanical question but an issue that bears heavily upon the interpretation of events. All the usual rules of thumb were employed continually for this problem. In general, subsoil containing some admixture of soil or flecks of charcoal was determined to be redeposited. "Dirty" subsoil was deemed redeposited, while "clean" subsoil was deemed undisturbed natural. This useful rule of thumb, however, cannot be taken as an invariable rule. Subsoil *can* be dug up and reposited without getting contaminated by soil or charcoal. Conversely, undisturbed natural can be infiltrated from above by earth and charcoal flecks filtering down crevices.

Anthony Ryan, a visiting geologist with considerable research experience of glacial till, introduced us to a cheap, simple, and very useful method of assisting a decision in cases of doubt. Most glacial till in Ireland contains small fragments of limestone, and this is certainly true at Dún Ailinne. Over time, these limestone particles are progressively dissolved, from the surface downward, by the slightly acid content of percolating rainwater.

Dilute hydrochloric acid, readily and cheaply available from local pharmacies, can be dribbled onto a disputed deposit of subsoil by means of an eyedropper: if there is bubbling and fizzing, then there are limestone particles; if not, then all limestone particles have already been dissolved out by rainwater.

On an exposed vertical section cut through undisturbed glacial till subsoil hydrochloric acid will produce no reaction near the surface. Lower down, however, reaction will begin to appear, as the acid reaches undissolved limestone particles. This simple test proved very useful in numerous places where it could not be decided by conventional rule of thumb means whether or not a given deposit was disturbed.

Trenches, Holes, and Pits

From the outset of excavation in 1968, we found traces of prehistoric construction, and these became very common as excavation progressed. We found most of these on the summit area, though a few occurred in the site entrance excavation area. These features appeared initially as discolorations and/or texture disconformities, such as concentrations of small stones, on the surface of the subsoil. Trowelling out the discolorations eventually produced holes of one sort or another. As work progressed it became increasingly clear that most of these features fell into one of four interpretive categories—post-holes, stake-holes, palisade trenches, and pits. A few could not be assigned to any of these categories and remain labeled simply as undefined features.

Post-holes were identified by vertical sides, sufficient depth to support at least a short post, and some evidence of both primary and secondary fill. The diameter of a post-hole is normally excavated larger than the post it is to receive. With the post in place it is then necessary to pack it around with material sufficient to hold the post firmly in place. This packing is the primary fill and very often contains many stones (for obvious reasons) where these are available, which is the case at Dún Ailinne. If the post rots *in situ*, the void will become filled with soft, stone-free humic material. On the other hand, the post may be extracted. In this case, (a) it is likely that the primary fill will be disturbed, and (b) the void will be deliberately filled in with whatever material lies to hand, such as loose soil and stones.

Stake-holes have no primary fill, for stakes are small enough to be driven directly into the ground. It may be more difficult, with stake-holes as opposed to post-holes, to determine whether the stake has been removed or has rotted *in situ*, since a stake may be withdrawn with relatively little effort to leave a clean void which, if it fills gradually with humic material, may be indistinguishable from a stake that has been left to rot in place. However, the gradual filling in of a stake socket is likely to result in the inclusion of some small stones and topsoil, which may serve to differentiate this fill from a stake that has rotted in place to leave a clean humic fill.

Palisade trenches, often called slot-trenches, are designed to receive a continuous series of close-set posts that, when completed, form a palisade. The construction method is the same as for post-holes: the trench is dug wider than the posts, which must then be packed in with primary fill to support them firmly in place.

Pits are holes that show no evidence of having supported posts or stakes. Their original purpose may be assessed either from their contents (such as storage pits, rubbish pits, burial pits) or possibly from their position in relation to neighboring features on the site (such as pits near houses may have been borrow-pits from which soil was dug to provide daub for house walls).

At Dún Ailinne almost every post-hole and palisade trench contained disturbed primary fill and loose, jumbled secondary fill. This showed that the posts originally set into these holes and trenches had been deliberately extracted. In many locations, the primary fill was so disturbed as to suggest that the post had been rocked to and fro to loosen it before it could be extracted.

It is on the basis of such evidence that we posit (a) that Iron Age activities on the summit of Dún Ailinne included the erection of large timber constructions, and (b) that these structures were dismantled rather than being left to rot away.

2
Excavation of the Summit Area

Bernard Wailes

The summit became the primary focus of excavation, as explained in Chapter 1 (Plate 2-1). During the first season's work, an area 80 m x 20 m was laid out across the low mound and stripped of sod (see Figure 1-1). Blackened soil, containing burnt stone, ash and charcoal, containing *inter alia* heavily corroded iron objects and glass beads, was exposed beneath the sod, and clearly showed some focus of intense prehistoric or early historic activities.

To the north of the low mound we found a section of palisade trench (516), but beyond that, to the north, there were no signs of activity beyond the occasional flint flake. The northern 18 m of this area, therefore, was backfilled. To the south of the low mound we found some indications of trenches, and left them to be examined at a later date.

As excavation progressed during subsequent years the outline of successive circular structures gradually appeared, partially covered by the low mound (Plate 2-2, 2-3). These structures extended both west and east of the 1968 excavation area, which was consequently expanded in those directions to the area shown in CD Figure 2-1.

The surface of the low mound exposed during the first season contained not only Iron Age artifacts, but also typologically Neolithic artifacts. These latter also occurred in the topsoil of areas surrounding the low mound. So from the start two things seemed very probable: that a Neolithic component would eventually be found on the summit, and that there had been considerable disturbance of the site to have brought Neolithic material to the surface.

Our primary purpose here is descriptive, so we will limit discussion to that necessary in order to explain the features and layers described, along with their relationships. More detailed discussion can be found in Chapters 16-18.

In this chapter, we give explanations for the relationships between the various cultural sequences. These correlations are shown in chart form at the end of the chapter in order to guide the reader (see Chapter 1 for the procedures used for recording stratigraphy).

Sequence

Table 2-1 shows the sequence ultimately determined for the summit area at Dún Ailinne. One section shows surfaces and layers and the other shows structures.

The summit excavation covered an area approximately 70 m x 80 m, with hundreds of features, many of which are stake-holes about 1 cm in diameter (Plate 2-4). In practical terms, it is impossible to publish an illustration of all summit area features on one plan at a scale that permits every feature, plus its identifying number, to be clearly visible. A reference plan, divided into four parts (CD Figures 2-2, 2-3, 2-4, and 2-5), that provides this information appears on the accompanying CD. In these plans, all features are included and all are numbered; where numbers did not appear on the original plans, the feature is designated on the reference plans with an "N" so that the reader un-

Table 2-1. Dún Ailinne Summit Area: Sequence of layers and surfaces.

PHASE	DESCRIPTION
Topsoil	Plowsoil. Contains artifacts of all periods from Neolithic on.
Flame	Uppermost level of low mound. Loose stones (many burned), ash, charcoal, much animal bone.
Dun	Light colored, gravelly, mainly /wholly redeposited "natural". "Paving" over part of area.
Upper Emerald	Very dark, much charcoal.
Crimson	Gravelly light-colored "occupation" surface between Lower Emerald and Upper Emerald. On east side covers Mauve palisade trenches. On south and west peters out within Emerald. To north continues beyond Upper Emerald and Lower Emerald to merge imperceptibly into Occupation.
Lower Emerald	Similar composition to Upper Emerald.
Harry*	Occupation surface below Lower Emerald.
Jade*	Occupation surface below Harry.
Niamh*	Occupation surface below Jade.
pre-Niamh	Definition uncertain; possible surface directly below Niamh.
Blue*	Old ground surface (compressed sod) below Niamh/pre-Niamh.
Occupation	Thin, patchy, dirty layer with occupation debris. Lies outside protective cover of low mound deposits and so is sandwiched between natural and plowsoil, and in places is destroyed by plowing. Contemporaneous with all phases between natural and plowsoil (except Violet?).
Violet	Lenses below and distinguishable from Occupation. Could be contemporaneous with Tan, Khaki, Blue, Niamh, Jade, or Harry.
Natural	Bedrock/undisturbed glacial till.

Dún Ailinne Summit Area: Sequence of features (trenches, pits) and/or evidence of various construction episodes.

PHASE	DESCRIPTION
Uaininn	post-Iron Age rig-and-furrow on east side of summit area. Medieval (?), early modern (?). Chronological relationship to Grey unknown.
Grey	Arc-shaped embankment and quarry ditch. Separated from Iron Age levels by thick buried sod. Medieval (?), very early modern (?). Chronological relationship to Uaininn unknown.
Mauve	Iron Age: last construction episode. Circular trenches 515, 516; circle of large posts 1-30; central circular structure 42. Partial contemporaneity postulated on geometric grounds.
Lemon	Two features (86, 411) cut into Rose, and cut into by Mauve.
Rose	Iron Age. Circular trenches 60, 513, 514; smaller circular annexe to south (trenches 519, 520 etc.); entrance (to east-northeast) flanked by antennae trenches 278, 341; between these antennae trenches are lines of post-holes and two short trenches, 2231, 2232.
White	Single circular palisade trench 512. No dating evidence (artifactual or radiocarbon), but presumed Iron Age because appears to have been dismantled and immediately replaced by Rose phase constructions and has entrance aligned east-northeast, like subsequent Rose and Mauve phase circular structures. Possibly may have small central arrangement of posts.
Khaki	Features cut through by White trench (512), but with no evidence to suggest Neolithic date. Shallow pit (2790) contains portion of food vessel (E.79.905/906).
Tan	Features such as 281 and 293 containing only Neolithic artifacts. No material suitable for radiocarbon dating.
Z	Features that cannot be related to any other phase by stratigraphy, artifacts, or geometry.

*Harry, Jade, Niamh, (and pre-Niamh?) and Blue exist *only* under the protective cover of Lower Emerald derstands that the number wasn't inadvertently left off. Plans referred to in the text, which are more general and at smaller scales, can also be found on the CD to provide over-all views of the summit area. These latter necessarily omit many smaller features, and most of the feature numbers are not included.

Also for reference, a section drawing was compiled that runs across the summit area, approximately bisecting the low mound and feature 42 (Mauve phase) and cutting across the end of the arc-shaped embankment. The exposed section faced north, so the drawing runs east to west. This is shown in Figure 2-6, also located on the CD.

The descriptions that follow are arranged in chronological sequence (from Neolithic through to modern). However, in the interest of clear discussion, it is not always possible to follow this sequential pattern exactly.

Blue Phase (Layer)

Blue phase is a surface below Niamh, pre-Niamh, Jade, and Harry surfaces (CD Figure 2-7). All survived as recognizable and separable entities only because they were protected by Lower Emerald layer. Blue layer covered a relatively small area. It was very compact, presumably due to the covering weight of the low mound levels above. Unlike Niamh, Jade, and Harry surfaces above it, Blue did not include a gravelly component but was a relatively soft, silty, humic, ginger-brown deposit, and it lay directly above the natural soil.

These factors strongly suggest that Blue layer was a surviving patch of the humus that developed over the glacial till in Late Glacial/earlier Holocene times, perhaps around 8000 BC, and was probably the surface that extended across the summit area when Neolithic activities began. If so, then Blue would have been earlier than, contemporaneous with, and later than the Tan and Khaki features.

Neolithic and Bronze Age: Tan Phase (Features)

The occurrence of Neolithic artifacts from the topsoil on down indicated from the start of excavation that, eventually, a disturbed Neolithic component would emerge. This proved to be the case. Tan phase features contain *only* typologically Neolithic artifacts, and two (281 and 293) are cut through by Iron Age features (CD Figure 2-8).

Feature 281

This is a curved ditch of an irregular pear shape, with the point at the southwest end (maximum dimensions 22 m x 26 m). Whether this pointed end was open or whether 281 originally continued is not known since the later feature 2432 was cut down here. The base of the pear, the northeast side, is completely missing, cut away by Mauve feature 42. The dimensions of 281 are also irregular: the width at its top varies between 1 m and 2 m; the depth varies, too, averaging about 0.5 m. The cross section of 281 is a shallow splayed U-shape, which does *not* resemble the later Iron Age palisade trenches. There are no traces of post-holes in its fill.

The fill of this ditch is unsorted, very hard, and compacted. There is little trace of any silt line at the bottom and no traces of upcast from the original digging of 281 in the vicinity. Taken together, these factors suggest that 281 was filled, probably not long after it was dug, largely with the material that had been excavated from it. This fill contained a number of Neolithic artifacts but, alas, nothing that could have been used for radiocarbon age determination.

The original purpose of 281 is obscure, since it does not resemble any known house-foundation of the Neolithic (or indeed any other period), nor does it resemble any form of tomb, Neolithic or otherwise. There are no post- or stake-holes inside its curving outline or in the immediate vicinity outside.

Feature 293

This *appears* to have been originally a pit about 2 m x 1 m in area, and perhaps about 0.7 m deep. It had been cut through by the southwestern stretch of Rose phase palisade trench 514. This destroyed most of 293, leaving only its two ends. The fill remaining in the northwest end contained a large portion of a Linkardstown-type decorated bowl and a small perforated stone bead. These Neolithic vessels are found mainly in southeast Ireland, in burial contexts, so we propose that 293 had been one of these burial pits.

Feature 2506

This is a pit discovered in the course of trowelling across the Rose phase entrance area. It contained a cache of 13 flints (including the projectile point E.79.3480), interpreted as a deliberate deposit of the Neolithic period.

Table 2-2. Dún Ailinne Summit: Composite Sequence Chart. Aspects Aligned Horizontally Are Considered Contemporary in Time.

MAIN STRUCTURES AND FEATURES	FEATURE 42, MAUVE CENTER	LAYERS AND SURFACES
		Flame
	Burning over Feature 42	Dun
20 m post circle (Mauve) dismantled	Feature 42 dismantled	
		Upper Emerald
		Crimson
		Lower Emerald
Mauve palisades dismantled	(Feature 42 possibly dismantled?)	Harry
		Jade
Mauve palisades and 20 m post circle erected	Feature 42 erected	Niamh
		pre-Niamh
Rose structures dismantled		Jade?
		Niamh?
Rose structures erected		pre-Niamh?
White structure dismantled		
White structure erected		?
Khaki (including food vessel deposit)		
Tan (Neolithic feature)		Blue

Neolithic and Bronze Age: Khaki (Features)

Feature 2780

This shallow pit contained conjoining fragments of a food vessel (E79.905/906) (CD Figure 2-8). There were no other associated artifacts or any fragments of bone. If this represents the remains of a burial, the pit is curiously shallow, but there are no indications that there had been any covering mound. Associated charcoal provided a radiocarbon age determination of 1270 BC ± 55 (sample no. SI 982—Stukenrath and Mielke 1973:399-400).

Feature 161

This pit is cut into by the White phase circular palisade trench. It contained no artifacts or any material that could be used for radiocarbon age determination.

Iron Age Features

Construction Features and Layers/Surfaces

This section presents the data for successive Iron Age *construction episodes* (see Chapter 1). There is some correlation with Iron Age *layers* (detailed later), so it is impossible to separate the two categories even at this descriptive stage. The interrelationships between the Iron Age constructions (features) and layers may be found later in this chapter.

Timber Structures: Construction and Dismantling

A great many of the Iron Age features on the summit were trenches and post- or stake-holes (see Chapter 1 for further discussion). Most of the trenches had originally held close-set upright timbers to form palisades and so are called "palisade trenches" (often called "slot-trenches" in the literature).

In not a single instance had the timber(s) in a post-hole or palisade trench been left standing to rot away naturally. In all but one example (burnt posts, see below) it appeared that the upright timbers had been deliberately extracted. The force required to loosen large timbers in their sockets prior to withdrawing them meant that usually the primary fill, including packing-stones, had been disturbed. In several instances it was clear that (a) trenches and holes had originally held posts, and (b) these had been deliberately removed:

- In a number of places enough of the primary trench fill remained intact to see clearly the outline of a portion of the timber that had been removed, with vertical packing-stones still in place.
- In a couple of places the base of the upright timber had left a clear impression in the bottom of a palisade trench.
- Occasionally a timber had been removed "cleanly" from its socket, leaving the primary fill intact and providing a complete imprint of the original timber.
- In only one place, in 341 (the south side of the Rose phase "antennae" entrance complex), a short stretch of contiguous timber stumps remained *in situ* in their sockets, where they had been burnt. This, of course, provided crystal-clear *positive* evidence for the original presence of upright timber posts. One supposes that they had not been removed simply because, being already burnt, this was unnecessary.

White Phase

Feature 512

This is a circular palisade trench, diameter 23 m, with an entrance to the east-northeast (CD Figure 2-9). It cuts across feature 281, a Neolithic trench (see above), in two places and is in turn cut across by features 60/513/514 of Rose phase (see below). The fill of 512 contains several Neolithic artifacts (pottery and flint), but also two pieces of iron (E79.1089 and. E79.2329) and a piece of slag (E79.3203). These latter indicate an Iron Age date for 512, as does the lack of any indication for a lapse in time between the dismantling of 512 and the construction of the subsequent Rose phase structures.

Feature 2302

At the center of 512 is what appears to be a composite feature (2302) consisting of two arcs of small freestanding posts. These *might* originally have formed a complete circle about 4 m in diameter. But their relationship to 512 cannot be established, and two of the post-holes are set into the fill of the Rose phase palisade trench 514. The reason for suggesting that this little complex might be contemporaneous with 512 is its position central to the 512 circular structure. We shall discuss this further below.

Rose Phase

After the White phase structure 512 was dismantled, a far larger and far more ambitious complex structure was erected: two conjoined circles of timber palisades, the larger having an elaborate entranceway to the east-northeast (CD Figure 2-10). This entranceway faced the main site entrance and its inner roadway (Chapter 3), and the geometric relationship between the Rose phase constructions on the summit and the site entrance and inner roadway suggest that these two complexes were laid out and constructed as a part of one design at the same time.

Rose Large Enclosure

This circular enclosure comprises three concentric palisade trenches (features 60, 513, and 514) with a maximum diameter of 38 m. Feature 60 is the innermost, the narrowest, and the least deep.

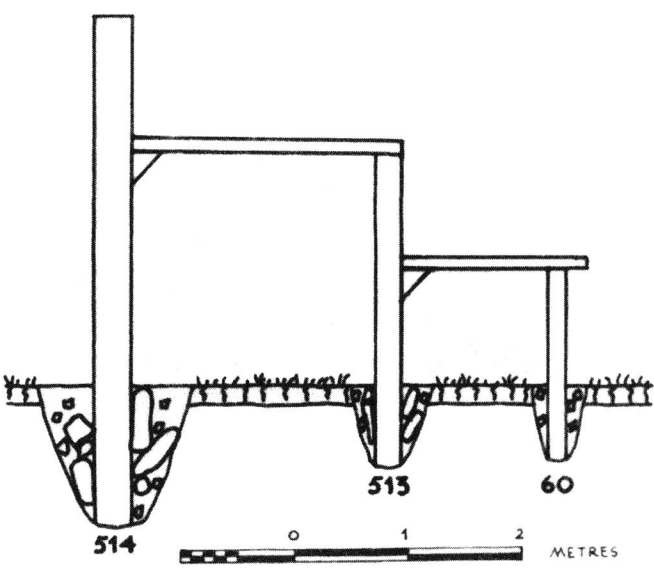

Figure 2-11. Possible reconstruction of Rose phase viewing platform.

Feature 513 is intermediate between the other two in position, width, and depth; there is a gap of about 20 m on its west-southwest side, more or less opposite the main entrance to this large enclosure. Feature 514 is the outermost palisade trench, and it is the widest and deepest. The three palisade trenches are set quite close to one another, with about 1 m between them.

This triple-walled structure is broken by a main entrance to the east-northeast, about 4.5 m wide, and a smaller gap to the south-southwest, where this larger Rose circle joins the smaller circle, or "annex," as it was dubbed. These two circles were laid out and constructed at the same time: on the eastern side of the entrance between Rose large circle and the annex its two outer palisade trenches (513 and 514) converge and join the outer palisade trench of the Rose annex (505) in one unit, with *no* stratigraphic sign that one was added to the other. Mercifully, this critical junction was left intact when the later Mauve palisade trenches (515 and 516) were cut either side of it. On the other (west) side of the entrance between these two Rose circles, the junction is largely obscured by the later Mauve large post-holes 22, 23, and 24.

The deliberate grading of these three concentric palisades of the larger Rose circle, from the smallest (60) on the inside to the largest (514) on the outside, suggest that they could have supported some sort of upper-works which were higher on the outside and lower on the inside. Two tiered platforms would be a possibility, to have created standing or seating space for upper and lower rows of people watching or participating in activities taking place within the circle. A possible reconstruction of such a feature is shown in Figure 2-11.

No features within this larger Rose circle (60/513/514) can be associated either stratigraphically or geometrically with the enclosing triple-ring palisade structure.

The Rose Phase "Annex"

As noted above, a smaller circle of palisade trenches (features 215, 217, 366, 505, 506, 518, 519, 520, 1267, 1422, and 1423) conjoins the larger circle (60, 513, 514) on the south-southwest side of the latter. The gap between the two circles is narrow, about 1.5 m. The annex also has its own entrance from the outside, about 2 m wide, on the east-northeast perimeter. The maximum diameter of the Rose annex was 21 m. A line of three post-holes within the annex runs north-northeast to south-southwest just inside the western side of the entrance from the larger Rose circle, along with a small scatter of stake-holes. These post-holes and stake-holes *might* have been the bases for some sort of fence just inside the gap between the annex and the larger Rose circle, but this is highly conjectural, not least since they have no demonstrable stratigraphic relationship to the Rose structures.

The annex circle was composed of two close-set concentric palisade trenches (the outer one being 505/520, the inner 506/519), with an intermediate palisade trench (1422) running between them from the southeast clockwise to the northwest. To the west, these three trenches are almost completely obliterated by feature 2432, but their bases could be just partly discerned.

Two alternative explanations have been put forward for this double/triple palisade trench construction. The first is that additional support was needed because of the very shallow nature of the palisade trenches around part of their perimeter. This, with little doubt, is because hard bedrock comes very close to the surface over part of this area of the summit. The second explanation (Lynn 1991) is that this Rose annex was modified or at least partly re-built at some stage, with earlier stretches of palisade being replaced using new trenches in which to set at least some of the new posts. The

Excavation of the Summit Area

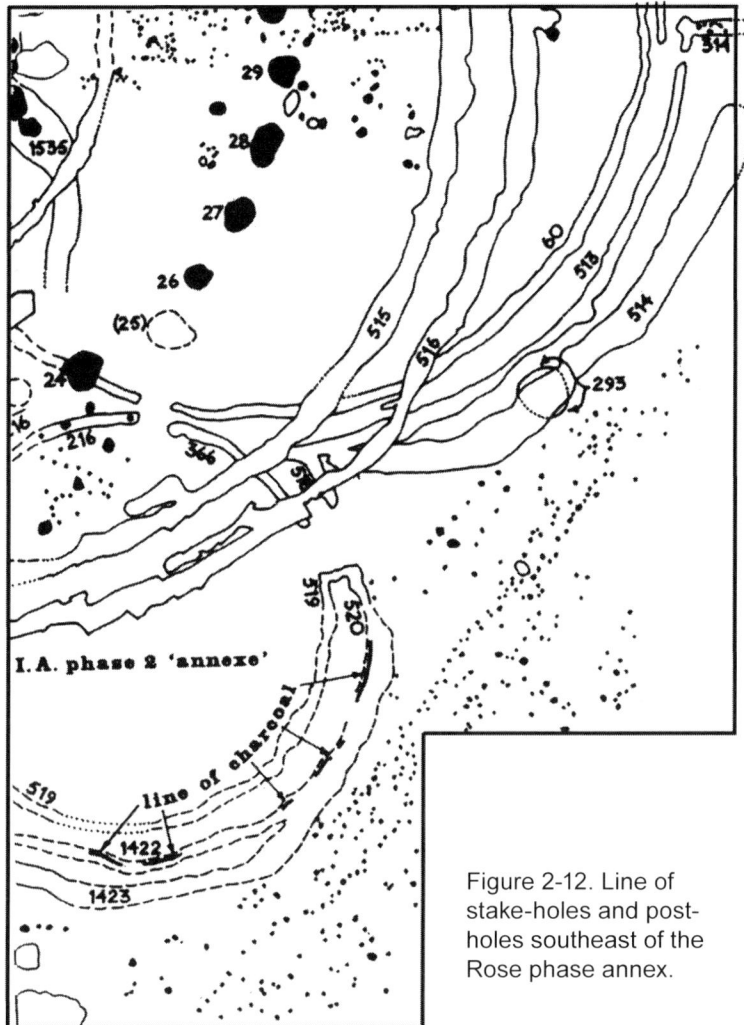

Figure 2-12. Line of stake-holes and post-holes southeast of the Rose phase annex.

very shallow stratigraphy (see above) of much of this area makes it impossible to decide between these two interpretations.

Linear Stake-Holes Southeast of Annex

Outside the Rose annex to the east lay a linear arrangement of multiple stake-holes and a few post-holes running roughly north-northeast to south-southwest (Figure 2-12). This line was tangential both to 520, the outer palisade trench of the annex, and to 514, the outer palisade of the larger Rose circular structure (Plate 2-5). The line continued beyond the place where it is closest to 520 and onward to the southerly limit of the summit excavation area.

It was impossible to link these stake-holes stratigraphically with either 520 or 514, but they come very close to both palisade trenches, strongly suggesting that the stake-holes were designed to brush against the palisade trenches. This impression is reinforced because these stake-holes do not continue past the points where they brush against palisade trench 514. For this reason this arrangement of stake-holes is assigned to Rose phase. If they are indeed Rose phase, their purpose is obscure, for if they represent some form of fencing, they would have effectively blocked the exterior entrance of the Rose annex.

Rose Entrance Complex Features

On the east-northeast of the larger Rose circle the outermost palisade trench (514) stops short of the middle (513) and inner (60) palisade trenches. The two latter end and join to leave a gap forming an entrance ca. 4.5 m wide.

Two linear palisade trenches (278 and 341) run perpendicular to feature 513. Feature 278 starts in a roughly northeasterly direction but bends gradually to run closer to east-northeast. Feature 341 runs nearly due east. Thus these two palisade trenches diverge and could be called antennae trenches. Only some stretches of 278 and 341 were excavated completely, but their continuous lengths were traced by excavating their fill sufficiently to define their edges. Those stretches that were excavated completely had originally held close-set upright posts, that is, palisades. One stretch of 341 contained the burnt stumps of several contiguous posts, still *in situ* (Plate 2-6). Both 278 and 341 were traced to the eastern limit of the defined excavation area and presumably continued at least some distance eastward down the slope of the hill.

Within the funnel formed by the two antennae trenches 278 and 341 ran two lines of post-holes forming an avenue, although they diverged very slightly as they progressed eastward.

Between the two rows of posts described above, and along the same axis, were a pair of short linear trenches, 2231 to the north and 2232 to the south. Each was about 3 m long, and each showed evidence of having originally held close-set vertical posts. These two trenches are about 5 m apart.

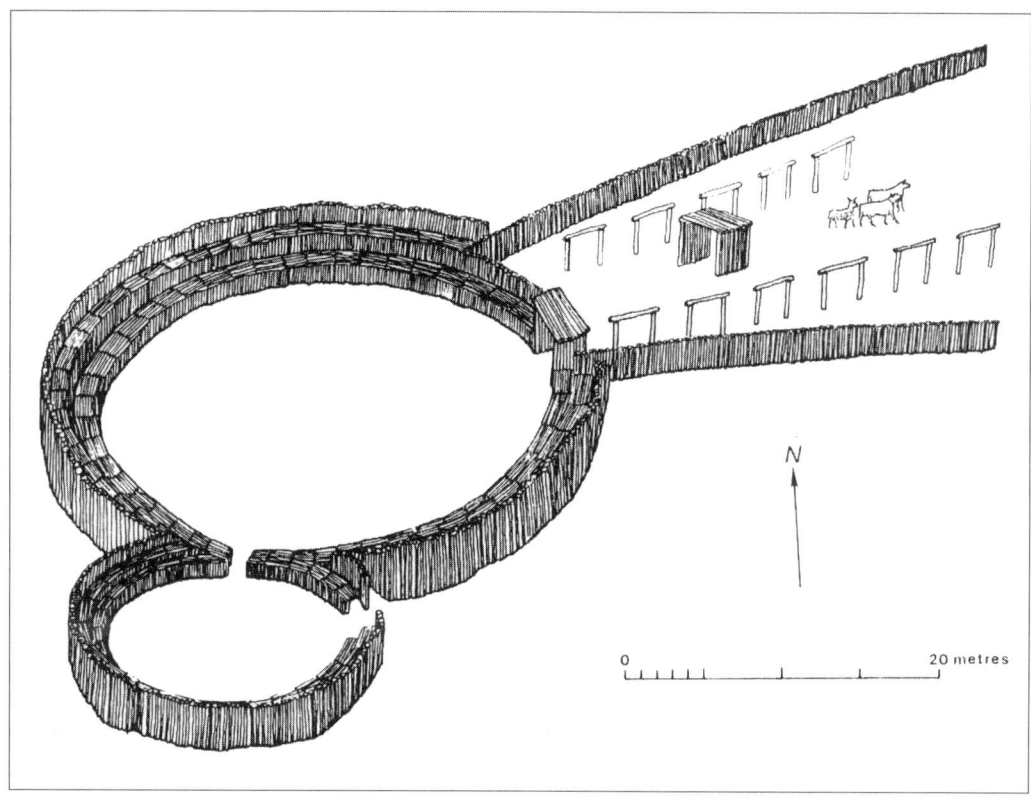

2-13. Possible reconstruction of the Rose phase structures.

There were no features between 2231 and 2232, but a mass of stake-holes and small post-holes ran north from 2231 to the northern antenna trench, 278, and a similar mass of stake-holes and small post-holes ran south from 2232 to the southern antenna trench, 341. Neither of these two concentrations of stakes and posts formed a very coherent pattern, but their general appearance is linear, and here and there within both groups distinct lines of holes could be discerned.

The avenue of post-holes, the two short palisade trenches 2231 and 2232, and the roughly linear masses of stake-holes and post-holes, cannot be related stratigraphically to the larger Rose circle. Nevertheless, their position leaves little doubt that they form an integral part of the same plan, so they have been included unhesitatingly with Rose. This complex must have presented a very impressive approach up the hillside from the original site entrance and its internal roadway to the east (see Chapter 3). Figure 2-13 shows a possible reconstruction of what the Rose phase structure might have looked like.

Lemon Phase

Three features—86, 406, and 441—cut into Rose features, but were in turn cut into by Mauve features. Both were irregular pits of no ascertainable purpose.

Mauve Phase

The last Iron Age building activities on the summit consisted of three concentric constructions (CD Figure 2-14). On the outside was a circle, 43 m in diameter, of double palisade trenches (inner 515, outer 516), with an entrance to the east-northeast. Inside this lay a circle of large free-standing posts (features 1-15, 19-30), 20 m in diameter. At the center was feature 42, a 6 m diameter circular palisade trench.

Mauve Chronology

While the concentric arrangement of these three main components briefly described above indicates that all three formed part of one design, the chronological history of Mauve is complicated. Stratigraphically, the trenches of the outer palisade circles (515 and 516) were dug at the same time as the holes for the 20 m circle of large posts. This was demonstrated because both were dug immediately before the deposition of the surface Harry (see below). Feature 42 is clearly post-Rose since it cuts into the Rose palisade trench 60. But the Harry surface was of limited extent, and did not extend as far as feature 42. Construction of the latter, then, remains a part of Mauve primarily on geometric grounds.

Over a limited area inside the eastern part of the circle described by the Mauve palisade trenches (515 and 516) Lower Emerald level was deposited above the Harry surface. Above Lower Emerald was Crimson level, and above Crimson was Upper Emerald. Lower Emerald and Crimson levels extended far enough to the east to cover the *secondary* fill of the inner Mauve palisade trench 515. Thus the posts of 515 (and probably the outer palisade trench 516) were extracted before the deposition of Lower Emerald. The 20 m circle of large posts remained standing during the deposition of Lower Emerald, Crimson, and Upper Emerald. Finally, the posts of the 20 m post circle were extracted, and Dun level laid over some of them (again, in the eastern area of the Mauve circle). The Mauve palisades (515 and 516) were dismantled, while the 20 m circle of large posts remained standing for a while longer.

The relationship of the central feature 42 to the sequence of events outlined above is uncertain because none of the low mound layers, except Flame, extended far enough west. Since it cut into Rose trench 60, it seems likely to be contemporaneous with the Mauve perimeter trenches (515 and 516) and the 20 m circle of large posts, which also cut into Rose features. Moreover, feature 42 is at the geometric center of the Mauve constructions. After the feature 42 structure had been dismantled there was intense burning over much of its floor and wall trench, leaving a layer rich in charcoal. Above this was Flame layer. The burning over dismantled feature 42, therefore, was almost certainly contemporaneous with Lower Emerald, Crimson, Upper Emerald, or Dun.

Mauve Circular Palisade

This consisted of two concentric trenches, 515 (outer) and 516 (inner) (Plate 2-7 shows a section of 515). The outer circle, 516, has a gap in its western side and another on its southern side. The entrance to this circle was about 2 m wide, to the east-northeast. This entrance was flanked by four short internal palisade trenches perpendicular to 515, suggesting that the entrance was built up into quite an elaborate gateway. Above ground level it is possible that 515 and 516 palisades were originally joined to form a parapet or viewing platform from which activities within the circle could be watched. Figure 2-11 shows a possible reconstruction of this for the Rose phase, and gives an impression of the kind of structure envisioned for the Mauve phase as well.

Mauve 20 m Diameter Circle of Large Posts

These large post-holes measured on average about 1 m diameter and were about 1 m deep (Plates 2-8, 2-9, and 2-10 show three of these post-holes). The primary fill in most of the holes was very badly disturbed when the posts were removed, but here and there sufficient primary fill and packing stones remained *in situ* to show that the original posts were about 0.5 m in diameter. As a comparison, a typical telegraph pole today is about 0.2 m in diameter.

Post-hole 30 provided a particularly good cross section (CD Figure 2-15). Worthy of comment is the intense burning that took place around this post on the surface (Harry) laid down over the primary fill (that is, shortly after this post had been erected), burning sufficiently intense that the surface turned white, grading into red and then pink as the diminishing heat penetrated farther into the ground. Nevertheless, the cross section shows quite unambiguously that post-hole 30 remained standing despite this intense burning and was not extracted until some time later (after the deposition of Lower Emerald, Crimson, and Upper Emerald layers around it).

Eventually 27 post-holes of this 20 m circle were identified (30 had been anticipated originally, with advance feature numbers 1–30, of which only feature numbers 1–15 and 19–30 were used), of which 26 were excavated and one (21) was defined at its surface level but not excavated. The southwest side of this circle was cut across by the northern end of the Grey phase feature 390, the quarry ditch which provided the material for the arc-shaped embankment. If there *had* been post-holes here, and they were equidistant with the other post-holes in this circle, feature 390 would have destroyed two. An original circle of 29 large posts is postulated,

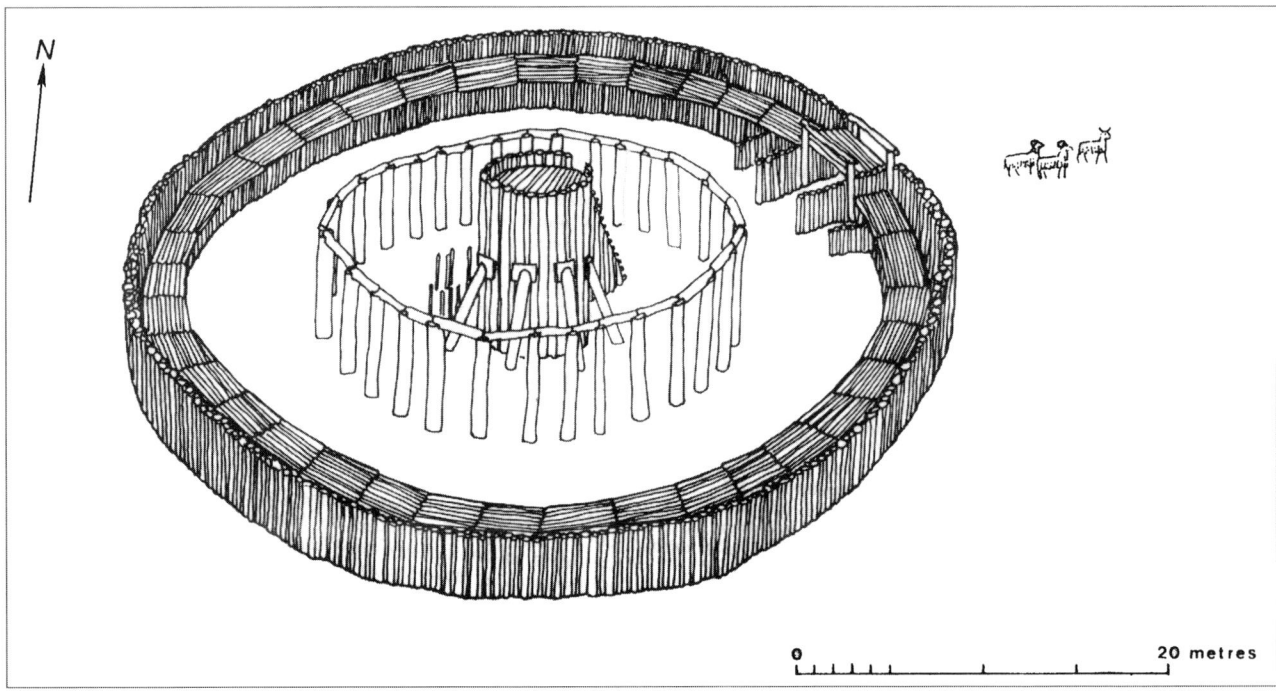

Figure 2-16. Possible reconstruction of Mauve phase structures.

therefore—an odd number in more than one sense.

As an exercise in reconstructing the methods used in the construction of this timber circle, we gave some thought to how a circle of 29 equidistant posts might be laid out. One possibility is first to describe a circle of the desired size on the ground. Second, a cord is laid on this circle, and markers are attached where the cord overlaps; the distance between these two markers is the circumference of the circle. Third, the distance between the two terminal markers is divided and marked at equidistant intervals: the cord is divided into two, then each half into thirds, and each third into fifths. Eventually there are 30 markers—the original two at each end and 28 intervening ones. The cord is then again laid down on the original circle on the ground, with the two end markers once more in the same place. The result is 29 points marked on this circle, at each of which a post is erected. Whether the designers and builders *intended* there to be 29 posts or 30 posts we do not know, of course.

Mauve Feature 42

This central feature of Mauve is of very curious plan and so, inferentially, reflects an unusual original construction.

- First, the circular wall trench was 6 m in diameter, small for a residential structure.
- Second, the wall trench was continuous: there was no sign of an entrance at ground level.
- Third, there was no domestic refuse inside 42, on the floor or trodden into it. Nor was there any sign of a hearth.
- Fourth, several well-preserved post-sockets in the primary fill of the wall-trench showed the posts to have been at least 10 cm in diameter, rather more robust than necessary for such a modest-sized structure if it had been a house.
- Fifth, around the perimeter of the wall trench nine pits were arranged radially. Five of these contained substantial remains of post-holes. The disposition of these post-holes was such that they *might* originally have supported wooden buttresses leaning against the outer walls of the 42 structure. These post-holes were not sufficiently well-preserved to show whether the original posts had been set vertically or on a slant, let alone in which direction they might have slanted.

The factors outlined above suggest that 42 was neither intended nor used for domestic purposes. If, as was evidently the case, it could not be entered at ground level, then was it a wooden tower? Figure 2-16 shows a possible reconstruction of such a tower, along with the "viewing stand" and freestanding post structure suggested above. The sturdy wall posts and the possible external buttresses also point toward this interpretation. Further, on the east-northeast side, facing the entrance through the outer Mauve palisade circle, the radial pit contains not one post-hole, but three. This suggests that perhaps some form of narrow ramp or stairway was originally erected at this point. If 42 represents a strongly constructed wooden tower, with external supporting buttresses and perhaps a ramp or stairway for ascent, then what was its purpose? After feature 42 had been dismantled, there had been intense burning over most of the floor and part of the wall trench.

Iron Age Layers/Surfaces

The low mound, identified at the outset of excavation was centered at about 48500 47500, and for this reason, an east-west balk was left standing along the east-west line 48300 North. This provided the major cross section of the low mound. Narrow balks were left on two north-south lines across the low mound for shorter periods of time. These balks provided stratigraphic control, but the primary evidence for layers and surfaces came from horizontal area excavation.

These layers and surfaces (listed below top to bottom) were of limited extent:
Flame: ca. 550 m^2 (by far the most extensive)
Dun: ca. 160 m^2
Upper Emerald: ca. 170 m^2
Crimson: ca. 60 m^2
Lower Emerald: ca. 75 m^2

The surfaces Harry, Jade, Niamh, and pre-Niamh were correspondingly quite small, too. By comparison, the area covered by the Mauve phase constructions was ca. 1,450 m^2.

A large number of minor features occurred beyond the protection of Lower Emerald/Crimson/Upper Emerald/Dun, including stake-holes, post-holes, pits, and shallow trenches. By far the largest concentration lies between the central Mauve feature 42 and the inner Mauve perimeter palisade trench 515 within the eastern part of the Mauve phase construction. Most are covered by Flame, providing a *terminus post quem*. Strictly speaking, they could be of any earlier date, but since very few occur *outside* the inner Mauve palisade trench 515, but are prolific *within* 515, it is reasonable to propose that most are contemporaneous with Mauve. If so, these numerous features are then probably contemporaneous with Harry, Jade, Niamh, and pre-Niamh, even though a strict stratigraphic correlation cannot be made. In effect, there is a continuous trampled surface, with numerous features, which can be disentangled stratigraphically only where protected by the low mound layers Lower Emerald, Crimson, Upper Emerald, and Dun.

This interpretation leaves us with a mass of features within the eastern part of the Mauve construction. In a limited area (protected by the low mound) they can be divided into three (possibly four) consecutive phases. Elsewhere no chronological distinctions can be made, although it seems intuitively likely that these features were not strictly contemporaneous. One can visualize intense activity, perhaps spasmodic, over a relatively short period of time. As the low mound layers began to accumulate, trampling ceased in that area, and so the features there remained more distinct and less confused (Harry, Jade, Niamh, pre-Niamh and Blue), whilst outside the protective cover of the low mound trampling continued and possible stratigraphic distinctions were irretrievably lost.

The uppermost level of the low mound, Flame was considerably more extensive than any of the levels below it, described in this section. Since Flame was of relatively loose composition, and its top had been disturbed by plowing, it is very likely that the extent of Flame found during excavation was rather more extensive than it had been originally. That is, it is highly likely that Flame had spread outward over the years due to natural erosion and to plow action.

The layers and surfaces below Flame, then, were preserved, and provided a complex sequence. The lowest of these—pre-Niamh, Niamh, Jade, Harry—were so thin that they are better regarded as surfaces than layers, although above them Lower Emerald, Crimson, Upper Emerald, Dun, and of course Flame were thick enough to be called layers.

Pre-Niamh, Niamh, Jade, Harry Surfaces

These are best treated together. Clearance of Lower Emerald revealed a light brown-orange, gravelly surface, composed largely of redeposited glacial till. This was labeled Harry (see CD Figure 2-14). Careful scraping showed a myriad of small, slightly darker, softer, stone-free patches. Most of these turned out to be stake-holes. These were excavated with the greatest care in order to distinguish between stake-holes (vertical) and what were probably root-holes (with bends down their extent).

Careful scraping of Harry surface revealed another series of stake-holes and root-holes in a matrix of the same composition as Harry, that is, redeposited glacial till. These were labeled Jade (CD Figure 2-17) and were excavated in turn.

The removal of Jade surface exposed another surface, mainly redeposited glacial till like Harry and Jade. This was Niamh surface, with yet another series of stake-holes and root-holes (CD Figure 2-18). Here and there, in small patches only, further careful scraping *seemed* to reveal more stake- and root-holes, but these proved extremely difficult to distinguish from the Niamh features. We designated them pre-Niamh, the uncertainty indicated by the name showing our doubt as to their existence as a separate surface (CD Figure 2-19).

Since these surfaces were all of the same color and texture, and less than 5 mm thick, it must be emphasized that they were distinguished one from the other solely because of the different levels of features exposed. There is little doubt, however, that there *were* different levels of stake-holes, because in a number of instances the surface on which one stake-hole was observed completely covered and obscured another stake-hole a centimeter or so away. This left little doubt that there really were successive surfaces in which stake-holes occurred.

Here and there Harry surface overlapped the primary fill of the inner Mauve palisade trench 515 but *not* the secondary fill. This shows contemporaneity between Mauve and Harry to the extent that the Harry surface existed whilst the Mauve palisades were standing. Whether these Mauve palisade trenches were cut whilst Harry was being deposited, or slightly before, it is impossible to say. None of the surfaces beneath Harry, that is, Jade, Niamh, or pre-Niamh, showed any stratigraphic relationship with any Mauve construction features, or with any pre-Mauve construction (such as Rose or White). So whether they too are approximately contemporaneous with Mauve construction, or were earlier, is unknown.

Below all these surfaces Blue was exposed, and beneath that glacial till (see above). The texture of Blue (stone free and relatively soft) was markedly different from that of the surfaces above it—pre-Niamh, Niamh, Jade, and Harry. Outside this limited area, protected by the low mound, no trace of Blue could be identified. This shows, more clearly than anything else, the degree of trampling that must have occurred *outside* the protection of the low mound.

Lower Emerald, Crimson, and Upper Emerald

Both Lower and Upper Emerald (CD Figures 2-20 and 2-21, respectively) are thin layers of heavily blackened soil containing much comminuted (i.e. pulverized into small fragments and scattered) charcoal. They were compacted and relatively damp compared to Dun and Flame above. Both Lower and Upper Emerald incorporated thin lenses of humic material (as did Flame) and patches of *in situ* burning. Crimson was a thin layer composed mainly of redeposited glacial till, providing good color and texture contrast with Lower Emerald below and Upper Emerald above. During excavation, Crimson was seen as a restricted lens within an Emerald layer. Only as excavation progressed did it become apparent that Crimson extended almost all the way across Emerald, and, consequently, Emerald was divided into Upper and Lower.

Lower Emerald and Crimson ran over the secondary fill of the inner Mauve palisade trench, 515, thus showing clearly that the Mauve palisade trench circle (515 and 516) had been dismantled by this time (no figure has been provided for Crimson because it contained few features and these were not of critical importance to the interpretation). However, since not only Crimson but also Upper Emerald accumulated against the big posts of the 20 m circle in this area (shown particularly well in the case of feature 30) it is clear that this timber circle was still standing for some time after the Mauve circular palisades 515 and 516 had been dismantled. The two posts (64 and 458) flanking the inner sides of the entrance into the Mauve palisade construction were also left standing after the rest of the Mauve palisade was dismantled and indeed remained standing through the deposition of Upper Emerald.

Finally, the patch of burning over the dismantled feature 42, although not stratigraphically connected to any of the low mound surfaces or levels, was covered by the more extensive Flame layer. This burning must relate to one of the pre-Flame layers of the low mound. There are patches of intense *in situ* burning in Lower Emerald, Upper Emerald, and Dun, and the burning over the dismantled feature 42 could correlate with any of these.

Dun Layer

Dun layer is composed mainly of redeposited glacial till, but it also has a smaller area of quarried stone slabs set close together to form a sort of paving (CD Figure 2-22). These slabs showed no signs whatsoever of abrasion on their upper, exposed surfaces, so if they were trodden upon it was not for long.

The big posts of the Mauve 20 m circle, as well as the posts (64 and 458) originally flanking the Mauve entrance, were extracted and the ragged sockets filled in loosely by Dun, that is, redeposited glacial till and the paving of quarried stones. As this loose secondary fill of the big post-holes settled and compacted, the Dun surface sank, leaving depressions. It is clear from this that these remaining posts of the Mauve construction were dismantled just before Dun layer was deposited. Dun thus marks the end of any Iron Age standing structures in the summit excavation area, with the exception of 287, a solitary post-hole of the Dun phase (the post was extracted before the deposition of Flame, and the socket was filled with Flame debris).

Flame Layer

Flame was the last Iron Age deposit on the summit area and so apparently marked the end of Iron Age activities here. It was composed of a relatively loose soil, blackened by the inclusion of much ash and charcoal (CD Figure 2-23). It also contained numerous stones, many of which were "burnt"—that is, had been subjected to considerable heat. There were no patches of *in situ* burning within Flame, so this burnt material had been derived from elsewhere. Further, artifacts from Flame included not only Iron Age but also Neolithic objects. All these factors show that Flame contained much redeposited material derived from some source or sources nearby which were not identified during the excavation.

Very thin, stone-free lenses of humic material occurred throughout Flame layer, and this indicates that there had been short periods of inactivity, during which patches of vegetation developed before being covered by another episode of deposition. A comparison might be made with the patchy vegetation that develops over a year or so on the spoil heaps at excavations. It seems clear that the deposition of Flame layer continued for several years.

Flame layer also contained very many animal bones, far more than from all other summit area contexts combined. To some extent this might be a factor of preservation: the soil of the summit area generally is mildly acid and so not conducive to good bone preservation—the pieces of bone from the damp Lower and Upper Emerald layers were in particularly bad condition. It is likely that the loose, and so relatively dry, composition of Flame layer permitted better bone preservation than elsewhere. A number of the animal bones from Flame were burnt, particularly at their ends, which indicates roasting over an open fire—as meat contracts during cooking, the ends of the bone are exposed directly to heat. This animal bone evidence, together with the copious ash, charcoal, and burnt stone in Flame, suggests that Flame layer accumulated largely as the result of periodic feasting, when quantities of meat were roasted. It seems likely that stones, brought to the spot from around the site, were used as an aid to heat retention during the roasting process.

Miscellaneous Features of Unknown Date

Feature 2935

On the southwest of the summit area excavation, a curved trench was discovered. If this was once part of a circle, the diameter would have been about 12 m. Immediately outside this arc, to the east-northeast, lay a pair of short L-shaped trenches. This complex shows general similarities to the sequential circular palisade structures that were completely excavated. So, though there is no dating evidence for 2935, an Iron Age date is suggested.

Patch of Burning at 44750 49350

In the far northwest corner of the summit excavation area there is a patch of burnt material, about 3 m x 3 m. It overlies Mauve palisade trenches 515 and 516 and so could be of any date after the dismantling of those palisades. In view of the burnt material in Lower Emerald, Upper Emerald, and Flame, it is plausible to suggest that this patch is most likely to have been deposited during one of those phases during the accumulation of the low mound.

Feature 229

On the extreme northwest of the excavated summit area two arcs of parallel stake-holes (or possibly very small post-holes) were uncovered. There appears to be a gap in this arc (an entrance?) facing east. If this arc is a part of a circular structure, its approximate diameter would have been in the region of 15 m.

There is no evidence for the date of feature 229: it is not cut into by, nor does it cut into, any of the Iron Age constructions described above; there are no associated artifacts; and there was no associated organic material from which a radiocarbon age determination might have been obtained. If it is indeed a portion of a circular structure, its form and structure do not indicate anything later than earlier medieval.

Post-Iron Age Activities

These are described briefly in the Introduction and Summary, and nothing useful can be added here. Post-Iron Age artifacts are discussed in Chapter 14.

The Iron Age Summit Sequence: Review and Discussion

The Timber Constructions

The most prominent features of the Iron Age sequence were the three successive construction phases—in chronological sequence (early to late) White, Rose, and Mauve. Each was defined by circular palisade trenches (or slot trenches), which had originally held upright timbers. The several intersections of the White, Rose, and Mauve palisade trenches provided unequivocal stratigraphic evidence for this sequence. Each construction was, in turn, dismantled, all indications being that White was replaced immediately by Rose, and Rose in turn by Mauve.

White was a relatively modest single circle (512) of 23 m with, possibly, a central feature of post-holes (2302) of 4 m diameter. The White circular palisade was dismantled (though 2302 may have been left at least partly standing) and replaced by the far larger and more complex Rose structures. These consisted of two contiguous palisade circles (the larger 38 m diameter; the smaller 21 m diameter) in a "figure-of-eight" plan, with an access gap between them where they adjoined. A very elaborate antennae entranceway led into the larger circle. The larger Rose circle was composed of three concentric trenches of diminishing size from outer to inner, suggesting that they supported a banked arrangement of two inward-facing platforms, an upper and a lower.

Mauve replaced Rose with a double palisade trench circle (515 and 516) of 43 m diameter. At the center of this large Mauve circle was feature 42, a 6 m diameter circular palisade trench with additional external post-holes suggesting buttresses. Feature 42 was clearly post-Rose, since it cut through Rose phase palisade trench 60, but it could not be demonstrated stratigraphically as contemporaneous with the Mauve 43 m circle. This contemporaneity is postulated because it lies at the geometric center of the Mauve phase 43 m circle. Between the Mauve outer circle and feature 42 lay a concentric circle, 20 m in diameter, of (probably) 29 massive (ca. 0.5 m diameter) free-standing posts.

Iron Age Layers/Surfaces: The Low Mound

Although the uppermost level of the low mound, Flame, had been to some extent eroded and spread laterally by plowing, enough depth remained intact to have preserved a series of superimposed levels beneath. The lower levels of the low mound (Lower Emerald, Crimson, and Upper Emerald) accumulated while the Mauve phase 20 m circle of large posts and the two posts (64 and 458) flanking the Mauve entrance were still standing, but the upper levels of the low mound (Dun and Flame) postdate the dismantling of all Mauve structures. Flame layer was considerably more extensive than the layers below and extended far enough west to cover the foundations of the dismantled feature 42.

The composition and contents of Flame indicated that it represented the redeposited residues of roasting of meat and feasting. This was periodic, since Flame contained within it several thin lenses of humic material, indicating short phases of inactivity, probably a few years at most. Below Flame, Dun layer was composed of redeposited glacial till and a rough paving of quarried stone slabs. In the restricted area of its deposit, Dun had been laid over the holes from which posts of the 20 m circle and posts 64 and 458 had been extracted.

Beneath Dun lay Upper Emerald, a relatively small area of black soil containing much fine charcoal. Below this lay Crimson, a very thin layer of redeposited glacial till, and below this again was Lower Emerald, of the same color and composition as Upper Emerald.

Iron Age Layers/Surfaces: The Surfaces pre-Niamh, Niamh, Jade, and Harry

Excavation of Lower Emerald revealed a surface of redeposited glacial till, dubbed Harry, containing a considerable number of stake-holes and other small features. Further scraping showed a sequence of similar surfaces below Harry—Jade; Niamh below Jade; and a fragmentary and elusive possible surface below Niamh, cautiously labeled pre-Niamh. This sequence represented sequential thin spreads of redeposited glacial till into each of which a number of upright stakes had been placed. All are so thin that the term "surfaces" seemed more appropriate than "layers." There were no evident traces of humus forming between these surfaces, so it is likely that they were deposited in relatively rapid succession.

Surface Unprotected by the Low Mound

Outside the cover of the low mound lay a mass of features, concentrated in the eastern part of the Mauve circle, mostly between feature 42 to the west and palisade trench 515 to the east. As argued above, most of these are probably contemporaneous with Harry, Jade, Niamh, and pre-Niamh underneath the low mound.

Iron Age Layers/Surfaces: Occupation

Here and there on the unprotected surface patches of "occupation" occurred. It is quite likely that some of these, at least, were very thin patches of Lower Emerald, Crimson, Upper Emerald, or Dun detached from their parent bodies. Some of these were quite extensive, notably where Flame layer had protected them from subsequent plowing. This occupation is stratigraphically undifferentiated, lying above natural and beneath Flame (where that occurred) or plowsoil. For example, on the northern edge of Lower Emerald, Harry surface (below Lower Emerald) and Crimson (above Lower Emerald) merged as Lower Emerald thinned and disappeared. The disappearance of Lower Emerald, of course, removed the very layer that distinguished Harry and Crimson—both composed of redeposited glacial till—from each other stratigraphically. At this point, both Harry and Crimson cease to be identifiable as distinct layers, and become occupation.

The Relationships Between Iron Age Structures and Iron Age Layers and Surfaces

The Harry surface overlay the inner edge of the *primary* fill of 515, the inner of the two Mauve perimeter palisade trenches. It also overlay the primary fill of the large post-holes of the 20 m circle. This established that the Mauve perimeter palisades (marked by the double trenches 515 and 516) and the 20 m circle of freestanding large posts had been constructed at the same time. Lower Emerald and Crimson, however, extended over the *secondary* fill of trench 515 and so were deposited *after* the posts in 515 had been extracted. But since Lower Emerald, Crimson, and Upper Emerald accumulated around the large posts of the 20 m circle and the Mauve entrance posts 64 and 458, it is clear that these had been left standing for some time after the Mauve 43 m perimeter palisade circle had been dismantled.

The central structure of Mauve, feature 42, lay outside the limited area covered by the successive surfaces pre-Niamh, Niamh, Jade, and Harry, and the successive layers Lower Emerald, Crimson, Upper Emerald, and Dun. As described above, after the dismantling of feature 42 a large patch of heavily burnt material covered much of the floor of feature 42 and parts of its wall trench. Above this, Flame layer extended right across feature 42.

If feature 42 had been constructed at the same time as the Mauve perimeter palisades and the 20 m circle of large posts, this burning must have been contemporaneous with Lower Emerald or Crimson or Upper Emerald or Dun. As we have noted, there is no stratigraphic connection between any of these layers and feature 42. This heavy burning over the dismantled feature 42 is suspiciously similar to the heavy burning around the large post 30, at the base of Lower Emerald (on Harry surface).

Mauve Feature 42: Interpretation

Summarizing the detailed description given earlier in this chapter, feature 42 was a very sturdy circular timber structure, 6 m in diameter, with *no* entrance at ground level, and no indication of residential use. It appears to have been surrounded by posts arranged in a radial fashion, suggesting buttresses. On the east-northeast, on the axis of the Mauve construction plan, there was a short line of post-holes. All of these factors are consistent with feature 42 having been a wooden tower with radial supporting buttresses and a ramp or stairway leading from ground level to the top on the east-northeast side.

The Low Mound and the Surfaces Beneath It: Interpretation

The superimposed pre-Flame levels of the low mound were *not* situated over the center of Mauve phase feature 42. This suggests that feature 42 was left standing at least while the lower levels of the low mound were deposited. Further, the two inner flanking posts (64 and 458) of the Mauve entrance were left standing even though the rest of the Mauve perimeter palisade (515 and 516) was dismantled. This suggests that the axis of Mauve, from the central feature 42 through the entrance to the east-northeast, was retained. The 20 m circle of large posts was also left standing after the dismantling of 515 and 516. Clearly, then, the dismantling of the complex multiple Mauve structures was a protracted process, not completed until the deposition of Dun layer.

If the location of the low mound seems anomalous in relation to the over-all concentric Mauve plan, this location can hardly have been fortuitous. On the contrary, while the lower levels of the low mound (Lower Emerald, Crimson, and Upper Emerald) were deposited, elements of the original Mauve complex remained—the 20 m circle of large posts, Mauve entrance posts 64 and 458, and (probably) the central feature 42. With the deposition of Dun layer, the last vestiges of Mauve construction were destroyed. The burning over the dismantled feature 42 can be no later than the deposition of Dun; Mauve entrance posts 64 and 458 were extracted; and the 20 m circle of posts was dismantled too. It may be particularly significant that the stone paving part of the Dun layer (on the northern part of Dun) lay right across the east-northeast axis of Mauve, deliberately covering the sockets of the remaining Mauve entrance posts 64 and 458. This, then, appears to be the final conclusion of Mauve, when the last remaining structures were not only dismantled but also covered over.

Lower Emerald, Crimson, Upper Emerald, and Dun are superimposed within a restricted area. Until the end of Upper Emerald, the Mauve 20 m circle was left standing, as were two posts (64 and 458) marking the Mauve entrance, and perhaps Mauve central feature 42 as well. Some of the Mauve constructions were deliberately left in place for some time, and the east-northeast Mauve axis was left unencumbered. Indeed, it is possible that Upper Emerald features 31 and 37 (both post-holes) were *deliberately* located more or less on the Mauve axis, as if to reaffirm it.

Why was the low mound not deposited somewhere that bore a relation to the geometry of the Mauve constructions? Alternatively, why was the low mound deposited where it was, rather than elsewhere within the general confines of the Mauve constructions or, indeed, outside those confines altogether? The only correlation that *can* be suggested for the position of the low mound is the geometric center of the Rose larger circle. While this is not a precise correlation, two sources of evidence provide tentative support for this suggestion. First, post-hole 30 lies very close to the center of the Rose larger circle, and there was heavy burning around this post during the accumulations of Lower Emerald. Second, the one and only post erected during Dun phase was also very close to the geometric center of the Rose larger circle. Was the Rose construction, dismantled some time previously, commemorated as a significant location throughout the deposition of low mound layers up to and including Dun?

The Summit Area: Summary and Interpretation

After the Neolithic activities on the summit there was no trace of human activity for some two millennia or more, apart from the deposition of a food vessel in a pit. In the later 1st millennium BC the summit became the focus of considerable activity for some time. The three successive phases of Iron Age structures (White, Rose, and Mauve) must be interpreted as ritual and/or ceremonial, even though some limited manufacturing did take place (see Chapter 18).

All three successive Iron Age structures were timber circles, constructed in the same manner, and all were oriented toward the east-northeast. But other aspects of these three successive constructions differed. White was a single circle, with a *possible* central feature. Rose was far larger and more complex, but had no structures inside either of its timber circles (the larger one and the smaller annex). Moreover, there was a very elaborate and imposing antennae entranceway to the larger Rose circle. Mauve, on the other hand, did have structures within its timber circle: feature 42, interpreted as the foundations of a wooden tower, and the 20 m diameter circle of very large posts.

Of White one can say little except that it *may* have had a central feature (2302) which was retained into Rose phase, after the White perimeter circle had been dismantled, and remained into Mauve phase after the Rose structures had been dismantled. But this is very speculative.

Rose and Mauve structures show marked contrasts. Rose had two conjoining circles, both open with no internal structures, and had an imposing antennae entranceway. The Mauve circle had two imposing structures within it but none outside. This suggests that rituals and ceremonies during Rose phase were open, while those held during Mauve phase were more restricted. In this respect, it may be significant that the entrance into the Rose larger circle was appreciably wider (ca. 4 m) than the entrance into the Mauve circle (ca. 2.5 m). The postulated tower at the center of the Mauve circle, moreover, hints that physical elevation may have been designed to emphasize social and/or political and/or ritual elevation. If this tower existed, perhaps it was the equivalent of the mounds at other royal sites—Site B at Navan, the conjoined Tech Cormaic and the Forradh at Tara, and the Rathcroghan mound at Croghan. Was it, for example, intended for inaugurations?

If it may be postulated that there was some change of emphasis or outlook from Rose to Mauve, it may on the other hand be argued that Rose continued to be commemorated throughout the use of Mauve phase, and indeed after it, by the location of the low mound levels roughly over the center of the Rose larger circle.

An Iron Age Just-So Story

The term Just-So Story is borrowed, in its archaeological context, from Kent Flannery for an archaeological interpretation that should not be inflated by labeling it a hypothesis, not least because it cannot be tested. The following scenario explains all the evidence, but cannot be tested in any real sense. We offer it as a plausible story, and leave the reader to judge its likely accuracy.

Perhaps some conflict or rivalry was operating to produce these contrasts—dynastic rivalry, for example. First, the Rose faction was dominant and constructed Rose phase. Then Mauve faction became ascendant, dismantled the Rose structures, and replaced them with a different design, reflecting a rather different set of values or beliefs, or at least a different emphasis from that of the Rose faction. Rose faction then regained a degree of power, dismantled the outer perimeter palisades (515 and 516) of the Mauve construction, and began to conduct activities over the approximate center of the (former) Rose larger circle—activities that resulted in the accumulation of the low mound.

Meanwhile, the Mauve 20 m circle of posts remained standing, and the Mauve axis from its central feature (42) through its entrance (between posts 64 and 458) appears to have remained marked. At this stage, both Rose and Mauve factions were able to display their claims to Dún Ailinne.

With the deposition of Dun layer, however, all traces of Mauve construction were swept away: the large posts of the 20 m circle were extracted; the Mauve entrance posts 64 and 458 were extracted and the entrance was obliterated by the deposition of the Dun stone paving; feature 42 was (probably) dismantled and a fire was set over its foundations; and a solitary post (287) was erected roughly over the former center of the Rose larger circle. These activities could mark the triumph of Rose faction and the defeat of Mauve faction.

The subsequent accumulation of Flame layer was still focused roughly over the former center of the Rose larger circle and so may mark continued Rose faction dominance. Alternatively, the extraction of Dun post 287 and the deposition of Flame may mark the gradual obliteration of Rose faction activities by a re-emergent Mauve faction. At all events, the deposition of Flame marked the latest-known Iron Age activities at Dún Ailinne and so, presumably, the decline of the site as a functioning royal site of the Laigin, the ancient people of Leinster.

3
Perimeter Survey and Excavation

Bernard Wailes

The perimeter of the site of Dún Ailinne is defined by an approximately oval bank and ditch. Since the bank is outside the ditch, the site is morphologically a henge, not a hillfort. We examined the entire perimeter carefully and conducted excavation at two locations on the eastern side, including the original site entrance. The bank is of simple dump construction, and there are no traces of external *chevaux-de-frise* (see Chapter 1) nor of a palisade on the inside of the ditch. The original site entrance has a short length of unexcavated roadway outside it, and a longer stretch of roadway inside, which runs some 70 m uphill toward the summit area. This internal length of roadway had been constructed by the excavation of a strip of subsoil about 8 m wide, with flanking stone kerbs.

Bank and Ditch: Survey

There are 23 gaps through the bank. Twenty-two of these did not have corresponding gaps or causeways across the ditch. In each case it appears that the gap in the bank had been made by pushing a portion of bank inward to form a spoil heap in that section of ditch.

Only one gap, on the east side of the site, appeared to have a causeway, and this therefore became the prime candidate for the one and only original entrance to the site. Early in the excavation, a small test trench determined that there was indeed a causeway here, interrupting the ditch. This cutting (feature 3133) subsequently was incorporated into a more extensive excavation of this original site entrance (see "Entrance Excavation" below).

On the inner face of the ditch bedrock was visible in many places, and elsewhere it was covered only thinly by hillwash (soils washed down from the sloping bank) and sod. In seven locations the inner face of the ditch had been quarried, and in each case there are gaps through the external bank opposite, or close to, these quarries. Excavation of the original entrance showed that both ends of the ditch had been quarried, and debris here showed clearly that quarrying was not ancient. No excavation was undertaken at any of the other quarries noted, so there is no information on their age. All are probably modern.

Bank and Ditch: Excavation

Bank and Ditch Construction

The location of cutting 21 (see Figure 1-1) was selected because here both bank and ditch were less eroded than in most other locations around the perimeter and there was no sign of modern interference with either bank or ditch. This cutting showed that the material from the ditch had been piled up on its downhill side to construct a simple dump bank (CD Figure 3-1). There were no signs of platforms, revetting, box construction, palisades, or timber lacing. Nor was there any sign that the ditch in this location had ever been re-cut or that the bank had been remodeled in any way. It was a simple quarry and dump, single-phase construction.

Cutting 22, just north of cutting 21, took advantage of a recent gap cut through the bank. This gap was slightly expanded and its south face cut back to expose the cross section through the bank. This exposure confirmed the simple dump construction of the bank shown in cutting 21.

Chevaux-de-Frise: *None*

Peter Harbison (Trinity College Dublin) suggested that we should excavate downhill, outside the bank, in order to see if there were any traces of timber *chevaux-de-frise*. A *chevaux-de-frise* is a defensive palisade composed of vertically placed stones set at angles known from hillforts such as Dun Aengus, Co. Galway (Waddell 2000:354–7), and the presence of such a feature would suggest a more defensive function for Dún Ailinne. The eastern (external, downhill) end of cutting 21 extended beyond the outer edge of the bank in order to check this possibility. There were no traces of post-holes that might have been the sockets for *chevaux-de-frise* timbers or stones.

Internal Palisade or Posts: None

Ó Ríordáin's (1954) excavations at Tara included a cutting across the northern perimeter of the Ráith na Ríg, and he reported post-holes along the inner edge of the ditch. At Dún Ailinne, we excavated cutting 23 in order to see if this occurred here, too. This cutting was situated right on the inner (interior, uphill) edge of the ditch just south of the western end of cutting 21. We found no traces of any post-holes or slot-trenches.

Entrance Area: Survey and Excavation

Confirmation of Original Entrance

As noted above, a small test trench (feature 3133) confirmed the presence of a causeway across the ditch, and thus that this was the original site entrance. More extensive excavation followed in order to ascertain, insofar as possible, the construction of the entrance and of the roadway that runs through it. The description and discussion of this area that follows starts at the east end (the outside of the bank, downhill) and progresses westward through the entrance (uphill, into the interior of the site).

The Outer Roadway

The outer roadway was planned but not excavated, as we had no permit for excavation here. About 40 m of this feature were visible at ground level (CD Figure 3-2). It is slightly sinuous, and veers from the alignment of the inner roadway inside the entrance (Plate 3-1). This suggests that it was laid out and constructed at a different time from the inner roadway. Although there is no direct evidence for this, the outer roadway has the appearance of an afterthought.

The Entrance through the Bank

The two ends of the bank (3104) flanking the entrance were not obviously disturbed since their original construction, though the low spur (3130) on the southern end of the bank might be a small spoil heap from some minor modification of the bank here. Neither end of the bank (3104) was excavated substantially so this remains speculation. On the south side of the entrance there is a low kerb, and a similar feature opposite, on the north side. The latter is less distinct and so is qualified with a "?" on the plan (see CD Figure 3-2). These two kerbs are about 7 m apart. Between them is a partly excavated shallow pit (3129), which does not relate stratigraphically either to the kerbs flanking it or to the bank (3104). Since its fill contained recent rubbish, this pit is presumably modern, having nothing to do with the original entrance.

A linear trench (3103) follows the line of the inner edge of the bank, across the entrance. Like 3129, this cannot be clearly related to the bank (3104) and so may have nothing to do with the original entrance. On the other hand, it lies on the line of the outer edge of the ditch and so may have originally been a marker for laying out the perimeter. Another possibility is that 3103 could have supported a fence or palisade across the entrance, since it contained numerous stones, which could have been packing stones to support timber posts.

The Causeway across the Ditch

We exposed the ends of the ditch in 3101 on the north and 3133 on the south, both of which contained modern debris and were thus clearly a part of modern quarry operations. This evidence, along with the very irregular ends of the ditch, showed clearly enough that the original ends of the ditch had been totally obliterated by quarrying. We may conclude that the entrance causeway is reduced—perhaps considerably—from its original width. This reduced causeway was left, one suspects, to provide continued access to the interior of the site for farm vehicles.

The causeway is hard bedrock (which probably explains modern quarrying in this area), bedded along the slope of the hill so the causeway is, in effect, a sheet of rock. Features 3114 and 3120 are small shallow pits pecked into this bedrock. Feature 3100 is a shallow slot trench, which *might* have had a pair to the south (see plan, CD Figure 3-2), quarried away in modern times. If so, then there *might* have been some timber structure here straddling the center line of the roadway through the entrance.

The Inner Roadway

Moving to the interior of the entrance, a cutting was laid perpendicular to the roadway in order to examine it and its flanking banks. The ground here slopes gently from north to south, as well as—more steeply—from west to east. The roadway was not simply a depression worn into the subsoil by many years of traffic but was a deliberate construction. A strip about 8 m wide had been excavated into the subsoil. The kerbs on either side were marked by linear concentrations of stones, indicating that these kerbs were originally revetted (propped up from behind for support). Along the southern kerb was a line of five stake-holes, which could be interpreted as reinforcement of the (probable) stone revetment. Feature 3131 was not excavated: its surface outline indicated a small trench running perpendicular to the line of the roadway. There was no trace of either a prepared surface (such as cobbling) to the roadway or any sign of wheel ruts.

On the south side of the roadway there is a low bank, presumably the upcast from the excavation of the roadway. A scatter of small pits and postholes was found both on top of and beneath this bank, but no evident patterning could be seen in either series, perhaps due to the limited area excavated. On the north side of the roadway excavation showed that there had *not* been any flanking bank. The dip down into the roadway here is due to the excavation of the roadway itself. In section, the fill of the roadway appears to be simple hillwash, with no sign of deliberate infilling.

As a visible surface feature, the roadway inside the entrance extends about 70 m uphill from the site entrance. Unlike the shorter, sinuous, outer roadway, this inner section of roadway is straight, as far as can be seen on the surface. Unfortunately, its surface indications peter out well before they reach the excavated summit area of the site, and we were unable to excavate any area between the visible uphill end of the roadway and the excavation area on the summit of the hill.

The Entranceway: Conclusion

The excavation of the entrance showed a few features that might have been the foundations for timber constructions, but no clear remains. We cannot say whether or not there had been a gateway, for example. The modern quarrying of the ends of the ditch either side of the entrance causeway might have destroyed any construction features here. The internal roadway had clearly been constructed. It is laid out in direct relationship to the entrance through the bank and across the causeway between the ends of the ditch, which strongly suggests that this internal roadway and the entrance were all part of one planned enterprise. The chronological relation of the shorter external roadway is not known, but we suggest that it was a later addition. The layout of the entrance and the internal roadway is clearly connected to the Iron Age structures on the summit.

Perimeter: Chronology

There are no datable artifacts (apart from modern rubbish deposits) from any of the excavated areas of the perimeter. There is no doubt that the entrance is original and that it is the *only* original entrance, but its relationship to the outer and inner roadways cannot be determined stratigraphically. There is one radiocarbon age determination, from buried sod beneath 3130, the low spur extending outward from the southern end of the bank (3104). The buried sod contained a humic fraction, used for dating, and is presumed to represent the date of the last vegetation growth on this sod before it was covered by 3130. This age determination is of the 5th century BC, which at least indicates that the bank and ditch were constructed in the later 1st millennium BC rather than during the Neolithic or early medieval times (see also Chapter 15).

The outer and inner roadways clearly relate to the entrance and so are unlikely to be earlier than the bank and ditch construction. But whether they are contemporaneous with the bank and ditch construction or later cannot be shown. The outer roadway is slightly sinuous and does not lie on the central line of the inner roadway, which suggests that it may be a later addition. The central line of the inner roadway, when projected up the hillside toward the summit, passes right through the elaborate Rose phase entrance and through the geometric center of the larger Rose phase circle. The most parsimonious interpretation of this is that the inner roadway and the Rose phase summit constructions were laid out as parts of one ambitious plan.

Since there is no demonstrated *chronological* sequence for the perimeter, but only a very limited *conjectural* sequence (outer roadway a later addition?), it cannot be divided into phases. As noted above, the construction of the inner roadway *probably* correlates with Rose phase construction on the summit. On the master site chronological chart (Table 2-1), then, only two tentative correlations are made between perimeter and summit.

4
Feature and Artifact Summary

Susan A. Johnston

General Distribution of Features

There were 2,851 feature numbers assigned to excavated features at Dún Ailinne. Since in some cases two or more features turned out to be the same feature (such as the several features numbered separately which all turned out to be portions of trench 281), this represents a largest possible number; the actual number would be smaller. Of these, 886 could not be assigned to a phase, while an additional 585 were of uncertain identification or could not be clearly assigned to a single phase (such as Crimson/Harry or pre-Mauve). This leaves 1,380 features whose phases could be identified. Table 4-1 shows the distribution of features by phase.

The three phases separated from the rest at the bottom of the table are those certainly or likely to be medieval or modern (see Chapter 2). Grey is the curved bank, probably medieval, and a quarry ditch; Uaininn comprises the post-Iron Age cultivation furrows in the eastern part of the site. In four cases—a depression, a pit, a quarry pit, and a ditch—features were simply designated "modern." Taking these out of the total of 1,380 leaves 1,367 total prehistoric features for further discussion.

General Summary of Features

As would be expected, relatively large numbers of features belong to Mauve and Rose, which are the main phases of Iron Age activity at Dún Ailinne. Adding White (which belongs to this sequence though has relatively few features), these phases produced 331 features, 24% of the total of known, prehistoric phases. By contrast, only four features were assigned to Tan, though other features are arguably also Neolithic in date; this total also includes trench 281, which is of course rather large.

The somewhat unexpected observation that Table 4-1 presents is the large number of features belonging to Harry and Jade. These two phases have by far the largest numbers of features, together comprising 905 or 66% of the total. While other features belong to these phases, the vast majority of each is comprised of post-holes and stake-holes. Indeed, when all types of features are examined, post-holes and stake-holes are the most common category by far. Table 4-2 shows the distribution of the various types of features as described in the feature log.

Stake-holes and post-holes together comprise 72% of the total of prehistoric features. The next closest (not counting uncertain and unknown types) is pits, with 178, a small fraction of the number of post-holes or stake-holes. Further, these features are the most common type in most phases. Table 4-3 shows the eight phases with more than five features. Features were categorized as post-holes, stake-holes, other types, and uncertain types.

In all but Crimson, post-holes and stake-holes are the largest categories. Since Mauve, Rose, and White represent phases in which timber structures were built, the predominance of post-holes makes some sense, but this does not account for all the post-holes and probably few of the stake-holes. While it is unlikely that all the post-holes and stake-holes can be accounted for by a single function, the possibility that a large proportion represents something more consistent remains. In Chapter 18, one

Table 4-1. Distribution, Features by Phase.

PHASE	N FEATURES
Blue	35
Crimson	29
Dun	4
Upper Emerald	3
Lower Emerald	5
Harry	533
Jade	372
Khaki	7
Lemon	4
Mauve	182
Niamh	40
Rose	141
Tan	4
White	8
Uncertain	585
Unknown	886
Grey	4
Uaininn	5
Modern	4
TOTAL	2,851

Table 4-2. Distribution, Types of Feature.

FEATURE TYPE	N FEATURES
Bank	2
Burned Area	24
Depression	15
Linear feature	7
Pit	178
Post	6
Post-hole	880
Stake-hole	1,162
Stones	8
Trench	108
Other*	8
Uncertain	280
Unknown	160
TOTAL	2,838

*Includes eight feature types where there was only a single example: animal run, hearth, hut, mound, plank, post support, stone paving, trackway

suggestion offered is that they represent temporary structures of some kind.

A further observation that can be made at this stage is that no features were assigned to the Flame phase (the widespread scatter of faunal remains, much of it burned, cannot be said to constitute a feature in the typical archaeological sense). This is notable given the staggering number of animal bones (18,000+) that came largely from this phase, most reasonably interpreted as feasting (see Chapter 13). It is possible that this phase is the result of repeated but very short-term episodes of feasting and so did not generate features. Another possibility is that any associated features were obliterated by the burning associated with this phase. It is also possible that there are features associated with this phase, but they lie outside of the excavated area.

Artifact Associations

In the finds register, each artifact given a number was also accompanied by context information. Ideally, this would include the phase with which the artifact was associated, as well as the feature type and number when it was recovered from a feature. In practice other issues sometimes intervened; in some cases, the associated feature was unclear on archaeological grounds, while in others, various context information was sometimes not recorded. Table 4-4 shows the general distribution of provenience information as recorded for this study. The table omits 14 artifacts and their associated features that were assigned to medieval or modern phases.

Most of these categories are self-explanatory. The first 3 are as indicated: artifacts from the surface (including contexts described as topsoil and plowsoil), artifacts from clearly identified features, and artifacts from the rather murky occupation levels. "Mixed" refers to contexts such as post-holes in trenches, where the exact provenience of the artifact could not be clearly distinguished. "No number" refers to the feature number; in these cases, the context of the artifact was described in a way suggesting that there was a feature involved (such as "fill of pit," "Mauve surface," or "loose soil above natural") but no number was indicated. This category represents 28% of the total. "Best guess" is shorthand for associated features designated with a question mark, such as "281?," which was taken to suggest that this was a likely context but uncertain. The remaining were unknown for a variety of reasons, most commonly missing context information, a missing artifact number, a page missing from the finds register, or the artifact was unprovenienced.

Table 4-3. Phases with >5 Features.

FEATURE TYPE	HARRY	JADE	MAUVE	ROSE	NIAMH	BLUE	CRIMSON	WHITE
Post-hole	84	35	100	60	8	5	15	3
Stake-hole	387	308	47	41	29	24	3	—
Other	46	20	16	37	2	5	6	2
Uncertain	16	9	19	3	1	1	5	3
TOTAL=1,340	533	372	182	141	40	35	29	8

Table 4-4. Distribution, Types of Provenience Information.

CONTEXT	N ARTIFACTS
Surface	378
Features	539
Occupation	250
Mixed	7
Best guess	76
No number	510
Unknown	77
TOTAL	1,837

Artifacts from the surface layers and those with missing or unknown context information provide no data for further analysis. Those from mixed and "best guess" categories, while providing some information, do not provide very useful data. That leaves artifacts from the occupation levels (14%) and those from actual, knowable features (29%), and in fact little can be said about the occupation levels. Despite their small number, however, the 539 artifacts which came from relatively precise proveniences can provide some insight into the character of Dún Ailinne.

As a first observation, of the total 2,851 features, a minimum of 92 (3%) produced artifacts. Including artifacts from numberless features would increase this total. There are 355 artifact numbers associated with features which had no feature number listed. If all of these came from features other than those already known to have produced artifacts, then the number of features with artifacts might be as high as 447. However, it is far more likely that many, perhaps even most, of these are other artifacts from the features already known to have produced artifacts, and so the number is probably not that high.

Obviously, this analysis can only deal with known, numbered features. Based on this, it is notable that the vast majority of features produced no artifacts. To some degree, this is a function of the large number of post-holes and stake-holes. While these can (and did) produce artifacts, they are less likely to do so, particularly the smaller stake-holes. This is demonstrated by Table 4-5, which shows that the vast majority did not produce artifacts. Omitting all post-holes and stake-holes leaves 627 features, 66 (10%) of which produced artifacts. Obviously this is significantly larger than 3%, but the conclusion is inescapable that most features at Dún Ailinne did not produce any cultural objects.

From another perspective, most of the features that did produce artifacts contained relatively few of them. Figure 4-1 shows this distribution for the 92 artifact bearing features. In numeric terms, 42 features (46%) produced only a single artifact, while only 16 (17%) produced more than 10. Leaving out those that produced a single artifact (since this would severely skew the results), the average

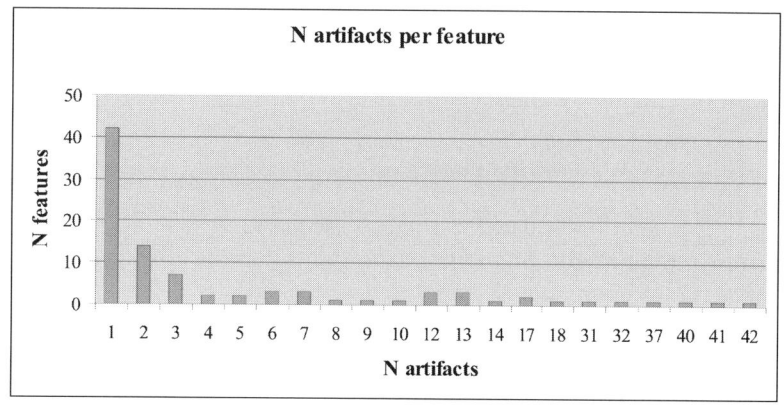

Figure 4-1. Distribution, number of artifacts per feature.

Table 4-5. Distribution, Post-holes and Stake-holes by Presence of Artifacts.

FEATURE TYPE	N WITH ARTIFACTS	N W/OUT ARTIFACTS
Post-hole	18	880
Post-hole?	3	143
Stake-hole	5	1,162
TOTAL	26	2,185

number of artifacts per feature is 9.94. Considering that a large number of these are small lithic flakes and bits of rusted iron, this is a very small number indeed, and underscores the observation that Dún Ailinne simply did not produce many artifacts.

It is possible that this has some taphonomic (deriving from environmental conditions after the artifacts were deposited) cause, but if so, such a cause is not readily apparent. Instead, it seems likely that the reason for this paucity of material remains is the behavior that took place at the site. As explored further in Chapter 18, this suggests that long periods of intensive use were not the case. Instead, whatever people were doing, they tended to take away with them what they brought to the site, with relatively few accidental losses or deliberate depositions.

Neolithic

The earliest evidence of the use of Dún Ailinne is the assemblage of Neolithic artifacts and a series of arguably Neolithic features. Given the scattered nature of the remains from the period, there is little that can be said about it with any certainty. Possible Neolithic features are discussed first, followed by the general characteristics of the Neolithic artifacts. The latter are considered in greater detail in Chapters 5 and 6.

Neolithic Features

This section is a more general discussion of features that might be assigned to the Neolithic based on their associated artifacts; artifacts are discussed in the following section. All of the features considered here produced such artifacts and cannot be ruled out as Neolithic on stratigraphic grounds. While this does not mean they must be Neolithic, arguments can be made about them with varying degrees of probability.

Somewhere between 31 and 35 features fall into this category. The uncertainty of the number stems from one context where the actual feature containing the artifacts is uncertain (it is listed as "418/419/420") and four others where the feature number is listed with a question mark (such as "1256?"). Omitting these leaves 31 remaining features.

Table 4-6 shows the types of features represented. At least two of the pits could also be post-holes, since they are recorded with a question mark in the finds register. Three of the features are variously described as "stone cluster" or "gravel spread"; the exact nature of these features is uncertain. Those listed as "uncertain" are features where the page is missing from the feature log, but the numbers are recorded in the finds register. In the latter, two are described as pits, one as a trench, and the other two are ambiguous.

Unfortunately, these are the kinds of features that are fairly generic. They could represent a wide range of behaviors, and quite probably do. Exceptions to this are Pit 293, which contained the Linkardstown burial (see Chapter 6) and Trench 281, which is sufficiently extensive to argue that it might represent an enclosure (see Chapter 2).

Figure 4-2 shows the distribution of the artifacts among these features. What is immediately apparent is that the majority of these features have only one or two artifacts of Neolithic type. In percentages, 11 features (35%) have a single artifact and four (13%) have only two. Grouped together, 21 (68%) have fewer than five Neolithic artifacts. While this does not inherently exclude these features as Neolithic, the disturbed nature of the Neolithic remains at Dún Ailinne would suggest that such small numbers should be treated with caution. It would be very easy for a few stray artifacts to become incorporated into a feature of a later period.

Table 4-6. Distribution, Possible Neolithic Feature Types.

FEATURE TYPE	N
Pit	11
Post-hole	7
Stake-hole	1
Trench	3
Stone/gravel cluster	3
Depression	1
Uncertain	5

Feature and Artifact Summary

Table 4-7. Artifacts in Possible Neolithic Features.

FEATURE #	FEATURE TYPE	ASSIGNED PHASE	TOTAL ARTIFACTS	ASSOCIATED ARTIFACTS
213	Post-hole	Unknown	13	9 sherds, 3 flakes, 1 implement
281	Trench	Tan	21	4 sherds, 13 flakes, 1 projectile point, 2 scrapers, 1 core
293	Pit	Tan	2	31 sherds of Linkardstown vessel, 1 slate bead
1517	Trench	Tan	14	14 sherds
2506	Pit	Tan	12	10 flakes, 2 projectile points
2568	Black gravel spread	Unknown	6	4 sherds, 1 flake, 1 scraper
2942	Pit?	Unknown	9	9 sherds
2962	Pit	Unknown	10	10 sherds
3106	Pit?	Unknown	5	5 sherds
3306	Pit	Tan	17	17 sherds

This leaves ten features with five or more Neolithic artifacts. Making the cutoff at five artifacts is obviously an arbitrary number, but this also represents a distinct drop-off in the data; after this point, each feature is unique in the number of artifacts it has. In addition, those features with five or more artifacts are the ones most likely to contain typologically identifiable artifacts. Often, those with a single artifact are single flakes, which could in theory date to any period of the site's use (though they are most likely to be Neolithic or Bronze Age). In the absence of any better criteria, five or more artifacts seems reasonable. The contents of these ten features are shown in Table 4-7.

Pit 293, discussed elsewhere in this volume, in Chapter 2 and Chapter 6, was the remains of a pit containing a Linkardstown burial, with the better part of a ceramic vessel surviving as well as a single slate bead. As such, it is probably the most securely identified Neolithic feature of the group, and was assigned to the Tan phase. Of the other four identified with this phase, they are for the most part those with the largest number of Neolithic artifacts. Trench 281 (Chapter 2) has the largest number, including artifacts of chert, flint, and quartz, and sherds probably representing two different vessels.

The remaining Tan phase features have gradually decreasing numbers of such artifacts: 3306 (17), 1517 (14), 213 (13), and 2506 (12). The first two of these contained ceramics only, representing respectively two and three vessels. Feature 213, which is variously described as a post-hole or stake-hole, contained both flint and quartz, as well as ceramics representing two vessels, while Feature 2506 contained lithics only, including two leaf-shaped projectile points. All of the remaining four features contained from five to ten artifacts, most of them sherds (though Feature 2568 produced two flints, a flake and a scraper). In the absence of any obvious stratigraphic indicators, these all may be considered Neolithic features.

Assuming that all 31 of the features are in fact Neolithic, their locations on the site can

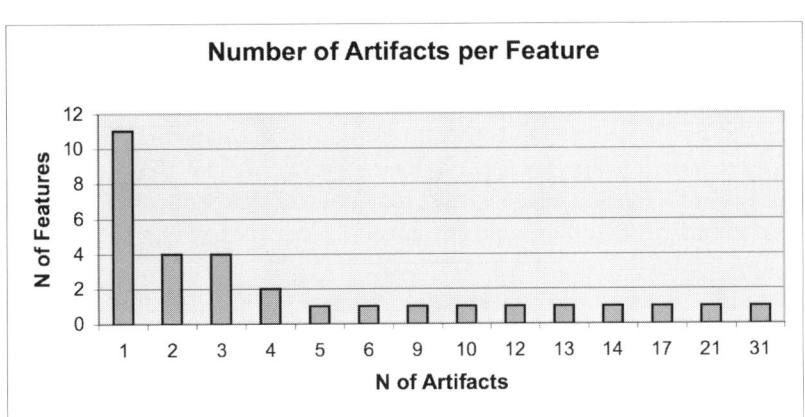

Figure 4-2. Number of artifacts in possible Neolithic features.

Table 4-8. Distribution, Types of Neolithic Materials.

MATERIAL	N
flint	488
chert	86
quartz	77
uncertain (flint/chert)	11
axes	10
granite	3
decorated ceramic (certain & probable)	39
undecorated ceramic	437
TOTAL	1,151

Table 4-9. Contexts of Neolithic Artifacts.

FEATURE TYPE	N
Baulk	9
Burned Area	2
Depression	2
Ditch	2
Embankment	3
Hut	2
Low Mound	1
Mound	18
Occupation	150
Palisade	1
Pit	155
Post-hole	173
Trench	153
Surface	196
Uncertain	241
Unknown	43
TOTAL	1,151

be mapped. CD Figure 4-3 shows the features, excluding the four trenches (which cannot be plotted as a single point). All but three of the features are within the main activity area of the central part of the site. The three outliers are Features 3106, 3108, and 3127. The latter two are post-holes, and 3106 is probably a post-hole also; it is listed as such in the feature log, but as "pit?" in the finds register. This small cluster of features may represent a discrete activity area, but there is no way to determine whether they are in fact contemporary.

Neolithic Artifacts: General Description

The artifact evidence of the Neolithic use of Dún Ailinne includes the typical range of material characteristic of the Irish Neolithic. This evidence consists of Neolithic pottery, lithic material, and stone axes, much of which is from unstratified contexts in the topsoil and from Iron Age levels. While there is other material that may be Neolithic, including stone balls and stone beads (Chapter 11), the date of this material is uncertain and it is not considered in this general section.

Also worth noting is a handful of animal bone recovered from pre-Iron Age contexts. A total of 136 fragments were recorded, 106 of them from the Blue phase, 23 from Tan, four from Khaki, and three from a mixed context (possibly representing Tan, Khaki, or White). Of these, only two were identifiable as to species, a cattle calcaneus from Khaki and a pig mandible from the mixed context. Tan is arguably Neolithic, while Khaki might be earlier Bronze Age (though this is highly tentative); Blue might also be Neolithic, though it is likely to be earlier (see Chapter 2). Thus some or all of these faunal fragments may date to the Neolithic. However, none was large enough to provide any useful information about the human use of the site; it is not even certain that all owe their presence there to human behavior. Therefore they do not factor into the interpretation of the Neolithic (or Bronze Age) use of Dún Ailinne and will not be considered further.

Based on ceramics, lithics, and stone axes, then, a total of 1151 artifacts could be considered Neolithic. The various categories of Neolithic artifacts are tabulated in Table 4-8, most by material (stone axes represent a number of materials and are therefore shown as a single category).

The largest categories of artifact are flint (including both debris and implements) and undecorated ceramic sherds (42% and 38%, respectively), together comprising 80% of the total. Much smaller are the other lithic categories (chert and quartz both coming in at around 7%) and decorated ceramics (3%). Stone axes contribute very little to the total (1%), and the granite hammerstones are negligible. Together, these categories represent the typical assemblage found at Neolithic sites all over Ireland and beyond (Chapter 5, Chapter 6).

Neolithic Artifacts: Distribution

As is true for all artifacts at the site, Neolithic artifacts came from a wide variety of contexts. Table 4-9 shows the various contexts. As always, a large proportion (480, 42%) are from unknown, uncertain, or surface contexts. Of the remaining artifacts, 481 came from pits, post-holes, and trenches; given the history of the site, the majority of these are likely to have been from later periods (though see above). A large number (150) also came from the occupation layer. This indicates that much of the Neolithic material was churned up during the various Iron Age phases. Interestingly, compared to Iron Age material, a larger proportion of Neolithic artifacts were from a known archaeological context, albeit not typically their original one. About 514 Iron Age artifacts were recovered (see Iron Age section below); 279 were from uncertain, unknown, or surface contexts, representing 54%. Compared to the 42% of Neolithic artifacts in these contexts, this suggests that Neolithic artifacts were more likely to end up in Iron Age contexts than in more modern or disturbed ones (such as surface layers). This is presumably taphonomic, perhaps having something to do with their being more deeply buried or indeed protected by Iron Age features.

While the distribution of Neolithic artifacts might seem scattered, it is worth noting that relatively few features produced such artifacts. The proportion can be calculated in various ways. The total number of features recorded from Dún Ailinne is 2,851; 13 of these were considered medieval or modern, leaving 2,838 potentially prehistoric. Of these, 1,367 could be assigned to a phase with relative certainty, and of these, 335 belonged to one of the 4 main Iron Age phases or the Neolithic (Tan) phase. Of these, 76 (23%) produced a total of 411 Neolithic artifacts. The rest of the artifacts came from surface, mixed, or uncertain contexts, or from the "occupation" phases. Put another way, the vast majority of features of any phase did not produce Neolithic artifacts.

It is difficult to assess how many of the artifacts might have come from Neolithic contexts. This is partly because the features were typically identified as Neolithic on the basis of the artifacts, an annoyingly tautological situation. As noted elsewhere, however, at least two features were identified as probably Neolithic, Trench 281 and Pit 293 (containing the Linkardstown burial). A number of other pits, post-holes, trenches, and other features, such as the stone cluster numbered 1536, produced only Neolithic materials and could not be excluded as Neolithic on stratigraphic grounds. These may also therefore have produced essentially *in situ* artifacts. Counting those recovered from Trench 281 and Pit 293, and adding those from the more likely of the uncertain features, as few as 30–35 and perhaps as many as 140 (counting all possible features as definite) of the typologically Neolithic artifacts may have been *in situ*. Even using the most generous number, however, it is clear that the majority of Neolithic artifacts, probably more than 80%, came from later features as well as both uncertain and surface contexts.

Another way of looking at this is through the distribution of Neolithic artifacts by phase, shown in Table 4-10. The majority could not clearly be assigned to a phase (779, 68%). Of the remaining artifacts, a small number (90, 8% of the total or 24% of those from identifiable phases) could be clearly assigned to the Tan phase, arguably representing the Neolithic. However, far more came from the most active Iron Age phases, the largest being Mauve, Rose, and White (170 combined), representing major Iron Age construction and ritual activity, and Flame (36), the final period of Iron Age use. Together, Iron Age phases represent about half (55%) of the known contexts in which Neolithic material was found.

The spatial distribution of Neolithic artifacts shows the pattern one would expect give this situation, with some artifacts in Neolithic contexts but the majority in disturbed contexts. CD Figure 4-4 shows the distribution of Neolithic artifacts (this figure excludes several outliers; see below), and as would be expected, Neolithic artifacts were recovered from most parts of the excavated section of the site.

This is emphasized by a small number of outliers not shown in CD Figure 4-4, which fall outside

Table 4-10. Distribution, Neolithic Artifacts by Phase.

PHASE	N
Tan	90
White	9
Rose	80
Mauve	81
Flame	36
Crimson	5
Dun	4
Grey	1
Harry	7
Jade	12
Khaki	18
Lemon	13
Lower Emerald	2
Upper Emerald	5
Niamh	1
Uaininn	8
Uncertain	256
Unknown	523
TOTAL	1,151

of the main excavated area defined on the grid as E-W 410000 to about 52000, and N-S 44000 to about 54000. All but one of these outliers (a surface find of a single flint projectile point at 46700 62900) are associated with the excavation of the Iron Age roadway leading from the main entrance of the site to the timber structures at the center (presumably; see Chapter 3). Excluding the projectile point just noted, there are a total of 18 artifacts (ten of flint and eight ceramic sherds representing three vessels) recorded from this outlying area. Six of the flints were surface finds and three of the remaining have missing or incomplete context information. The final flint, a tertiary flake, and the sherds all come from small pits or post-holes. One pit (3519) may be Neolithic (see Features discussion, above). The other three (3106, 3108, 3127) are small pits or post-holes, all of which produced only Neolithic artifacts and which could not be ruled out as Neolithic on stratigraphic grounds.

Although the majority of the Neolithic artifacts are lithic remains, the distribution of both lithics and ceramics essentially mirrors the aggregate distribution; this is shown in CD Figure 4-5. The distribution of stone axes, shown in CD Figure 4-6, is marginally different, having a slightly more scattered pattern, but this is more likely to be due to sample size than some behavioral or chronological difference.

As is noted above (and Chapters 5 and 6), this assemblage overall says little that is specific about either the date or the use of Dún Ailinne in the Neolithic. All can be assigned to the Neolithic on typological grounds; and, with the exception of the burial in Pit 293, all would be consistent with a domestic context, a larger funerary context, or a non-funerary ritual context.

Bronze Age

There are very few features and artifacts that can be assigned with any certainty to the Bronze Age at Dún Ailinne. Stratigraphically, large numbers of features cannot be assigned to any period, so associated artifacts become the basis for determining the date of at least some features. However, because of the generalized nature of most of the pre-Iron Age artifacts which were recovered, the situation with the artifacts is no more satisfying. Flint flakes, chert cores, and even stone beads might come from any period from the Neolithic through the Iron Age, thus it is impossible to be certain what time periods they represent. By the same token, with the exception of the food vessel, no artifacts were found whose typology was confined to the Bronze Age. In the end, it is likely that some, even many, of the features and artifacts suggested as Neolithic in the preceding section are in fact Bronze Age in origin.

Having said that, there are at least a few artifacts and their associated features for which a somewhat more convincing argument can be made. The first is of course the food vessel (E.79.905). This is discussed in Chapter 6, but the vessel itself and its associated pit, Feature 2790, are the only definitive evidence of Bronze Age activity. As such, it suggests that the behavioral context during this period was a ritual one.

Other artifacts are far less certain, and the three which are noted here were not recovered in any proximity to the food vessel. It is suggested in Chapter 11 that the amber bead (E.79.1915) likely represents the Bronze Age, though such an attribution is far less certain than the food vessel. This bead's context is somewhat unclear; it is recorded as coming from the lower mound, with no other more specific information known.

A second possibility is E.79.1832, a flint projectile point with asymmetrical barbs. This is discussed in Chapter 5, where it is noted as matching typologically with a point associated with a food vessel at Coney Island in Lough Neagh. This may suggest it also dates to the Bronze Age—or it may not! Since the Dún Ailinne point came from the topsoil, there is no associated feature that might also be assigned to this period.

Finally, the possibility is suggested in Chapter 9 that E.79.115, a turquoise glass bead, might be from the Bronze Age. As noted there, beads of this color, though of a lighter shade, have been recovered from Bronze Age contexts. Since the Dún Ailinne bead was found in the topsoil, this is obviously tentative.

In the end, while it can be noted that there is definitive evidence of at least one episode of Bronze Age behavior at Dún Ailinne, the extent and character of other activity at the site in that period remains unknown.

Iron Age

Despite traces of activity from other periods, Dún Ailinne remains in essence an Iron Age site. The trenches and post-holes which represent the several phases of timber structures form the main evidence for analysis of this period. However, other features represent other aspects of the site's use in the Iron Age. The timber structures discussed in more detail in Chapter 2 will not be discussed further here. Other features which are likely Iron Age in date have already been noted above, such as the large number of post-holes and stake holes. Most of these belong to the Jade and Harry phases, which are arguably contemporary with the Rose and Mauve timber structures, respectively (see Chapter 2). They thus represent Iron Age activity.

Other categories of feature are less clear. Leaving out features associated with the Mauve and Rose phase structures, and the post-holes and stakeholes of Jade and Harry phases, there is a small handful of features which produced arguably Iron Age artifacts. There are nine total, including two post-holes, five actual or probable pits, one possible trench, and a copper alloy fragment from the low mound. In addition, given the overall Iron Age character of the site, it is likely that a significant number, and probably the majority, of features which did not produce artifacts but could not be assigned stratigraphically also belong to the Iron Age. These have already been discussed in more general terms.

Iron Age Artifacts

In absolute numbers, by far the largest quantity of artifacts from Dún Ailinne came from the Neolithic and Bronze Age, rather ironic since most of the activity at the site dates to the Iron Age. Using a rough number based on "artifact counts" (see Preface), a total of 1851 artifacts were recovered from the site. Of these, 1151 (62%) of them are largely comprised of pottery fragments and lithic remains from the Neolithic, while only 514 (28%) included glass, iron, copper alloy, and other materials attributable to Iron Age activity. Unlike the analysis of Neolithic objects, where missing objects were not included, three missing Iron Age objects were included here. These are E.79.338, E.79.2268, and E.79.3017, for which there is relatively reliable information.

Obviously the disparity between Neolithic and Iron Age artifact numbers is to a great extent a function of taphonomic and other factors. The nature of lithic production and maintenance produces a large amount of waste, and this is indeed a large percent of the recovered Neolithic material. Similarly, the tendency of pottery to fragment also augments this total. By contrast, the more fragile nature of iron, while on the one hand causing the total number of artifacts in this category to increase (see Chapter 7), also undoubtedly means that a number of iron artifacts did not survive in any form, fragmentary or otherwise.

Table 4-11. Numbers of Probable Iron Age Artifacts.

OBJECT	N
Beads, bead fragments	24
Binding strips	3
Blades (probable and certain)	4
Bracelets and bracelet fragments	14
Casting debris	4
Disk	1
Fastener	1
Fibula	2
Fitting?	1
Ingot?	2
Nails (probable and certain)	73
Needles (probable and certain)	8
Pendant	1
Pin fragments	10
Rings, ring fragments, ring beads*	37
Shafts (possible pins, needles, nails)	111
Spearhead	1
Sword	1
Toggles	8
Tools (chisels, spikes, hooks, tracer)	9
Uncertain (fragments, strips, wire)	198
Weight?	1
TOTAL	514

*This includes both rings meant to be worn, such as bronze spiral rings, and more utilitarian objects, such as iron ring fittings of various kinds; about 19 are in the former category and 18 in the latter.

At the same time, the range of categories of artifact represented by the Iron Age remains is far greater than that for the Neolithic and Bronze Age (largely ceramic vessels, stone axes, lithic implements and debris, and possibly some or all of the stone beads and balls). This suggests that the complexity of the behavior associated with the Iron Age use of the site far outstrips the more ephemeral and somewhat uncertain nature of the Neolithic and Bronze Age activity. Table 4-11 shows the broad categories of probable Iron Age remains, including objects made from iron, copper alloy, glass, lignite, and gold.

While the exact character of many of these artifacts is typically uncertain, about half of them can be described as personal items, such as beads, weapons, and rings. This presumably reflects the possessions of those in attendance at the various rituals carried out at Dún Ailinne. The other half are more utilitarian in nature. Many nails and tools may repre-

Table 4-12. Distribution, Iron Age Artifacts by Feature Type.

FEATURE TYPE	N OBJECTS
Hut	2
Mound	68
Occupation	74
Pit	20
Plank	2
Post-hole	9
Trench	60
Surface	145
Uncertain	112
Unknown	22
TOTAL	514

Table 4-13. Distribution, Iron Age Artifacts by Phase.

PHASE	N OBJECTS
Dun	11
Flame	87
Harry	6
Jade	2
Lower Emerald	7
Mauve	36
Rose	24
Upper Emerald	18
White	2
Uncertain	56
Unknown	265
TOTAL	514

sent the actual construction of the various Iron Age structures; others, such as casting jets, glass toggles (see Chapter 9), and the tracer, reflect a degree of small-scale manufacturing being carried out. Still others may inhabit several of these categories, such as tools and needles, which may be both personal possessions and evidence of manufacturing.

Iron Age Artifacts: Distribution

As would be expected given the disturbed nature of the site, the largest number of artifacts (279, 54%) came from uncertain or surface contexts. Most of the remainder came from the occupation layers, the mound, and the trenches and pits attributable to the Iron Age. Table 4-12 shows the distribution of artifacts by the type of feature.

As with Neolithic objects, the majority of Iron Age artifacts did not come from features. Of the 514 Iron Age artifacts, only 69 (13%) were recovered from clearly identifiable features. The rest came from the surface (145, 28%), mixed, uncertain, or unknown contexts (226, 44%) or from the occupation phases (74, 14%). Compared to the total recorded features at the site, the Iron Age artifacts show a similar pattern to the Neolithic: of the arguably 331 features that could be clearly assigned to the four main Iron Age phases, only 24 (7%) produced artifacts. This number is even smaller than the 23% of prehistoric features that produced Neolithic artifacts, noted above. On the other hand, by contrast with the Neolithic, all of the Iron Age artifacts came from Iron Age features, a point that means little given the far larger number of artifacts that were recovered from disturbed contexts.

As would be expected, the phases represented by Iron Age objects are those which showed the majority of the Iron Age activity. Table 4-13 shows the artifacts which could be associated with a phase. Leaving aside the 321 found in uncertain or surface contexts, 149 (77%) of the remaining 193 are from the three major phases represented by timber structures (Mauve, Rose, and White) and the final phase characterized by extensive feasting (Flame).

We charted the distribution of artifacts from those phases that had more than five separate data points to show their spatial distribution. Each point represents a single find spot, and not necessarily a single artifact. The distributions are shown in CD Figure 4-7. The distribution of artifacts in each of these phases shows a pattern that mirrors the major features by which the phase was identified. Artifacts from both Lower and Upper Emerald are limited to the area of the mound in which those layers were preserved. For artifacts recovered from Flame, the distribution is more scattered, reflecting the scatter of burned material associated with that phase. For the Rose and Mauve phases, the artifact distribution mostly hugs the circular pattern of the trenches which define them. This is not unexpected; for Rose, 22 of the 24 artifacts securely attributable to this phase came from the concentric trenches, while for Mauve, 31 of 36 artifacts had this provenience.

Beyond this, there may be some clustering of the Mauve phase artifacts. CD Figure 4-8 shows only the Mauve phase objects, and there do seem to be three to four distinct clusters of objects. Whether this represents something real deriving from Iron

Table 4-14. Types of Artifacts from Mauve Phase Contexts.

OBJECT	N
fragment	3
hook	1
nail	3
needle	1
pin fragment	1
ring	4
shaft	9
sword	1
TOTAL	23

Age activity or not is uncertain. Table 4-14 shows the kinds of artifacts recovered from Mauve phase contexts. As with the iron objects overall, it is difficult to determine the original character of most of the artifacts represented, most of them being shaft fragments (perhaps pins or nails), unidentified fragments, or rings of unknown function. However, it also includes the sword, arguably a ritual deposit (see Chapter 7). Perhaps some of the other items, particularly those of a personal nature, might also derive from a similar cultural context, that is, with the clusters produced by specific deposits rather than random loss. In that case, the various clusters may represent the location of such deposits. There is no way to determine this with any degree of certainty.

Missing and Discarded Artifacts

As would be expected of a project completed decades ago, a number of finds recorded in the finds register could not be located while this report was being written. Approximately 346 objects are considered missing ("approximate" because the finds register sometimes indicated that there were multiple objects, for example, "fragments of glass," but not the exact number). These are discussed further below. An additional 72 numbers were assigned to objects (again, approximately 84 objects in total) that were later determined to be natural and discarded. All but one of these were fragments of stone, sometimes listed as flint or chert and sometimes just as stone. Table 4-15 shows the numbers of these.

The four objects listed as "flint/chert" actually represent a single number given to three fragments of flint and 1 of chert, discarded as natural. The two objects listed as "stone?" were both originally identified as crucibles but later discarded as natural. The "uncertain" object was originally designated "stone," which was then changed (somewhat mysteriously) to "soap?" before being marked as natural and discarded. The rest were presumably collected as possible lithic artifacts but were ultimately proven not to be artificial. An indeterminate number of other objects, all listed in the finds register as modern—typically glass, metal, and other debris—were also noted as discarded but were not counted since they were never given numbers.

Table 4-15. Objects Noted as Discarded.

MATERIAL	N
chert	11
flint	7
flint/chert	4
stone	59
stone?	2
uncertain	1
TOTAL	84

The number of missing objects, officially 346, represents about 15% of the total artifacts collected and given numbers (2281, including artifacts, missing objects, and discards, but not faunal or botanical remains, or soil or other kinds of samples). Of this total, about half were either certainly or probably modern, while a smaller number were either probably ancient or were impossible to assign. Table 4-16 shows these categories.

Missing objects were entered into the database essentially verbatim from the finds register. The information available for analysis therefore varies considerably, from very general ("glass") to fairly specific ("finely worked flint projectile point"). In addition to basic descriptive and context information, some attempt was made to assign this material to chronological periods. Most periods were recorded with a question mark to indicate that cer-

Table 4-16. Distribution, Missing Objects by Likely Period.

PERIOD	N
Iron Age?	39
Modern	183
Modern?	9
Neolithic?	54
Uncertain	61
TOTAL	346

Table 4-17. Numbers of Missing Neolithic Artifacts.

MATERIAL	N	TYPE	N
chert	6	flake?	7
flint	39	fragment	33
quartz	7	hollow scraper	1
quartz?	2	projectile point	2
TOTAL	54	projectile point?	3
		scraper	1
		scraper?	6
		uncertain	1
		TOTAL	54

tainty was impossible. The exception was modern objects, many of which were identifiable from the description, such as clay pipe fragments and bullet casings. Some objects, such as "green glass" and "bottle glass," were assumed to be modern. Context was also used, so that surface or topsoil finds listed simply as "glass" were likely to be modern; these were listed as modern but with a question mark. Iron, stone, and some other miscellaneous fragments were more problematic. If they were recovered from a clearly Iron Age context, they were designated as such; those that were unstratified or were from less clear contexts were recorded as uncertain. All flint, chert, and quartz was assigned to the Neolithic category, though of course they could well be from other periods. It should also be noted that 31 objects have lost their numbers over the years; these objects were given new numbers (see Preface), but presumably some of the "missing" objects are actually among the re-numbered group.

Table 4-16 shows that 192 of the missing objects, which represent 55% of the total, are modern or probably modern. These are considered more fully in Chapter 14. A proportion of the uncertain objects (which are 18% of the total missing objects) are also presumably modern, while others may be ancient; obviously this cannot be narrowed any further. That leaves a total of 93 missing objects which are possibly or likely to be ancient, 27% of the total missing objects or 4% of the artifact total as noted above.

Missing Neolithic Objects

The missing Neolithic category is comprised solely of lithic artifacts. The materials represented and the artifact types are listed in Table 4-17. The overwhelming majority of these (72%) were identified as flint, with much smaller numbers of chert and quartz. The two pieces identified as "quartz?" were described in the finds register as "crystal," presumably (but not certainly) meaning quartz crystal. Looking at the type of artifact, most (61%) were categorized as "fragment." This designation was used for entries that listed something like "flint" or "piece of flint." It is difficult to know the character of these pieces. Some examples of flint that were later determined to be natural were discarded, as noted above, so presumably there was some belief that those listed here might have been artifacts. However, since other pieces were described as flakes, possible flakes, or implements, it must be assumed that these "fragments" were not recognizable types. They might have been cores, or they might ultimately have been determined to be natural.

The implements were listed with a question mark to indicate that they were not positively identified as such in this study. This includes three possible projectile points (one said to be of quartz) and six possible scrapers, as well as seven possible flakes. The "uncertain" artifact listed was described only as a "chert object." The fate of the other four objects (two projectile points, a scraper, and a hollow scraper) is somewhat more mysterious. A note among the files, dated August 1972, indicated that they had been sent to the University of Missouri for possible thermoluminescence dating. However, there is no record of such a TL date, and the lab there has no record of the artifacts. A possible scenario is that the technique was attempted and the artifacts destroyed in the process, but no date was produced for any number of valid reasons.

Missing Iron Age Objects

As with the known Iron Age artifacts from the site, the missing objects that are possibly Iron Age in date are also more varied than the Neolithic category. Table 4-18 shows these objects. To some extent this variety is a result of the way the objects were categorized. Of the 13 categories, eight could be from other periods. This comprises a total of 19 objects (49% of those attributed to the Iron Age), and includes everything but the glass, iron, copper alloy, and slag. In addition, the wood is likely to be Iron Age as well. It is described as burned fragments, possibly of posts, which could date to any use of the site; however, though neither fragment is associated with the post-holes of the Iron Age timber structures, the presence of these structures makes an Iron Age attribution somewhat more likely.

Table 4-18. Numbers of Missing Iron Age Artifacts.

MATERIAL	N	TYPE	N
antler	1	bead fragment?	1
bone (faunal/human)	3	bead?	2
charcoal	1	bracelet fragment?	2
clay	1	fossil	6
copper alloy	1	fragment	18
glass	6	nail?	2
iron	9	pin?	1
slag	2	shaft	3
stone	4	slag	2
stone?	1	uncertain	1
uncertain	7	weight?	1
unknown	1	TOTAL	39
wood	2		
TOTAL	39		

Most of the other categories are comprised of objects which could well be natural. An exception is the antler fragment, which was worked and used possibly as a handle (see Chapter 10; the antler was examined and described at some point after it was recovered but cannot now be located). Its context was somewhat uncertain, but it was believed to have come from a post-hole in a trench assigned to the Harry phase. That makes it likely to have come from the Iron Age, though there is always the possibility that it dates to an earlier period and was only later incorporated into this context.

The remaining objects were recorded in the finds register with generally vague descriptions, such as "smoothed bone," "charcoal fragment with a hole in it," "pockmarked stone," or "burned clay." The artificial nature of any of these could only be determined by direct examination. By contrast, objects in the "unknown" and "uncertain" categories are at least more readily identifiable. Of the seven in the latter group, six are crinoids, fossils whose presence at the site may be coincidental. As noted elsewhere (Chapter 11), these might have been used as beads or deliberately collected for some other reason, or they might be there naturally. The other "uncertain" listing, E.79.3738, was described as "vitreous material," something whose true nature is obscure. The "unknown" object is described as "red bead." Little else can be said about this, except that the possibilities are endless. It could be an ancient specimen of red glass, in which case it is most unfortunate it was lost. It could also be modern, and have been made from anything, including plastic.

For the faunal bone, the possibility may be noted that some or all of it is not actually missing. The bone fragments listed here were recorded as missing if (1) they were not among the worked bone but (2) were described in the finds register in a way that suggested they were possibly more than food remains etc. However, if they were determined to be food remains rather than worked or artificial *after* they were listed in the register, it is unlikely that the finds register would have been modified to reflect this, and the bones would now be stored with the large faunal collection. The faunal collection is composed of over 18,000 fragments, and individual faunal bone numbers were not recorded in the analysis that was conducted on them. Thus to determine whether the objects listed here as missing might now be among the faunal collection, it would have to be located among the individual pieces; frankly it is unclear that this would be worth the effort. Since the faunal analysis carried out on the existing collection was quite thorough, it seems likely that worked bone would have been identified. The conclusion to be reached is that these are either misidentifications or the bones went missing before the faunal analysis was carried out. There is now no way to determine what the relative proportion of each might be.

More problematic is a missing fragment of human bone. There is a very small fragment (E.79.5) that could be human that was examined in this study (see Chapter 13), but there was also a larger fragment that might have been human bone (Wailes 1990:29). This would appear to be E.79.722, which is described in the finds register as a possible fragment of human skull and was recorded in a photograph (see Chapter 13, Plate 13-1). A brief and informal examination by a physical anthropologist at the University of Pennsylvania not longer after the fragment was recovered suggested that it was a portion of parietal. Unfortunately this bone cannot now be located for any further analysis.

Descriptions in the finds register are not necessarily accurate in detail with regard to the identification of artifacts. Basic descriptions are certainly reliable, but specific details depend to a great extent on the individual knowledge of the person who did the listing. Possibilities were noted, exaggerations are undoubtedly included; and since the finds register was destined to be superseded by more definitive analyses and the final report, it was not consistently changed to reflect the most current information. Thus while the descriptions are broadly reliable, they are not a true substitute for the artifact itself.

It is with this in mind that a few words can be said about the remaining missing artifacts. The copper alloy object (E.79.3017) is easily dispensed with. It was described (see Chapter 8) as a "domed object," possibly a weight, and was destroyed in the process of being mounted for a PIXE analysis. The other metal category, iron objects, is more problematic. While the exact state of the nine iron objects listed was not described, it is certain that they were no better preserved than any of the iron from Dún Ailinne. Of the three listed as "fragments," two were described as indeterminate pieces of iron (one of them "curved"). While the other six were listed in the finds register as possible pins, nails, or shafts, all were presumably rusted fragments that were longer than they were wide, and so given a designation based on the perception of the person who entered them. These shapes are sufficiently generic that they could have been anything, from any of the later periods of use of the site. They were assigned to the Iron Age based on context, but the disturbance at Dún Ailinne makes even this less than certain.

The exception among the iron is E.79.3663, which is described as "two iron fragments, possibly fibula." They came from trench number 2936; however, the pages from the feature log which would have included this number are also missing. It seems difficult to imagine that something that could have been a fibula would have been treated so cavalierly, and the inclination here is to assume that the finds register description was hyperbole on someone's part. However, to be consistent, it is noted here as a possible fibula, and listed as missing.

The remaining category is glass, a material that is as problematic in its own way as iron. It must be one of the most common modern finds in archaeological sites, and so the possibility of modern glass being initially mistaken for ancient is high. Further, it may be noted that the criteria used here for assigning period meant that anything described as "green glass" was considered modern; some of this glass could theoretically be ancient. Thus there may be ancient glass among the modern or modern glass among the ancient; since all of the fragments being discussed here are missing, it is perhaps a moot point.

In any case, there were six fragments of glass that stood out among the veritable barrage of bottle and green glass, and so warrant further (brief) discussion. Two of them were described as beads or fragments of beads, both (E.79.692 and E.79.1221) said to be blue glass. A third number, E.79.2804, was given to two fragments of "L green glass bracelet," the "L" presumably meaning "light" (since they were not described as joining, or even certainly from the same artifact, they were entered as two objects). The remaining two fragments were both from the Flame phase occupation layers, and were assigned to the Iron Age on that basis; one, E.79.503, was described as "blue glass" while the other, E.79.473, was simply listed as "glass."

It is difficult to know what to make of these, particularly the first four. Blue beads (17, some with additional colors added as decoration) and a fragment of a light green glass bracelet (E.79.1927) were recovered from Dún Ailinne (see Chapter 9), so these are not out of place. As with the supposed "possible fibula," however, it seems hard to imagine that these would have been lost, given their potential significance to the interpretation of the site, as well as the care the other glass objects received. In the absence of further detail, this too must remain a mystery.

5

Lithic Remains

Susan A. Johnston

The lithic assemblage from Dún Ailinne is comprised of a total of 665 pieces of flint, chert, quartz, and granite, including both production waste in the form of debitage and a range of implements. An additional 403 pieces of flint, chert, and quartz and 76-78 pieces of unidentified stone were also collected from the site, all judged to be natural; 22 of the flint, chert, and quartz fragments were discarded, and 61 of unidentified stone fragments. That left 381 natural fragments of flint, chert, and quartz, and 15-17 fragments of unidentified stone in the collection. Basic descriptive statistics of the positively identified flint, chert, and quartz fragments (323 total) are provided in Table 5-1 for the sake of completeness, but they are otherwise not included in the analysis. The stone axes are considered further below.

It is worth noting that some of the pieces judged to be natural may also be lithic production products. A specialist analysis of this collection would certainly reveal additional useful information.

A number of objects were recorded in the finds register but are now missing (and were not included in the analysis below). These are discussed more fully in Chapter 4, but they include 54 pieces of flint, chert, and quartz, 21 of them possible or probable implements. Among the implements, seven scrapers, five projectile points, one hollow scraper, and seven flakes were listed (the remaining implement was listed only as "chert object"). Of these, four are the implements apparently sent for TL dating which were probably destroyed in the process (see Chapter 4 for their numbers and descriptions). These were likely to have been described accurately, but it is impossible to know whether the rest were correctly identified based solely on their description in the finds register, so all have been excluded. Given their relatively small number, they would have not have affected the implement counts or conclusions in any significant way. Whether they would have been typologically interesting is of course now moot.

The focus of this analysis is the flint, chert, and quartz material, but three possible granite hammerstones should be noted. All (E.79.693, E.79.1812, E.79.2710) are glacially worn round cobbles, and two (E.79.693 and E.79.2710) are artificially rubbed, per Ivor Harkin (personal communication). Their dimensions are given in Table 5-2. As can be seen, they are approximately the same size; the artificial rubbing of the surfaces of two of them suggests they were used for something, if not as hammerstones proper.

General Context: Flint, Chert, and Quartz

Excluding the possible hammerstones, then, leaves 662 pieces of flint, chert, and quartz. Table 5-3 shows the distribution of materials. This number includes 11 pieces whose material could not be determined, but which certainly belong in the general class of flint and/or chert. The flint was generally in the brown and gray range, but occasional examples of other colors occurred (such as a very pink round scraper and several honey colored examples). The chert ranged from fairly coarse grained examples to very fine grained ones. Quartz showed a similar

Table 5-1. Descriptive Statistics (mm), Natural Stone Collected from Dún Ailinne.

FLINT=230	L	W	T	CHERT=56	L	W	T	QUARTZ=37	L	W	T
Mean	25.8	17.6	9.4	Mean	25.1	17.4	10.5	Mean	18.2	12.2	6.8
Median	24.0	15.5	9.0	Median	23.5	15.0	9.5	Median	16.5	11.0	6.5
Mode	19.0	15.0	10.0	Mode	24.0	14.0	7.0	Mode	16.0	10.0	5.0
Range	10-87	7-70	3-32	Range	12-62	10-34	3-26	Range	10-40	6-23	2-12

range, from very coarse and cloudy examples to extremely clear, glass-like prisms.

Lithics were found scattered throughout the site, in a variety of contexts. Table 5-4 shows the distribution of those pieces found in reasonably certain contexts; a further 401 pieces were in uncertain or unknown contexts (counting surface finds), and 24 came from features of uncertain character.

While most of these artifacts are in disturbed contexts, at least some of these features are arguably Neolithic (see Chapter 4). This is clearly problematic since the presence of lithics is in part what suggests this date for these features. It seems likely that at least some of this material dates to the Bronze or Iron Ages (see below), which sets up an unavoidably tautological situation. Having said this, however, of the various pits, post-holes, and trenches that produced lithics, several can be assigned to the Neolithic with at least some certainty (see Chapter 4). Trench 281 and its continuation, trench 1282, produced 20 examples, and 12 pieces came from pit 2506. Other examples are noted in Chapter 4. Even accepting these as all Neolithic, however, the fact remains that the majority of lithics, perhaps as much as 90-95%, are from secondary contexts.

Another way of looking at this is to examine the archaeological phases associated with the lithic contexts. Figure 5-1 shows the archaeological phases associated with lithics at Dún Ailinne. As is clearly represented, the majority of lithics with reasonably certain phase associations (127 or 63%) came from Iron Age phases Flame, Mauve, and Rose. Some lithics may actually date to this period, but it seems unlikely that this many can be attributed to the Iron Age. By contrast, Tan, the arguably Neolithic phase, only produced 31 artifacts (15%).

Some hint as to the dynamics of site formation is provided by comparing this distribution to that of Neolithic ceramics (see Chapter 6). For one thing, far more phases are represented (15 versus 9 for ceramics), suggesting that the lithics are far more scattered. This may be the result of their being smaller to begin with compared to sherds (particularly if the sherds are the result of the disturbance of whole vessels rather than individual sherds). It may also result from the fact that the majority of the lithic remains are arguably waste products, and so might have been more scattered to begin with. In addition, while the top four phases in terms of lithic numbers are Rose (57), Mauve and Flame (35 each), and Tan (31), ceramics show a slightly differ-

Table 5-2. Hammerstones, Basic Dimensions (mm).

NUMBER	LENGTH	WIDTH	THICKNESS
E.79.693	73	63	50
E.79.1812	71	69	62
E.79.2710	72	65	58

Table 5-3. Distribution, Artifacts by Material.

MATERIAL	N
chert	86
flint	488
quartz	77
flint/chert?	11
TOTAL	662

Table 5-4. Distribution, Lithic Contexts

FEATURE TYPEN	OF LITHICS
Burned Area	2
Embankment	2
Hut	2
Mound	1
Occupation	85
Pit	27
Post-hole	21
Trench	100
TOTAL	240

Lithic Remains

Table 5-5. Distribution, Lithic Materials by Phase.

CHERT	N=22	FLINT	N=142	QUARTZ	N=28
Crimson	1	Crimson	3	Flame	2
Flame	2	Dun	4	Harry	2
Mauve	7	Flame	28	Jade	1
Rose	9	Grey	1	Mauve	7
Tan	1	Harry	4	Rose	9
Uaininn	2	Jade	3	Tan	5
		Lemon	1	Uaininn	1
		Lower Emerald	1	White	1
		Mauve	20		
		Niamh	1		
		Rose	37		
		Tan	24		
		Uaininn	4		
		Upper Emerald	5		
		White	6		

ent pattern in terms of individual sherd frequencies: Mauve (46), Tan (24), Rose (21), and Khaki (18).

While the pattern of sherd distribution varies, however, the number of actual vessels disturbed matches the lithic distribution much more closely: Rose (8 vessels), Mauve (4 vessels), and Khaki (2 vessels). To a great extent this pattern is probably the result of the fact that the greatest amount of ground disturbing activity occurred in Rose and Mauve phases, during which the large timber structures were constructed. Finally, there is the difference in the actual phases represented. While a number of lithics were included in Flame phase features, no ceramics came from this phase. In comparison, the two vessels from Khaki phase are from a single pit, and no lithics are represented there. A likely reason for this is the greater general scatter of lithic remains over the site, which then became incorporated in what appears to have been fairly large scale activity represented by the Flame phase.

There seems little patterning in the way different materials were distributed over the site. Table 5-5 shows the distribution of materials by phase (where both material and phase could be determined with some certainty). The more artifacts there are, the more phases are represented, but the four phases that show the most artifacts for each material, Flame, Rose, Mauve, and Tan, are essentially the same for all three materials. Thus it seems that the various materials were also equally distributed around the site, to be disturbed by Iron Age activity.

There are a number of examples of burned flint, though none of burned chert or quartz. A to-

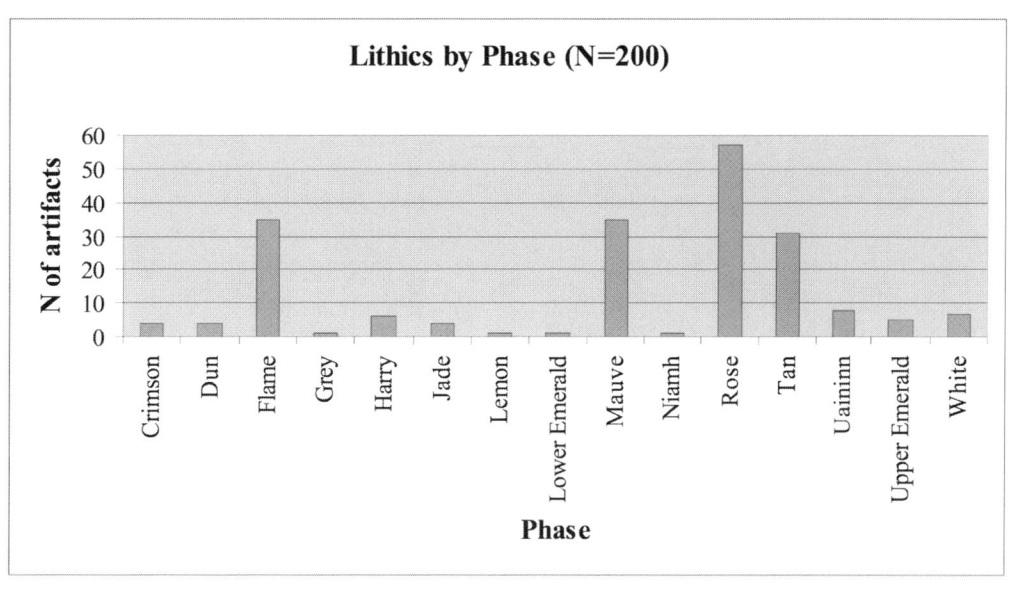

Figure 5-1. Distribution, lithic artifacts by phase.

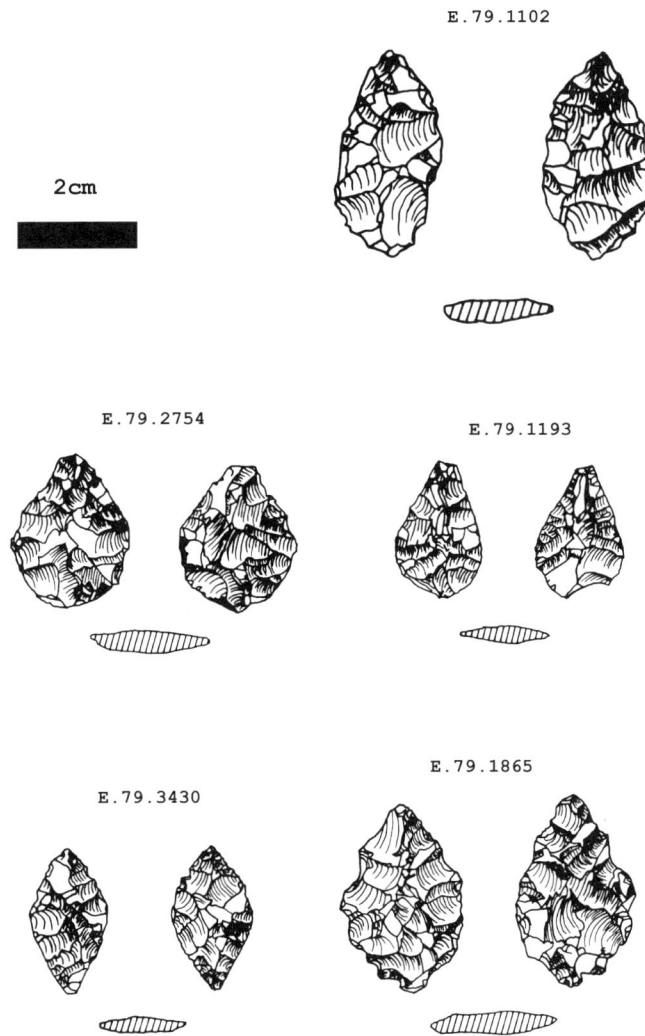

Figure 5-2. Leaf-shaped projectile points from Dún Ailinne.

tal of 58 flakes and implements show possible evidence of burning, both in discoloration and in fracture patterns. This may have something to do with material pre-treatment, though this assemblage has not been examined specifically for this possibility. That heat treating can improve the knapping quality of flint and chert has been attested experimentally, typically reducing the incidence of step and hinge fractures (see Whittaker 1994:72-73); both are evident in the waste material at Dún Ailinne. Presumably heat treating occasionally goes wrong, perhaps producing the kinds of lithic examples seen here. In the context of the distribution of artifacts within phases, a pertinent observation is that only one artifact (a small fragment of flint, E.79.414) came from a Flame phase feature, a phase where significant burning took place. Given that almost half (26) of the burned lithics are from unknown phases, this number could certainly be larger, but even if all of these were originally within Flame phase features, that still leaves a significant number of artifacts. This suggests that the burning happened before the artifacts were deposited, rather than being post-depositional conditions. While some of them may be the result of accidents associated with hearths etc. certainly some experimentation with heat treating may have happened here.

Implements

Of the 662 lithic artifacts, 220 (33.2%) could be identified as implements or possible implements, including cores and quartz prisms (these were included in this analysis despite being natural, because they may have been deliberately collected).

Altogether, nine types of implements were recorded for the Dún Ailinne assemblage:

Projectile points: includes smaller points and one "javelin head"
Hollow scraper: scrapers made on flakes with at least one concave retouched hollow
Round scraper: scrapers, round or oval shape and cutting edge, retouched along some portion of the circumference
Straight scraper: scrapers retouched along one straight edge, either an end or a side
Scraper: scraper that did not fall into any of the other scraper categories
Borer: retouched implements that have a point on one end, resembling awls
Core: with one or more flakes removed
Implement: retouched implements that did not fit into any other defined type
Retouched flake: flakes with a few flakes removed but no obvious attempt at shaping.

Table 5-6 shows the distribution of these types for all materials, including the uncertain examples. For this table, possible and certain examples are grouped together. Flint shows by far the larger range of implement types as well as num-

Table 5-6. Distribution, Lithic Artifact Types by Material.

CHERT	N=14	FLINT	N=173	QUARZ	N=29	UNCERTAIN	N=4
borer	1	borer	5	core	8	core	3
core	4	core	31	prism	13	round scraper	1
projectile point	5	hollow scraper	12	retouched flake	7		
retouched flake	2	implement	11	scraper	1		
round scraper	1	projectile point	20				
scraper	1	retouched flake	22				
		round scraper	44				
		scraper	12				
		straight scraper	16				

ber, presumably reflecting material preference, availability, or both. While the overall number of implements for quartz is higher than chert, this is artificially inflated by the addition of the prisms. Without these, the only real implements (leaving aside cores) are retouched flakes and a single possible scraper. Again, this presumably displays a material preference, perhaps reflecting the fact that quartz is more difficult to work than either flint or chert, and seems to have been available in smaller nodules etc. Chert shows a similarly low frequency of implement types with the exception of projectile points; there are five of them, more than the other chert implement types combined (leaving out cores). Assuming this distribution is not a result of collection bias, flint seems to have been by far the preferred material, with chert and quartz a distant second. For projectile points, chert seems to have been marginally more preferred than for other implements.

Length, width, and thickness were recorded to the nearest millimeter for all implements. Length was taken along the axis from the bulb of percussion (or as near as could be established) to the opposite, distal end, and width was the maximum measurement perpendicular to length. Where the axis could not be determined, length was measured as the maximum dimension and width was perpendicular to this. Thickness was taken as maximum thickness.

Projectile Points

There were 25 whole or broken projectile points in this collection. The majority (15, 13 of them complete examples) are of the leaf-shaped or lozenge-shaped type characteristic of the 3rd and 4th millennia in Ireland (Green 1980; Waddell 2000:49) (Plate 5-1). All but two chert examples are flint. There are in addition three broken tips from projectile points, and of these at least one (flint) probably was also leaf- or lozenge-shaped. An additional artifact may also belong with this group (E.79.621; see below). The complete examples range in size from large and rather lumpy examples to small and quite delicate points. Table 5-7 shows the overall statistics for the lengths, widths, and thicknesses of the complete leaf- and lozenge-shaped points (this excludes two examples which are clearly leaf-shaped, but one is missing a tip and the other is missing a butt).

Of the complete examples, five are well-executed in good quality material, three of flint and two of chert (Figure 5-2). The three flint examples (E.79.1193, E.79.3430, and E.79.1102) are also the smallest in this assemblage. E.79.1102 is an elongated oval shape, while E.79.3430 is the sole clearly lozenge shaped example. E.79.1193 is classically leaf shaped and has a slightly hollow base which is just offset from center. It looks deliberately retouched, but may be the result of accidental chipping. The other two examples are both chert. E.79.2754 is also classically leaf-shaped and quite well-made, very thin and symmetrical. E.79.1865 is a more elongated leaf shape, and has a small tang.

Two additional points are broken, but were also leaf-shaped (Figure 5-3). Both are flint, well-

Table 5-7. Dimensions (mm), Projectile Points.

N=13	L	W	T
Mean	29.6	20.8	4.4
Median	31.0	20.0	4.0
Mode	25.0	20.0	5.0
Range	21–38	13–30	2–7

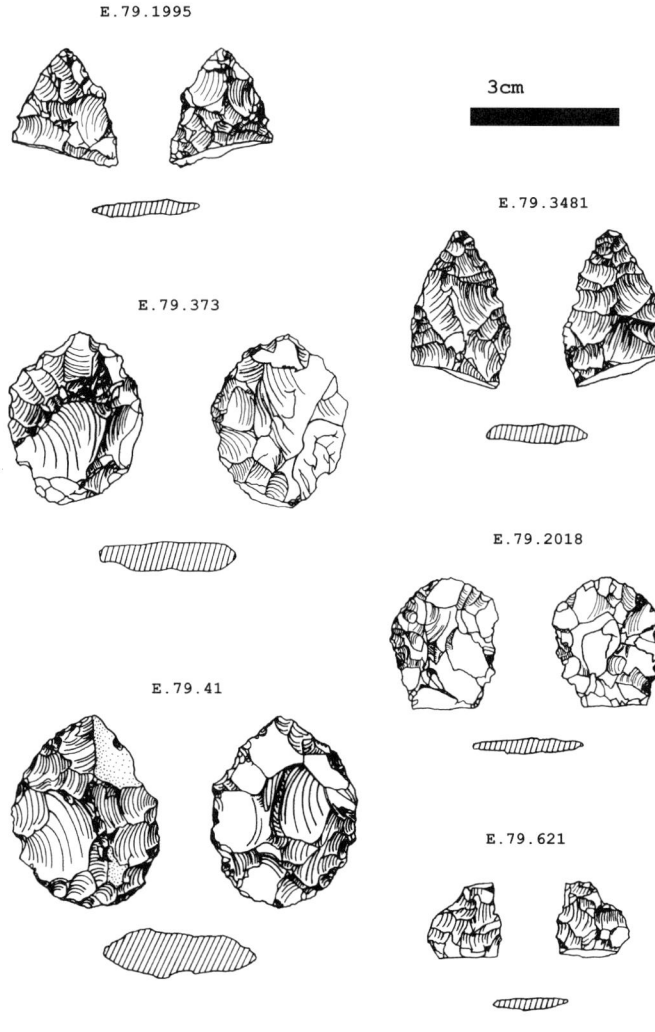

Figure 5-3. Leaf-shaped projectile points from Dún Ailinne.

The remaining eight leaf-shaped points are generally larger and fashioned on poor quality flint, suffering from hinge fractures and flaws in the material. All of these are flint, significantly thicker, and asymmetrical (Figure 5-4 shows some of them). E.79.1185 and E.79.262 are not retouched on one face, and only minimally retouched on the other, while E.79.3021 is sufficiently rough that it may not be a point, or may have been rejected because of material flaws.

Leaf-shaped arrowheads are extremely common in the British and Irish Neolithic. In Ireland, their context is more frequently sepulchral, occurring most often in the court tombs traditionally associated with the first half of the Neolithic (Green 1980:76, 219). The association between leaf-shaped arrowheads and early Neolithic pottery in Britain is close to exclusive, the exceptions being occasional examples of the former in Beaker habitation sites, food vessel contexts, and other 2nd millennium BC sites (Green 1980:94–6; Waddell 1990).

In addition to leaf- and lozenge-shaped points, there are also at least four additional types. Three examples (Figure 5-4) are longer and narrow, quite unlike the leaf shape seen in the bulk of the assemblage. One of these is complete, E.79.1. It is flint, and has a pointed base, set slightly off-center. This shape may have been dictated by a material flaw that appears right at the point on the base. E.79.3695 (see Plate 5-2) is the same size and shape, but the base is flat and has been snapped. Whether this was deliberate or not is unclear. E.79.1905 is a chert point with the tip missing. It too is narrow, but has a slightly concave base that appears deliberately produced. Given the way the piece is tapering to its tip, it was probably the same shape and about the same size as the other two just described.

made, very thin and largely symmetrical. E.79.3481 is snapped at an angle across the butt end, and E.79.2018 is missing its tip. E.79.1995 (Figure 5-3) is a flint tip, well made and probably originally leaf shaped, though not enough survives to be certain. E.79.621 (Figure 5-3) is a rather problematic piece. It could be the butt end of a small point, preserving what looks like a squared tang. However, if this is a tang, it was placed deliberately to one side of the butt, with no distinction between the tang and the side of the point. This is evident by the clear retouch along both remaining sides of the piece. The end opposite the "tang" is snapped, so its original shape is unknown. Thus if it was a point it was somewhat unusually shaped.

The remaining three complete points are each of unique type (Figure 5-5). E.79.1832 (Plate 5-2) is a flint arrowhead with asymmetrical barbs. It is small, only 23 mm long from the longer barb to the tip. While the shorter barb may have been broken off and subsequently retouched, there is a point of exactly the same type reported from Coney Island in Lough Neagh (Addyman 1965:84–87 and his fig. 8). There it was associated with food vessel sherds, mainly of bowl type, in a context interpreted as domestic. While it was not so associated at Dún Ailinne (it was found in the topsoil), sherds

Lithic Remains

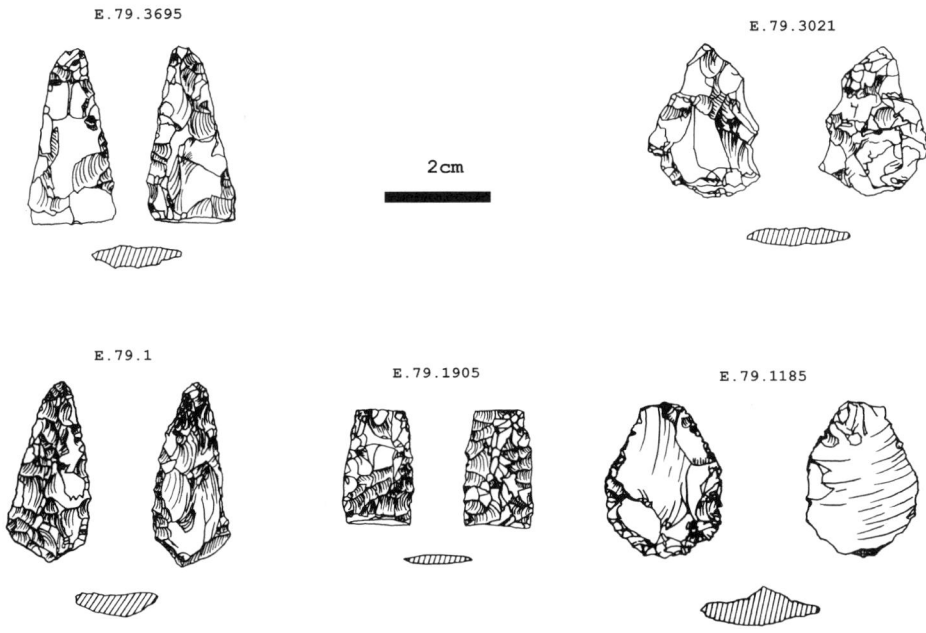

Figure 5-4. Projectile points from Dún Ailinne, other types.

of an undecorated bowl food vessel were found at the site, though some 30 m away (see Chapter 6). It is possible therefore that this point also dates to the earlier Bronze Age, providing further evidence of the use of this site during that period.

E.79.2850 (Plate 5-2) is a large point of the type known as a "javelin" or lance head. It is 83 mm long by 29 mm wide and 6 mm thick, and so exceeds the minimum length of 5 cm defined for the type by Collins (1981:111). In-

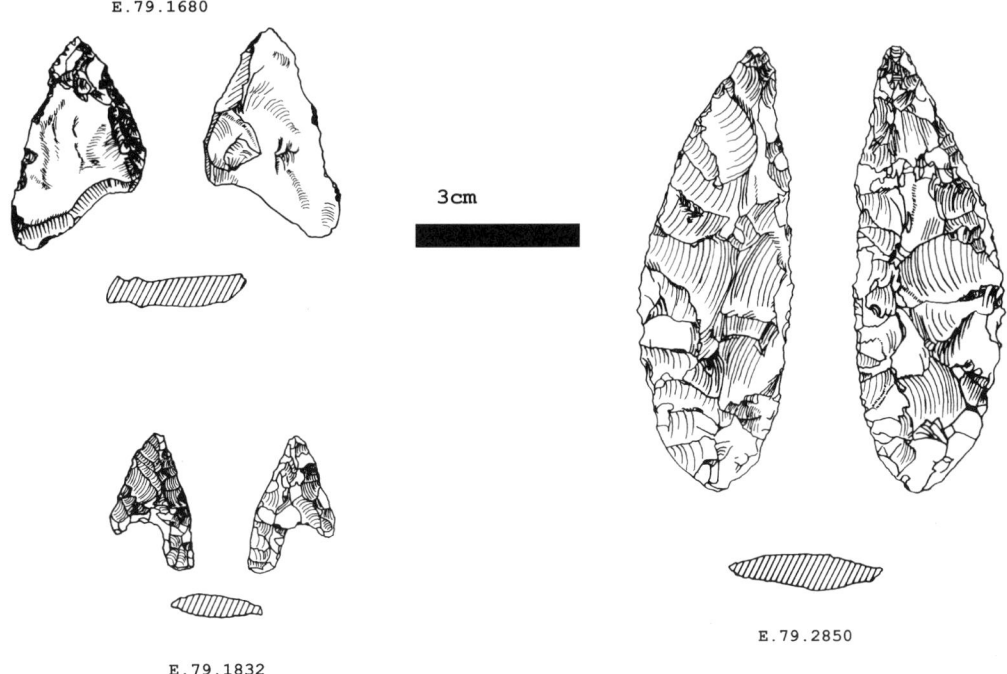

Figure 5-5. Three unusual projectile points from Dún Ailinne.

deed, it may be at the longer end of the range; Collins (1981) does not tabulate the lengths of the examples he describes, but assuming that his drawings are 1:1, the Dún Ailinne example exceeds the length of most of those that are illustrated. In shape it conforms to his type A, a leaf-shaped version lacking obvious angles or shoulders (1981:113). This example is asymmetrical, being quite flattened on one side compared to the other. Otherwise it is generally well made, bifacially worked on good quality material with only slight hinge fracturing on one face. Unlike some types found in Ireland, the surface is not polished (Green 1980:75), also a characteristic of Collins's type A (1981:115). As with leaf-shaped points, javelin heads are typically found in tombs, particularly court tombs, but are also found in domestic and industrial contexts (Collins 1981:120). For example, 49 complete and fragmentary examples were recovered from Dalkey Island, Co. Dublin (Liversage 1968). Compared to other find spots, the Dún Ailinne example is at the edge of the most typical geographic range for javelin heads, which are most commonly found in sites in the northeast of the island but which does extend to a few sites in the southeast (Collins 1981:122).

The final complete projectile point, E.79.1680 (Plate 5-2), may be classified as a *petit tranchet* derivative (PTD), although it is only minimally retouched; it may also be considered what Green (1980:100) calls the "Irish oblique," where it falls into what Flanagan has described as the "pointed" type (1966). It is made of chert on a single flake which is somewhat curved. The longest edge (31 mm) is at the distal end. This edge has the majority of the retouch, which is very slight, and there is also some retouch along the adjacent lateral edge, both on the ventral surface. There may also be some slight retouch along the opposite lateral edge as well. With the exception of a few possible tiny

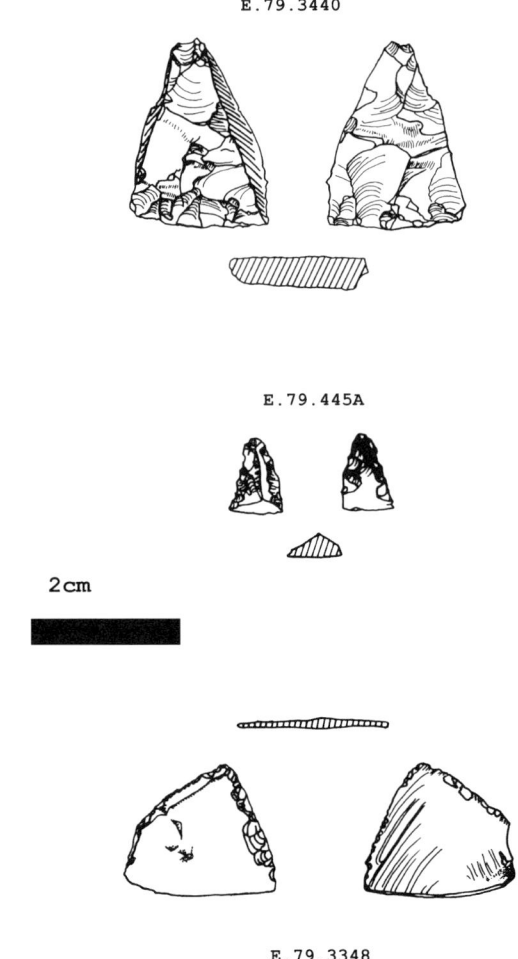

Figure 5-6. Uncertain projectile points from Dún Ailinne.

flake scars along the distal end, there appears to be no retouch on the dorsal face. The small amount of retouch may mean that the piece is unfinished.

This type of point has an almost uniquely Irish distribution, hence the name given it by Green; rare examples from Britain are suggested as being im-

Table 5-8. Distribution, Scraper Types by Material.

CHERT	N=2	FLINT	N=84	QUARTZ	N=1	UNCERTAIN	N=1
round scraper	1	hollow scraper	12	scraper	1	round scraper	1
scraper	1	round scraper	44				
		straight scraper	17				
		scraper	11				

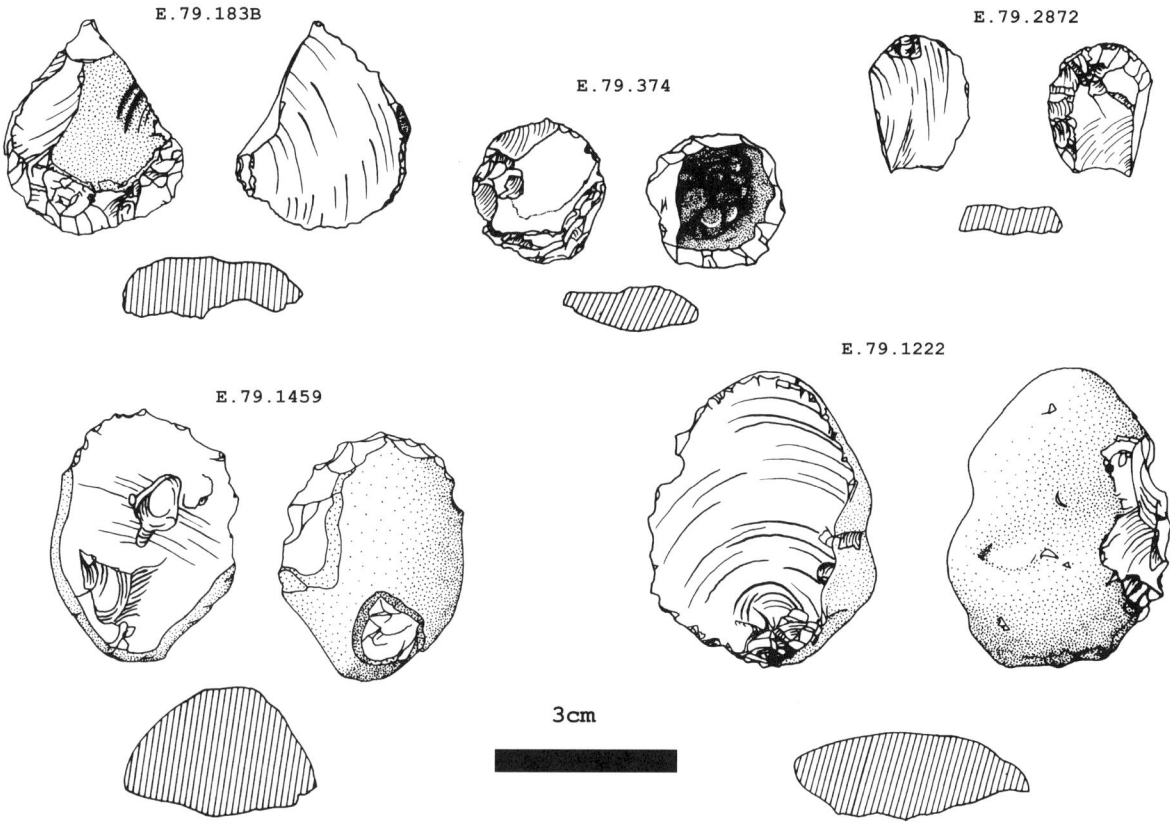

Figure 5-7. Round scrapers from Dún Ailinne.

ports or anomalies (1980:103). At the time of his writing, almost all "Irish oblique" points were made of flint, with only one example cited made of black chert (Green 1980:65). Assuming this is still true, that makes the Dún Ailinne example quite unusual. It is perhaps worth noting that a point classified as a PTD, but made of "black flint," is reported from Meare Lake Village (St. George Gray and Cotton 1966:361 and pl. LXII), but this example is shaped quite differently. Interestingly, another point that appears very similar to the Dún Ailinne PTD appears in fig. 87 in the same Meare publication, described simply as "flint."

PTDs are known from a number of sites, sometimes in relatively large numbers. They are the fourth most common implement type at Newgrange (O'Kelly, Cleary, and Lehane 1983:147), and were also numerous at Monknewtown (Sweetman 1976); several were also recovered from sites in and around Lough Gur (Ó Ríordáin 1954a; Woodman and Scannell 1993), and at Lough Eskragh, Co. Tyrone (Collins and Seaby 1960). Their function is somewhat debated, with projectile points or possibly knives being the most likely (Woodman and Scannell 1993; Green 1980:102-3; O'Kelly, Cleary, and Lehane 1983:147-50).

The remaining two points are tips (Figure 5-6), one (E.79.3348) flint and the other (E.79.445A) chert. E.79.3348 is an unusual piece, being what appears to be a single extremely thin flake with very fine retouch along three edges; the fourth edge is snapped. The two longer intact edges converge making a point, and on this basis this may be the remains of a very fine projectile point, possibly even a javelin head. However, the surviving piece is too small to suggest any particular original shape with any certainty. The same is true for E.79.445A, which is a very small (13 mm) chert piece. It is fairly thick (4 mm) and is bifacially retouched along both intact edges. Given how narrow it is, it is likely that the original point was also narrow, like the three examples described above and unlike the more typical leaf-shaped points.

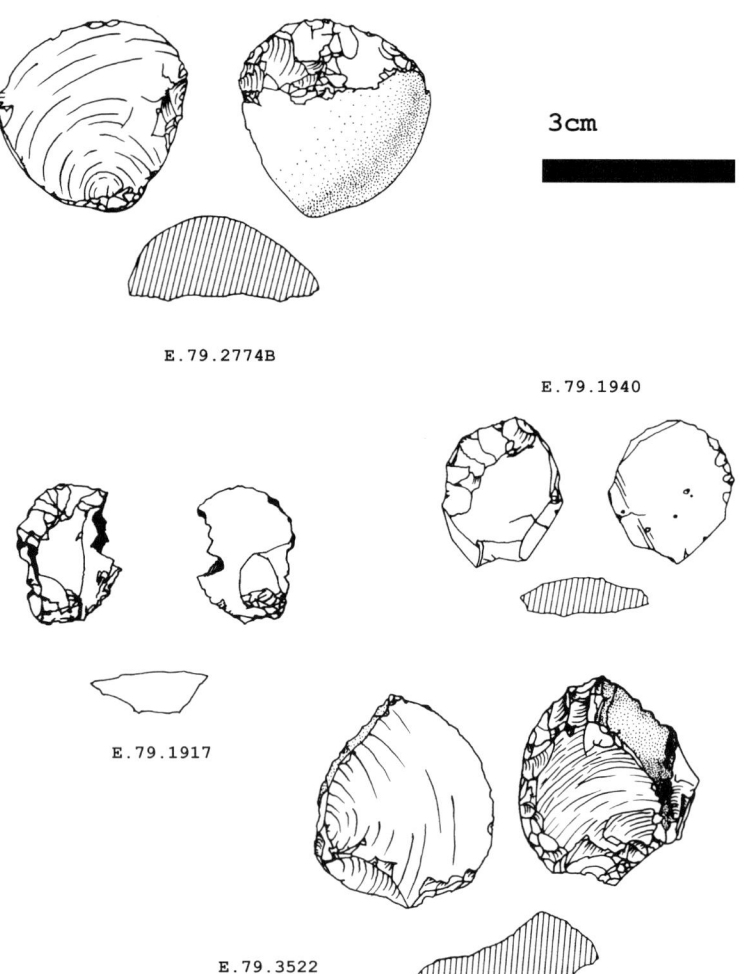

Figure 5-8. Round scrapers from Dún Ailinne.

E.79.3440 may also belong with the projectile points (Figure 5-6) (Plate 5-3). It is a bifacially worked piece that appears to be snapped obliquely across what may have been the middle of a flake; alternatively, it could have been snapped in two places across the body of the piece. If this is the remains of a projectile point, its size suggests a spear point or javelin head. However, there is not enough of the piece surviving to be certain of the original shape, and it could be some other implement, such as a plano-convex or other knife.

Scrapers

A simplified system for classifying scrapers was used here, modeled on several which appear in the literature (see O'Kelly, Cleary, and Lehane 1983; Bradley 1970). This was done for two reasons. First, the total number of scrapers was not high (88) and so a simple system seemed more appropriate. Second, it has always seemed to be somewhat arbitrary to use the location of the retouched edge as the basis for classification, since there is no way to know if these various "types" were functionally the same or different to the tools' makers and users. So scrapers were divided into four groups based on shape of both cutting edge and the artifact itself: hollow scrapers, round scrapers, straight scrapers, and a 4th category of uncertain types simply called "scrapers."

Table 5-8 shows the distribution of the various scraper types according to material (both certain and uncertain examples were combined for this table). Scrapers, while not large in overall number, are the largest single category of implement. This probably reflects both the generic nature of the identification (anything with a retouched edge that does not conform to any obvious type might be called a scraper) and the probable usefulness of the tool itself. The 88 scrapers from Dún Ailinne represent 40% of the total of implements. Flint was the preferred material for scrapers, as for implements in general. Further, all hollow scrapers were made from flint, perhaps reflecting their overall delicacy and the greater difficulty in achieving this quality in chert or quartz.

Round Scrapers

The largest category of scraper is the round scraper, represented by 46 examples at Dún Ailinne (sev-

Table 5-9. Dimensions (mm), Round Scrapers.

N=40	L	W	T
Mean	31.4	26.1	10.7
Median	30.5	26.0	10.0
Mode	34.0	32.0	10.0
Range	16–64	15–41	6–17

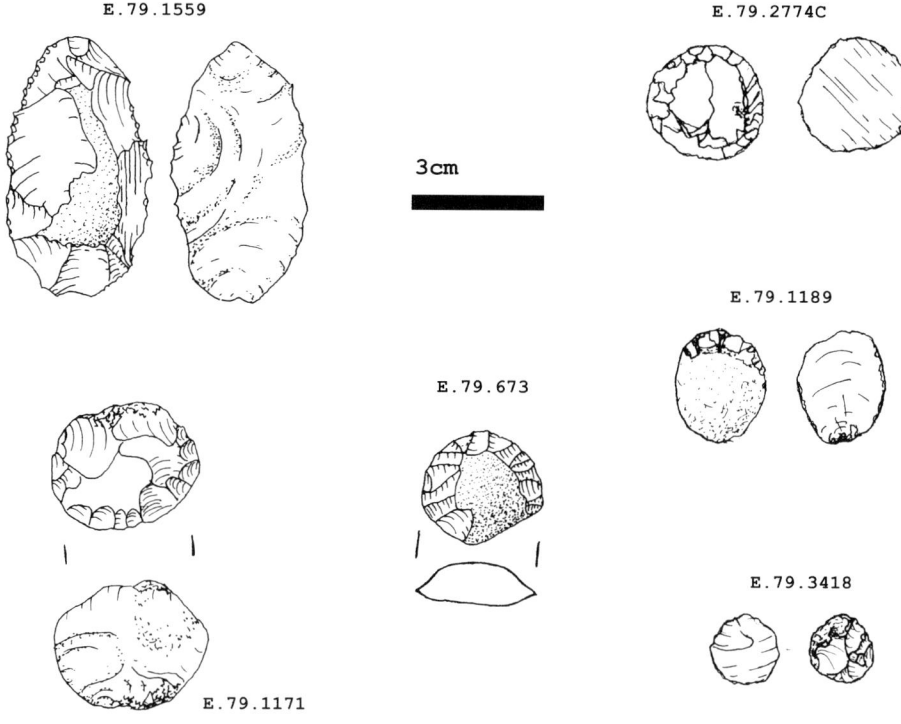

Figure 5-9. Round scrapers from Dún Ailinne.

eral round scrapers are shown in Plate 5-3) (Figures 5-7, 5-8, and 5-9). Round scrapers comprise 20% of the entire implement total and 53% of scrapers, being the largest single category of implement. Again, this may be an indicator of the usefulness of this particular tool. Many of the round scrapers are made from primary flakes, with the cortex left in place where not retouched. In size, they range from relatively small examples (including the "thumbnail scrapers") to relatively large ones. Table 5-9 shows the statistics for these artifacts (only the 40 certain examples, all flint, are included here).

A scatter plot of the dimensions (length versus width) of the round scrapers shows their general uniformity (Figure 5-10), with length and width largely correlated. The smaller "thumbnail" scrapers cluster at the lower left of the diagram, while the largest examples are the outliers at the upper right. A subjective assessment of the steepness of the retouch shows that the majority of the certain examples (32 or 80%) show steep retouch on at least part of their circumference. This may be typologically significant, or it may be the result of re-sharpening. As the edge gets re-sharpened, one would expect it to become increasingly steep. If one attributes the prevalence of steep retouch to intensity of use and resharpening, then this fits with an overall picture of implements being used intensively at Dún Ailinne (see below). Statistically, a comparison of the means of these two groups shows no significant difference for length or width, but thickness is significantly different at a 0.001 level. This makes sense given that it is necessary to have a thick piece in order to produce steep retouch.

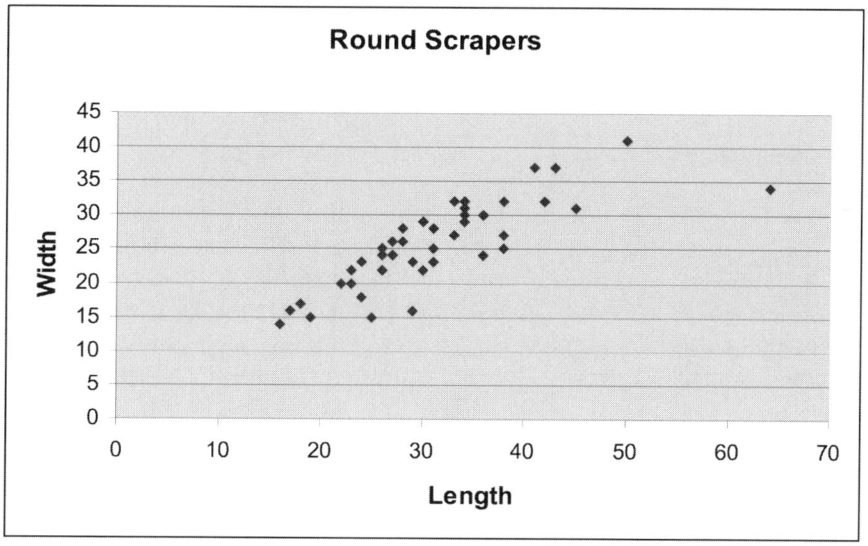

Figure 5-10. Round scrapers, length by width.

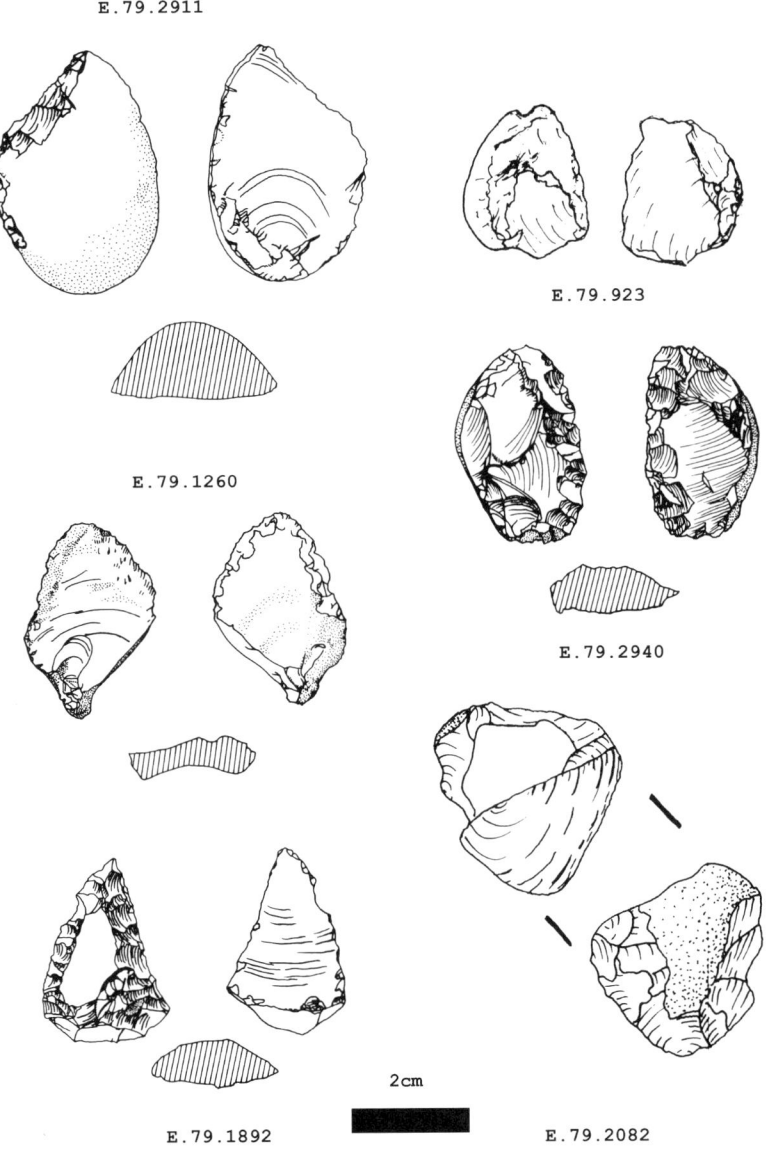

Figure 5-11. Scrapers from Dún Ailinne, other types.

Straight Scrapers

The next largest group in number is straight scrapers (Figure 5-11). There were 17 examples of this category, all flint. Three of them have uncertain retouch, but the other 14 show retouch along at least one straight edge. In shape they can be roughly divided into three kinds. Three examples (E.79.4003, E.79.1892, and E.79.20) have two retouched edges that converge to a point, while another three (E.79.3700, E.79.4000, and E.79.5013) are more blade-like, with parallel retouched edges. Those with convergent edges may be typologically intentional or may indicate a more intensive degree of re-sharpening in these cases. While they do come to a point, like those identified below as possible boring implements, they are somewhat different in shape, being more triangular and less like an elongated teardrop.

Ten of the remaining 11 are generally rounded or irregular in shape; all have some degree of cortex remaining on some portion of the edge opposite the retouched edge, as in backed implements. This ranges in extent from relatively thin bands of cortex to one example where most of the dorsal surface is covered. On the basis of a purely subjective assessment, the cortex would have contributed to the ease of using the cutting edge. The final implement, E.79.1260, is somewhat intermediate, with a rounded shape and cortex covering most of the dorsal surface, but with two retouched edges converging to a very rounded point.

Statistics for the 14 certain examples are presented in Table 5-10.

Hollow Scrapers

There are seven certain and five possible hollow scrapers from Dún Ailinne (Plate 5-4). The certain examples are of the well-known class of insular Neolithic implements (Flanagan 1965) found at a variety of Irish sites of the period. The classic form has a retouched concavity (the hollow) most commonly at the distal end of a flake, though variations occur (see Flanagan 1965; O'Kelly, Cleary, and Lehane 1983:132–42). Of the Dún Ailinne examples, three (E.79.2860, E.79.1138, and E.79.1853) show this configuration (Figure 5-12), conforming to what Lehane has called the "winged" variety (O'Kelly, Cleary, and Lehane 1983:132). Of the other four (Figure 5-12), three have hollows on their lateral edges, two (E.79.3067 and E.79.3170) on the left edge of the bulbar surface and one (E.79.3011) on the right. E.79.3391 (Figure 5-13) is somewhat unusual, being significantly larger than the others

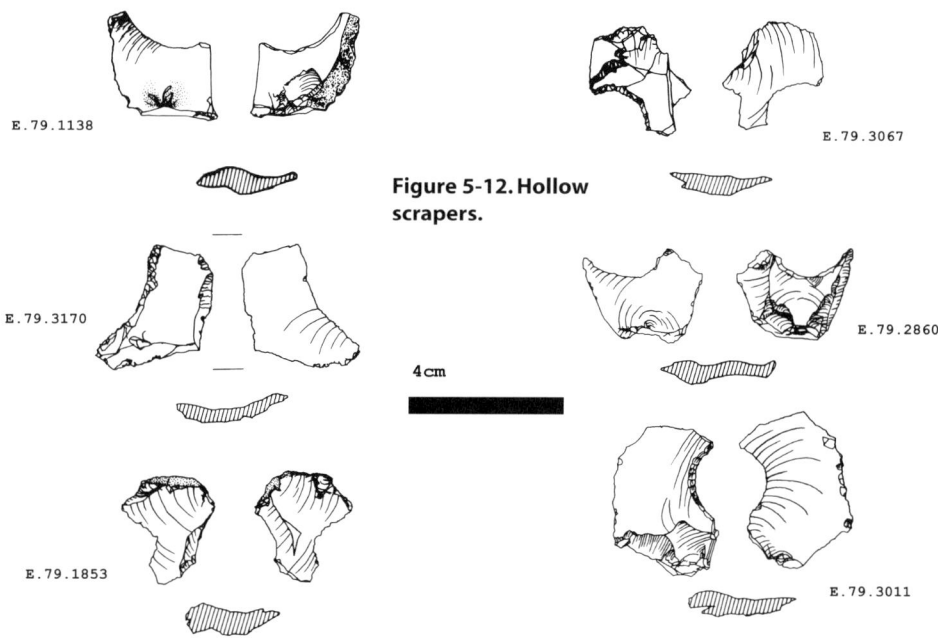

Figure 5-12. Hollow Scrapers from Dún Ailinne.

(71 mm long versus the longest at 39 mm) and having several retouched areas besides the hollow; the hollow is on the left lateral edge, but the area below this is snapped, and below this and on the opposite edge there is additional slight retouch. This implement may have functioned as a knife in addition to a hollow scraper.

The other five examples (three are shown in Figure 5-13) are uncertain for a number of reasons. All have hollows on the distal ends, but they are not typical. E.79.2812 has what appears to be a retouched hollow but it is only very slightly curved. The retouch in the hollow of E.79.436 is very slight and difficult to determine with certainty. E.79.1032, E.79.1596E, and E.79.2863 all have hollows that are not retouched; E.79.2863 has retouch along a short area adjacent to the hollow but it is not concave. These last three may be blanks that were never completed. Blanks of this type were described in the flint hoard from Killybeg (Woodman 1967) and in the court tomb at Ballynichol, Co. Down (Flanagan 1965:324).

The hollow scrapers in this assemblage are noticeably thinner and more delicate than the other scrapers from Dún Ailinne, conforming to the general characteristics of the group, which are typically 2–3 mm thick (Flanagan 1965). This can be demonstrated by comparing them to the other scrapers. The average thickness of the hollow scrapers (both certain and uncertain examples) is 3.75 mm, while that of round scrapers is 10.7 mm and straight scrapers is 8.24. Both of these are statistically significant to a very high degree ($P>0.001$).

Hollow scrapers are ubiquitous on Irish Neolithic sites, and their use also continued into the Bronze Age (Flanagan 1965). They are found in tomb contexts, where they often outnumber projectile points (Herity and Eogan 1977:36), in hoards (Woodman 1967; Flanagan 1966), and on domestic sites such as Lyles Hill (Evans 1953) and Island MacHugh (Davies 1950). Hollow scrapers are commonly associated with the typical range of Neolithic implements, including leaf-shaped points, *petit tranchet* derivative implements, stone axes, and javelin heads (Flanagan 1965). While they are generally accepted as belonging to the large class of scrapers, their specific function remains obscure.

Table 5-10. Dimensions (mm), Straight Scrapers.

N=14	L	W	T
Mean	38.1	23.2	7.9
Median	37.5	23.0	7.0
Mode	36.0	23.0	7.0
Range	25–51	11–33	4–14

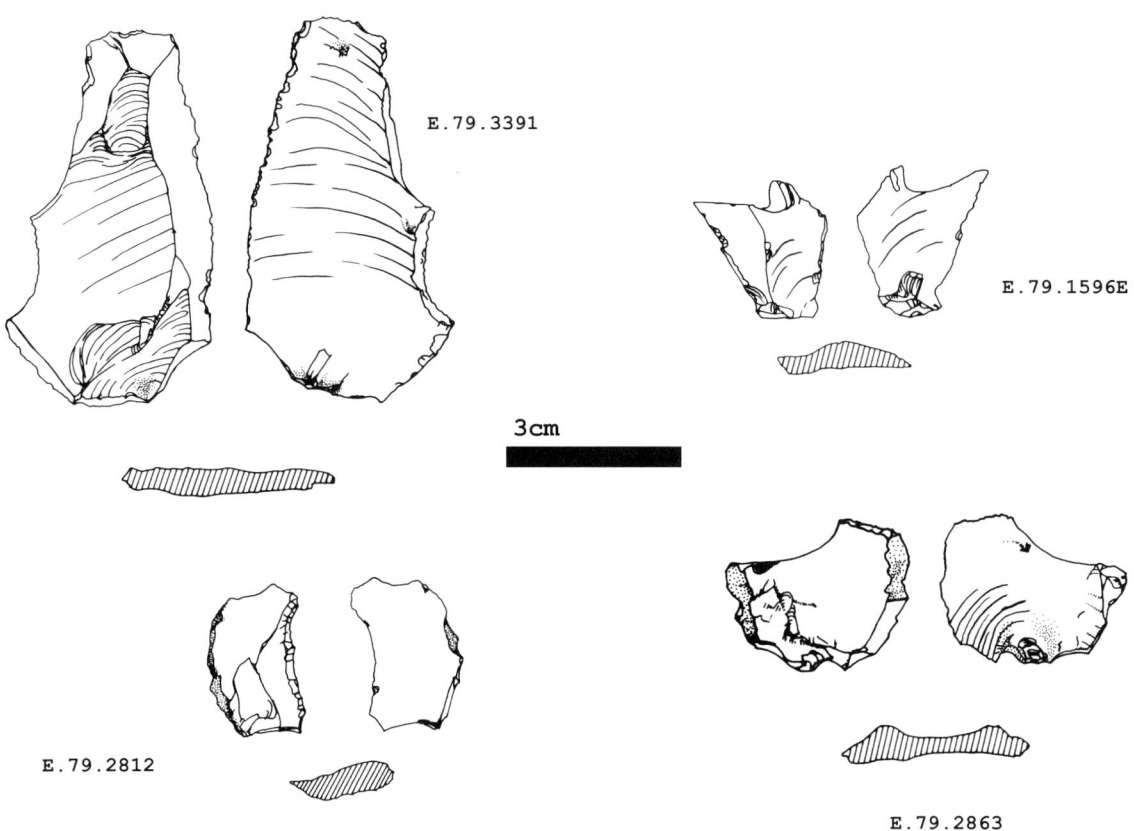

Figure 5-13. Hollow scrapers from Dún Ailinne.

Suggestions have been made that they may have been carried in a standard "set," rather like modern wrenches (Flanagan 1966). The apertures from the Dún Ailinne sample range from 16 mm to 31 mm, with an average of 21 mm. Hollow depths range from 3 mm to 8 mm, but five of the seven examples are either 4 mm or 5 mm deep (average 4.9 mm). These dimensions do not, therefore, mirror the fairly regular gradation of sizes found by Flanagan, making it unlikely that the group from Dún Ailinne can be interpreted in this way.

Other suggestions are that they were used as small saws, to prepare wooden rods (for example, arrow shafts), to make bone pins, or even to make fire (Waddell 2000:52; Flanagan 1965:328). Gloss has been noted on some examples (Eogan 1963:45), suggesting the possibility that they were used as sickles, but as Flanagan points out, gloss would also be the result of most of the other uses noted (Flanagan 1965:326); in any case, gloss is not evident on the Dún Ailinne examples. Presumably the average thinness of the hollow scrapers has something to do with function. Assuming thickness is an indicator of the robusticity of a scraper's use, then hollow scrapers were presumably used for something that did not require a thick, heavy tool. What this might have been is of course anyone's guess.

Scrapers

The remaining scrapers (13 examples) did not conform to any of the three types described above. In some cases they are broken while in others they are simply irregular in shape and in retouched edge form. All but two are flint. Statistics are shown in Table 5-11.

Table 5-11. Dimensions (mm), General Scrapers.

	L	W	T
Mean	31.1	22.3	8.8
Median	30.5	21.5	9.0
Mode	22.0	18.0	9.0
Range	22–46	13–34	5–12

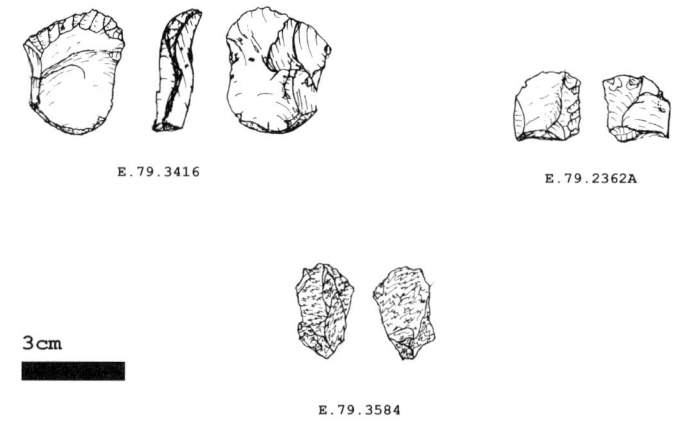

Figure 5-14. Three unusual scrapers from Dún Ailinne.

E.79.2362A (Figure 5-14) is a small, irregular chert scraper that is retouched on two convergent edges; E.79.3584 (Figure 5-14) is the only example of a quartz implement (see Plate 5-3), with a curved retouched edge that was added to what appears to be a core (Julio Mercador, personal communication). Nine of the flint scrapers in this group can be divided based on shape, those that are rounded (E.79.2854, E.79.1820, E.79.2872, E.79.1542, E.79.2774D) and those that are more blade-like (E.79.626, E.79.217, E.79.2403, E.79.3784). Of these, E.79.2774D is broken; it may have been a round scraper or possibly a borer. E.79.3416 (Figure 5-14) is irregular, notable because of its shape; apparently because of the way the flake was struck, there is a hollow on the dorsal surface opposite to the retouched edge that fits the thumb (or at least, my thumb) perfectly, making it easy to hold. Finally, E.79.3669B is an uncertain example, with retouch that appears almost haphazard.

Borers

The term "borer" is used here to mirror the usage established at Newgrange (O'Kelly, Cleary, and Lehane 1983:153). There are six implements that have been classified as possible borers (five are shown in Figure 5-15; Plate 5-5) and a seventh, E.79.2774D, may also belong with this group. These all share the characteristic of having a point, apparently intentionally, but not being the proper shape for a projectile point. The points vary from very blunt ones (possibly broken?) to one example (E.79.466) that is quite sharp. Except for a single chert example, all are flint. In shape they can be divided into two groups. One includes four examples (E.79.2767, E.79.3665B, E.79.3296, and E.79.5001) that are broadly teardrop shaped, while the other two (E.79.466 and E.79.3435) are longer and narrow. The former range in size from smaller to larger, while the latter group are about the same length and width but are substantially different in thickness. Table 5-12 shows their dimensions.

Of the teardrop shaped examples, E.79.2767 and E.79.3665B are similar in shape, though the former is about half the size. Both are made on primary flakes with cortex left over the dorsal surface, and both are blunted at the tip. The tip of E.79.2767 is quite distinctly shaped, while that on E.79.3665B is more uncertain. E.79.3296 is made on a flake with no cortex remaining and its tip also appears deliberately blunted. The chert piece, E.79.5001, has several patches of cortex over its surface. It also has a distinct curve to the right, presumably to facilitate holding it. These pieces resemble several examples recovered from Newgrange, for example E.56.149, which are described as "spurred implements" (O'Kelly, Cleary, and Lehane 1983:153-54, fig. 65).

The other two are different. In contrast to the other borers, E.79.466 is quite thin and sharp, and it is unclear if its shape is intentionally pointed. While there is retouch along one edge of the point, the other appears to have been snapped; whether this is intentional or not is unknown. E.79.3435 is

Table 5-12. Dimensions (mm), Borers.

Artifact Number	L	W	L
E.79.5001	38	22	13
E.79.2767	20	22	8
E.79.3296	37	23	6
E.79.3665B	35	30	12
E.79.466	41	15	4
E.79.3435	42	15	8

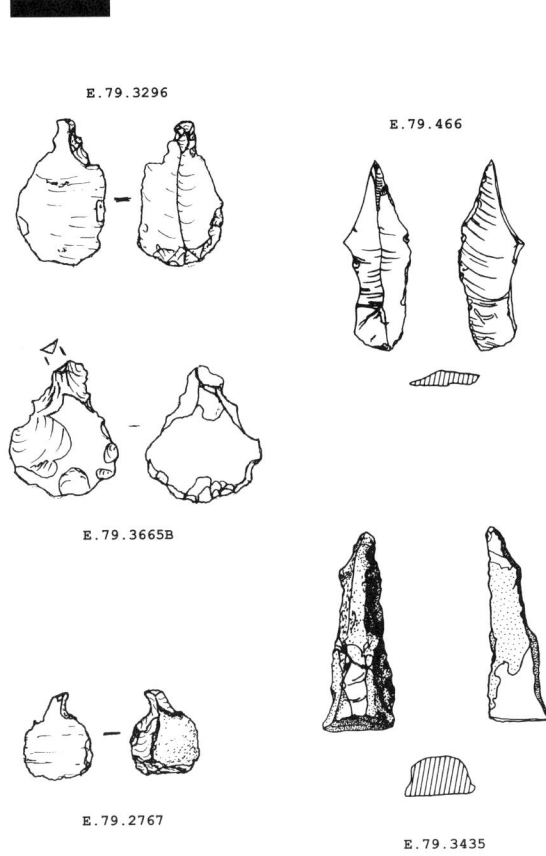

Figure 5-15. Borers from Dún Ailinne.

essentially the same width and length but is twice as thick. It is a plano-convex piece with one surface almost completely flat, whose overall shape appears to have been deliberately produced with retouch. Its tip is a rounded point that certainly could have been used as a borer; however, obvious parallels to this implement are not forthcoming.

The fact that all of these implements would have been useful in making holes is the reason they are grouped together as borers. Whether they were actually used this way remains unproven. Assuming they were, however, it is arguable that the teardrop shaped versions might have been for coarser materials, such as wood or bone, since they have blunt points (E.79.2767 does have a slight spur which is somewhat sharper). The same is true of E.79.3435, whose point is more rounded. Alternatively, the blunting of the point might be from use, and so be the reason why they were discarded. E.79.466, being sharper and thinner, would have been more suitable for finer materials. Lehane notes that borers and spurred implements have been found at sites from the Paleolithic through to the Bronze Age (O'Kelly, Cleary, and Lehane 1983:153).

Implements (Uncertain Types)

Ten retouched pieces do not conform to any of the typical implement types described so far. Some of these have uncertain retouch, while others simply have unusual shapes. All are flint and five (four are shown in Figure 5-16) have definite retouch:

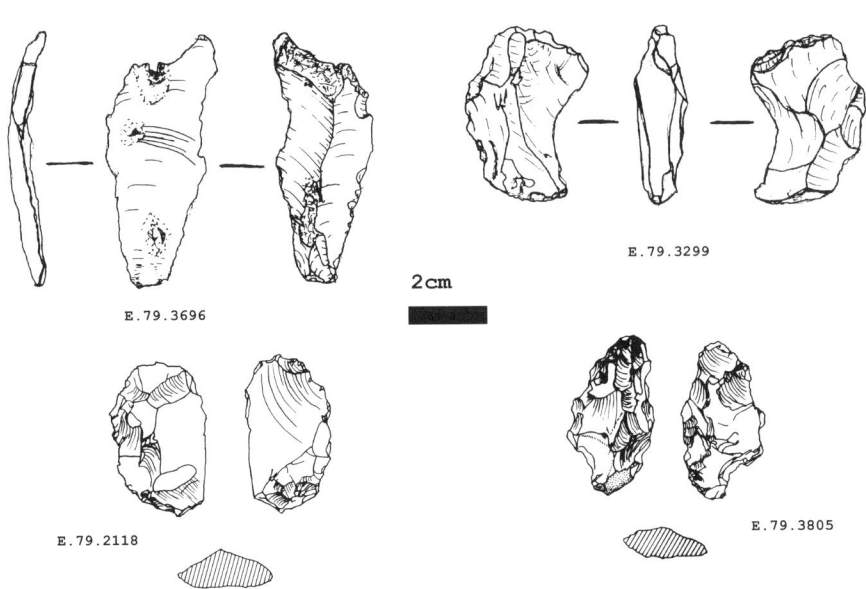

Figure 5-16. Implements from Dún Ailinne, uncertain types.

E.79.1327. A broken implement, dark brown flint. There is retouch on one lateral edge and possible retouch on the opposite edge; this edge may also have been deliberately blunted. It appears to have been snapped at the end.

E.79.2118A. The dorsal surface has been modified, and there is retouch in several places on the edge. The edge is also damaged, possibly from use.

E.79.3299. This is an irregular piece, with several large flakes removed from the dorsal surface and what appears to be retouch along the distal end. There is also a distinct hollow along one lateral edge, and this suggests that it might be a rough-out for a hollow scraper. However, the shape is unlike the typical hollow scraper.

E.79.3696. The longest of these implements at 75 mm, this is a flake with retouch on both lateral edges (see Plate 5-3). Some is quite fine and some deeper, making the piece look serrated. This suggests it might have been a saw. There is cortex on the distal end, and a number of material flaws are scattered throughout the piece.

E.79.3805. A flint implement with convergent sides heavily retouched to produce denticulate edges. A small patch of cortex was left on the proximal end. The piece looks like a small saw, but it is possible that it was a rough-out for a projectile point.

The remainder have uncertain retouch. Of these, E.79.64 may also be a saw, with one edge looking decidedly denticulate. E.79.1749C is a small,

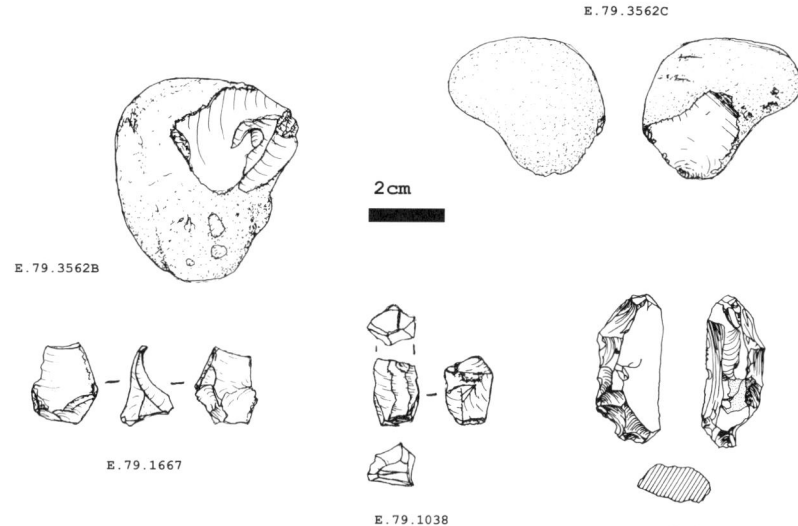

Figure 5-17. Cores from Dún Ailinne.

irregular, thick chert piece whose shape suggests a chisel. The other three (E.79.1711A, E.79.1036, and E.79.3358) are all irregular and show some uncertain retouch along various parts of their edges.

Cores

A total of 34 cores and 12 possible cores were recovered from Dún Ailinne (five cores are shown in Figure 5-17; Plate 5-6). As shown in Table 5-6, all three materials are represented, with the majority being flint and roughly equal numbers in chert and quartz. The degree to which the cores had been worked was somewhat variable, but overall they were quite small and well worked down. Figure 5-18 shows a scatter plot of core length by width (only those that were certain examples), and it is evident that most cores group around values for length less than 40 mm and width less than 30 mm. The six examples that inhabit the area above 40 mm in length and 30 mm in

Table 5-13. Dimensions (mm), Cores by Size.

Small Cores (N=28)	L	W	T	Large Cores (N=6)	L	W	T
Mean	29.6	22.0	12.0	Mean	51.5	39.0	29.2
Median	28.5	21.0	12.0	Median	49.5	35.0	30.5
Mode	37.0	21.0	9.0	Mode	47.0	33.0	—
Range	18-49	12-31	6-19	Range	42-67	33-57	16-43

Table 5-14. Small Cores, Dimensions (mm) by Material.

CHERT (N=3)	L	W	T	FLINT (N=21)	L	W	T	QUARTZ (N=4)	L	W	T
Mean	32.3	24.3	11.0	Mean	29.9	22.3	12.2	Mean	26.3	18.8	11.5
Median	33.0	25.0	11.0	Median	28.0	21.0	12.0	Median	25.0	15.5	12.0
Mode	—	—	—	Mode	37.0	21.0	14.0	Mode	—	14.0	13.0
Range	29-33	21-27	6-19	Range	20-49	12-31	6-19	Range	18-37	14-30	9-13

Table 5-15. Dimensions (mm), Retouched Flakes.

N=31	L	W	T
Mean	25.6	17.7	5.7
Median	23.0	16.0	5.0
Mode	18.0	14.0	5.0
Range	13-56	9-32	2-16

width are all flint. Three of them (E.79.3562A, B, and C) are almost complete flint nodules with 1-2 flakes removed. The other three (E.79.2670B, E.79.3291, and E.79.3292) are half cortical, again with only 1-2 flakes removed. The 28 remaining examples were all more intensively used. Table 5-13 shows the statistics for these, with the six largest examples just noted shown separately in the section to the right.

Comparing the larger cores with the more heavily utilized ones suggests some observations about intensity of use. For length and thickness, the average dimensions of the more utilized cores are half, or less than half, of the average sizes of the larger cores, while for width, the larger cores are close to twice the size (actually 1.7 times larger). Since the majority of cores (82.3%) fall into the former group, this suggests that the cores were typically worked down as far as possible before being discarded.

Comparing the smaller 28 cores by material shows little difference between the groups (Table 5-14). None of the differences were statistically significant, but this may be due to the low samples size of quartz and chert cores. That said, of the three materials, chert cores are larger on average than flint cores, and quartz cores are the smallest. This might indicate the original size of nodules available for use, or it may represent the intensity of use of particular materials. If the latter, then quartz cores were worked the most intensively and chert the least; this might indicate preference, availability, or relative value.

Retouched Flakes

Among the flakes were 31 which had varying degrees of retouch, but which did not conform to any of the typical categories of implement types. Most of these were flakes with a few areas showing definite or possible retouch, perhaps modified quickly for some immediate, temporary purpose after which they were discarded. Some of the examples may have been intended as implements, but were abandoned fairly quickly in the manufacturing process. Descriptive statistics are shown for the retouched flakes in Table 5-15.

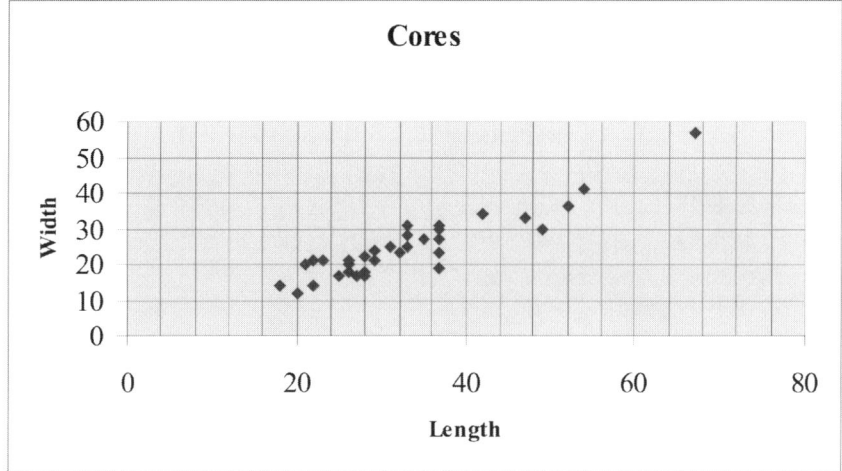

Figure 5-18. Cores, length by width.

Table 5-16. Dimensions (mm), Retouched Flakes by Material.

FLINT (N=22)	L	W	T	QUARTZ (N=7)	L	W	T
Mean	26.9	18.1	5.9	Mean	18.9	14.4	5.1
Median	24.5	16.0	5.0	Median	18.0	12.0	5.0
Mode	19.0	14.0	6.0	Mode	18.0	—	7.0
Range	13-56	9-32	2-16	Range	13-23	9-22	2-7

Table 5-17. Distribution, Unretouched Flakes by Material.

CHERT	N=72	FLINT	N=316	QUARTZ	N=48	UNCERTAIN	N=7
Flakes	55	Flakes	247	Flakes	32	Flakes	3
Flakes?	17	Flakes?	69	Flakes?	16	Flakes?	4

Of the 31, two were chert, seven were quartz, and the remaining 22 were flint. Just under half (13 examples) showed some degree of cortex on the surface. In all but two (E.79.1612 and E.79.495B) these were thin patches left on the edge, and in some cases this could have been deliberate backing.

Meaningful comparisons of dimensions with chert are not possible due to the small number of examples, but Table 5-16 compares quartz and flint. Of these, only the length is different in a statistically significant way, at a 0.05 level. The quartz retouched flakes are clearly shorter, reflecting perhaps in part the smaller size of the original cores noted above.

Prisms

There were 13 clear quartz prisms recovered from Dún Ailinne, none showing any evidence of human modification. Quartz forms crystals naturally in the shape of hexagonal prisms with pyramidal ends, and where it is pure it is glassy and clear (Whittaker 1994:67). While there is no evidence that the Dún Ailinne prisms reflect human activity, it is possible that they were deliberately collected. The possible symbolic significance of quartz in the Neolithic has been noted at sites such as Newgrange (Bradley 1998:104, 110), where the quartz appears non-local and so was deliberately brought to the site (Meighan, Simpson, and Hartwell 2003). In the same vein they are noted here. All of the prisms are small, with a mean length of 20.7 mm and a range of 13-33 mm. Of the 13, seven were found in the plowsoil, two were from the occupation levels, three were found in probable Iron Age contexts, and the last came from a feature of uncertain date.

Unretouched Flakes

As with most assemblages of lithics, the bulk consisted of unretouched flakes. There were 443 that were classified in this group, comprised of 337 certain and 106 uncertain examples. For this analysis, flint and chert flakes were catalogued as primary (wholly cortical), secondary (partially cortical), or tertiary (non-cortical) flakes, following the system used at Newgrange (O'Kelly, Cleary, and Lehane 1983:124). An additional nine flakes were identified as probable bifacial thinning flakes. Quartz flakes were simply categorized as flakes or fragments. Three additional flint flakes were inadvertently classed only as "flakes"; these are now in the National Museum of Ireland, Dublin. Measurements to the nearest millimeter were taken in the same way as described for implements; flakes less than 10 mm in length were not measured. Where 1-2 flakes were grouped under a single number, the largest flake was measured. Altogether, this produced a measured group of 332 flakes. In addition, where possible, platforms were examined for width, thickness, and general shape. Platform morphology is one of the factors which the flint knapper consciously controls to produce flakes of particular sizes and shapes. For example, it has been shown experimentally (Dibble and Whittaker 1981) and in actual lithic assemblages (Dibble 1985) that, along with other factors, platform width and thickness are correlated respectively with flake width and thickness.

Table 5-18. Distribution, Unretouched Flake Types by Material.

FLAKE N=35		PRIMARY FLAKE N=42		SECONDARY FLAKE N=122		TERTIARY FLAKE N=129		THINNING FLAKE N=9	
flint	3	chert	5	chert	23	chert	27	flint	9
quartz	32	flint	37	flint	99	flint	99		
						uncertain	3		

Table 5-19. Dimensions (mm), Unretouched Flakes.

N=332	L	W	T
Mean	23.3	16.7	4.8
Median	22.0	15.5	4.0
Mode	24.0	14.0	4.0
Range	2-70	3-52	1-17

As with implements, the majority of unretouched flakes are of flint, followed by chert, quartz, and a few uncertain types. Table 5-17 shows the distribution of materials for unretouched flakes (both certain and uncertain examples). Looking only at those examples that are certainly identified, Table 5-18 shows the breakdown of types of flake by material.

While the overall percentage of secondary and tertiary flakes is essentially the same for flint and chert, the percentage of primary flakes is slightly higher for flint than chert (16% versus 9%). This may reflect sampling bias, or it may have something to do with the nature of the material, the technology, or both. For example, if flint cores are smaller than chert ones (as suggested above), then one would expect that there might be more flint primary flakes, since each flake struck from the core would remove a larger portion of the cortex than for a larger chert core. The larger number of bifacially worked flint implements (primarily projectile points) accounts for the absence of thinning flakes in other materials.

Descriptive statistics for the assemblage of unretouched flakes overall is shown in Table 5-19 and is broken down by material in Table 5-20. Overall, length and width are strongly correlated (R=0.81). Chert flakes are the largest in all dimensions, while flint is second and quartz is the smallest. All of these differences are significant at a level greater than 0.001. Possible reasons for this difference might be cultural preference for larger or smaller implements or something deriving from the material itself, such as technological considerations or core size.

There was no statistically significant relationship between the type of platform (single, dihedral, or multiple facet) and the resulting length, width, or thickness of the flake. However, both width and thickness of platform were correlated with flake width and thickness, respectively. Table 5-21 shows the statistics for these comparisons. The widths are highly correlated; platform thickness is not so strongly correlated with flake thickness, although the R value is significant at a 0.05 level. In general, these two comparisons support the experimental and other data cited. The weaker correlation between platform width and flake width may be due to some aspect of raw material which differs from that of the other two studies, or perhaps to a difference in the technique employed in flake production.

The ratio of flakes to implements is somewhat different depending on the material. While both

Table 5-20. Dimensions, Unretouched Flakes by Material.

Chert (N=55)	L	W	T	Flint (N=244)	L	W	T	Quartz (N=30)	L	W	T
Mean	29.5	22.1	6.3	Mean	23.1	16.3	4.7	Mean	15.0	10.6	3.0
Median	26.0	21.0	6.0	Median	22.0	15.0	4.0	Median	15.0	10.0	3.0
Mode	24.0	16.0	5.0	Mode	21.0	14.0	3.0	Mode	11.0	10.0	2.0
Range	13-70	10-52	2-17	Range	10-52	5-38	1-16	Range	10-24	3-23	1-6

Lithic Remains

Table 5-21. Correlation, Platform Width and Thickness Versus Flake Width and Thickness.

COMPARISON	N	CORRELATION	R SQUARED	SIGNIFICANCE
Platform Width vs. Flake Width	120	.507	.257	0.0001
Platform Thickness vs. Flake Thickness	125	.163	.027	0.34

Table 5-22. Number of Unretouched Flakes Compared to Implements by Material.

MATERIAL	N IMPLEMENTS	N UNRETOUCHED FLAKES	% FLAKES (TOTAL ASSEMBLAGE)	RATIO, FLAKES/IMPLEMENTS
Chert	10	55	85	5.5:1
Flint	141	247	64	1.7:1
Quartz	8	32	80	4:1

chert and quartz have a large number of flakes/implements, flint is rather lower. Table 5-22 shows, for each material, the number of implements compared to the number of certain unretouched flakes, along with the percent of flakes and the ratio of flakes to implements.

It is certain that sampling bias plays some part here. However, if there is any validity to it, it could suggest several things. The smaller ratio of flint flakes to implements implies that not as much work was being done on these implements than on those in other materials, where greater amounts of waste were being produced. This is particularly noteworthy when there is such a difference in the overall number of implements in flint versus the other two. One would expect greater amounts of flint waste, not lesser. Possible reasons for this include greater efficiency in the use of flint, a situation which would be required if flint was harder to obtain; or less need to maintain, re-sharpen, or otherwise modify flint implements, whether technologically, culturally, or both. While there is no obvious way (or indeed no particular need) to choose between these two, it might be noted that some other evidence hints at a general lack of flint raw materials. Thus the former might be a more likely explanation.

It is interesting in this regard to note that a comparison of the average length, width, and thickness of the unretouched flakes (Table 5-19) with those of the retouched implements (Table 5-23) shows differences which are all statistically significant at a level greater than 0.001. This is not unexpected, and it provides some insight into the process that produced the flakes. In all dimensions, the unretouched flakes are smaller than the implements, a pattern that is supported by looking at the cumulative frequencies of the length of flakes versus implements in all material (Table 5-24).

While only 5% of unretouched flakes are longer than 40 mm, almost 18% of implements exceed this length. Thus the implements are as a group significantly longer than unretouched flakes. This is the reverse of what would be expected if the unretouched flakes were essentially blanks intended for implement production. One reason for this is that clearly some flakes, particularly the secondary and tertiary ones, are the result of tool maintenance and resharpening. As for the remainder, they were not blanks intended for further use, but were rather those that had been rejected, at least initially, on the basis of size or quality. The latter in turn may imply that everything that was suitable for making

Table 5-23. Dimensions (mm), Retouched Implements.

N=129	L	W	T
Mean	32.6	23.4	8.0
Median	31.0	23.0	8.0
Mode	26.0	15.0	4.0
Range	13–83	8–41	2–17

Table 5-24. *Cumulative Frequency, Length of Unretouched Flakes Compared to Implements.*

FLAKES (N=332)			IMPLEMENTS (N=129)		
RANGE	FREQUENCY	CUM. %	RANGE	FREQUENCY	CUM. %
0-5	1	0.30	0-10	0	0.00
6-10	7	2.41	11-15	2	1.55
11-15	59	20.18	16-20	6	6.20
16-20	69	40.96	21-25	20	21.71
12-25	87	67.17	26-30	35	48.84
26-30	47	81.33	31-35	20	64.34
31-35	34	91.57	36-40	24	82.95
36-40	12	95.18	41-45	12	92.25
41-45	6	96.99	46-50	5	96.12
46-50	3	97.89	51-55	1	96.90
51-55	6	99.70	56-60	1	97.67
56-60	0	99.70	61-65	1	98.45
61-65	0	99.70	66-70	0	98.45
66-70	1	100.00	71-75	1	99.22
			76-80	0	99.22
			81-85	1	100.00

implements was used, with few flakes of acceptable size and/or quality being discarded. This is consistent with the discussion of raw material (below) that suggests that good quality flint was not readily available. In such circumstances, one would not expect to find potentially useful flakes being discarded. As always, preservation is a confounding factor here, considering the severity of the disturbance of the Neolithic features.

Raw Material

A visual examination of the collection shows a large number of flakes with cortex remaining on the surface. Numerically, of the 302 unretouched chert and flint flakes (cortex was not noted for quartz) 42 (14%) were primary, with total cortex on the dorsal surface, and 122 (40%) were secondary, with at least some cortex evident. Put another way, just over half (54%) of the unretouched flakes have at least some amount of surface cortex. This may suggest that small nodules were commonly used in implement production, resulting in many of the waste flakes being from the fairly limited outer surface of the original core.

The degree to which good quality flint and chert were available in the area around Dún Ailinne is somewhat unclear. The major sources of good quality flint occur in the northeast, where flint deposits underlie basalt flows, and are also exposed in a number of large outcrops both on the coast and inland (Woodman 1988). At least one open-cast mining site has been identified, where there is evidence of both flint extraction and the production of implements (Waddell 2000:49) and evidence of flint mining has occurred on other sites as well, such as Ballygalley Hill, Co. Antrim (Collins 1978). Traditionally it was assumed that, the farther away from these areas a site was, the more likely that good quality raw materials were hard to come by. However, as Woodman (1988) has pointed out, this is probably too simplistic. Sources which in the past might have been more productive might not have survived into more recent times, and while the material available from glacial drift, river gravels, and beaches might not be as high quality, it was likely both generally acceptable and also sometimes abundant. In addition, particularly in the Neolithic, there seems to have been some choice to use the more easily available sources from beaches, rivers, and glacial drift in preference to those which were of higher quality but harder to acquire, perhaps as the result of increased sedentism (Woodman 1987; see also Collins 1978).

Despite these observations, there are several aspects of the Dún Ailinne assemblage that suggest that raw material, particularly flint, was not readily available here. As has already been noted, there is the intensity with which cores were worked, the apparent efficiency with which flint implements were re-sharpened and maintained, and the number of flakes with remaining cortex. To this can be added the high incidence of hinge fracture and material flaws that are visible in both flakes and implements. Since we are looking at what was discarded rather than what was preserved, this last may be illusory, showing us instead what was rejected and not what was utilized. But if this is indicative of what was generally available, it suggests that good quality material was hard to come by.

It would be interesting to see if the relationship between the shape of projectile points and distance to raw material sources, analyzed for Britain by Green (1980:58–59), also holds for Ireland. Green observed that projectile points that were farthest away from flint sources in Britain were smaller and more squatter in shape, while those from nearby were more elongated. While this was not measured at Dún Ailinne, a visual examination of the arrowhead forms does show a tendency for rather squat shapes (though sample size and preservation are problematic).

Chronology and Context

Unfortunately, while some of the lithic types represented at Dún Ailinne are characteristic of the Neolithic, many types also have greater longevity. Most of the implements described here have been recovered from Neolithic and Bronze Age sites, in particular the asymmetrical projectile point, straight and hollow scrapers, borers, PTDs, and leaf-shaped points, and so offer little in terms of chronological indicators except in the broadest sense. It might also be noted that the appearance of metal does not mean that stone stopped being used to make tools. While no systematic study appears to have been done, it is likely that flint, chert, and perhaps quartz as well continued to be used into the Iron Age. At Haughey's Fort, McCormick (1988) argued that some of the animal bones recovered from the enclosure ditch showed cut marks that were probably made with flint tools. This site dates in part to the later Bronze Age (Mallory 1988, 1991).

The site of Loher, Co. Kerry, suggests that flint continued to be worked into the Early Christian period, at least until AD 1000 (Woodman 1988), and the possibility of things like strike-a-lights etc. provide additional contexts for the use of both new flint tools and collected flint implements from earlier times. While there are not (to my knowledge) any typical flaked implements of these later periods, it would not be unexpected to find that flint and chert continued to be worked, and so that at least a portion of the unretouched flakes might date to this period. So while it is assumed that the bulk of this material dates to the Neolithic and some to the Bronze Age, the appearance of flint, chert, and quartz in Iron Age features at Dún Ailinne might not necessarily be secondary in nature.

That said, the majority of lithics must still be considered in disturbed contexts. Given this, overall lithic distribution cannot reliably indicate much about the spatial aspects of lithic activity. The only possible suggestion is offered by those few cases where a groups of lithics were found together, indicated by the use of the same number for a group of artifacts. CD Figure 5-19 shows the locations of those numbers that were assigned to three or more artifacts (implements and flakes). This represents a total of 30 locations including 118 artifacts, ranging in group size from three to ten artifacts for each location. Three of these locations are associated with trench 281, but most of the rest are from surface contexts (such as plowsoil) or later Iron Age features. Whether these represent actual activity areas or not is problematic, but it may begin to suggest something about the location of Neolithic activity.

The nature of the activity that produced the lithics at Dún Ailinne is largely obscure. The presence of every stage of lithic production, from cores to thinning flakes, suggests that such production took place, though the primary activity seems to have been tool maintenance. But the context in which this happened remains uncertain. The main evidence is negative—there is no evidence of occupation structures, and the only evidence of ritual structures is the burial in pit 293 and the possible enclosure trench 281. The latter did produce some lithic material, and so perhaps a portion may be associated with this use of the site. The remainder may be best considered largely ephemeral, the result perhaps of casual tool production and maintenance behavior largely secondary to whatever ritual activity is indicated by the enclosure, or alternatively independent short-term site use associated with gathering and hunting in the area. This would fit with the idea noted above that the main activity was not tool production, but rather tool maintenance.

Another way of examining this is to compare the lithics at Dún Ailinne with those from other sites. Woodman and Scannell (1993:59, their table 5-6.5) have provided a useful list of the major implement types from a number of Neolithic and earlier Bronze age sites. These were grouped into four categories (hilltop settlements, other Neolithic settlements, henge-like and related sites, and the Dundrum Sandhills) in order to compare them to the lithics from Lough Gur. Comparison with these sites suggests that Dún Ailinne does not fit well with any of them. The closest match is the hilltop sites, which would fit with Dún Ailinne's location. Proportionally, the approximately 2:1 ratio of axes to points seen at Lough Gur (considered to be similar to the hilltop sites) is also seen at Dún Ailinne, as is the low number of PTDs. However, the number and proportion of scrapers is not mirrored at Dún Ailinne; the approximately equal numbers of straight and hollow scrapers is quite different from the large number of straight scrapers at Lough Gur and the absence of hollow scrapers. All of the other sites listed have similar distinct differences. This may indicate that the disturbance of the Neolithic artifacts at Dún Ailinne is severe enough to prevent any accurate assessment, or (perhaps more likely) it suggests that the Neolithic activity at Dún Ailinne was not associated with larger-scale settlement.

Parallel Sites

The most obvious comparison for the Dún Ailinne lithics is the other royal sites in Ireland. The recent publication on Navan (Emain Macha) suggests that this site has comparable lithic materials (Waterman 1997:61–66). There were more than 430 worked flakes, scrapers, and other implements of flint reported from the site, closely comparable to the 488 flint pieces described here. The vast majority were flakes, followed by scrapers in a variety of forms. The small number of cores (7), leaf-shaped arrowheads (3–4), and the single javelin head are all also closely comparable in overall proportion of the assemblage, though Dún Ailinne has greater numbers in most categories. Typologically these are also broadly similar, with one or two types (such as the fabricator from Navan, or the transverse arrowhead from Dún Ailinne) being confined to one site or the other. Navan also produced some earlier material, namely two Bann flakes and a possibly early fish-tail scraper, suggesting perhaps a longer period of use than Dún Ailinne. Most of the Navan lithics were found at the base of the fossil plowsoil, which may be Neolithic in date (though it is uncertain; Waterman 1997:13), the rest coming from the post-hole fill of later prehistoric features.

Tara (Newman 1997:71-75) is a rather different situation, since there is a passage tomb of Neolithic date on the site. This produced a characteristic passage tomb assemblage, which does not typically include worked flint implements or flakes (Herity 1974; Eogan 1986). A single chert end scraper has also been reported as a surface find, from just north of Rath Maeve and very near the monument, but this cannot be closely dated (Newman 1997:211–15). Thus there is no comparable lithic assemblage from Tara, which is reasonable given that it seems to have had a rather different character in the Neolithic than either Navan or Dún Ailinne (see below).

Beyond these royal sites (Cruachain has not been excavated), there are a wide variety of Neolithic sites to choose from for comparisons. Unfortunately, given the disturbance of the Neolithic phase of Dún Ailinne, it is difficult to know what would serve as appropriate comparisons. Looking at implement types, the typical Irish Neolithic lithic assemblage is such that it is uniform over most types of sites, particularly in the earlier half of the period. Considering instead the relative proportion of various implement types, it has been observed that there really is no such thing as a typical Neolithic assemblage, given the variety of the distribution of forms (Woodman and Scannell 1993:58). A few descriptions of the variety of lithic assemblages illustrate the point.

The best-known sites of the earlier Irish Neolithic are funerary or ritual in nature. Of the chamber tombs, most produce flint implements of some type. That at Barnes Lower contained various types of flint knives, a javelin head, two round scrapers, a broken leaf-shaped arrowhead, and three hollow scrapers (Collins 1966a); those at Carnanbane (Evans 1939), Knockiveagh (Collins 1957a), Edenville (Collins 1957b), and Knockmay (Collins 1952) showed a similar assortment. A number of generally "ritual" sites also produced lithic implements, but in smaller quantities (Davies 1935–36; Case 1953). Excavations at Goodland revealed a late Neolithic knapping floor associated with the ritual site there (Case 1973).

Habitations sites are not much more helpful, producing similar implements but in larger quantities. Neolithic houses at Ballycastle (Ó Núalláin 1972), Ballynagilly (ApSimon 1969a), and Slieve Breagh (Herity and Eogan 1977:49) all produced quantities of lithic implements, including end scrapers, round scrapers, hollow scrapers, and various types of leaf arrowheads. The series of houses at Lough Gur showed the same types in large numbers (Ó Ríordáin 1954a), as did the enclosed habitation site at Donegore (Mallory and Hartwell 1984). The sites noted in the study by Woodman and Scannell (1993) have already been discussed.

The material from Dún Ailinne (and from Navan for that matter) compares well with these in range of types, but the remains are far more numerous than in the tombs and far less numerous than in the long-term habitation sites. Better comparisons may be provided by several sites in which, like the royal sites, occupation from later periods overlays Neolithic material. At Feltrim Hill, primarily an Early Christian site, a large quantity of flint and chert, including non-utilized flakes, leaf arrowheads, and various types of scrapers, including one hollow scraper, was recovered from underlying Neolithic levels (Hartnett and Eogan 1964). The large quantity of unretouched flakes suggested to the excavators that flint knapping was a major activity. Evidence of Neolithic use of the Early Medieval site at Langford Lodge, Co. Antrim, has some parallels with Dún Ailinne. Along with flint waste, cores, and a handful of scrapers and other implements, the traces of pits, stake holes, stone settings, and a possible ditch were interpreted by the excavator as having had a ritual character (Waterman 1963). Similar traces of Neolithic occupation occurred at the Early Christian site of Dressogagh Rath (Collins 1966b).

What all of this suggests is that very little can be derived from the Dún Ailinne lithic assemblage to illuminate the probable character of the site in the Neolithic. The evidence suggests that it was more short-term than long term, and included tool production and maintenance, unless the disturbance can be argued to have removed truly large quantities of evidence. Beyond this, all that can really be said is that the character of the lithic assemblage is consistent with Neolithic assemblages in general, and matches well with the remains at other royal sites.

Stone Axes

Stone axe heads at Dún Ailinne are represented by three complete and 7–8 fragmentary examples (four are shown in Figure 5-20; Plate 5-7). As with the other categories of earlier prehistoric material, these were also found mostly in unstratified or disturbed contexts. Only three were found associated clearly with features, two (E.79.156 and E.79.243) below the embankment and the third (E.79.833) in stony fill above the gravel layer (Flame phase). Plate 5-8, a photograph from 1968, shows one of the stone axes, almost certainly E.79.243, *in situ*. A fourth (E.79.767) was recovered from Crimson phase layer. A fifth (E.79.2805) was associated with Trench 290 and its associated post-holes, but

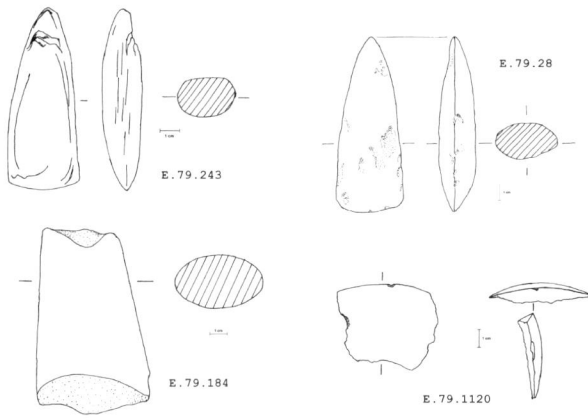

Figure 5-20. Stone axes from Dún Ailinne.

its exact stratigraphic context was uncertain. The remaining six examples were unstratified, coming from surface layers.

Since ground stone axes are generally considered to date to the 4th and 3rd millennia (Cooney and Grogan 2000:51; Sheridan et al. 1992; Waddell 2000:45), the appearance of such axes in Iron Age contexts suggests disturbance. It is worth noting however that ground stone axes have been recovered from pre-Roman Iron Age, Roman, and Romano-Celtic sites in Britain and on the Continent (Adkins and Adkins 1985). Some of these are arguably votive or other ritual offerings. While there is little evidence of such a practice in Ireland, the general absence of Romans being only one problem (though see Carson and O'Kelly 1977 with regard to Roman artifacts at Newgrange), the idea that axes might have been deliberately collected and incorporated into Iron Age levels at Dún Ailinne is not without merit.

Context and Description

Most of the axes are of igneous rock, the majority (six) being tuff; an additional two are probably gabbro and the other two are schist and siltstone (Ivor Harkin, personal communication). While the results of the Irish Stone Axe Project are still preliminary, a predominance of tuff was not mirrored in the sample they examined (Cooney and Mandal 1998). In the group discussed in their first volume, Co. Kildare was characterized by a predominance of mudstone axes, followed by shale and dolorite/pelite (Cooney and Mandal 1998:107). This may have many explanations, including preservation, non-random discovery, or the actual character of the Neolithic use of Dún Ailinne. Further work is clearly needed.

Cross section could be determined for all but two axe fragments (E.79.833 and E.79.1120). All were oval except for E.79.112, which is distinctly D-shaped. Only three of the axes are complete. E.79.28 and E.79.2805 are both made from tuff and both show considerable wear on their cutting edges, presumably from use. E.79.2805 has a large depression on one surface of its cutting edge, while E.79.28 is more battered, showing numerous small nicks, dents, and chips over much of its surface, though concentrated on the cutting edge. E.79.243, a green flecked schist, is in better condition. It has some fracture on the butt and the surface is pitted, but the cutting edge appears fairly sharp and polished, though whether from use, resharpening, or representing the original surface treatment is unknown. The butt of E.79.2805 is rounded, while E.79.243 and E.79.28 both are more pointed (the latter particularly so). Using the categories established by Cooney and Mandal (1998:17), E.79.243 has an asymmetrical face, while E.79.2805 is more symmetrical, and shows straight, splayed sides. E.79.28 is harder to classify due to damage, but it too is possibly best classified as asymmetrical.

Three axe heads is not much of a sample for comparison, but their dimensions do fall at the low end of those described so far by the Irish Stone Axe Project. There, while the overall range was quite large, 73.7% of the complete specimens fell between 8 cm and 16 cm. The majority of widths (77.4%) was between 4 cm and 7 cm, and thicknesses (67.6%) between 1.8 cm and 3.4 cm (Cooney and Mandal 1998:39-40). Table 5-25 shows statistics for the 3 complete axes from Dún Ailinne.

Whether this has any implications for function is debatable. It has been argued that larger axes were used for tree felling while smaller ones were for smaller-scale woodworking, for example carpentry (Harding and Young 1979:105), an observation refined to refer specifically to axes in the 8-20 cm range (Cooney and Mandal 1998:53). This is presumably based on the idea that axes outside this range would be too large or too small to be truly functional. If so, this indicates tree felling was not one of the things people did at Dún Ailinne during the Neolithic, unless of course the axe head fragments are the remains of larger axes used for this purpose. Certainly the generally worn state of the axes (fragments included) suggests use, possibly heavy, and so supports a utilitarian context.

Table 5-25. Dimensions (cm), Complete Stone Axes.

ARTIFACT NUMBER	MATERIAL	L	W	T
E.79.28	tuff	11.7	4.4	2.6
E.79.2805	tuff	10.8	5.1	2.9
E.79.243	schist	9.5	3.9	2.1

Caches of axes, presumably of a ritual nature, are well known (Cooney and Mandal 1998:51-52), but there is no evidence of this at Dún Ailinne.

Of the seven certain axe fragments four are from the middle part of the axe head. This includes E.79.184, E.79.1120, E.79.112, and E.79.2880. E.79.184 appears to represent most of the axe head, with only the cutting edge and butt broken off (or possibly the butt was flattened?). E.79.112 is a short section from the middle of the axe head; it has a D-shaped section, and may in fact have been an adze. E.79.1120 is a small fragment from the mid-shaft, and is also broken through the middle, perpendicular to what was presumably the cutting edge. E.79.2880 is also broken at both ends, but part of one end shows a slight bevel, and so may represent the butt.

The remaining three fragments appear to be from the axes' ends. E.79.767 is clearly incomplete, but the slight depression (from use?) at the broader end seems to suggest this was the cutting edge. E.79.833 is most of the cutting edge of the axe. It is fairly sharp and appears unworn. E.79.2220 is clearly broken at one end. At the other end, the remains of a bevel suggests that this might be the butt, an identification supported by the fact that the sides, while mostly parallel, are beginning to diverge, presumably towards a cutting edge.

E.79.156 is a small fragment whose material has not yet been determined. Its identification as an axe fragment is unclear; one surface has some polish, but the opposite surface is fractured and uncertain. If it is a fragment of axe head, it is from the middle, and does not represent either cutting edge or butt.

Most of the fragments are too small to determine their shape. E.79.184 has sides which are not parallel, but since the butt is damaged it is difficult to tell if it was originally asymmetrical or had splayed sides (though on balance, the former seems more likely). E.79.2220 has sides that appear quite straight, and so may originally have been parallel sided. However, the hint of divergence that appears to be starting at one end may belie this. The remaining fragments are too small to even hazard a guess.

Table 5-26. Dimensions (cm), Stone Axe Fragments.

ARTIFACT NUMBER	MATERIAL	L	W	T
E.79.184	gabbro?	10.4	6.3	4.4
E.79.767	gabbro?	8.7	7.2	5.0
E.79.1120	tuff	4.4	5.6	1.0
E.79.112	siltstone	4.9	5.9	1.5
E.79.2880	tuff	7.4	5.1	3.4
E.79.2220	tuff	9.2	5.8	3.8
E.79.833	tuff	7.5	3.6	2.3
E.79.156	uncertain	8.7	4.5	2.5

Table 5-26 shows the dimensions of the stone axe fragments, and Table 5-27 shows the means and medians (there are insufficient examples to calculate the mode). Again comparing the axe fragments from the Irish Stone Axe Project, those from Dún Ailinne fit well with these (Cooney and Mandal 1998:39–41). Little else can be said about the fragments, except that the majority are truly fragmentary, the exception being E.79.184. This may indicate heavy use, as noted. The small number would also support accidental loss, though it has been suggested that broken fragments of axes might be saved for more symbolic reasons (Cooney 1998:110).

The exact chronological position of the stone axes here is perhaps debatable. As noted above, stone axes are associated with sites ranging from Mesolithic to Bronze Age, and they are also apparently found on Early Christian and medieval sites (Sheriden et al. 1992; Cooney and Mandal 1998). Given the presence of a possible food vessel burial at Dún Ailinne, it is worth noting that axes have been found associated with such burials (Cooney and Mandal 1998:38). It is thus not impossible that one or more of the examples might originally derive from this Bronze Age context.

Curiously, in their note on the chronological range of stone axe finds, Sheriden et al. (1992:400) do not note any from Iron Age sites. Whether this is an oversight or has instead some archaeological meaning is a question worthy of further investigation. In general, while the axes found through the Bronze Age are known (or sometimes assumed) to have been used, those from the later periods are said to be either residual finds from earlier occupation or the result of deliberate collection for various purposes. Certainly the idea that the Dún Ailinne stones axes are in fact of Iron Age date cannot be ruled out *de facto* on stratigraphic grounds, and given the large amount of timber needed for the Iron Age structures, stone axes might have been useful. Such a question certainly cannot be answered on present data, but it is an interesting possibility.

Be that as it may, the majority of stone axes known from Irish sites are associated with the Neolithic (Sheridan et al. 1992; Cooney and Mandal 1998), and thus it is most likely that they represent that period of use at Dún Ailinne. As to the behavior that they represent, some thoughts on function have already been noted. All but one example appear used, so they are not the survivors of a deliberate deposit of ceremonial axes. There is no evidence that they represent a cache, though given the disturbance of the Neolithic contexts at Dún Ailinne, there is always the possibility that such a cache could have been disturbed. A polished stone axe was associated with the burial at Linkardstown, Co. Carlow (J. Raftery 1944; Sheriden et al. 1992:395), and so the probable Linkardstown burial found at Dún Ailinne (see Chapter 6) provides a possible context for one or more examples. Again, however, only one example could be described as polished (E.79.833), and since it is fragmentary the character of the original surface is unknown. In the absence of any direct evidence, the most likely context would seem to be a utilitarian one, with the axes representing the lost or discarded remains of woodworking tools, or perhaps, in a broader use of the term "utilitarian," weapons.

Table 5-27. Descriptive Statistics (cm), Stone Axe Fragments.

	L	W	T
Mean	7.6	5.5	3.0
Median	8.1	5.7	2.9
Range	4.4–10.4	3.6–7.2	1.0–5.0

6

Ceramics

Susan A. Johnston

Neolithic Pottery

The assemblage of Neolithic pottery from Dún Ailinne can be considered in two groups. The first consists of the remains of a pot of Linkardstown type, found in Pit 293 along with a green disc-bead. Given the circumstances of the find (see below), this pot and the bead are likely to have been *in situ* when found. The other category is 433 individual sherds, representing 89 vessels, plus a (literal) handful of small, crumbled fragments that were not counted as sherds. While the majority of these sherds (295, or 68.1%) were found associated with features, most of these features were assigned to the Iron Age on the basis of stratigraphy.

Trench 281, its possible continuations in trenches 1282 and 1517, and possibly four other pits are all arguably Neolithic. Altogether, five of these seven features (two contained only lithics) produced 28 sherds representing ten vessels. The remaining 405 sherds must be considered in disturbed contexts. With the exception of a single sherd found in the topsoil, these were found mixed into Iron Age levels and included in the somewhat problematic occupation material. Figure 6-1 shows the distribution of these sherds according to feature type (the figure excludes the sherd from the topsoil and two other isolated sherds, one in a small depression and the other in the low mound). As the figure shows, the largest group among these sherds (157 or 38.9%) was found incorporated into various post-holes and probable post-holes, indicating that they were disturbed by the successive building of timber structures in the Iron Age. Of the remainder, 136 (26.8%) are from pits and trenches (definite and likely), 66 (16.4%) from the occupation levels, and the rest (71 or 17.9%) were from unknown or uncertain contexts.

Illustrating this another way, Figure 6-2 shows the distribution of sherds by their phase. The figure shows 166 sherds for which chronological phase could be identified with some degree of certainty; two phases, Lower Emerald and Harry, each had one sherd, and are not included. As noted in the chapter on lithics, this distribution differs somewhat from that one. The detailed discussion can be found in Chapter 5, but several observations can be summarized. In particular, there are far fewer phases with ceramics than with lithics (15 versus seven, or nine with Lower Emerald and Harry), suggesting that ceramics were far less scattered. This was attributed to several possibilities: that lithic waste was more scattered than ceramic vessels to begin with, that flakes etc. are smaller and lighter than sherds and so would be expected to scatter more widely, and that, while the pattern of sherd distribution varies, the number of actual vessels disturbed matches the lithic distribution much more closely.

It might also be noted that the large number of sherds in the Tan phase is partly the result of the Linkardstown vessel having been attributed to this phase. Removing the 31 sherds of this vessel brings the number of sherds in Tan to 28, and so below Mauve (46) and closer to Rose (21) in number. Another difference is the large number of lithics incorporated into Flame phase features versus the absence of ceramics from this phase. This was suggested to be the result of the greater scatter of

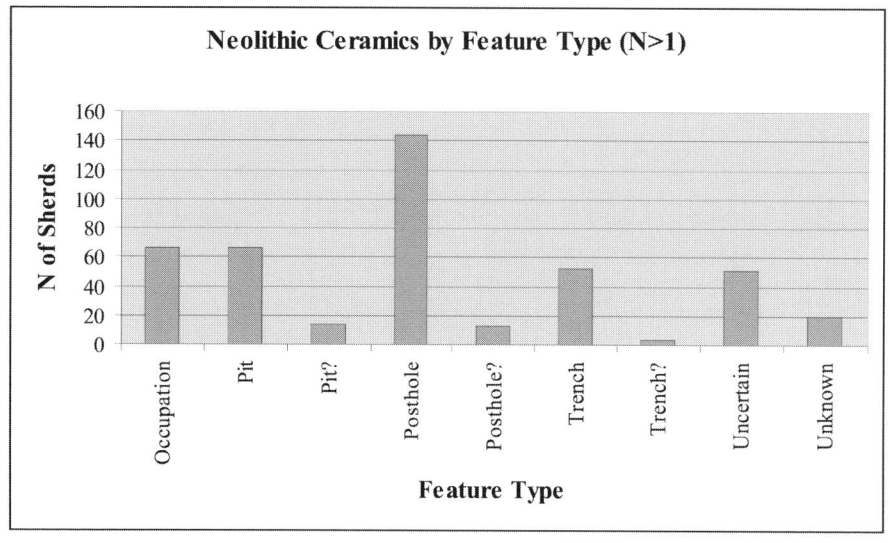

Figure 6-1. Distribution, Neolithic ceramics by feature type.

the lithics which were then mixed into the Flame phase activities.

All sherds were given a number during excavation; where a group was thought to be the remains of a single vessel the group was given a single number. Diagnostic sherds, and sometimes others as well, were also given individual letter designations (such as "E79.1747D"), though not consistently. Based on this record 89 vessels are represented in this assemblage, 30 (33.7%) by a single sherd and 59 (66.3%) by two or more sherds. Figure 6-3 shows the distribution of sherds per vessel, excluding the Linkardstown pot (which was represented by 31 sherds). As is evident, this assemblage was very fragmentary, which can also be demonstrated by the overall statistics on sherd size. This is shown in Table 6-1.

All sherds larger than 10 mm were measured to the nearest millimeter. Where the sherd could be oriented, such as a rim or shoulder sherd, maximum length was measured parallel to the rim and maximum width was measured perpendicular to length. For body sherds, maximum length was the maximum dimension and maximum width was measured perpendicular to length. Maximum thickness was also recorded for all sherds measured. Any sherd that had been given a letter designation was measured separately; where there were a number of body sherds included under a single number, the largest was measured to represent the group. Using these guidelines, a total of 181 sherds were measured for Table 6-1.

As the table shows, while a few sherds were large, most were under a few centimeters in overall length and width. Mean length and width are 25.6 mm and 21.2 mm respectively, and most sherds were under 30 mm in length and 23 mm in width. Thickness, which is less affected by preservation, averages 7.9 mm, but the most common thickness is 6 mm. This underscores the disturbance suffered by the Neolithic remains on the site.

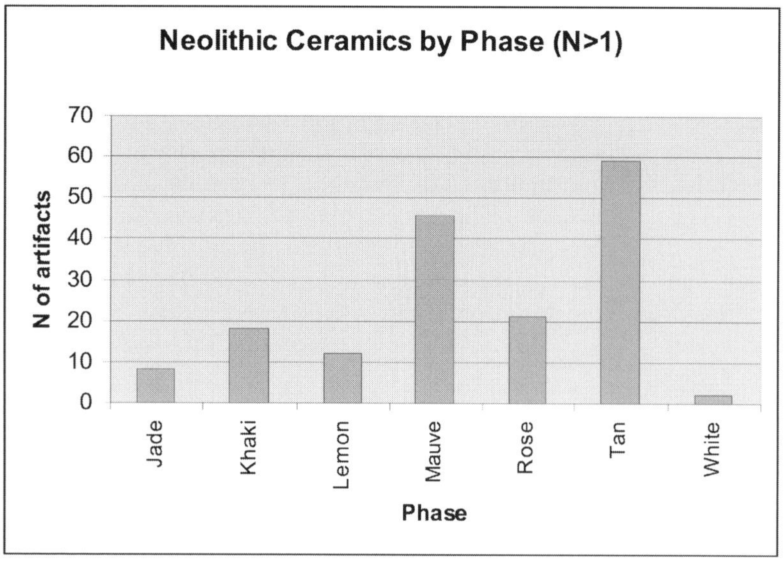

Linkardstown Vessel

In the fill of pit 293, on its west side, were a number of sherds of a shouldered bowl and a small green slate bead (Figure 6-4; Plate 6-1). The occurrence of large sherds in

Figure 6-2. Distribution, Neolithic ceramics by phase.

Table 6-1. Dimensions (mm), Neolithic Sherds.

N=181	L	W	T
Mean	25.6	21.2	7.9
Median	24.0	20.0	8.0
Mode	17.0	19.0	6.0
St. Dev.	10.9	10.0	2.7
Range	11–82	7–72	4–18

close proximity to each other suggests that, while they were disturbed, they were not dug up and reburied in the course of later activity. This suggests that the pot was largely *in situ*, a point supported by the otherwise fragmentary character of the rest of the Neolithic pottery.

The bead is dark green slate, composed of phyllite or mica and chloride. It is flat in section and round, though flattened on one side. It measures 1.1 cm at its maximum diameter, and is 2 mm thick. The perforation (4 mm diameter) is now somewhat asymmetrically placed, but this may be an illusion caused by wear on the side of the bead nearest to the perforation. There are striations visible on the inside of the perforation, presumably from drilling the hole, and it is V-shaped, drilled from one direction. The surface is polished.

The pot is represented by a total of about 31 sherds, many of which join to form larger fragments. There are five from the rim, which is strongly inverted, representing about 4/5 of the circumference. A

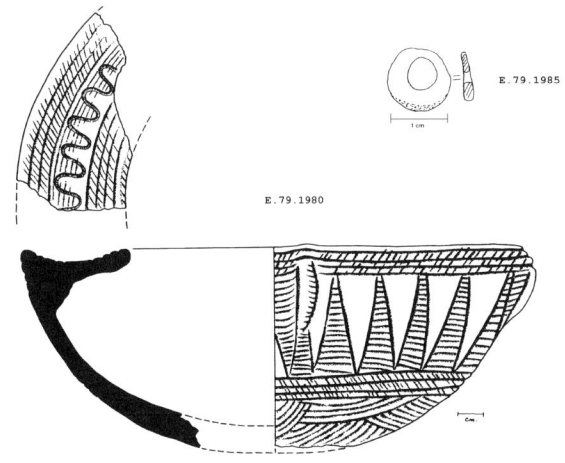

Figure 6-4. Linkardstown vessel and associated bead from Pit 293.

number of the body and base sherds could be joined into three large fragments extending in at least one place from rim to base. The outside is slipped and burnished, and shows blackening; the inside is reddish brown, and also shows some blackening. The neck is slightly concave and set perpendicular to the body, with a strongly pronounced shoulder. The original vessel was fairly small and shallow, with an estimated rim diameter of 9.5 cm, shoulder diameter of 17.8 cm, and a height of 8.2 cm. It is fairly thin, with an estimated wall thickness of 0.5 cm.

Where the surface has survived, most of the sherds show some decoration, suggesting it originally covered most of the vessel's interior and exterior surfaces. The decoration on the body is fairly complex, with a combination of impressed cord markings, vertical ribs, ridges, and channels in both angular and curvilinear patterns. The base is finished with curved nested arcs producing a basketry effect. Both pot and bead were included by Herity in his discussion of decorated Neolithic pottery, and he provides a detailed description of the decoration (1982:298 and his fig. 23). In style the vessel most closely resembles that from Balintruer More (Co. Wicklow) and is similar to those

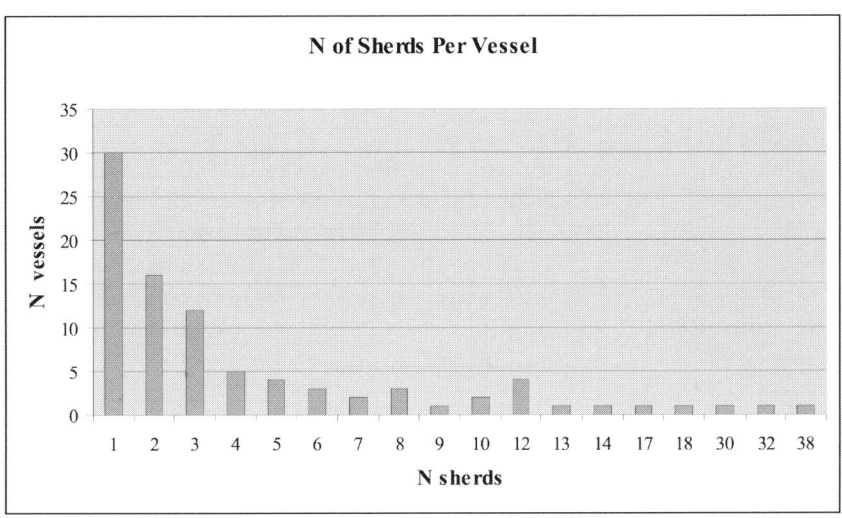

Figure 6-3. Distribution, number of sherds per vessel.

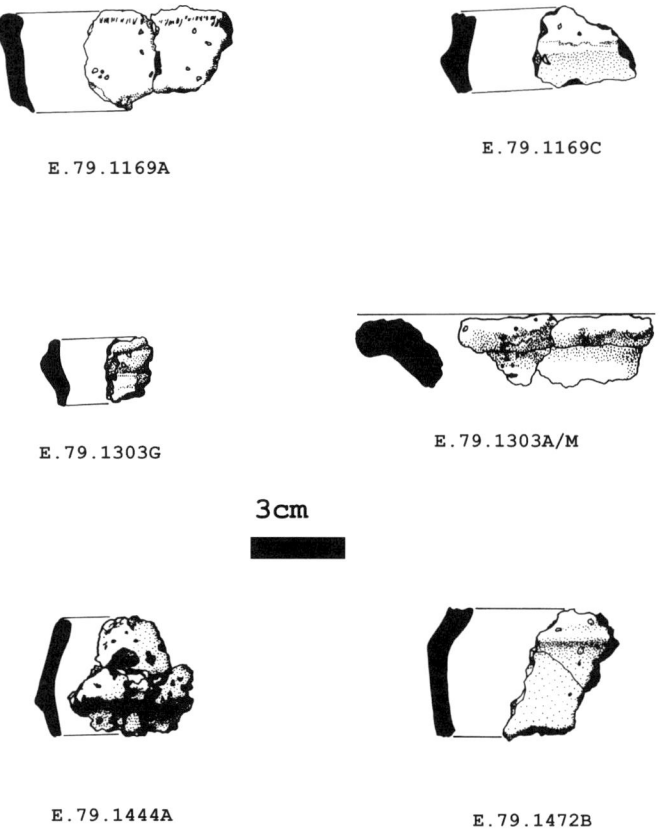

Figure 6-5. Undecorated Neolithic pottery from Dún Ailinne.

from Linkardstown (Co. Carlow) and Jerpoint West (Co. Kilkenny) (Wailes 1971:7).

The suggestion has been made that the pit containing the pot and bead is the remains of a burial (Herity 1982:298; Newman 1997:147). This seems to have been widely accepted, and the feature appears as a probable Linkardstown burial in the publication defining the variation in this burial type (Brindley and Lanting 1989-90). Here, where the pot is noted along with ten other similar sites, it is identified as being of Drimnagh style, and as such is argued to be early in the sequence. It is suggested that this style of pot was developed in Ulster and was subsequently adopted for funerary purposes in Munster and Leinster, where they became dominant as burial goods. The most likely time span given for these burials here, based on radiocarbon age determinations, is between 4800 and 4600 BP, or 2850-2650 Cal-BC.

There is certainly no reason why Pit 293 could not have been a burial. The degree of disturbance of the Neolithic levels, as evidenced by the fact that most of the pit was destroyed, provides an explanation for why there is no surviving skeletal material (though the fact that so much of the pot survived does make this somewhat puzzling, if the two were originally in proximity in the pit). A fragment of bone which appears to have been from a human skull (E.79.722) was recovered from the site, but was not in any way associated with Pit 293 (see Chapter 13 and Plate 13-1). It came from the Flame phase occupation layer and was not particularly near any of the Neolithic features (about 10 m from Trench 281 and 20-30 m from Pit 293). There is thus no compelling reason to associate it with the Linkardstown vessel.

There is also no direct evidence of any mortuary structure or mound accompanying the pit (the boulders noted at the site do not appear to have been shaped, and their original position is unknown; Wailes 1976), but this does not necessarily undermine the interpretation. The Linkardstown burial at Martinstown (Hartnett 1951), for example, also lacked any covering mound or any other surface evidence of a burial, though its original occupant was present and accompanied by pottery. Although the possible enclosure indicated by trenches 781, 1535, and 1282 does not enclose the pit, it is possible that it served as the functional equivalent of a mound, that is, as a marker of some kind.

In their discussion of Linkardstown burials, Brindley and Lanting (1989-90) note that, while there is a significant degree of variation in the type, the presence of characteristic pottery (notably Drimnagh style vessels) is still the most reliable indicator of a Linkardstown burial. Dún Ailinne also falls geographically into the main range of this type. Taken together, while the case is far from proven, it seems reasonable to argue that Pit 293 may have been the remains of a burial of Linkardstown type. As such, it provides a broad date range for the Neolithic use of the site, and suggests that, whatever other activity may have characterized the Neolithic at Dún Ailinne, burial was one use to which the site was put in this period.

Other Neolithic Pottery

As noted, preservation of the remainder of the Neolithic sherds was not good. A large proportion of the collection consists of small, rather featureless, body sherds, comprising 80% of the total. Of

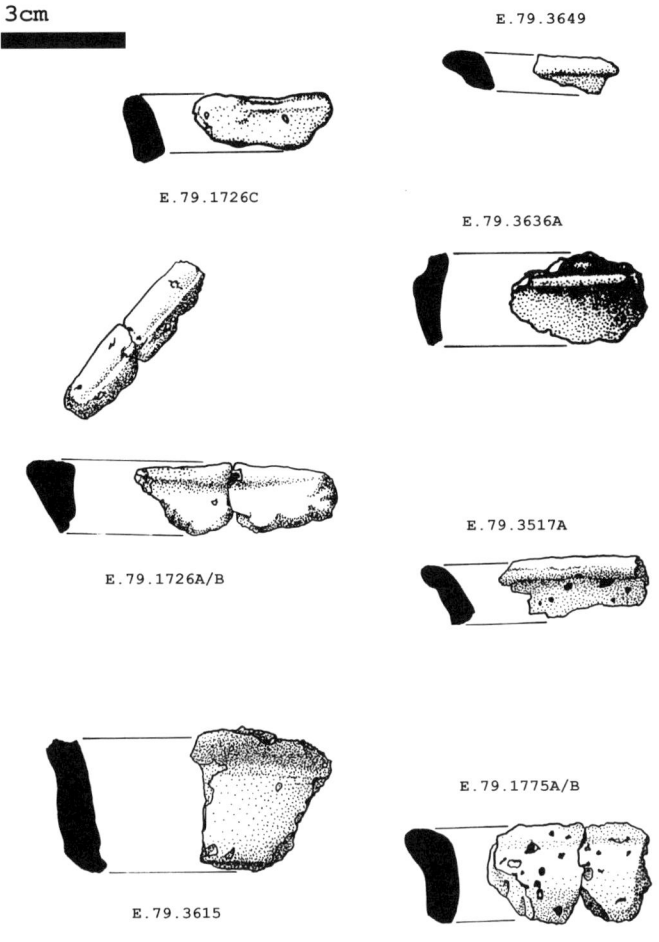

Figure 6-6. Undecorated Neolithic pottery from Dún Ailinne.

the rest, 32 (7.4%) are rim sherds, 15 (3%) are base sherds, and 19 (4%) are fragments of shoulders (Figures 6-5, 6-6, and 6-7, and Plate 6-2 show a selection of the undecorated Neolithic ceramics). The remaining 19 are various possible but uncertain rims, shoulders, and bases. Figure 6-8 shows the distribution of sherd types, with and without the large number of body sherds.

Among the vessels represented, 10 were indicated solely by their bases, 23 by rims, and 52 by body sherds. As noted, the majority of vessels (30) are represented by a single sherd (see Figure 6-3). A further 28 vessels are indicated by 2-3 sherds, while most of the rest (26) had between four and 14 sherds. The remaining five vessels had much larger sherd totals, from 17 to 38 each. This indicates the generally fragmentary condition of the assemblage, an observation supported by the overall size of the sherds. Even though there are some vessels represented by a fairly large number of sherds, the sherds themselves are still fairly small.

Sherd color was somewhat varied. The most prevalent shade was an orange-brown, where the orange appeared to be mixed with the brown, showing in patches. Fifty (56.1%) of the vessels represented showed this color. Also fairly common was a more yellowish brown or yellowish buff color, accounting for an additional 26 vessels (29.2%). The remaining sherds were varying shades of brown, from light to dark, and there was one sherd that appeared to be black.

Virtually all sherds showed some degree of blackening, on one or both surfaces. The core was also commonly black, either on its own or in conjunction with surface blackening. Where the interior surface showed this, it may be due to the vessel's use as a cooking pot; in other cases, it may be the result of preservation, or perhaps a byproduct of the firing process.

Sherd fabric was also varied; 28 (31.5%) of the vessels were represented by sherds that were fairly hard and smooth, while 34 (38.2%) were rough, eroded, crumbled, or generally deteriorated, possibly indicating a softer fabric (though differential preservation conditions might also be responsible). Among the vessels, eight (9%) showed relatively well preserved (though small) sherds that were still fairly coarse compared to the majority of thin to medium wall thickness. Of the remainder, eight other vessels appeared rough and gritty, but with fairly hard fabric, while ten were represented by sherds with one smooth and one eroded surface. A final group was problematic, consisting of 11 sherds, five of which were hard and smooth and six of which were rough and eroded.

Gritting appeared in all sherds. Particles were almost invariably of quartz or quartzite and mica, but varied considerably in size from small and almost unnoticeable to large and protruding. An SEM examination of two sherds (E.79.1444 and E.79.3792) showed that, in one example (E.79.3792), the inclusions were probably a biotite mica, based on their constitutive elements (Patrick McGovern, personal communication).

In some sherds, the gritting may have fallen out, leaving them with a "corky" appearance. In others, these may be the result of air bubbles due to im-

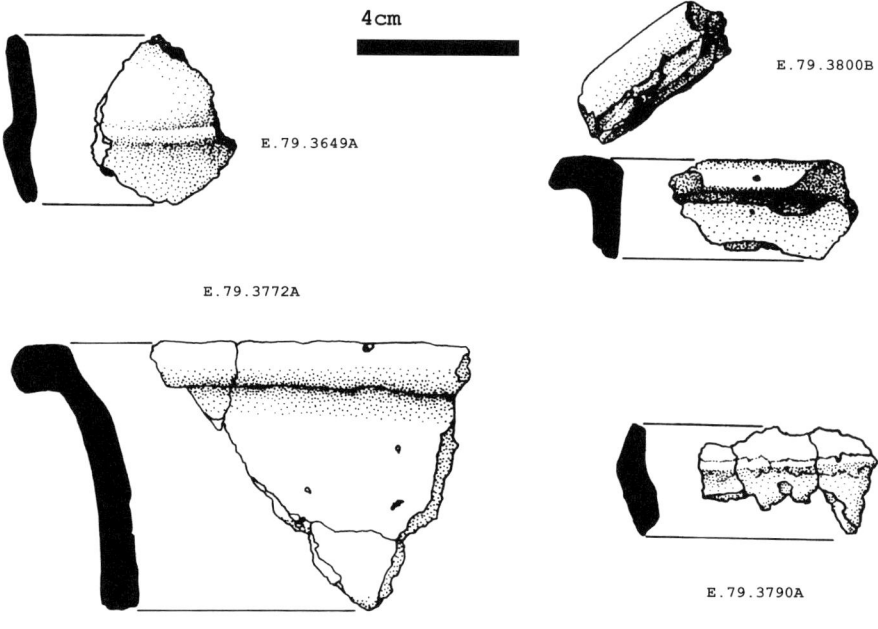

Figure 6-7. Undecorated Neolithic pottery from Dún Ailinne

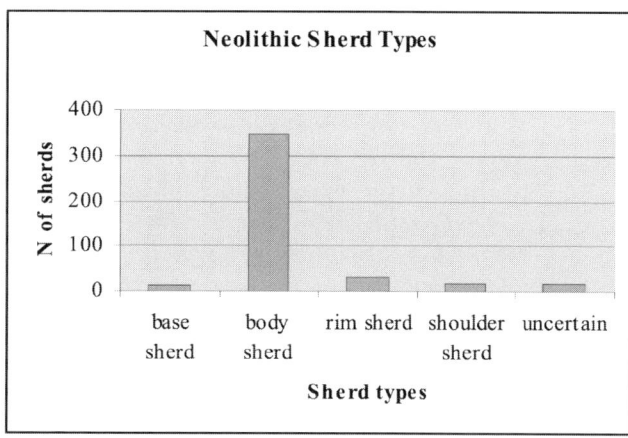

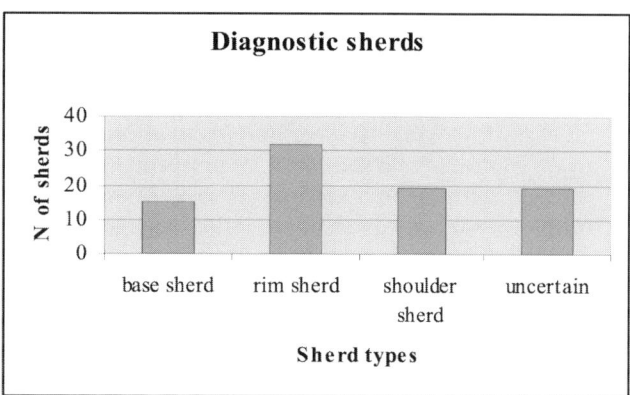

proper drying before firing. Again, the SEM examination of one sherd (E.79.1444) suggested this, given that 1) there was no trace of reaction rims from the disintegration of a mineral, and 2) the shapes of the voids makes them unlikely to be the result of burned out organics (Patrick McGovern, personal communication). This may in turn indicate that the ceramics were being manufactured on or near the site. Presumably these sherds are from vessels which broke on firing, or at least were of inferior quality. Since it is difficult to imagine someone deliberately acquiring such vessels, at least some sherds may be waste from on-site manufacture of ceramics. The SEM examination of the two sherds also suggested that they were fired below 750° (Patrick McGovern, personal communication), suggesting a fairly low-tech manufacturing environment. A number of sherds also showed traces of plant fibers. While it is theoretically possible that these are the remains of grass or other vegetable temper, it is more likely that these are the remains of roots that intruded from the surrounding soil.

Because of the assemblage's poor state of preservation, vessel profiles are largely conjectural. Of the 23 vessels represented by rims, 16 (69.6%) showed simple, rounded rims (see Figures 6-5 through 6-7). These were either upright or everted, and flattening occurred to varying degrees on the top or edge of the rim. Two examples appeared to be slightly bulbous, and one appeared

Figure 6-8. Numbers, Neolithic sherd types (all and diagnostic sherds only).

to show a slight internal bevel. Four of the remaining vessels showed pointed rims (two slightly everted, one everted, and one upright); the other three were represented by one rectangular rim (very pronounced), one slightly beaded example, and one flattened rim with an internal bevel.

Few vessels allowed reconstruction of their bases. Of the ten that were identified, five appeared to be from flat-based vessels and four from round-bottomed pots (the other was indeterminate). It should be remembered that most of these fragments are small, and any given sherd might not represent accurately the base profile.

Fifteen of the vessels were identified as shouldered, a typical Neolithic form. In general, the shoulders were not very pronounced. Most were rounded, and of the rounded examples most were simple angles produced by the joining of the neck to the body. Of the total, eight fell into this category; four were rounded and slightly stepped, while two were rounded and stepped; one was also stepped, but angular.

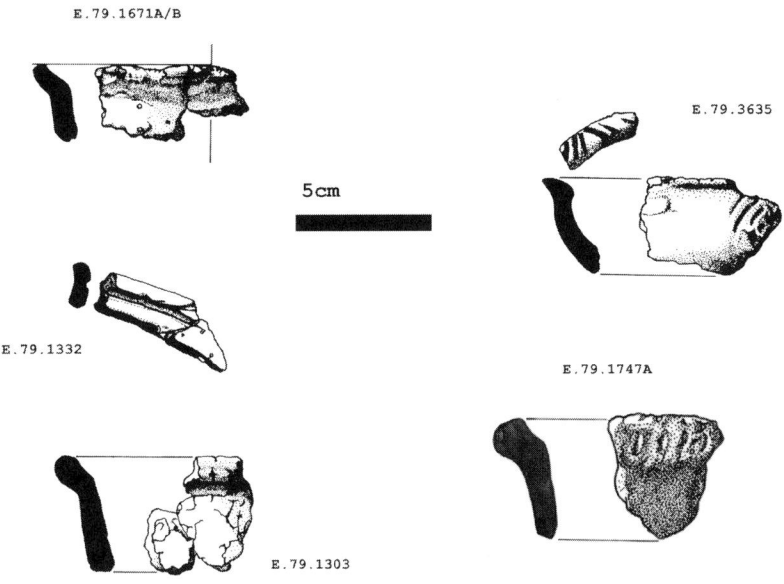

Figure 6-9. Decorated Neolithic pottery from Dún Ailinne.

From these diagnostic sherds, and from some of the better preserved body sherds, it was possible to identify approximately 26 (29.2%) of the vessels as having a rounded profile, suggesting the typical Neolithic bowl shape. Four appeared to have been flat-walled, or slightly concave, and eight sherds came from vessels with concave necks.

Decoration occurred extremely rarely, with only one sherd showing clear motifs; an additional seven sherds showed various grooves that may be the remains of decoration (Figure 6-9, Plate 6-3). All of these were rims, though not all decoration appeared on the rim itself. The most highly decorated piece (E.79.3635; Figure 6-9, Plate 6-4) was a rim that was pointed and everted. Cord impressions appeared on the flattened top of the rim, in a pattern of two groups of parallel hatch marks. Each group contained three hatch marks, and the two groups were oblique to each other such that the innermost formed an inverted V. Decoration also occurred on the external surface, on the body just below the rim, where three (possibly four) grooves formed concentric arcs.

The decoration on the other sherds is far less clear:

E.79.1747A. A rounded and strongly everted rim sherd, the interior of which is decorated with four parallel grooves perpendicular to the rim and ending where the rim bends. There is also some decoration on the top of the rim, but it is eroded and hard to define (possibly two concentric arcs or wavy lines, and several dots or stab marks).

E.79.1303B. Rim sherd with 2–4 incised parallel lines visible on the interior surface, just under the rim and running oblique to it.

E.79.1671A. Rim sherd with the remains of a ridge, and possibly 2–3 ridges, running perpendicular to the rim on the interior surface. Slight depressions on either side of the ridges suggest finger impressions.

E.79.1332 A & B. Two joined sherds. A is a rim sherd, and has a deep groove running parallel to the rim, about 8 mm under it, on the inner surface. This grooves appears to expand at the end into a Y-shaped, possibly triangular depression. There appears to be a second parallel groove at the lower edge of the sherd, about 9 mm below the first, which continues onto B (which is from the vessel's neck) along the lower edge of the interior surface of the sherd.

E.79.3683 A & C. Two rim sherds with grooves running just under the interior of the rim. Whether these are decorative, functional, or the result of wear is uncertain.

Typological Parallels

The Neolithic pottery from Dún Ailinne falls into the general category traditionally known as Western Neolithic; using more recent terminology, all but the few decorated sherds noted would fall under the undecorated Carinated Bowls (Waddell 2000). The recent three-fold scheme proposed by Sheridan (1995) updates the traditional version of Case (1961, 1963) and others who have addressed this issue. These typologies are all based largely on rim form and vessel profile, with decoration becoming significant in separating regional substyles. Unfortunately, the rim forms of the Dún Ailinne assemblage do not fit neatly into any of these various schemes due to the incomplete state of the sherds. Overall they have the simpler rim forms of Case's Dunmurry style, and so would fit into Sheridan's Phase 1. The usual thickness of the sherds, which averages about 8 mm, would also fit with this group. However, their shoulders lack the more angular, pronounced profile which seems to characterize it. Similar observations can be made regarding Sheridan's Phase 2 (including Case's Lyles Hill and Limerick styles), though again a markedly angular shoulder is lacking at Dún Ailinne. At the same time, while the typical profiles offered in these various publications do not provide a convincing match for this assemblage, the drawings in, for example, the publication on Lough Gur (Ó Ríordáin 1954a:328–29), which shows a more comprehensive range of variation, do seem to compare more favorably. Thus while it is uncertain to which style Dún Ailinne's ceramics belong, perhaps Sheridan's Phase 2 is the most convincing match. If so, then this would also date the assemblage to 2900–2500 BC, about the same part of the Neolithic as the Linkardstown pot.

Parallel Sites

Despite the fact that the Neolithic is not the period of most extensive use at these sites, it is appropriate to start comparisons with the other royal sites. At Tara (Newman 1997:71–75), Neolithic pottery was limited to the passage tomb (the Mound of the Hostages). Excavations there produced Carrowkeel ware, the pottery generally found in such tombs, and also various Bronze Age forms associated with later burials inserted into the tomb's covering cairn. Nothing parallel to the type of pottery found at Dún Ailinne has been reported.

At Navan, the situation is rather different. Here, sherds from at least 20 vessels were recovered from the middle to late part of the Neolithic. Most were of the carinated or uncarinated bowls typical of the period, and were assigned to Sheriden's category of Modified Western Neolithic pottery or Case's Sandhills Western ware. Three of the vessels were decorated: one carinated bowl with shallow striations on the outside of the rim and neck; a single decorated rim and undecorated body sherd, the former with whipped cord impressions and four shallow incised or impressed lines; and a sherd of incised coarseware of uncertain date, though possibly middle to late Neolithic. There is also a plain, uncarinated pot with a collar-like rim, fitting into Case's Sandhills: Dundrum or Herity's Broad-rimmed vessels (Waterman 1997:67–69)

An additional 97 small, featureless plain sherds from an indeterminate number of pots, all heavily abraded, were also recovered. The presence of a sooty encrustation on the interior surface of many sherds suggested their use as cooking vessels, while the remainder were presumably for storage or serving food and drink. A tentative date was suggested of 2750–2250 BC for the assemblage. As part of a larger study, some of the Navan sherds were also examined microscopically and petrologically. Comparing both the lithic inclusions in the ceramics and their chemical composition to local clay sources suggested a strong possibility that they were manufactured locally. However, none of the sampled clays were themselves a likely source of the material (Waterman 1997:67–72).

Of the two, then, Navan seems more directly comparable to Dún Ailinne. Typologically, chronologically, and perhaps functionally, the two assemblages match well, and while overall Dún Ailinne had a larger assemblage, the proportion of sherds to vessels and to decorated sherds was largely parallel. Other factors, such as the generally poor state of sherd preservation, the blackening on the surface of some sherds, and even the presence of quartz inclusions all indicate that the Neolithic presence at these two sites, at least as indicated by these ceramics, was closely comparable. There is, however, nothing at Navan that provides a parallel to the possible burial associated with Pit 293.

Assuming Pit 293 is the remnant of a Linkardstown burial, the surviving pottery compares well with that from other burials of this type, as already noted. Beyond this, the disturbance at Dún Ailinne of the probable Neolithic trench and other possible

Neolithic pits and post-holes by Iron Age activity renders them somewhat unhelpful in determining the character of the site's use in that period; in any case, most of the pottery did not come from these features, but rather from disturbed contexts in later phases.

The other features and Trench 281 might indicate a more general, non-funerary, ceremonial use, if Trench 281 is in fact the remains of an enclosure. However these features are also not inconsistent with a domestic context. The ceramics would seem to indicate that a domestic component was present, and that it was perhaps more significant in terms of the use of the site. However, this is based largely on the presence of ceramics manufacture and the suggestion from blackening that cooking was part of the Neolithic activity. While this might indicate a domestic character, there are many possible scenarios where cooking could be part of a ritual use as well. Thus the choices are annoyingly ill-defined in terms of appropriate comparanda (see Sheridan 1995 for a useful summary of the range of sites which have produced Neolithic pottery in Ireland and abroad); in the end, neither a domestic nor a non-funerary ritual use of the site would be inconsistent with the Neolithic ceramic assemblage.

Food Vessel

The food vessel described here was found in what can be described as the remains of a very shallow pit (2790). Very little of the pit survived later Iron Age activity. It is described in the feature log as having some associated charcoal, and being approximately 35 cm in diameter.

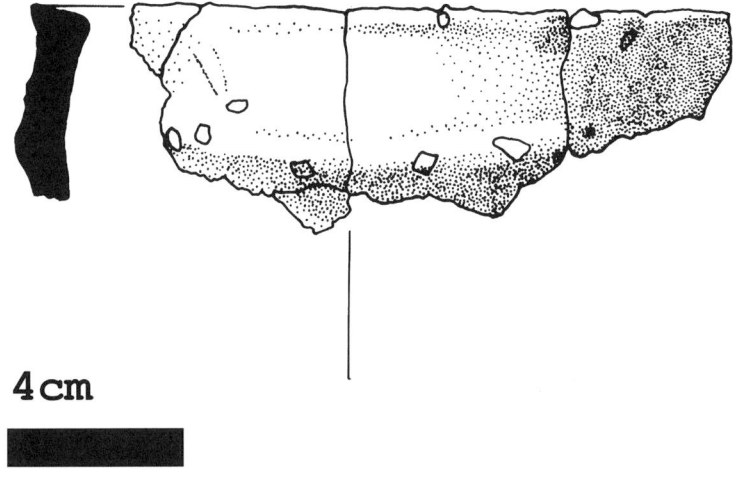

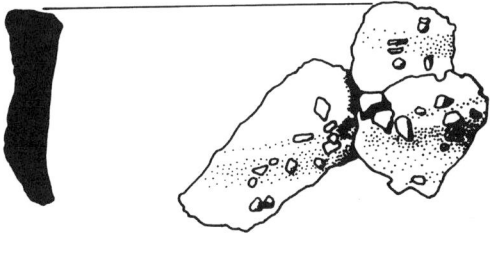

Figure 6-10. Food vessel from Dún Ailinne.

Description

The food vessel (E.79.905–906, but catalogued as E.79.905) is represented by a total of 14 sherds (the largest sherds are shown in Figure 6-10 and Plate 6-5). Nine of these are conjoined rim sherds, forming a single piece representing about one third of the vessel's rim. Of the other five sherds, three could also be fitted together; one of these is from the rim while the other two are body sherds from the vessel's shoulder. These three sherds are from another location along the rim, and could not be joined with the others. The remaining two sherds are loose, undiagnostic body sherds whose exact location on the vessel is unknown. The largest of the 13 sherds is 4.8 cm x 4.0 cm, while the smallest ones are less than 1 cm^2. They range in thickness from 0.6 cm to 1 cm depending on the degree of erosion.

The vessel's fabric is reddish-brown, ranging in shade from a darker brick red to a lighter, more orange color. All sherds have a blackened core, a characteristic common among food vessels which suggests that the vessels were incompletely oxidized during firing. This in turn is probably the result of using open bonfires to fire the vessel over a relatively short period of time (Sheridan 1993). Both inner and outer surfaces are extremely eroded and rough, and densely gritted with large white inclusions. Many of the inclusions are as large as 0.5 cm, and several are as large as 0.7 cm, at the large end of the range typical of food vessels but not outside it (Sheridan 1993:50). There is no trace of decoration on either surface. Although there are food vessels that lack decoration, the vast majority carry a variety of linear designs including incised and impressed motifs. (ApSimon 1969b; Harbison 1973; Waddell 1990; Ó Ríordáin and Waddell 1993). Thus it is possible that the Dún Ailinne vessel was originally undecorated, but it is also likely that the lack of decoration is due to poor preservation.

The rim is flat and both pointed and slightly everted. Its thickness ranges from 0.6 cm to 1 cm. Based on the approximately one-third of the vessel's mouth that is represented by conjoined rim sherds, its original diameter was ca. 14.5 cm. About 3.5 cm below the rim is a shoulder which, though distinct and very slightly stepped, is not particularly pronounced. It suggests a more globular shape for the vessel rather than a biconical form. None of the sherds extends more than 1 cm below the shoulder, so the shape of the vessel below this point is conjectural, and the original height remains unknown.

The fabric, as well as the portion of the profile which survives, undoubtedly places it in the class of food vessels. These vessels show a great deal of variation in type, and their proper classification remains the subject for debate (Ó Ríordáin and Waddell 1993; Harbison 1969; ApSimon 1969b; D.D.A. Simpson 1968). There is, however, general agreement that there are two basic forms overall, the bowl form and the vase form. Both rim and shoulder of the Dún Ailinne food vessel suggest that it belongs with those of bowl form; the rim is only slightly everted and the shoulder is insufficiently pronounced for it to be classified with the vase type.

Context

Beyond the fact of a Bronze Age presence at Dún Ailinne, little else is certainly indicated by this food vessel. The majority of food vessels have been found in burial contexts (Ó Ríordáin and Waddell 1993; Waddell 1990; ApSimon 1969b; O'Kelly 1989:195), and thus it is likely that this was also a burial. As with the possible Linkardstown burial discussed above, however, all that remains of this activity is the shallow pit and the vessel itself, barring the possible association of a human skull fragment already noted in the section on the Linkardstown vessel (see also Chapter 13). This fragment was not found near the food vessel in Pit 2790, but rather some 20 m away in Flame phase deposits, so there is no particular reason to associate the two. Also discussed elsewhere (Chapter 11) is the cupmarked stone, and the possibility remains that this is the sole survivor of a cist (stone lined) burial. However, this seems unlikely given the complete lack of evidence for the stone sockets from a cist wall and also the lack of proximity between the find spots of the stone and the food vessel (which were found almost 25 m apart). However, since leaf-shaped points, small scrapers, and stone axe heads have also been found associated with Bronze Age burials (Waddell 1990), it is possible that some of the material discussed in Chapter 5 might have come from such a burial.

Food vessels have also been recovered from domestic contexts (Ó Ríordáin and Waddell 1993:5 notes some 15 sites). At Dalkey Island, Co. Dublin, food vessel sherds, along with other Neolithic and Bronze Age pottery types, were interpreted as representing intermittent, short-term, domestic occupation throughout this period (Liversage 1968). Food vessels have also been found at Newgrange, associated with domestic remains (O'Kelly et al. 1983; but see Bradley 1998:102–103). At Coney Island, Lough Neagh, food vessel sherds of bowl type (though decorated) were found associated with the remains of a number of pits and two rectangular structures, all of uncertain character but interpreted as domestic (Addyman 1965). Interestingly, the food vessel sherds from one of these structures were associated with an asymmetrical arrowhead. An arrowhead of exactly the same type was found at Dún Ailinne (E.79.1832), although in an unstratified context (and some 30 m away from the food vessel). If the Coney Island association means anything, it might suggest that the association of bowl food vessel and asymmetrical arrowhead at Dún Ailinne indicates a similarly domestic character for the earlier Bronze Age activity here.

In the absence of any evidence for structures to support such an argument, however, it seems more likely that this is the remains of a burial. Bowl food vessels are predominantly found in burial contexts, the majority coming from cist or pit graves (Ó Ríordáin and Waddell 1993:5). While vase food vessels are more likely to be found with cremations, the bowl variety may be associated with either inhumation or cremation (Ó Ríordáin and Waddell 1993:19; Cooney and Grogan 1994:109–10); the latter might explain why there is no trace of a burial's occupant at Dún Ailinne. Bowl food vessels are also more commonly found in Leinster, again fitting with the Dún Ailinne vessel (Cooney and Grogan 1994:113–14). Many of these form what Ó Ríordáin and Waddell have identified as a noticeable concentration of unburned burials in Leinster (1993:19). It may also be noted that, in a study carried out by Mount (1995), men were more likely to be accompanied by bowl food vessels than either women or children; however, this was attributed to the larger number of men receiving formal burial treatment overall. In other words, while more males than females overall had associated bowl food vessels, the percentage of males with bowls was only slightly larger than that of females and children.

Based largely on associated finds, bowl food vessels are older than the vase form which superseded them, though there is significant overlap. The radiocarbon evidence agrees with this conclusion, showing that the two forms were in general use at the same time. The bulk of the available radiocarbon age determinations fall in a range of 3800–3600 BP, but both earlier and later examples are known (Ó Ríordáin and Waddell 1993). Charcoal found in association with the Dún Ailinne food vessel sherds gave a C^{14} age determination of 3220 ± 55 BP (1623–1400 Cal-BC) (SI-982). This is somewhat later than the typical range indicated, but not completely out of line. While the disturbance that characterizes the site may be the reason for this somewhat anomalous date, it may simply be that this vessel is a late survival of the bowl type. There is a reported C^{14} age determination of 2900 ± 100 BP (GrN 11450) for a bowl from Altanagh, Co. Tyrone (Williams 1986), and while this date may be anomalous, it may also show that the Dún Ailinne bowl is not entirely unique.

Clay Pin

One other ceramic object may also be considered with the pottery. E.79.2304 is a pin fragment which is either clay or ceramic, a very light tan or beige in color (Plate 6-6). It is composed of the head and about 14 mm of the shaft, and was found in two pieces (now repaired). The shaft is 5 mm thick. A groove running across the width of the end of the shaft does not appear deliberate. The head is somewhat rounded and is 7 mm in diameter. The pin was found in pit 409, which was assigned to the Crimson phase. This phase was one of the thin lenses comprising the low mound and is probably, though not certainly, Iron Age.

Parallels for this piece have not been forthcoming. It would presumably not have functioned literally as a pin, and it might perhaps be better described as a peg, possibly for some decorative use. The material is very soft, so it would not have been particularly robust for securing anything. In overall shape, it is not unlike the bone or antler pins found in some passage tombs (see Herity 1974:135, fig. 97, nos. 3–10), which are described as "phallic" and have a presumed symbolic significance. The Dún Ailinne example is of course a different material, and there is no passage tomb at the site. However, given the disturbance at the site and the presence of other Neolithic material, it is not impossible that E.79.2304 could be Neolithic and related to these better-known artifacts.

7
Iron

Susan A. Johnston

A total of 403 artifacts and fragments of iron were recovered from Dún Ailinne. Nine additional iron objects are listed in the finds register but are not now among the collection (see Chapter 4); two—E.79.338 and E.79.2268—are included in this analysis because there was more information about them than simply finds register entries.

This iron count has some inherent limitations. First, while modern objects were specifically excluded from this analysis, some may still have been included unintentionally. The corroded state of the iron meant that detailed typologies for many objects were impossible. Objects like nails, which might be identified more precisely by section or head shape, cannot be definitely dated. Other objects which are more generic in shape, like hooks, might date from almost any time period, a situation exacerbated by the sometimes disturbed context of the finds. Those "objects" which are unidentifiable, often little more than corroded lumps (here called "fragments"), could equally represent any period of the site's use.

Since the condition of the iron was fairly poor (despite some notable exceptions) deterioration of artifacts subsequent to excavation also occurred. This made counting artifacts an uncertain process. The following guidelines were used in this count:

- If the larger of the fragments in a single bag (with a single number) could be joined together, they were counted as a single object (smaller "crumbs" could not realistically be treated this way); otherwise, the fragments were considered separate objects and counted as such.

- If the finds register was definite about the object having been recovered as a single artifact (such as "iron ring") but the bag currently contained fragments, this was counted as a single artifact; the same is true if a drawing of the object, made at the time of discovery, showed a single object.

- If the finds register was equivocal about the nature of the artifact (such as "iron fragment"), the number of fragments was counted separately; this was due to the possibility that "fragment" could stand for more than one fragment in excavation shorthand.

This system is admittedly subjective, and error is clearly on the side of separate fragment counts rather then single artifacts. Thus clearly there were originally fewer (and perhaps significantly fewer) iron artifacts represented in the archaeological record than the number given here, and it would be legitimate to consider this number a maximum. As a rough indicator of the effect of this issue, there are a total of 31 artifact numbers that have iron counts of greater than one. Altogether, these account for 259 individual iron pieces, or 64% of the counted total. While there is no reliable way to know whether or not each of these numbers originally represented a single object, the potential for over-estimating numbers is clearly illustrated.

The state of the iron is illustrated by the fact that, of the 403 counted, 158 (39%) were catalogued as "fragment," indicating that the original character could not be identified. Where there were multiple fragments under a single catalogue number, the larg-

Table 7-1. Dimensions (mm), Iron Fragments.

N=33	L	W	T
Mean	30.2	12.4	6.3
Median	26.0	11.0	6.0
Mode	20.0	6.0	3.0
Range	11-85	6-30	1-15

est fragment was measured. This produced 33 sets of measurements representing the largest unidentified fragments. Using this as an indicator, Table 7-1 shows the statistics for fragment size, indicating how small even the larger fragments were, while Table 7-2 shows the identifiable categories of iron object.

The categories are separated according to the certainty with which the objects could be identified, those on the right being probable but not certain. They may be understood essentially as a "best guess" at the original shape. "Uncertain" was used where the object seemed to have an intentional form, but a descriptive name for the object was illusive. "Shaft" refers to an object of the requisite shape (long and relatively thin), but with no details to allow more definitive identification. These could have been pins, nails, or something else.

General Context

A majority of the iron objects (including fragments) were recovered from either unknown or uncertain archaeological contexts. A chronological phase could not be identified for 273 (68%) artifacts; 48 artifacts and fragments (12%) were from mixed or uncertain contexts and the remaining 225 (56%) were unknown. The 130 artifacts and fragments (32%) whose phase could be identified are shown in Table 7-3.

The majority of these artifacts come from 3 of the 4 main phases of activity at the site, Flame, Mauve, and Rose (100 total, or 77%), with the largest number (58, or 45%) coming from Flame. An additional two artifacts come from the much shorter White phase. As the phases where there were arguably larger numbers of people involved at the site (in both its construction and use), this makes sense. Greater numbers of objects were more likely to be deposited, discarded, or lost where there were greater numbers of people present to deposit, discard, or lose them. This would apply to personal possessions, such as needles, knife blades, and the occasional decorative item such as a small iron finger ring (E.79.1039) from a Rose phase trench, as well as objects, such as nails, which derive from building activities.

The types of features represented by these artifacts are shown in Table 7-4. This table shows both identifiable contexts and artifacts from unstratified and uncertain (including mixed or unidentifiable) contexts. While the inability to identify most objects makes the significance of this difficult to judge, at least one pattern is evident in this data. While there is little difference between identifiable objects and fragments in unclear contexts, fragments are far less likely to come from known con-

Table 7-2. Types of Iron Artifact.

OBJECT	N	OBJECT	N
binding strip	3	blade?	1
blade	1	chisel?	3
disk	1	finger ring?	1
knife blade	1	fitting?	1
nail	19	hook?	3
needle	5	knife blade?	1
ring	13	nail?	54
ring fragment	2	needle?	3
shaft	83	pin?	3
spearhead	1	pin fragment?	2
spike	2	ring?	3
strip	4	shaft?	24
sword	1	TOTAL	99
uncertain	10		
TOTAL	146		

Table 7-3. Distribution, Iron Artifacts by Phase.

PHASE	N
Dun	10
Emerald	1
Flame	58
Harry	3
Jade	1
Lower Emerald	3
Mauve	27
Rose	15
Upper Emerald	10
White	2
TOTAL	130

Table 7-4. Identifiable Iron Artifacts and Fragments by Feature Type.

CONTEXT	N	IDENTIFIABLE	FRAGMENT	CONTEXT	N	IDENTIFIABLE	FRAGMENT
Hut	2	2	—	Baulk	43	3	40
Mound	52	47	5	Surface	125	63	62
Occupation	47	39	8	Uncertain	53	44	9
Pit	7	4	3	Unknown	22	11	11
Post-hole	7	6	1	TOTAL	243	121	122
Trench	45	26	19				
TOTAL	160	124	36				

texts, while identifiable objects are far more likely to do so. Put another way, fragments are far more likely to come from disturbed contexts than more clearly definable ones.

The most obvious explanation for the difference in pattern is preservation of the original objects. Objects in surface contexts may have been more likely to be reduced to fragments precisely because they are less protected, while those in mixed or uncertain contexts are likely to have been disturbed. That this may be a factor can be demonstrated, albeit rather crudely. Table 7-5 shows the individual fragments of unidentifiable objects, comparing the type of feature they were found in with the number of artifact numbers assigned to them ("N Obj #" in the table).

While this is an imperfect comparison, the fact that all of the fragments were found in a single location (the reason they were given a single number), might indicate that they were originally one object. The table also shows the ratio of artifact numbers to fragments, assuming that each number equals one object. As can be seen, the ratio of "objects" to fragments is in most cases significantly higher for unstratified and uncertain contexts (at the top) than for sealed deposits (at the bottom), even though the number of "objects" is not all that different. This suggests that, while the absolute number of objects does not differ noticeably, objects in unstratified or mixed contexts were more likely to decompose into larger numbers of fragments (and so become unrecognizable) than those in sealed deposits.

That said, there may still be other factors at work. One other possibility is that at least some of the recognizable artifacts may have been deliberate deposits; this is arguable for the sword (E.79.630; see below), and possibly for other objects. This may suggest factors such as the object being in better condition when originally deposited, and thus being better preserved when recovered.

In terms of the general character of the objects, their state of preservation makes it impossible to determine whether they were primarily personal possessions versus economic or constructional debris, as was done for copper alloy. Of the total iron objects (403), only 33 could be securely identified as to original form. The various "shafts" could be nails or pins, while most of the rings, strips, and disks are unidentifiable beyond this general attribution. Nevertheless, most of what is identifiable are personal possessions; this includes needles (five), binding strips (three), the two certain blades, the sword, and the spearhead; the probable finger ring also belongs here. The only categories which are presumably not personal are three spikes and 19 nails. So while the comparison is not entirely secure, this does suggest that, as with other categories of artifacts, iron also is characterized by a significant presence of personal items. These presumably represent, for the most part, the possessions of those in attendance at the various functions held at the site.

Table 7-5. Iron Fragments Versus Accession Numbers by Context.

FEATURE	N OBJ	N OBJ #	RATIO
Baulk	40	2	20.0
Surface	62	8	7.8
Uncertain	9	2	4.5
Unknown	11	3	3.7
Mound	5	4	1.3
Occupation	8	5	1.6
Pit	3	3	1.0
Post-hole	1	1	1.0
Trench	19	5	3.8

Description, Iron Objects

Among the identifiable objects, there are several which stand out in that they are known objects in a reasonably good state of preservation. These are the sword, the spearhead, the blades, a finger ring, three binding strips, and the needles. Other categories of objects can be described more generally, including the nails, the spikes, and the various rings, strips, and other items of unknown function. The remainder of the iron artifacts will only be considered in general terms.

Sword

The most noteworthy of the weapons recovered from Dún Ailinne is a largely complete sword, E.79.630 (Figure 7-1, Plate 7-1). It was recovered from deep in the fill of a Mauve phase trench (516), the palisade trench forming the outermost circle of the timber structure (Plates 7-2, 7-3). It was almost against the side of the trench, and while it was not absolutely clear whether the fill was primary or secondary, its position so close to the trench wall suggests it was primary.

The sword is essentially intact, lacking only the hilt, and it is completely oxidized (minimal conservation was done on site at the time it was found). Since hilts of this period appear to have been typically organic (Rynne 1983), it is likely that this sword also had such a hilt. The sword's total length is 44.6 cm, with the blade being 38 cm and the tang 6.5 cm. The blade's thickness averages about 9 mm. The blade is somewhat triangular, converging fairly rapidly toward the point; its maximum width, near the hilt, is 39 mm and it narrows to about 16 mm at the tip. The hilt guard mount appears to be of iron (Plate 7-4), making it the only known example in this material, bronze being the norm (Rynne 1981:93; B. Raftery 1984:65); indeed, Scott (1990:61) describes it as a "skeuomorph" of copper alloy forms. It is bell-shaped (campanulate), rising fairly shallowly to the center of the hilt. In cross-section, the blade is essentially oval, though pointed at the edges.

Typologically, the sword is clearly La Tène, falling into Raftery's Type 1 (1984:66-70) and Rynne's Type A (1981). Both are based on hilt and blade shape. This places it in the same group as, for example, the swords from Lisnacrogher, Co. Antrim (Munro 1890:382-84; Wakeman 1884:386-88; 1891:542), Edenderry, Co. Offaly (B. Raftery 1984:63), and Cashel, Co. Sligo (Rynne 1960). Comparing only the hilt guards, those from Cashel and

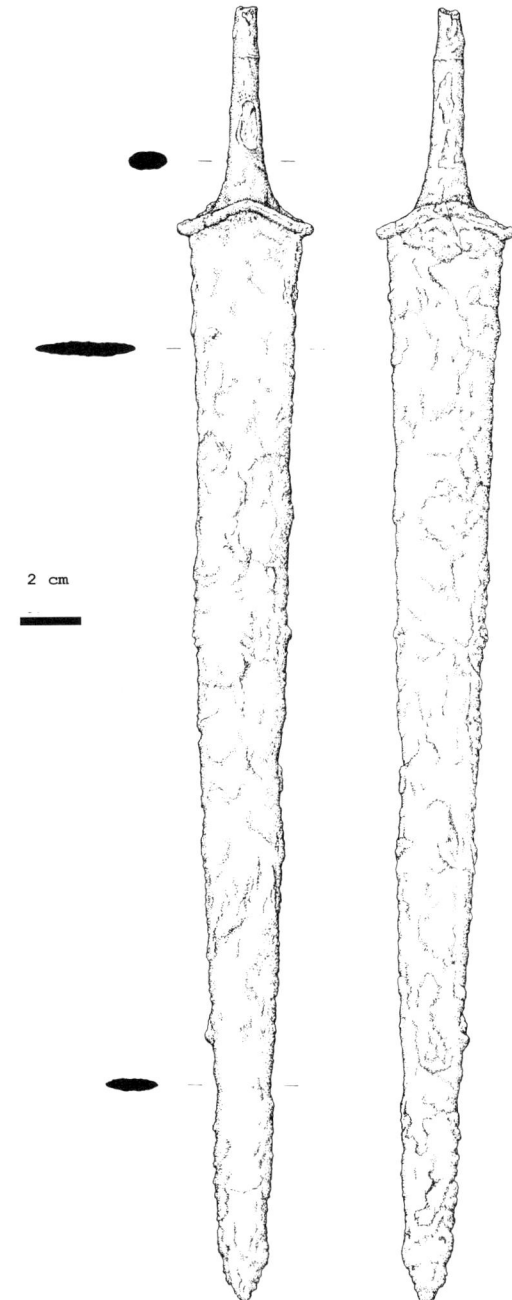

Figure 7-1. Iron sword from Dún Ailinne.

Edenderry are particularly close parallels, and the blade of the sword from Cashel is also short. Scott also notes a similarity to the sword from Drinagh, Co. Laois (1990:65). Purely on typological grounds, there is nothing about the Dún Ailinne sword to suggest anything other than a native origin (B. Raftery 1984:66). Type I swords are said to belong to the

3rd to 2nd centuries BC, though the Dún Ailinne example suggests (the problematic radiocarbon sequence from the site notwithstanding; see Chapter 15) they may extend into the 1st century AD (B. Raftery 1983:83, 1984:66-70; Scott 1990:65).

While it is must be considered a sword based on its characteristics, it is unusually short; indeed, Raftery describes it as "little more than a dirk" (B. Raftery 1984:65). Irish swords in general are known for being short (Scott:1990:61; B. Raftery 1994:141; Waddell 2000:304). B. Raftery (1984:67) lists that from Balinderry, Co. Westmeath, as the longest, with a blade just over 46 cm. The bottom of the range is anchored by Cashel at about 37 cm (B. Raftery 1984:67) and Dún Ailinne at 38 cm. While "dirk" is perhaps an overstatement, it is certainly a short-bladed weapon. European and British swords of "Celtic" type span a range of 55 cm - 95 cm (Pleiner 1993:63), longer than the group of Irish swords and significantly longer than the Dún Ailinne example.

This has raised the question of the effectiveness of these swords in battle (see B. Raftery 1984:67; Scott 1990:95). Similar questions have been raised with regard to the quality of the metal, and this has been investigated experimentally. In this case, replicas certainly held up well enough to inflict serious damage (Pleiner 1993:163-64). This does not take account of the shortness of the swords, however, and it has been suggested that serious fighting was done with spears, while swords were intended to a significant degree for display and the occasional close combat (Waddell 2000:304).

This may have relevance for the other significant use of swords, as votive deposits. The deposition of metalwork in the Iron Age is well known (see Bradley 1990 as a fairly recent synthetic treatment), and swords in particular have received this treatment (Pleiner 1993:59-60). In Ireland, all but two swords (Dún Ailinne and the burial at Lambay Island) were recovered from various wet sites (Cooney and Grogan 1994:197-98). While a portion of these could be explained by loss, it is unlikely that people were so careless with their possessions that this would be common. This suggests that such ritual deposition was a primary means by which Irish swords entered the archaeological record. The Lambay Island sword, associated with a burial, also falls into the general class of "ritual deposit," leaving Dún Ailinne as the only example that is not in a clearly ritual context (though it is arguable that its context is also ritual in nature; see below).

The idea that Irish Iron Age swords primarily functioned in a ritual context does not rule out the possibility that they were associated with combat, whether symbolically or actually. Indeed, it is problematic how swords would have taken on symbolic significance without some practical context; if swords were never used in combat, what is their symbolic significance? That said, with the exception of the excavation of a battlefield, what would the archaeological context of a sword used only in battle look like? Pleiner (1993:157-64) notes that "Celtic" swords in general sometimes are notched and damaged, suggesting they were used. But this does not rule out their ultimate deposition in ritual contexts. In the end, swords may have had simultaneous ritual and secular cultural meanings, and perhaps we should not be too quick to overemphasize the fact that we typically only see them in the former context archaeologically. This may have been the typical end of the use life of an Iron Age sword, which otherwise had a secular function until such deposition.

The circumstances under which the Dún Ailinne sword came to be deposited in a palisade trench are of course unknown. It is difficult to imagine a situation in which something of this size would have been accidentally lost, though perhaps one could envision it being accidentally left behind under some circumstance of great haste or confusion. The same can be said for deliberate discard, though there is perhaps a somewhat greater latitude for the imagination here: say, theft, or a dramatic gesture of some sort. However, on balance the most likely option seems to be deliberate deposition, along the lines of a votive deposit. Such a deposit in an earthbound setting, as opposed to a watery location, is unusual (Cooney and Grogan 1994:197-98, 211-13). It is possible that it represents something more like a foundational deposit for the construction of the Mauve phase timber structure, rather than an offering made in a context analogous to the better-known water deposits. Whatever the actual associated rite and its timing with regard to the Mauve phase construction, however, the likely association of Dún Ailinne with ritual and secular power makes the deposition of an object evocative of male warrior status seem appropriate.

Spearhead

The spearhead (E.79.2305) was found in mound material, from a Flame phase context (Figure 7-2, Plate 7-5). It is now in five pieces; three of them are small, and the tip has been removed for analysis (a sample mounted for PIXE analysis is also

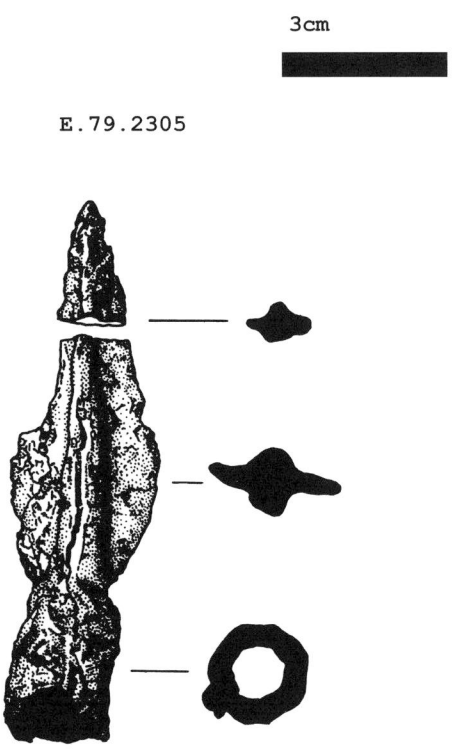

Figure 7-2. Iron spearhead from Dún Ailinne.

stored with it). It is 13.1 cm long, which is relatively short, and 27 mm wide by 22 mm thick at its widest and thickest points. Although it is somewhat deteriorated, it is leaf-shaped, with a fairly pronounced midrib running the entire length, and socketed. The socket has an internal diameter of 19 mm and an external diameter of 29 mm.

Because of the generalized nature of their form and its longevity, spearheads are not closely datable (Scott 1990:66; B. Raftery 1994:74), and the Dún Ailinne example is no exception. Stratigraphically, it belongs to the latest Iron Age phase at the site, and so in the later part of the Iron Age. Typologically, it compares in very general terms to most leaf-shaped examples, such as those illustrated by B. Raftery (1983:109-10, figs. 114-5; 1984:109, fig. 58), though it lacks evidence for any decoration or other elaboration. However, it also compares to examples from Lagore, which are possibly later in date (Hencken 1950:96, fig. 30). In detail, however, none of the illustrated examples provide a close parallel, and as such the spearhead contributes little to a discussion of the site's chronology.

Swords and spearheads are the most common iron objects found from this period in Ireland (B. Raftery 1994:149), but this is not to say that they are common overall. By comparison with the more numerous bronze examples from previous periods, iron weapons are surprisingly rare. Since they are typically found in watery contexts, this may account for some of the lack of numbers; in some wet locations, iron can disintegrate in as little as a century (Waddell 2000:285-86; Cooney and Grogan 1994:197). They are also commonly found in other ritual locations, such as burials on the Continent, typically associated with swords (Pleiner 1993:39). At the same time, they presumably derive their symbolic meaning for these contexts from their cultural use as weapons. As already noted, it has been suggested that spears, rather than swords (whose usefulness as weapons is debated), were the primary tools for combat (Waddell 2000:304).

As with the sword, the circumstances under which the spearhead was deposited are uncertain. It was not in a feature, and so deliberate deposit is more difficult to argue. Compared to a sword, it is somewhat easier to envision the accidental loss of a spearhead, which is smaller than a sword, though when hafted this difference is obviously eliminated. Its apparent association with the feasting that characterized the Flame phase may suggest a social context (admittedly subjectively conceived) where such a loss might occur (drunkenness? darkness? competition?). That said, a deliberate deposit cannot be ruled out, and the general ritual nature of Dún Ailinne may suggest that the spearhead too is a ritual deposit of some kind.

Binding Strips

Three pieces were identified as probable binding strips (two are illustrated in Figure 7-3 and all three in Plate 7-6). A fourth piece, E.79.1769, may also belong with this group and is described with them.

E.79.1453. Fragment of iron binding strip. The shaft is 8 mm high by 4 mm thick, with a rounded attachment plate at one end; the total piece measures 40 mm x 12 mm. One side of the plate has a 2 mm diameter depression which no longer appears to perforate to the other side. The piece was broken into three fragments (now repaired).

E.79.2951. Fragment of iron binding strip. One end is broken and the other end has a rounded attachment plate. Perforations are no longer visible on the plate except for a possible slight depression on one side. This piece is 47 mm long by 8 mm wide and 7 mm thick.

E.79.2229. Fragment of what is probably a binding strip, bent at a right angle. Its total length is 79 mm and it is 7 mm wide by 6 mm thick.

E.79.1769, which is also u-shaped, may also belong with these pieces. It is 27 mm L x 7 mm W x 5 mm T. It is lumped together with the general discussion of "fragments," but its shape suggests it might have had an edge-binding function.

Binding strips from shields or scabbards are not well known from Ireland, although an example was recovered from Navan (Waterman 1997:85 and Fig 39.1). The Navan piece is longer and somewhat more complete, having two more intact attachment plates along its 107 mm length. Otherwise, it compares well with the Dún Ailinne examples, being about the same width. B. Raftery (1997:93) cites the closest parallels for the Navan piece as being from various late La Tène and Roman shields recovered from sites in Britain, such as Cadbury Castle (Alcock 1972) and the Continent, where they are associated with shields (B. Raftery 1984:129). Bronze examples that are somewhat similar to the iron Dún Ailinne examples are among the objects recovered from Glastonbury (Bulleid and St. George Gray 1911:232

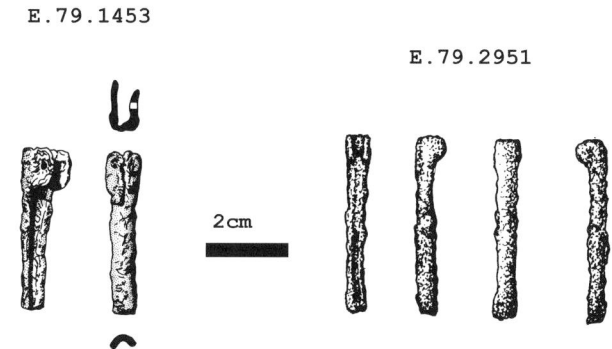

Figure 7-3. Two binding strips from Dún Ailinne.

and pl. XLIII). The only comparable object noted from Ireland is a smaller bronze binding strip recovered from the River Shannon near Athlone, Co. Westmeath. This piece was not associated with a shield, however, and a similar use for the Navan piece is uncertain due to its size (B. Raftery 1984:128-29). Whatever their use (shields, scabbards, or something else), it is tempting to regard the binding strips from Navan and Dún Ailinne as somehow uniquely associated with royal sites, at least in Ireland. The context for such an association however remains unknown.

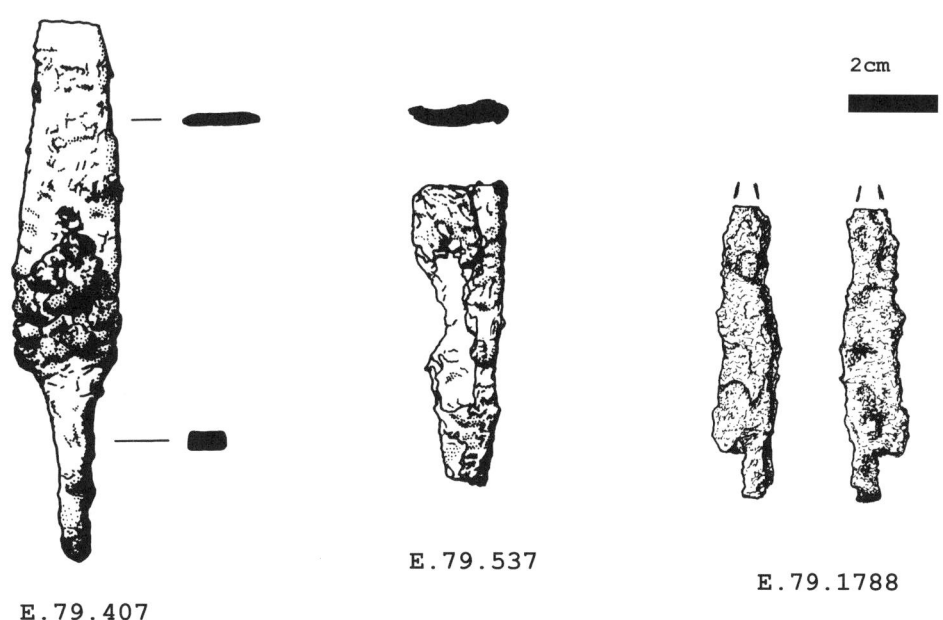

Figure 7-4. Iron blades from Dún Ailinne.

Blades

There are four blades, two certain and two possible, from Dún Ailinne (Figure 7-4, Plate 7-7).

E.79.407. Knife blade, with the tip removed for analysis (see Scott 1990:88–91 and Chapter 12 for a description of the results of metallurgical analysis). The total length of the object is 13.4 cm long, and it is 26 mm at the widest. The blade is 4 mm thick. The tang, which is centrally placed, is rounded at the end and 46 mm in length. The blade itself was found broken in two pieces and was repaired.

E.79.1788. 27 fragments of a single-edged iron blade. It appears to be a knife. Most of the fragments are small, flat, and irregular in shape. The one large piece is a blade which is 75 mm in length and 16 mm at the widest point; it is 5 mm thick. It has an asymmetrically placed tang which measures 11 m long by 7 mm wide. The blade tip was removed for analysis and is bagged separately.

E.79.537. Flat iron strip plus 11+ additional small fragments, which probably belongs to a knife blade. Although the large piece is corroded, it appears to be broader at one end and tapering to the other end, with slightly curved edges. A drawing from 1971 shows the tip to be intact, but it is now broken off. The large piece measures 76 mm by 22 mm by 4 mm thick.

E.79.5004. 20+ fragments of an iron object, all very fragile. Eight of the fragments are relatively large, and some of them appear to join. The largest fragment is 76 mm long by 31 mm and 5 mm thick. Its shape is irregular and the piece is damaged, but it does appear blade-like and ends in a rounded point.

The stratigraphic context of two of the blades is problematic. E.79.1788 is from the topsoil, while E.79.5004 had no number when it was examined for this study (see Preface), and so lacks provenience information. Both E.79.537 and E.79.407 came from the Flame phase. It is tempting in this regard to speculate that the latter two artifacts were associated with food consumption, the Flame phase being associated with extensive feasting activity. However, the generic form of these objects makes it difficult to ascribe any particular function to them, and it is indeed probable that they were used for multiple purposes. Further, the likely resharpening of them adds to the typological problems (Scott 1990:3). As a comparison, knife blades not unlike the Dún Ailinne examples were recovered from the Rath of Feerwore (J. Raftery 1944:fig. 4) and from the lake villages at Meare (St. George Gray and Bulleid 1953:235–36) and Glastonbury (Bulleid and St. George Gray 1917:382 and Pl. LXI). As B. Raftery notes (1984:238), the largely unchanging form of artifacts such as these also obviates their usefulness for chronological discussion. As if to underscore this point, J. Raftery notes, in his discussion of excavation at the Rath of Feerwore, that iron knives like these have been found in contexts ranging from 300 BC to AD 1400 (1944:36).

Finger Ring

While most of the iron rings from the site are large, thick, and fairly flat, suggesting a more utilitarian function, E.79.1039 appears to be a finger ring (see Figure 7-6).

It is fairly small and delicate, flat in section, and has an outside diameter of 19 mm; the interior diameter varies 15–16 mm. Its height also varies slightly at just over 2 mm. It appears to be a band, with no evidence of a bezel or any other flattening along its circumference. The surface is eroded so it is impossible to determine if it ever had any decoration. The ring was recovered from the fill of trench 60, the innermost of the three palisade trenches that constitute the main Rose phase timber structure.

Apart from pin fragments, which may be largely functional, this is the only example of iron jewelry from the site. Beyond this, there is no surviving detail that would allow anything further to be said about this ring. Its context places it in the Rose phase, though how it came to be there in unknown. It is possible it represents a deliberate deposit, but it is equally likely that it represents discard or loss.

Scott notes that iron personal ornaments are essentially absent from B. Raftery's 1983 Iron Age *corpus*, particularly notable given the general lack of iron objects overall; of 478 objects in the *corpus* potentially made of iron, only 47 are reported (Scott 1990:64–65). Iron jewelry seems little reported in the literature, apart from the more numerous pins. Iron spiral rings are reported from Glastonbury (Bulleid and St. George Gray 1911:216–17), but these are quite different from the Dún Ailinne example, which is not of spiral design.

In a study of Early Christian metal finger rings, Mulhall (1998) reports only one iron example out of

100 rings (a second example is reported from the Viking mass burial at Donnybrook, Co. Dublin, but is now missing; Mulhall 1998:132; Frazier 1879:51). This ring was recovered during early excavations at Uisneach, Co. Westmeath (Macalister and Praeger 1928), and is said to have been unstratified (Mulhall 1998:109). Now in the National Museum of Ireland, this ring is quite different from the Dún Ailinne example, being much thicker and penannular, with ends that currently overlap. Thus it does not provide much of a parallel for the Dún Ailinne ring, except in the very broadest sense.

Johns (1997:74) has noted, in the context of the Snettisham hoard (where the rings were mostly silver and also provide no useful parallels for the Dún Ailinne example), that it is likely that iron was more widely used for personal ornament than is now realized. This may be attributed to an archaeological focus on more expensive metals, as a reflection of more modern tastes. It is possible that the Dún Ailinne ring is a more functional item and not a personal ornament, but its overall delicacy and size certainly suggests the latter. If it is an ornament, then it seems to be a fairly unusual one, at least based on currently available artifact inventories.

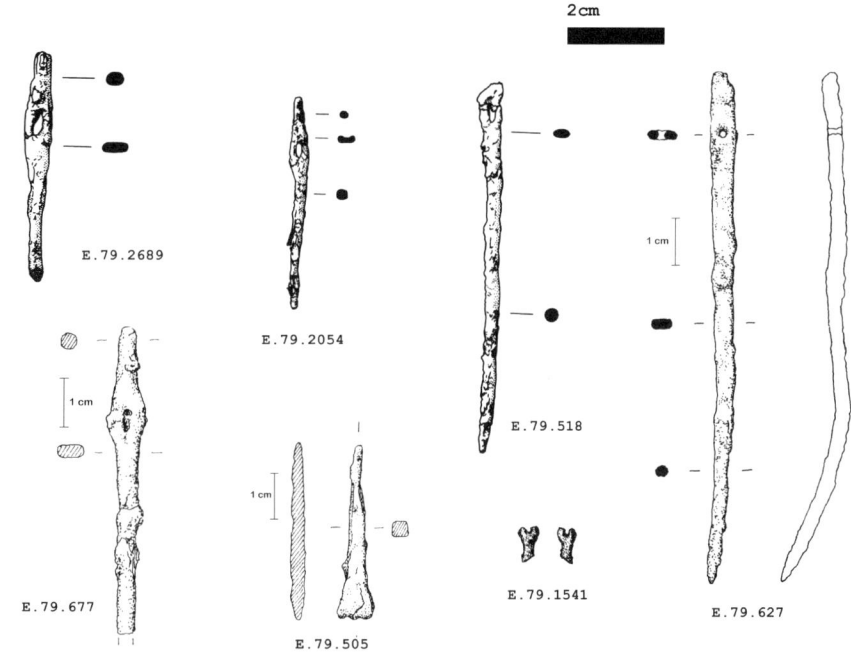

Figure 7-5. Iron needles from Dún Ailinne.

Needles

There are five examples of needles (Figure 7-5, Plate 7-8), plus three possible fragments. It is likely that some among the group of undifferentiated "shafts" are also the remains of needles. Of the five clear examples, four are essentially complete, though they are heavily corroded.

E.79.518. Iron needle, essentially complete. The top, at the end of the oblong perforation (2 mm), is broken. While the material at the end may be the broken piece cemented on with corrosion, it is also possible that this is only corrosion, and the broken fragment is missing.

E.79.627. Long iron needle with small, round perforation at one end (diameter 1 mm). The shaft is flattened and tapered, subrectangular in section though more rounded at the narrower end. The end opposite the perforation is curved.

E.79.677. Iron object, broken in two pieces. One piece is expanded in the middle of the shaft and has a discolored, indented oval area that looks like the eye of a needle, rusted closed.

E.79.2054. Large iron needle with an oblong perforation (5 mm diameter) about 3/4 along length. The opposite end is blunted.

E.79.2689. Fragment of what is probably an iron needle, broken in two pieces through the eye. While this does look like a needle, the area at what would have been the "top" does extend unusually far (12 mm) beyond the perforation rather than having the usual rounded end.

Of the three uncertain examples, two (E.79.1037 and E.79.1541; the latter appears in Figure 7-5) are shaft fragments with one bifurcated end suggesting a fractured perforation (or, in the case of the latter, possibly a ring-headed pin). The

Table 7-6. Dimensions (mm), Iron Needles.

ARTIFACT NUMBER	L	W	T	PERF.
E.79.505	40	7	4	—
E.79.518	81	6	3	2
E.79.2054	93	8	5	5
E.79.627	105	6	3	1

Table 7-7. Dimensions (mm), Iron Nails.

N=73	L	W	T
Mean	33.7	9.0	7.3
Median	32.0	8.0	6.0
Mode	54.0	10.0	6.0
Range	14-67	5-17	3-15

other, E.79.505 (Figure 7-5), is shaped very much like a needle, narrowing from a fairly flat, broader end to an almost pointed opposite end. The broad end has some discoloration on the surface that is circular and appears on both sides, suggesting an eye rusted solid.

As a group, the contexts of these objects are fairly unsatisfying. Considering both certain and uncertain examples as a group, four are from the Flame phase, though the specific context of one (E.79.1541) is uncertain and the other three (E.79.518, E.79.505, and E.79.627) are from the problematic occupation layers. Only one, E.79.2689, is from a secure context, Trench 515 of the Mauve phase structure, and this is a somewhat problematic piece due to its shape. The remaining three are from either unknown or uncertain contexts.

Of the eight total objects, the dimensions of four can be determined with some accuracy, though they may not be technically complete. The other four are clearly broken. Table 7-6 shows the dimensions of the four relatively complete pieces. Both width and thickness are quite consistent, while length varies in two ways: three are fairly close in length while the fourth is less than half of the smallest of the other three. While this may be related to preservation, it may indicate something about function, suggesting perhaps that the three needles of similar dimensions represent a common need associated with the activities at Dún Ailinne.

Perforations are particularly susceptible to closure by corrosion, but where these could be measured they are also shown in Table 7-6 (under "Perf."). Again, if this means anything, it may undercut the previous suggestion, since the dimensions of a needle's eye are directly related to the material which can be threaded through it. Thus arguably two of these needles might have threaded material of a similar quality, while the third is would accommodate something significantly thicker. Interestingly, the bone needle, E.79.417 (see Chapter 10), also has a perforation which is 5 mm in length; this needle is broken, so its length is not comparable (though the surviving segment is 30 mm long). The two sets of perforation sizes may indicate that there were two basic groups of materials in use at the site.

What these needles might have been used for is speculative (though "running repairs on druids' robes" is not entirely without merit; Wailes 1990). At least one (E.79.627) is curved at one end, though this may be the result of post-depositional factors and not original form. Needles may have been personal items normally carried around by members of a society where textiles were a common possession and perhaps in need of periodic repair. They may also have had symbolic value, particularly if textiles and/or those who produced them were associated with status or economic gain (as for women in later periods; see Bitel 1996:126-131). However, they also may be part of the pattern of artifacts indicative of low-level manufacturing at the site— slag, copper casting debris, glass toggles, spindle whorls, etc. As noted elsewhere, these may indicate something on the order of craft production associated with the other activities at Dún Ailinne. This is explored more fully in Chapter 18.

Nails

This is a problematic category, since the degree of corrosion of the identifiable nails from Dún Ailinne prevents the identification of any typological characteristics that would allow them to be assigned to a cultural or chronological context. In addition, some of the unidentifiable "shafts" are also certainly nails, though how many is unknown. Certainly nails have presumably been used since the production of iron met the needs of timber structures, and since there is little room to vary the shape of a nail, the differences tend to be subtle. Subtle differences are the very ones destroyed by iron oxidation, so there is really no way to determine whether all the nails identified from Dún Ailinne date to the Iron Age use of the site. Given the presence of timber structures, however, it is likely that at least some of them do, and so for the sake of

Iron

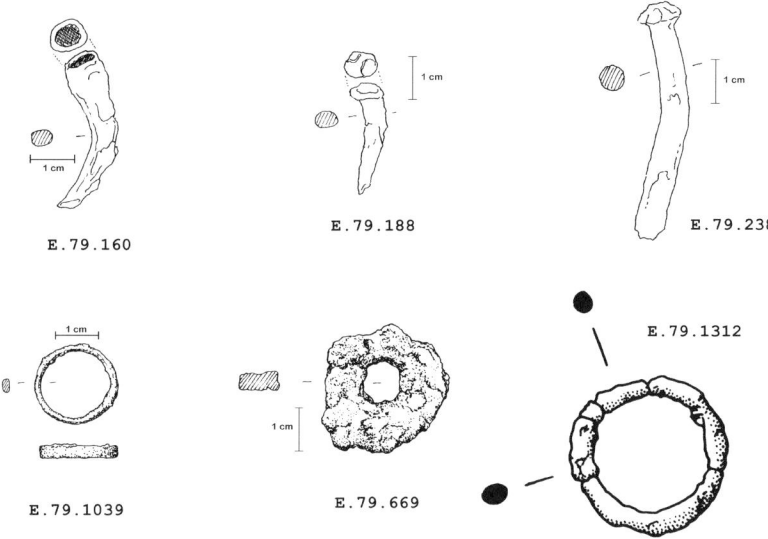

Figure 7-6. Iron nails and rings from Dún Ailinne.

of nails and nail fragments (88%) came from unstratified or uncertain contexts. This reflects the degree of disturbance overall but may also be the result of the repeated reconstruction of timber structures at the site. Presumably as each building phase was replaced a certain number of nails used in its construction were lost. However, since there is no way to know if and/or how many nails were used in building these structures, little else can be said. Indeed, it is likely that, while some of the nails are survivors of the timber structures, others were used in other contexts, such as in temporary structures erected during construction or connected with the other activities carried out at the site.

analysis they will be treated as a single group. The only exception to this is one example (E.79.38) that is almost certainly modern.

This group contains a total of 73 nails and probable nail fragments (Figure 7-6 shows several representative examples). It is difficult to determine how many of them are complete, and most of them clearly are not. Their dimensions (Table 7-7) thus give only an impression of minimum sizes for nails at the site. Table 7-8 shows both the types of features and the phases associated with nails and nail fragments (a single nail fragment, now E.79.5009 but originally with no number, has no context information and was omitted from this table). A small number (four) came from the Mauve and Rose phases, perhaps a result of the construction of those timber structures, and about the same number came from the Flame phase. However, the large majority

Possible Pins and Shafts

The generic category of "shaft" includes all those objects that lacked any defining characteristics other than being significantly longer than they were wide. These could be nails, pins, or some other type of artifact (Figure 7-7 shows a number of representative examples). There were 107 of these altogether, 24 of them uncertain. Table 7-9 shows the dimensions of 39 shaft fragments whose measurements were taken (where more than one fragment was listed under a single number, the largest fragment was measured, and any fragment less than 1 cm in length was not measured).

As can be seen, while their lengths are relatively short on average, they do cover a wide range. The longest is over 19 cm in length, almost double the next shortest (104 mm). This artifact, E.79.1926, which could be described as a shaft or a rod, is

Table 7-8. Distribution, Iron Nails by Feature Type and by Phase.

FEATURE	N	PHASE	N
Hut	1	Flame	5
Occupation	4	Mauve	3
Surface	39	Rose	1
Trench	4	Rose?	21
Uncertain	24	Upper Emerald	1
		Unknown	41

Table 7-9. Dimensions (mm), Iron Shafts.

N=39	L	L <194mm	W	T
Mean	45.1	41.2	6.5	5.4
Median	38.0	37.5	6.0	5.0
Mode	33.0	33.0	4.0	4.0
Range	21-194	21-104	4-13	3-11

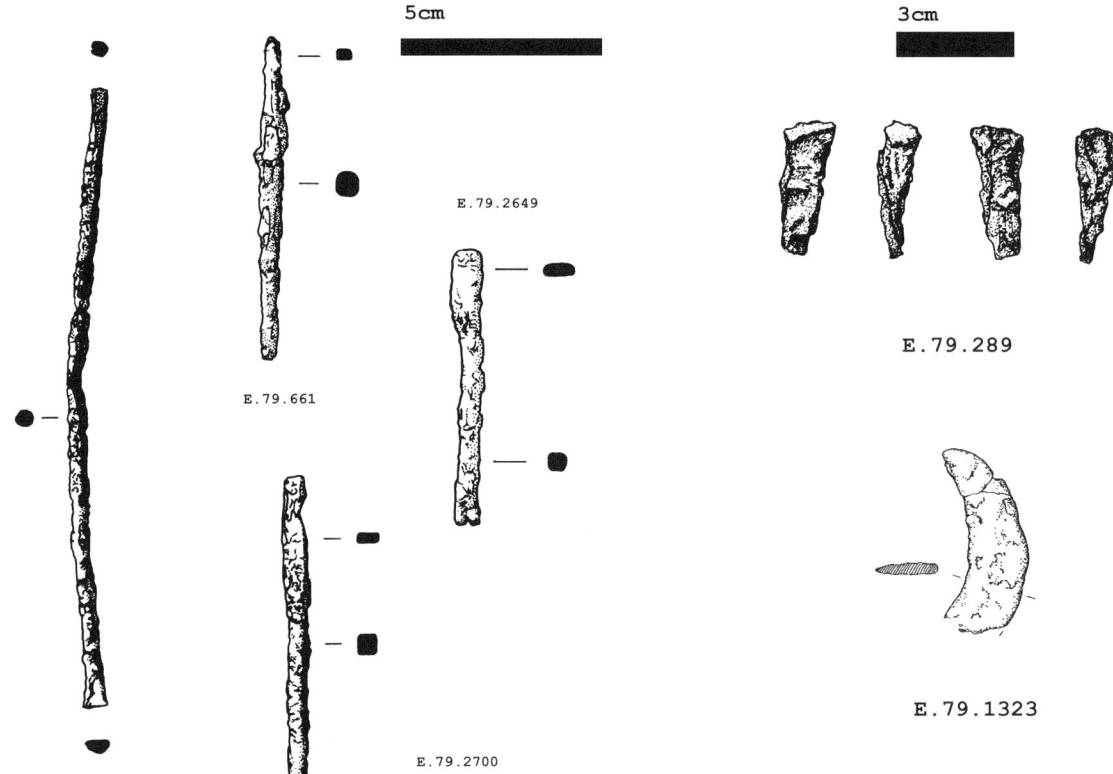

Figure 7-7. Iron shafts from Dún Ailinne.

Figure 7-8. Iron chisel and possible sickle blade.

slightly curved, round in section at one end and flattened at the other. Its shape and size suggest that it is unlikely to have been a nail or pin. It was subject to metallurgical analysis (see Scott 1990:88–91), and while this did indicate that the characteristics of the metal make it unlikely to have been effective as a metalworking tool, its function still remains unclear. Since it is so much longer than the other shaft fragments, the group length statistics have also been shown without this object ("L<194"; its width and thickness do not significantly alter those group statistics).

Table 7-10. Dimensions (mm), Possible Iron Pins.

ARTIFACT NUMBER	L	W	T
E.79.1336	61	5	5
E.79.1752	33	5	4
E.79.1942	81	8	8
E.79.2649	43	5	4
E.79.3098	23	5	4

Five additional fragments were considered possible pins or pin fragments, mostly on intuitive grounds; they tended to be thinner and more pointed than the nails and needles. Due to preservation, little else can be said about them. Their dimensions are shown in Table 7-10.

Tools

While some of the above artifacts might also be considered tools (such as the blades), this category includes three possible chisels and two spikes. Only one (E.79.289) was found in an archaeological context (the occupation layer); the others were surface finds, and given their rather generic shape it is possible that (some of) these are modern.

E.79.289 Thick (10 mm), short (35 mm long) fragment of iron, shaped like a chisel (Figure 7-8).

E.79.359 Thick (9 mm) iron object, very corroded (many fragments are broken off). It has a blunted point at one end like a chisel and is possibly broken at the other end. Its outline is irregular but it is roughly rectangular in section, and is 85 mm in length.

E.79.3438 Iron object shaped like a chisel. It is square at one end and becomes thin at opposite end. It is accompanied by 20+ fragments; the largest fragment is 65 mm long and 10-11 mm thick.

E.79.1417 Fragment of an iron spike, with 15+ fragments that appear to be part of it. It is heavy, and narrows from one end to the other. The longest piece is 72 mm long, 20 mm wide, and 14 mm thick.

E.79.2891 Fragment of iron spike, square in section (13-14 mm), narrowing to blunt point at one end. The opposite end appears to be broken. The piece is 93 mm long, and has also numerous fragments and crumbs which apparently belong to it.

E.79.1323 Ten fragments of iron, plus crumbs; most are flat, and one appears pointed. A drawing (Figure 7-8) shows this was originally a single piece, curved and flat with a blunt point. It may have been sickle blade.

Iron tools are relatively uncommon from this period in Ireland, particularly compared to objects arguably ritually deposited (B. Raftery 1994:149); the reasons for this lack remain obscure. In addition, they are, as Scott (1990:2) describes them, "typologically non-descript." Detailed descriptions of them in the literature are equally sparse, exceptions being the chisels noted from Feerwore, Co. Galway (J. Raftery 1944, fig. 4) and from Meare Lake Village (St. George Gray and Bulleid 1953:239 and pl. LI). As with the nails (and assuming they are Iron Age), the examples from Dún Ailinne may have been associated with the construction of the various timber structures or with any number of other subsequent activities, including the low-level manufacturing noted elsewhere.

Miscellaneous Objects

The remaining iron objects are a group of variously shaped pieces (about 37 altogether) whose original form and/or function is unclear. About half of these objects, shown in Table 7-11, (those in the top section on each side) were found in reasonable archaeological contexts. While little can be said about the artifacts in disturbed contexts, those in more secure contexts represent a variety of aspects of Iron Age material culture. Unfortunately, their preservation and/or generic shapes prohibit any more detailed discussion of those aspects.

Table 7-11. Unidentified Iron Artifacts by Feature Type and by Phase.

FEATURE	N	PHASE	N
Hut	1	Dun	3
Mound	9	Flame	6
Occupation	2	Mauve	5
Pit	1	Upper Emerald	3
Trench	5	White	2
Baulk	1	Uncertain	3
Surface	10	Unknown	15
Uncertain	8	TOTAL	37
TOTAL	37		

Table 7-12. Dimensions (mm), Iron Rings.

N=10	Ext. Diam.	Height
Mean	31.4	5.3
Median	31.5	4.5
Mode	41.0	3.0
Range	15-46	3-10

The largest category in this group is complete or partial rings (Figure 7-6 shows two of these). There are 16-18 of these (excluding the finger ring already noted), depending on how these are counted. Of these, ten are essentially complete, that is, they are now complete or nearly so, or were when found, or could be reconstructed. Five others are fragmentary; one of these (E.79.1088) may be from 2 to 3 different rings (and was counted as such). The final example, E.79.338, disintegrated during processing, and there appears to be no surviving description of it.

It was possible to take external diameters and heights on the ten complete or nearly complete examples. Table 7-12 shows the summary statistics for these. As can be seen, these are relatively small, none being more than 5 cm wide or a centimeter thick. The functions of these rings are unknown, but they are presumably various fittings or component pieces, possibly for personal dress, harnesses, or for more utilitarian purposes.

Of the remaining iron objects, nine are generic shapes of uncertain original form and ten were categorized as uncertain (a selection is shown in Figures 7-9 and 7-10). The first nine are a disk, a fit-

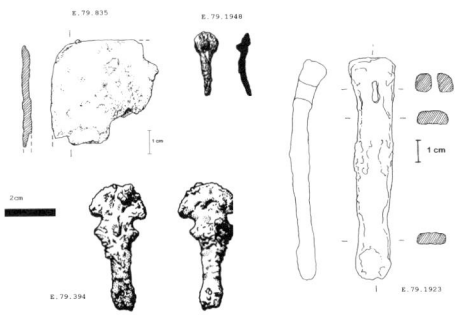

Figure 7-9. Uncertain iron objects from Dún Ailinne.

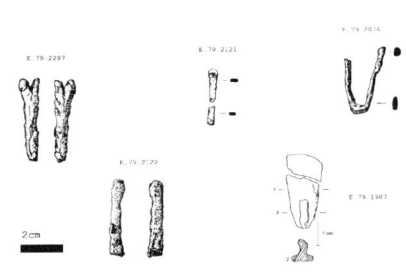

Figure 7-10. Uncertain iron objects from Dún Ailinne.

ting, three possible hooks and four strips:

E.79.2329. Iron disk, slightly concave on one surface and rounded on the opposite surface. It was originally broken in two pieces but now has been repaired. This may be a nail head. Its external diameter is 16 mm and it is 4 mm thick.

E.79.394. Iron object which appears to be a fitting of some kind (Figure 7-9). It is slightly curved; the shaft (ca. 32 mm L) is flattened and has a 1 mm perforation through it at the end. The piece expands to two lateral points at the other end of the shaft. Above this, the end is a flattened semi-circle reminiscent of the decorative end of a key. 57 mm long x 27 mm wide x 4 mm thick.

E.79.2074. Bent piece of iron, possibly a hook (Figure 7-10). A small depression at a flat place on the bend may indicate where something else was fastened. 52 mm long x 6 mm wide x 3 mm thick.

E.79.1016. Fragment of iron, somewhat square in section, and bent at about 1/4 of its length from the end. It looks like a hook, but both ends are broken so its original form is unknown. 39 mm long x 4 mm wide x 3 mm thick.

E.79.1089. Cylindrical fragment of iron, bent at about 1/3 of its length from the end. It looks like a hook, but both ends are broken so its original form is unknown. 69 mm long x 4 mm wide x 3 mm thick.

E.79.535. Iron strip, now broken in four pieces. At least three appear to join, and a drawing shows this was originally a single piece. 41 mm long x 11 mm wide x 7 mm thick.

E.79.2100. Thin, flat fragment of iron. Although generally irregular in outline, one end is slightly concave while the opposite end is rounded. 35 mm long x 26 mm wide x 1 mm thick.

E.79.2121. Flat piece of iron, now broken in five pieces (Figure 7-10). The largest is rounded at one end. 29 mm long x 8 mm wide x 3 mm thick.

E.79.2761. Flat strip of iron, plus numerous smaller pieces (8+ relatively large, plus crumbs) which appear to have come from it. Both ends have indentations that suggest they may have broken in the middle of oblong perforations. 95 mm long x 17 mm wide x 1 mm thick.

The ten uncertain pieces all have definite shapes, but a descriptive name is elusive:

E.79.160. Iron object, partially hollow. It is bent and shaped like horn or hook. 35 mm long x 10 mm wide x 8 mm thick.

E.79.835. Flat fragment of iron representing the rounded corner of a flat object (Figure 7-9). Along one part of the broken edge there is a raised "bubble." At this point, the interior is visible, showing that the object was partially hollow. It is uncertain if this was intentional or a result of corrosion. While the fragment is quite small, it is possible that it is a fragment of a chape with a squared end. The "bubble" would then be the space left for the blade. However, it is rather different in shape than other chape fragments reported in the literature (such as Glastonbury; Bulleid and St. George Gray 1917:389 and Pl. LXII). 47 mm long x 42 mm wide x 4 mm thick.

E.79.1723. 40+ fragments of iron, plus crumbs. The finds register describes this as a "socketed axe head." Now, however, it is mostly irregular fragments, and there is no evidence of what the piece might have looked like when found. Several of the fragments are cylindrical and twisted, but do not appear wide enough (at 1–2 cm internal diam.) to have been the socket for an axe. 44 mm long x 23 mm wide x 16 mm thick

E.79.1923. 40+ fragments of an iron object (Figure 7-9). The drawing shows this was originally a single piece, about 10 cm long x 2 cm wide x 1 cm thick. It had an oval perforation (about 1 cm max. diameter), and the end with the perforation was curved. The opposite end was rounded. Now, there is one large and heavy fragment representing the end of the piece with the perforation. The rest of the fragments are much smaller and are also flat.

E.79.1948. A piece of an iron object composed of a curved shaft, ca. 17 mm long, which ends in a round, flat disk (Figure 7-9). The latter has a small, round boss or projection on one side. The piece rather resembles the expanded terminal of an armlet, but much smaller. It is unclear if (or how) this goes with the other object with this number. 31 mm long x 12 mm wide x 4 mm thick.

E.79.1948. Flat, narrow fragment of iron, broken in two pieces. It is rounded on both ends and curved. It was originally in a separate bag, and it is unclear if (or how) it goes with the other object with this number. 28 mm long x 9 mm wide x 4 mm thick.

E.79.1987. Flat, triangular piece of iron with a small projection at one end (Figure 7-10). The projection is slightly curved toward the side of the piece at one end; the wider end of the piece has been repaired. 32 mm long x 15 mm wide x 5 mm thick.

E.79.2122. Fragment of iron object (Figure 7-10). It is long and narrow, rounded but flattened. One end is also rounded, and appears split into two, possibly intentionally. The other end is broken and the ends appear almost folded. It may be a shaft, but its shape is unusual. 41 mm long x 9 mm wide x 5 mm thick.

E.79.2297. Short, thick iron object, irregular in outline (Figure 7-10). It is blunted and oblique at one end and bifurcated at other end. 44 mm long x 10 mm wide x 9 mm thick.

E.79.2748. Flat iron fragment with both ends broken and bent in the same direction, perpendicular to remainder of piece. 27 mm long x 7 mm wide x 2 mm thick.

Little else can be said about these various objects except that they represent a small fraction of what was undoubtedly a large and complex iron material culture at Dún Ailinne.

8
Non-Ferrous Metals

Copper Alloy

Susan A. Johnston

Dún Ailinne produced 55 whole and fragmentary objects of copper alloy. Metallographic analysis of 11 of these artifacts (reported in Chapter 12) has shown that at least these 11 are bronze, and so it is likely that all or most of the remaining objects are too. Since they have not been analyzed, however, "copper alloy" is being used here to err on the side of caution.

The largest single category was comprised of unidentified fragments, but of the identifiable objects (38), most (30) were personal items (Table 8-1). Rings were predominant, but there were also 2 fibulae, a bracelet fragment, and a number of pin fragments (shafts and heads). The remainder seem to be more economic in nature, including a tracer, casting debris, possible ingots, and a possible weight. Table 8-1 shows the distribution of the various types, divided into personal and economic categories.

As with most artifacts at Dún Ailinne, copper alloy objects were found in a wide variety of contexts, many of them unstratified. Of the 55 objects, 16 (29%) were either in surface layers or in features of uncertain character; eight were from the occupation layers and nine were from the low mound. The remaining 39 (71%) were from various pits and trenches, most commonly from those associated with the construction activities of Rose and Mauve phases at the site. Table 8-2 shows the distribution of those objects with reasonably certain contexts, while Table 8-3 shows how the copper alloy artifacts are distributed according to phase.

A total of 29 objects could be assigned with some certainty to a phase (Table 8-3). Of these, the largest group (11 or 38%) came from Flame phase features. Mauve and Rose phases were each represented by five objects, Upper and Lower Emerald with three each, and Harry with two. This pattern makes sense in terms of the interpretation of the Flame phase as one of periodic feasting (see Chapter 13); since most of the copper alloy objects are objects of personal dress, they may have been lost during such occasions. In particular, some of them, such as fibulae, rings, and bracelets, may be those objects typical of more formal occasions, when people might have chosen to wear more elaborate or expensive items. The overall number of objects that are both identifiable and have secure contexts (21) is not sufficient to assess this with any certainty, particularly since most of the economic objects were unstratified or in uncertain contexts (Table 8-4). But it is perhaps noteworthy that, of the three probable economic objects with secure proveniences, only one came from a Flame phase feature. The other two are from Harry and Upper Emerald. The remaining personal objects (18) came from a total of six phases, with the largest group from the Flame phase.

This suggestion would also apply to those objects recovered from Rose and Mauve phases, since it is likely that these phases were also characterized by group participation in ritual and other activity. In fact, it is the economic objects, suggestive of small scale manufacturing, that are somewhat out of place. This issue is explored in detail in Chapter 18, but idea that Dún Ailinne was a place for ceremony (particularly in the Mauve and Rose phases) may imply the

Table 8-1. Distribution, Types of Copper Alloy Artifacts.

PERSONAL	N	ECONOMIC	N	UNKNOWN	N
bracelet	1	casting debris?	2	fragment	14
fastener	1	casting jet	2	strip	3
fibula	2	ingot?	2		
pinhead	3	tracer	1		
pinhead?	2	weight?	1		
ring	12				
ring fragment	1				
ring?	2				
shaft	4				
wire	2				

Table 8-2. Copper Alloy Objects by Feature Type.

FEATURE TYPE	N
Mound	9
Occupation	8
Pit	12
Plank	2
Post-hole	1
Trench	7
TOTAL	39

Table 8-3. Copper Alloy Artifacts by Phase.

PHASE	N
Flame	11
Harry	2
Lower Emerald	3
Mauve	5
Rose	5
Upper Emerald	3
TOTAL	29

presence of people in attendance, perhaps wearing their most elaborate clothing and ornaments. That would account for the preponderance of personal ornaments among the copper alloy objects.

By way of general parallel, some 31 whole and fragmentary objects of bronze are reported from the royal site at Navan Fort (Waterman 1997:83–85). While 19 of them appear to be uncertain fragments of sheet bronze, wire, and other uncertain forms, the remaining 12 can be roughly assigned to the same categories as above, personal versus economic. Only one object, a sickle blade, is clearly economic in nature; two others, a projectile head and a socketed axe, are ambiguous, having a broadly economic function but also possibly being items of personal adornment. The remaining objects, including pins and pin fragments, bar toggles, and a chape fragment, are items which could be expected to be worn by individuals at the site. In this way, Navan mirrors Dún Ailinne, suggesting the same image of well-dressed people attending ceremonies and/or other activities there.

Report On Copper Alloy Objects

G.C. Fisher (with contributions from S. A. Johnston)

The following report was prepared by Fisher in November of 1984 (it also included the gold strip; see below). Obviously there have been many discoveries of copper alloy artifacts since then, and so there are more recent parallels that could be cited. However, the basic conclusions for most of the categories described remain essentially the same; spiral rings still are too generic in form for dating purposes, and the unidentifiable objects are still unidentifiable. That said, the eye of a specialist in this material provides sufficient detail to make the occasional anachronisms a reasonable price for the descriptive material. Updated comments on Nauheim brooches have been added (obvious where the references are more recent than 1984) and any tables and figures showing counts, measurements, or distributions are also recent additions.

Brooches

E.79.743. Tapered bow brooch (Figure 8-1; Plates 8-1, 8-2). The fragmentary brooch is missing its axis bar, pin, and portions of its head and catchplate. The long, flat bow is tapered and twisted to form the narrow foot and triangular catchplate. The head is rolled upwards to house the pin attachment. The bow is decorated along its length with an incised herringbone design which changes, at the foot, to a series of transverse lines. The bow is 56 mm in length, 8 mm in width, and 1 mm thick. The brooch was recovered from a lens or layer of sediment above a layer of stones, which was assigned to Flame.

Irish parallels to this Dún Ailinne brooch are not easily identified due to its fragmentary condition. The tapered bow recalls the form of other "Nauheim" and derivative brooches (Hawkes 1981:65), and, despite its condition, it may be considered part of this class. It is similar to the brooch from Loughey, Co. Down (Jope and Wilson 1957), but not enough survives of the Dún Ailinne example to provide an exact parallel. The same can be said for the isolated brooch from Derrybeg, Co. Sligo (J. Raftery 1973:204), to which the Dún Ailinne brooch also bears a distinct resemblance. At Colchester, Essex, brooches like the Dún Ailinne example, classified as Camulodunum type VII (Hawkes and Hull 1947:312-13), were datable to the third quarter of the 1st century AD. Hawkes (personal communication) draws attention to a similar Roman-German brooch, typed as Camulodunum VIA, in which a taper is created by a simple twist of the strip bow; a single example of this group was found in Colchester in a ditch filled at the time of the conquest (Hawkes and Hull 1947:312, pl. xcii, 52). Tapered bow brooches have been found at several Wessex sites (Hawkes,

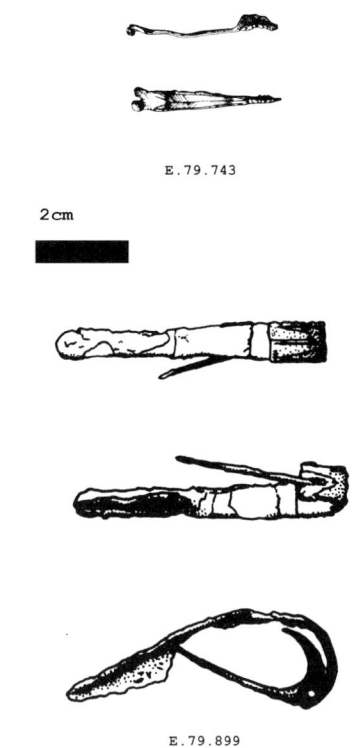

Figure 8-1. Copper alloy fibulae E.79.743 and E.79.899.

personal communication), including both hillforts with Roman occupation such as Hod Hill, Dorset (Brailsford 1962:8, fig. 7, C33-39), Ham Hill, Somerset (cited by Brailsford 1962:8), and Maiden Castle, Dorset (Wheeler 1943:261, fig. 84, 17-22), and native settlements such as Gussage All Saints, Dorset (Wainwright 1979:111-13, fig. 86, 3016, 3061).

More recently, in his discussion of brooches from Britain, Haselgrove (1997) places Nauheim brooches in the 1st century BC They form a significant proportion of brooches in some periods of the British Iron Age and are particularly noted at the wetland sites of Meare and Glastonbury in Somerset; the derivative form was associated with largely non-military sites in central and southern England (1997:59-65). Indeed, Britain is a likely source for at least some of the brooches, though of course the Continent probably played a part as well. Whatever the source, however, it is worth noting that there is no reason to assume that the individual who brought/wore the brooch to Dún Ailinne was Roman (see Warner 1991:50). Lacking any other concrete evidence of a Roman presence there, it seems far more parsimonious to suggest that the brooch itself rather than the

Table 8-4. *Types of Artifacts by Phase.*

ECONOMIC PHASE	N	PERSONAL PHASE	N
Flame	1	Flame	6
Harry	1	Harry	1
Upper Emerald	1	Lower Emerald	3
		Mauve	3
		Rose	4
		Upper Emerald	1

whole person was imported to the site.

Nauheim brooches are generally considered to be artifacts worn by women on Continental sites since they are often found in female graves (Collis 1984:53, 60). In Ireland, the situation is somewhat less clear. There are several Nauheim derivative brooches known from Ireland, including one from Derrybeg, Co. Sligo (J. Raftery 1973:204; B. Raftery 1984:147, 151-52) and a possible fragment from Castleskreen, Co. Down (B. Raftery 1984:147; Jope 1961-62). Two others were more definitively associated with burials, but in both cases the occupant's sex is uncertain. For the first, from Loughey, Co. Down (Jope and Wilson 1957), the cremated individual was not preserved when the burial was found, though it is commonly considered to be female apparently on the basis of the large number of beads (a problematic assumption at best). It is uncertain if the cremation from Ballydavis, Co. Laois (Keeley 1999), is amenable to sex identification, but if so it remains to be published (though the excavator did note that the burial was likely to be female on the basis of the brooch).

While the assumption that Nauheim derivative brooches in Ireland are associated with women thus seems far from certain, the continental associations may suggest the possibility. This in turn might provide tentative evidence of a female presence at Dún Ailinne. Given the brooch's recovery from a Flame phase layer, it perhaps points to the inclusion of women in the associated feasting activity.

E.79.899. Strip bow brooch (Figure 8-1; Plates 8-1, 8-2), a fragmentary brooch missing portions of bow, foot, and catchplate. Overall, the brooch is 97 mm long, 10 mm wide, and 1 mm thick. The flat, arched bow widens slightly to form a spatulate foot and, at the other end, is rolled downwards to house the axis bar of the hinged pin. The bow is decorated longitudinally along each edge with a raised border; at the head, two incised median lines converge with two incised diagonal lines. The attachment area for the hinge was broken and repaired in antiquity with a gray-colored solder, probably silver alloy. Hawkes (personal communication) suggests that at the time of damage the original pin may have been lost and a replacement pin, now part of the brooch, was substituted. The new pin, with its extremely long spur, would have transferred pressure away from the damaged area of the head to the undamaged area further up the bow, thus reducing the risk of future injury.

A copper alloy strip, extending at least 2.3 cm toward the brooch's foot, was attached to the underside of the bow at the spur's point of contact. Although both brooch and foot are now transversely broken below the two gray metal nails which secure the head end of the strip to the bow, the absence of a complementary means of attachment at the foot end indicates that the purpose of the strip was to reinforce rather than repair the bow.

The exact find spot of this brooch was not recorded in the finds register. However, based on the grid reference, it can be reconstructed as probably coming from feature 801. This is a trench assigned to the Harry phase, characterized predominantly by post-holes and stake-holes contemporary with the Mauve phase timber structures (see Chapter 2). Since this association for the fibula was reconstructed it remains uncertain, but if correct, it suggests a context somewhat different from the Flame phase context of E.79.743. Rather than the feasting implied by the latter, the Mauve phase structure implies (perhaps) a more formal ritual context for the introduction of E.79.899 to Dún Ailinne. Whether, in this context, it was lost, discarded, or deliberately deposited is unknown.

While the owner of E.79.899 cannot be identified any further, there is an exotic element implied in the character of the piece since it cannot be easily paralleled in Ireland. Hawkes (personal communication) assigns this piece to a group of early strip-bow brooches, classified as Camulodunum type VIB (Hawkes and Hull 1947:312, pl. xcii, 53-54). Like the "dolphin" brooches of Camulodunum type V (Hawkes and Hull 1947:311-12, pls. xci-xcii, 44-51), the bow of the Dún Ailinne brooch is humped above the hinge. This treatment was also given to Nauheim derivative brooches, as is evidenced by a hinged example also from Colchester (Hawkes and Hull 1947:313, pl. xcii, 61). The Dún Ailinne brooch combines the humped hinged attachment area with a parallel-sided strip bow.

Hinged strip bow brooches are frequently encountered in Wessex sites; Hawkes (personal communication) notes examples from Hod Hill, Dorset (Brailsford 1962:8, fig. 7, C34, C36-37, C39), Maiden Castle, Dorset (Wheeler 1943:261-62, fig. 84, 19, 22, 26, fig. 85, 35), and Gussage All Saints, Dorset (Wainwright 1979:111-12, fig. 86, 3026, 3058), contemporaneous with those from Colchester. As with the potential Roman character, however, while some type of contact is clearly indicated, these parallels need not imply the presence of people from these areas.

Bracelet

E.79.257. Approximately one quarter of a solid cast bracelet, total length 50 mm, 6 mm high and 4 mm thick (Figure 8-2; Plate 8-3). The bracelet is flattened on the inside surface; the rounded outside surface is decorated with narrow, regularly spaced transverse ribs. Projecting the circumference suggests a diameter of between 4.5 and 5 cm.

This bracelet has no exact Irish parallels. Two copper alloy bracelets decorated with alternating wide and narrow transverse ribs are said to have been found near Antrim; however, one of the pair is now lost and the provenience of the extant singleton is not firmly established.

Stead, citing British examples from Crosby Garrett, Cumbria (Greenwell 1877:386–87; Challis and Harding 1975:177, fig. 8, 14), Hengistbury Head, Hants. (Bushe-Fox 1915:pl. xxx, 15), and Arras, Yorks. (Stead 1979:75, fig. 28, 2–3) notes that bracelets with transverse ribbing are "not common in Britain" (1979:77). The ribbed decoration of the Crosby Garrett and Hengistbury Head bracelets is incised rather than cast and, although the former is rather worn (Challis and Harding 1975:4), the modeling of both bracelets shows minimal similarity to the high relief of the Dún Ailinne bracelet. In addition to the Arras bracelet, a closer insular parallel for the raised cast ribbing may be found on an example recovered from quarry debris at the site of Sutton Walls, Herefords. (Kenyon 1953:fig. 25, 3), which was occupied between the mid-1st century BC and the 4th century AD

On the Continent, these bracelets appear in numerous La Tène contexts. Hawkes (personal communication) notes a La Tène I/II example from Caranda, France (Déchelette 1914:1220, fig. 517, 5) and Stead (1979:77), drawing attention to their distribution from Burgundy to Czechoslovakia, points to parallels from the grave assemblages at Hallstatt, Austria. Several bracelets from Hallstatt are decorated with narrow, regularly spaced ribs (Kromer 1959:pl. 9, 26, pl. 13, 7, pl. 45, 6, pl. 71, 2, pl., 73, 9) that strongly recall the modeling of the Dún Ailinne example.

Pins and Studs

E.79.1763. Domed stud or pin head with rectangular shank scar on center of base (Figure 8-2).

E.79.2339. Pin shaft of square section. One end is broken; the other end is slightly bent and tapers to a point (Figure 8-2).

E.79.2695. Pin shaft of irregularly circular section. One end is broken, leaving a nipple at the end; the other end is spatulate with a rectangular section (Figure 8-2).

E.79.2742. Irregular fragment, possible pinhead (Figure 8-2).

E.79.2844. Pin or stud with domed head and square-sectioned shank (Figure 8-2; see also Plate 8-6).

E.79.3718. Two fragments of a bent pin shaft or circular section (Figure 8-2).

Table 8-5 shows the measurements for the three pinheads and three pin shafts. As Hawkes (1982:51) notes, the dress pin has a long history in Ireland. The two fragments of E.79.3718, tentatively identified by Hawkes from a color slide as together forming a swan's neck pin, cannot in fact be so reconstructed. The less bent fragment, which probably represents the pin shaft, shows clear breaks at both ends. The crux of the problem lies with the

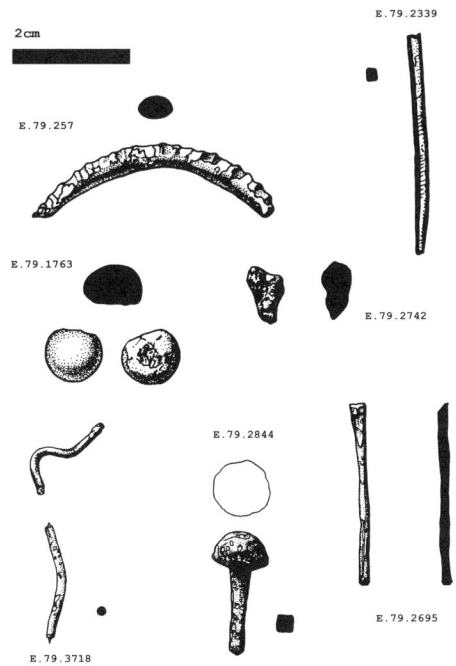

Figure 8-2. Copper alloy bracelet, pins, and studs.

crooked fragment; it is broken at the bent end but appears intact at the straight end. In order for this fragment to constitute the crook of a swan's neck pin, the straight end would have to show a break. That end could then join downwards with the pin shaft while the crooked end would wind upwards to form the remainder of the S-bend of the pin's head. However, unless the apparently intact end of the crooked piece is deceptive in its integrity, the Dún Ailinne fragments of E.79.3718 must represent some other form of pin. Consequently, this pin must join the remains of E.79.1763, E.79.2339, E.79.2695, and E.79.2844, whose fragmentary condition precludes any meaningful discussion.

Table 8-5. Dimensions (mm), Pinheads and Pin Shafts.

PINHEADS	L	W	T	PIN SHAFTS	L	W	T
E.79.1763	11	10	7	E.79.2339	39	3	3
E.79.2742	10	7	5	E.79.2695	32	3	2
E.79.2844	22	10	10	E.79.3718	21	2	2

Spiral Rings

E.79.514. Spiral ring of oval section, wound for two coils (Figure 8-3; Plate 8-4). Both ends are tapering and unbroken. Undecorated.

E.79.667. Ring of circular section with overlapping ends (Figure 8-3). Worn. One end is rounded, the other end is stepped.

E.79.902. Spiral ring of oval section, wound for two coils (Figure 8-3, Plate 8-4). Both ends are tapering and unbroken. Undecorated.

E.79.904. Spiral ring of sub-rectangular section, wound for one coil (Figure 8-3, Plate 8-4). Both ends are tapering and unbroken. Ring is decorated with three raised longitudinal lines, between each of which runs a punched zigzag design.

E.79.1466. Spiral ring of circular section,

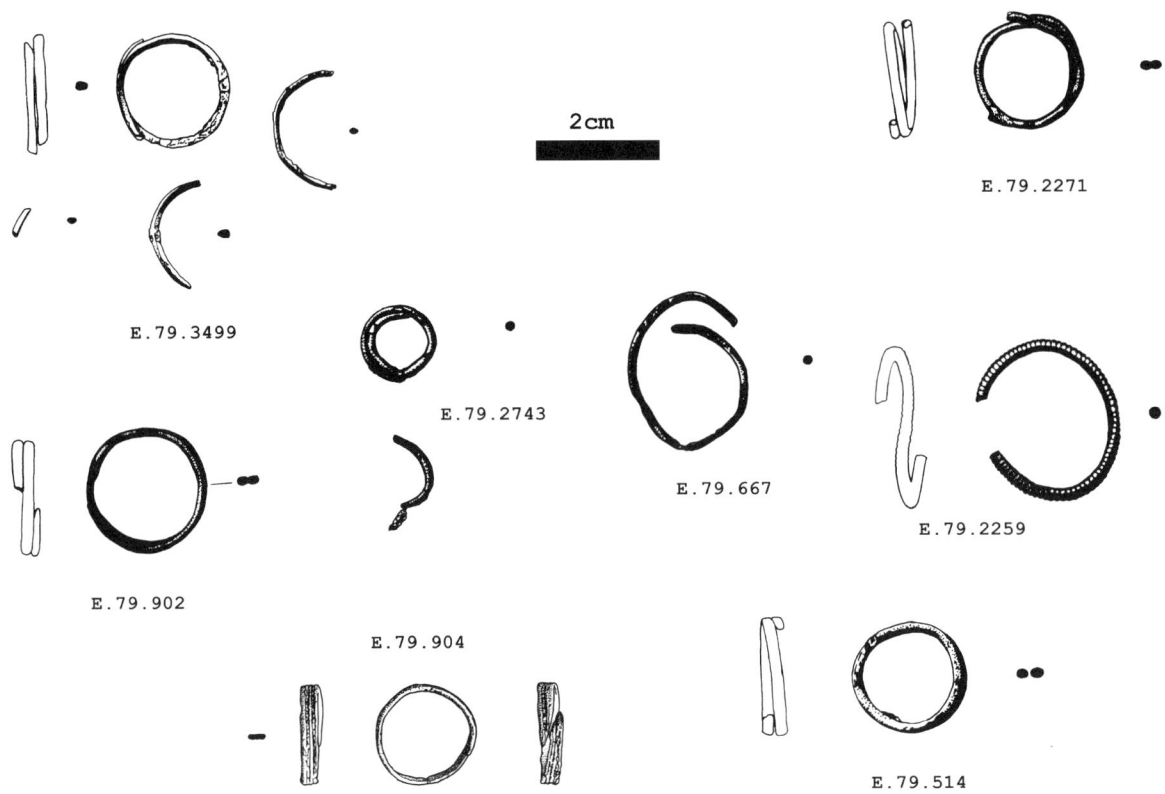

Figure 8-3. Copper alloy spiral rings from Dún Ailinne.

wound for 1-½ coils. Both ends are pointed. Undecorated.

E.79.2259. Fragmentary spiral (?) ring of circular section (Figure 8-3; see also Plate 8-3). One end is blunt, the other end is broken. Ring is decorated with transverse milling.

E.79.2271. Spiral ring of oval section, wound for 1-¾ coils (Figure 8-3, Plate 8-4). One end is broken, the other end intact and tapering. Undecorated.

E.79.2743. Fragmentary spiral ring of circular section, wound for at least two coils (Figure 8-3). One end is blunt, the other end tapers to a point. Undecorated.

E.79.3499. Fragmentary spiral ring of sub-rectangular section, wound for 2 ¼ coils (Figure 8-3). Both ends are unbroken and pointed. Undecorated.

Table 8-6 shows the descriptive statistics for the rings from Dún Ailinne. This includes both the nine spiral rings and the three other rings listed below. The spiral rings belong to an artifact type which, because of its uniformity over time and space, is of little chronological significance. As Jope and Wilson (1957:79) remark in their discussion of spiral rings from Iron Age contexts, they "are simple things used at different periods for different purposes."

Spiral rings have been found in a variety of contexts in Ireland. However, not all examples are informative parallels to the Dún Ailinne rings. The undated gold spiral rings in the collection of the National Museum of Ireland, Dublin (Wilde 1862:80-82, fig. 610; Armstrong 1920:97, nos. 453-54, pl. xiv, 233-34; J. Raftery 1951:fig. 235) show slight affinity in form or scale with the Dún Ailinne examples.

Warner (1976:288-89) dates the copper alloy spiral rings from Feerwore Rath, Co. Galway (J. Raftery 1944:33, 42, fig. 4, 26) and the passage grave of Loughcrew H, Co. Meath (Coffey 1897:29, fig. 1; Herity 1974:147, 235-37), to the early Iron Age. Like the Loughcrew H ring, Herity (1974:147) cites an example from Knowth, Co. Meath, as evidence of continued visits to passage graves by Iron Age people. The copper alloy wire ring of 1¼ coils found in the cairn at Loughash, Co. Tyrone (Davies 1939:266-67, fig. 3, 134), similarly, may be considered another example of this practice.

Copper alloy spiral rings of circular section have been found at Lisnacrogher, Co. Antrim (Wakeman 1883:398; Wood-Martin 1886:109; JRSAI 1890: pl.ii, 16), Clougher, Co. Tyrone (Warner 1976:288), and Loughey, Co. Down (*Arch Journ.* 13 (1856):407; Jope and Wilson 1957:79-81, fig. 1, 3, pl. v). Warner (1976:288) suggest that, like their associated material, the Loughey and Clougher rings may be imports of the 1st centuries BC to AD. A copper alloy spiral ring of plano-convex section and 1½ coils was found in the surface soil near an oval cashel on Feltrim Hill, Co. Dublin (Lucas 1967:12, fig. 7).

At Newgrange, Co. Meath, two silver spiral rings of three coils were found, the middle coil of each being decorated with transverse milling (Carson and O'Kelly 1977:46, pl. viii, a). Carson and O'Kelly's (1977:49) comparison of the decorated Newgrange rings with examples from native British and Romano-British sites such as Hod Hill, Dorset; Glastonbury, Somerset; Traprain Law, East Lothian; and Maiden Castle, Dorset, lends some support to Warner's (1976:289) earlier suggestion that the Newgrange rings are 3rd century AD imports. Closer parallels to the Newgrange rings, however, may be found among several Scottish examples. A copper alloy silver ring with similar transverse milling on its central coil was found at Dún an Fheurain, Argyll (Ritchie 1970-71:102, fig. 3). In assigning the Dún an Fheurain ring to the 1st to 2nd centuries AD, Ritchie cites a similarly milled ring dated to the 2nd century AD from the dun at Kildalloig, Kintyre (1970-71:102-3). A silver spiral ring with apparently identical decoration was tentatively dated to the first half of the 3rd century AD at the broch of Vaul, Inner Hebrides (MacKie 1974:50, 132-33, fig. 17, 237). However, as Clarke (1971:28) notes, this milled decoration is of limited chronological significance, as it also appears on silver rings from the Norrie's Law, Fife, hoard of late Roman and Pictish silver.

The Early Christian sites at Garranes, Co. Cork (Ó Ríordáin 1942:100, fig. 4, 176), and Site III, Dalkey Island, Co. Dublin (Liversage 1968:125, fig. 32, 533), produced copper alloy spiral rings of which Warner remarks, using his terminology, that they "are most unlikely to date differently from the other material from these sites—later Iron Age 1 and later [meaning the 5th century AD and later]" (1976:289). The possibility that the Garranes and

Table 8-6. Dimensions (mm), Copper Alloy Rings.

RINGS (N=12)	DIAM.	T
Mean	20.8	1.8
Median	20.5	2.0
Mode	19.0	2.0
Range	14-27	1-3

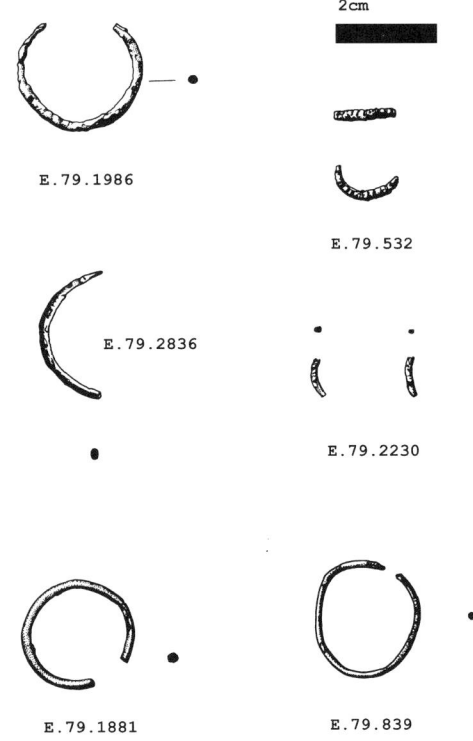

Figure 8-4. Copper alloy rings from Dún Ailinne.

Dalkey Island rings originally adorned pins or lachets, as was popular during the Early Christian period (Warner 1976:289), cannot be excluded.

Outside of Ireland, copper alloy spiral rings are well known in contexts ranging temporally from the middle of the Bronze Age to the Early Medieval period (Clarke 1971:261) and spatially from Northern Italy to Britain (Bulleid and Gray 1911:209; Gray and Bulleid 1953). The artifact type's ubiquity in the archaeological record and, paradoxically, its absence from any firmly datable Irish context prevents the Dún Ailinne spiral rings from being closely dated on the basis of their form alone. The meager Irish evidence suggests that, lacking any evidence to the contrary, the Dún Ailinne rings may tentatively be assigned to the first centuries BC to AD.

Rings

E.79.839. Penannular ring of circular section (Figure 8-4). Worn. Both ends are pointed. Band is decorated with a faint incised zigzag line for approximately one-half of its length.

E.79.1881. Penannular band of circular section with blunt ends (Figure 8-4). Undecorated.

E.79.1986. Penannular band of circular section with tapering ends (Figure 8-4). Undecorated. Worn.

The wasting and erosion of one area of the circumference of ring E.79.1986 may have resulted from it suspension from another object. A penannular wire ring exhibiting this characteristic wear pattern was recovered from the Rath of Feerwore (J. Raftery 1944:33, fig. 4, 29).

E.79.532. Fragmentary ring or earring of plano-convex section (Figure 8-4). One end tapers, and both ends are broken. Ring is decorated on rounded surface with an incised herringbone design.

E.79.2230. Two fragments representing approximately one-quarter of a ring of circular section (Figure 8-4). Undecorated.

E.79.2836. Fragment representing approximately one-half of a ring of circular section (Figure 8-4). One end is broken, the other end tapers to a point. Undecorated.

Tracer

E.79.1061. Tracer of square mid-section (Figure 8-5; Plate 8-5). One end is rounded with an oval section, the other end is tapering with a circular section. It is 31 mm long, and 4 mm in both width and thickness.

Metalworking tools similar to this tracer were used by Irish smiths from the later Bronze Age; an example is among the contents of the hoard from Bishopsland, Co. Kildare (Ó Ríordáin 1946:161, pl. xiii, 14; Eogan 1964:340, fig. 5, 9; Herity and Eogan 1977:fig. 68, 9). A similarly shaped tool was found in an unspecified context at Site V, Dalkey Island, Co. Dublin (Liversage 1968:91-92, fig. 18, 2495). As with the Dún Ailinne example, both ends of the Dalkey Island tool were modified. Without finding the tool's tang wedged into its handle, the identification of the working edge can be difficult. Liversage, arguing that the flattening of the mounted end of the Dalkey Island tool is logical only if the working end has a tendency to twist, a weakness to which an awl is not prone, and noting that this flattened end carries a nick which may have resulted from use, suggests that the flattened end of the tool was used as a tracer. Harbison (1967:97), in contrast, has characterized several Early Bronze Age copper alloy

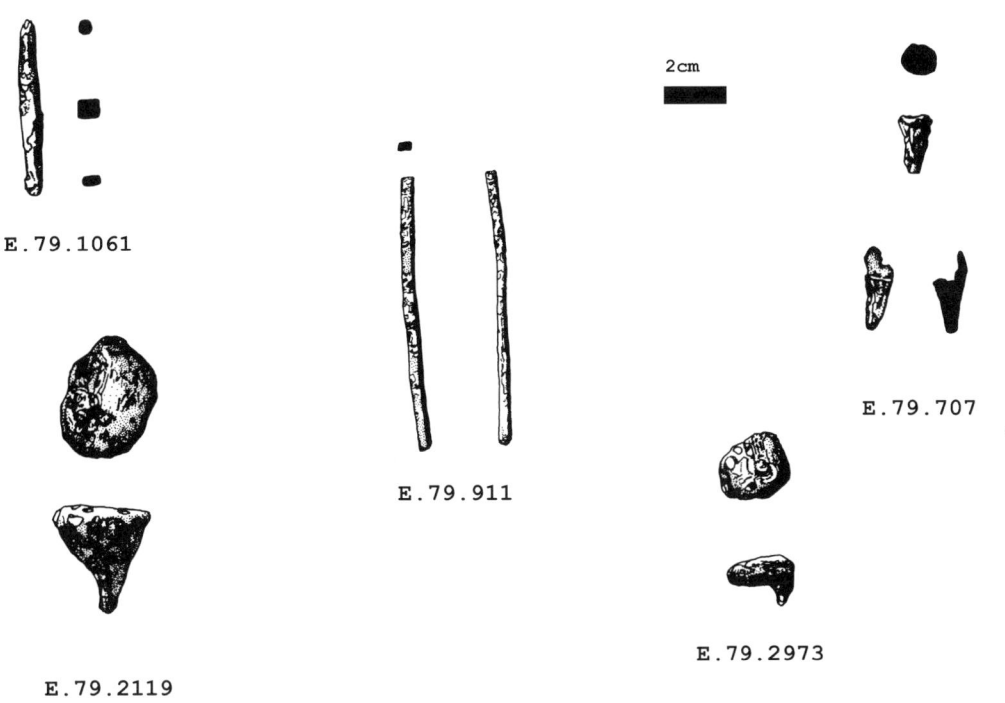

Figure 8-5. Copper alloy tracer, ingots, and casting jets.

tools of square mid-section which are flat at one end and pointed at the other as members of his Carigillihy type of awl. While, in view of their well-defined ends, it is difficult to take issue with Harbison's assessment of the tools from the type site in Co. Cork (O'Kelly 1951:81, fig. 9, 1) and at Site C, Lough Gur, Co, Limerick (Ó Ríordáin 1954a:382–83, fig. 31, 2–3), the function of the fragmentary tool from the Stone Circle at Lough Gur, which is represented only by a portion of its square-sectioned mid-shaft (Ó Ríordáin 1951:48, fig. 2, 3) is more difficult to assess.

Elsewhere in the British Isles, tracers have been found in equally early contexts, such as the later Bronze Age hoards from Glentrool, Kirkudbrightshire (Callendar 1920–21:31, fig. 1, 5), and Heathery Burn, Co. Durham (Evans 1881:166, fig. 191). Finds of similar tracers at Traprain Law, East Lothian (Curle 1919–20:71, fig. 8, 12) demonstrates the tool's limited use as a chronological indicator.

Tracers are used to produce relief or repoussé designs by bossing the surface of a metal sheet. The round-sectioned end of the Dún Ailinne tracer would have originally been mounted in a bone or wooden handle. The tool would have been held in one hand and the oval-sectioned working edge moved along the surface of the metal sheet as the tool's handle was tapped with a hammer held in the other hand (Maryon 1955:119–20). Rather than cutting or engraving the metal, these tools push the metal aside. For this reason, the working edge of the tool need not be sharp, nor need the tool be as hard as one which can cut metal (Lowery et al. 1971:174). Copper alloy tracers can be used to work copper alloy sheet although, as Lowery et al. (1971:170) note, experiments demonstrated a need for frequent resharpening of the tool's working edge.

Bars (Ingots?)

E.79.416. Bar (ingot?) of sub-rectangular section at one end and square section at the other end (Plate 8-5). It is 44 mm long, 6 mm wide, and 4 mm thick.

E.79.911. Bar (ingot?) of square section with slightly tapered ends (Figure 8-5, Plate 8-5). This one is more than twice as long (95 mm), though similar in width (5 mm) and thickness (4 mm).

Copper alloy bar ingots and blanks are occasionally encountered on Iron Age and Early Christian sites in Ireland. From Lambay Island, Co. Dublin, comes a small bar ingot (J. Raftery 1951:fig. 244). Another rod-shaped copper alloy ingot was among the contents of the Early Iron Age hoard found in Somerset townland, Co. Galway (J. Raftery 1960:4, frontispiece, 164). Ó Ríordáin (1948:71, fig. 9, 193) records a copper alloy rod from Carraig Aille II, Co. Limerick, which he suggests may be a blank. The discovery at Carraig Aille II of three complete clay crucibles—two of which were stained green, presumably from copper oxide residues—as well as almost 50 crucible fragments (Ó Ríordáin 1948:91–92) indicates the activities of a bronzesmith.

The metalworking site at Garranes, Co. Cork, likewise produced 12 copper alloy strips ranging in cross section from flat to rectangular to round. Moreover, Ó Ríordáin records from the site several fragments of sheet bronze and an unspecified number of "formless lumps of bronze which are obviously waste from casting processes, or rough pieces not yet cast into ingots when lost" (1942:100). Stone molds found at Garranes support Ó Ríordáin's contention that ingot casting was done there; indeed, a fragmentary copper alloy ingot found during excavation fit into the hollow of one of the molds (Ó Ríordáin 1942:108).

Casting Jets and Debris

E.79.2119. Funnel-shaped casting jet with head of roughly elliptical outline and single obliquely positioned runner (Figure 8-5; Plate 8-5). It is 23 mm long, 17 mm wide, and 19 mm thick.

E.79.2973. Funnel-shaped casting jet with flattened head of roughly pentagonal outline and single obliquely positioned runner (Figure 8-5). This one is smaller, at 9 mm long, 12 mm wide, and 11 mm thick.

E.79.707. Two cone-shaped fragments (casting debris?), each with a depression on the top surface (Figure 8-5). The side of one fragment rises to form a hooklike appendage. The copper alloy has oxidized to a slightly whitish metal. The larger of the two is 15 mm long, 6 mm wide, and 5 mm thick.

Casting jets, the metal residue left at the mouth of a mold after the molten metal has been poured, cannot be closely dated. In Ireland, an example with a single runner was found among the metalworking debris at Garranes, Co. Cork (Ó Ríordáin 1942:100, fig. 4, 279). Casting jets with single runners have been recorded in Britain among the contents of the Late Bronze Age hoard from Felixstowe, Suffolk (*Inventaria Archaeologica* 1956:16, 2(2), 12) and Stourmouth, Kent (Coombs and Bradshaw 1979:187, fig. 10.1, 20), the pre-Roman pits at Castle Hill, Scarborough, Yorks. (Smith 1927:180, fig. 2; Wheeler 1931:22, fig. 16, 1), and the 4th century AD deposits at the Romano-British villa at Shakenoak Farm, Oxon. (Brodrib et al. 1971:114, fig. 50, 120).

It is interesting to note with regard to these that some evidence of smithing, and possibly smelting, was provided by slag recovered from Dún Ailinne (see Chapter 12). Taken together with these casting jets, this suggests that some low level manufacturing was being carried out at the site.

Fastener

E.79.72. Fastener in the form of a ring with bent shank ending in a stylized zoomorphic head (Figure 8-6; Plate 8-6). It is 21 mm long, 11 mm wide, and 5 mm thick.

The ring-and-hook form of this fastener indicates that the object must have functioned as a fastener. While no close parallels are readily forthcoming, the fastener shows a general affinity with the British Iron Age button-and-loop fasteners of Gillam's type A (1958:79–80) and Wild's Class I (1970:137–38, fig. 1, 1). Wild characterizes the members of his group by a solid double boss hook end attached to a heavy ring loop, although a variant form found at Glastonbury, Somerset (Bulleid and Gray 1911:219, pl. xlii, E151), terminates in a single heavy boss. These fasteners were manufactured, most likely by native Britons, during the pre-Roman period and at the beginning of the Roman occupation (Wild 1970:138).

The function of these button-and-loop fasteners is by no means decided. While general agreement has been reached that the objects served to connect two pieces of fabric, leather, or textile, a narrower delineation of their role is not yet possible. Proposed uses for the button-and-loop fasteners include dress fasteners, harness fittings, girth strap fasteners, and shield fittings (Wild 1970:145–46).

Wild notes the formal similarity between these fasteners and the so-called ring belt-hooks (*Ringgürtelhaken*) from the Continent discussed by Werner (1961). In Britain, examples of these fasteners, which are almost twice the size of their insular Wild Class I cousins, have been found in pre-Flavian contexts at Hod Hill, Dorset (Brailsford 1962:17, pl. ix, I97) and Waddon Hill, Dorset (Web-

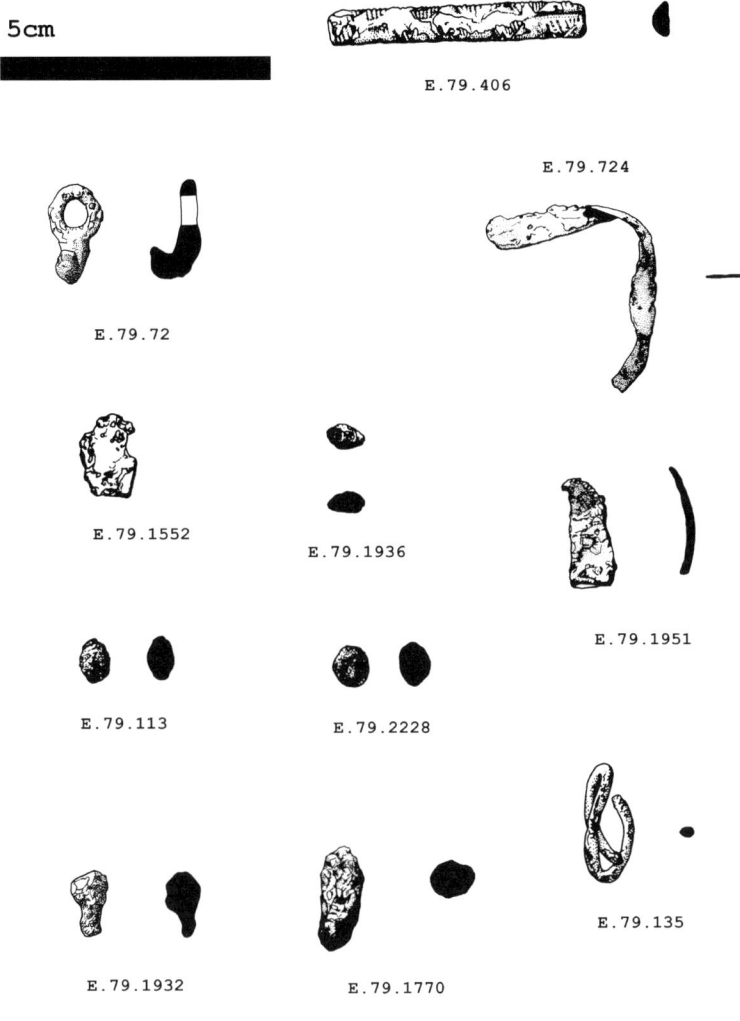

Figure 8-6. Selection of copper alloy objects from Dún Ailinne.

ster 1965:145, fig. 6, 11), as well as in the La Tène III "warrior" burials at Owslebury, Hants. (Collis 1968:25-26, pl. ix, 6; 1973:126-27, fig. 4, 5), Whitcombe, Dorset (Collis 1973:125-26), and North Grimston, Yorks. (Mortimer 1905:354-55, fig. 1019). A *terminus post quem* in at least the mid-1st century BC for these insular "belt-hooks" (Collis 1973:130) is supported by another example found at Hengistbury Head, Hants., in association with Roman coins issued ca. 91 BC (Bushe-Fox 1915:25, 61, pl. xxix, 8). The position of the sword and belt-hook in the graves at Owslebury and Whitcombe, where accurate plans were made, indicates that the weapon was suspended from a baldric slung diagonally between shoulder and hip (Collis 1973:130). In contrast, on the Continent, the sword belt was apparently worn around the abdomen (Werner 1961:145).

Hengistbury Head also produced a copper alloy fastener with a bent shank hook (Bushe-Fox 1915:61, pl. xxix, 7) which, although not completely satisfactory, most closely parallels the Dún Ailinne example. Fasteners of this type, commonly of iron and generally measuring twice the size of the Dún Ailinne piece, are well known in Continental late La Tène contexts (Werner 1961:149). Examples from male cremation burials at Grossromstedt, Germany (Eichhorn 1927:213-14, 1908E, 1911, 131), Rzadz, Poland (Anger 1890:47, taf. 15, 3; Kostrzewski 1919:62, abb. 48), and Bretzenheim, Germany (*Mainzer Zeitschrift* 23 (1928):72, abb. 5); from a male inhumation at Ornavasso (S. Bernado), Italy (Graue 1974:58, 201, 215, taf. 12, 4); and from the oppida at Staré Hradisko, Czech Republic (Meduna 1970:abb. 7, 4-5), and Bad Nauheim, Germany (Quilling 1903:53, taf. xvi, 1330) terminate with a semispherical projecting knob. Other members of this group recorded at the cremation cemetery at Hornbeck, Germany (Rangs-Borchling 1963:97, 106, 120, 126, taf. 17, 133, 134, taf. 31, 260, taf. 42, 366, taf. 50, 468, taf. 57, 556), and again at Stradonice, Czech Republic (Pič 1906:pl. xxxiii, 13, 18, 20, 31) end with a simple bend in the shank.

To summarize, both British and Continental parallels indicate a late La Tène date for this fastener. The recovery of the fastener at Dún Ailinne is of particular interest in view of Rynne's (1976:232-34, 243) suggestion of a discovery on Lambay Island, Co. Dublin, in 1927 of a late example of that group of British "warrior" burials which includes among its members the burials from North Grimston (mistakenly referred to as Grimthorpe by Rynne) and Whitcombe, discussed above.

Wire

E.79.134. Fragment representing approximately one-half of a wire ring of circular section. Worn. Undecorated, but found with a blue glass bead (also numbered E.79.134). The wire is mostly thin, but considerably thicker and elongated at one end. The thicker portion has a small piece of additional material (unknown type) wrapped around it. It is 15 mm in total length, and its maximum diameter is 2 mm. While the finds records are not specific about the physical relationship between the wire and the bead, a photo from 1968 shows the bead strung on the wire (see Plate 9-3).

E.79.135. Twisted wire (Figure 8-6; Plate 8-6). Both ends are blunt, one end is broken. Undecorated. It is 22 m long with a diameter of 2 mm.

Uncertain Objects

E.79.406. Cast flat strip of plano-convex section, broken at one end (Figure 8-6; Plate 8-6). The rounded side is decorated longitudinally with 2 rows of triangles; alternating triangles in each row are filled with incised transverse lines to form a checkered pattern. The fragment is 48 mm long, 7 mm wide, and 3 mm thick. It is possible that this is the remains of a bracelet, given the decoration, but it is quite flat, and it seems unlikely that this is due to post-depositional forces.

E.79.3017. Domed object (counter or weight?) with round outline and flat underside. This object was mounted for PIXE analysis and so is no longer available for measurement, but it was reported to be 13 mm in diameter and 6 mm thick.

Objects of Unknown Function and Fragments

E.79.452. Flat strip
E.79.724. Bent strip (Figure 8-6, Plate 8-6)
E.79.1951. Bent strip (Figure 8-6)
E.79.1552. Flat sheet (Figure 8-6)
E.79.113. Rounded object, flattened oval in section (Figure 8-6)
E.79.1506. Small fragments, may once have been a bead
E.79.1770. Roughly oblong fragment (Figure 8-6)
E.79.1932. Irregular fragment (Figure 8-6)
E.79.1936. Irregular fragment (Figure 8-6)
E.79.2228. Roughly spherical fragment (Figure 8-6)

Little can be said about these 10 fragments. They can be grouped broadly into flatter pieces (E.79.452, E.79.724, E.79.1951, E.79.1552), rounder pieces (E.79.113, E.79.1770, E.79.2228), and irregular fragments (E.79.1506, E.79.1932, E.79.1936). Their overall statistics are given in Table 8-7. Unfortunately, they are all too fragmentary to even guess at their original shape, and so their original function.

Table 8-7. Dimensions (mm), Unidentifiable Fragments.

FRAGMENTS (N=10)	L	W	T
Mean	17.7	8.2	3.3
Median	13.0	7.0	3.0
Mode	7.0	7.0	1.0
Range	4–65	2–19	1–6

Gold

Susan A. Johnston

A single piece of gold was recovered from Dún Ailinne (Figure 8-7; Plate 8-7). Though it was unstratified, it was found in the topsoil in the area of Trench 520, which formed one of the palisade trenches of the Rose phase annex. The piece is 16 mm long by 7 mm wide by 1 mm thick.

As the report below (written in November 1984) concludes, this piece is difficult to place in time. Given that the bulk of activity at Dún Ailinne dates to the Iron Age, it seems likely that it dates to this period as well. This would fit with its identification as an item of decoration, possibly of personal dress, a category that includes most of the metal artifacts from the site. However the presence of a food vessel at Dún Ailinne also means that a Bronze Age date cannot be ruled out.

Gold Decorative Strip

G. C. Fisher (November 1984)

E.79.2770. Sheet gold decorative strip, broken at one end. Decorated along its length with two parallel rows of repoussé dots separated by a raised median line and bounded along each edge and at the intact end with an identical raised line. A hole is punched through the sheet from front to back at the intact end.

Irish smiths began to produce objects of sheet gold and to decorate those objects with *repoussé*

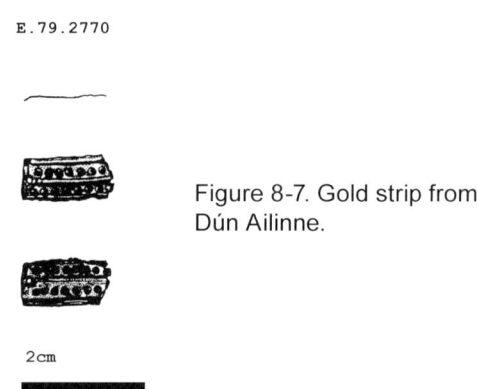

Figure 8-7. Gold strip from Dún Ailinne.

work at the beginning of the Bronze Age. Some examples of this early gold work display designs that combine rows of *repoussé* dots with raised lines in a manner similar to that of the Dún Ailinne strip. On the pairs of gold "sun discs" from Tedavnet, Co. Monaghan (Frazer 1899:41; Armstrong 1920:84, nos. 330-31, pl. xix, 425-26; Taylor 1980: pl. 5,e), an unidentified find spot in Co. Wexford (Frazer 1899:40; Armstrong 1920:84, nos. 328-29, pl. xix, 432-33), and Cloyne, Co. Cork (Day 1889:416; Armstrong 1920:85, nos. 334-35, pl. xix, 436-37), and on an unprovenienced singleton in the National Museum of Ireland, Dublin (Wilde 1862:94; Armstrong 1920:85, no. 337, pl. xix, 438), the line and dot decoration is raised from both sides of the metal sheet, thus producing a "*repoussé* effect" (Taylor 1980:23). Similarly, the gold dagger hilt band from Topped Mountain Cairn, Co. Fermanagh, found in association with a Food Vessel, carries along its length five parallel raised lines of which the outer two have been notched, thereby creating the appearance of a dotted line (Plunkett and Coffey 1898:653, fig. 3; Armstrong 1920:92, no.399, pl.X, 60; Taylor 1980: pl.28, e-f).

Despite the increasing popularity of the more massive gold ornaments, objects of sheet gold continued to be manufactured into the later Bronze Age (Herity and Eogan 1977;173-76; Taylor 1980:51). Among the contents of the Bishopsland phase hoard from Derrinboy, Co. Offaly, were a pair of sheet gold broad penannular bracelets decorated with alternating plain *repoussé* ribs and lines of *repoussé* oval ridges (J. Raftery 1961:pl.5, 1-2; Taylor 1980:pl. 29, a-b). Similar to the Derrinboy bracelets are single examples from Skrene, Co. Sligo (Armstrong 1920:93, no. 410, pl. vii, 43; Hartmann 1970: taf. 20, 994; Taylor 1980:pl. 29, e, g) and Dysart, Co. Westmeath (Armstrong 1920:44, 93, no. 409, pl. viii, 42; Taylor 1980:pl. 29, d, f).

With the characteristically Irish gorgets of the Dowris phase, *repoussé* work assumed a preeminent role in the Bronze Age goldsmith's technical repertoire (Eogan 1981:352-53). Although many of the gorgets are decorated with rows of *repoussé* dots, occasionally alternating with a raised rope-pattern line, only rarely on Late Bronze Age gold work, as in the example of a disc thought to be from Co. Armagh (Armstrong 1920:58, no. 45, pl. x, 46; Hartmann 1970:taf. 22, 1088) is the motif of plain raised lines and *repoussé* dots encountered.

Later examples of sheet gold objects, such as the La Tène strip found on Lambay Island, Co. Dublin (Wilde 1862:39, fig. 568; Baring 1907:17, fig. 1; Armstrong 1920:42, 91, no. 389, pl. x, 51; Armstrong 1924:123, fig. 16 top; J. Raftery 1951:fig. 242; Rynne 1976:232-33, pl. xxxii, 1), are decorated in a fluid, vigorous style of relief work best paralleled by contemporaneous British sheet bronzes. Indeed, it may be from the area of the Brigantes in the 1st century AD that the Lambay Island strip derives (M. Simpson 1968:250; Rynne 1976:232). Possibly allied chronologically with this example is an unprovenienced gold strip in the National Museum of Ireland, Dublin, decorated with *repoussé* dots in a line along each edge and in an arrow-like design at one end (Armstrong 1920:91, no. 390, pl. x, 52; 1924:123-24, fig. 16 bottom).

The function of the Dún Ailinne strip is difficult to determine from its form alone. The perforation at the intact end indicates, not surprisingly, that it must have been attached to a backing. However, the nature of that backing and the character of the larger object of which the Dún Ailinne strip is but a fragment remains unknown. While the *repoussé* work on the strip shows affinity with the gold work of the Bronze Age, neither a date nor a function can be more closely ascertained from either the object's form or decoration.

Postscript

Analysis of the gold strip is ongoing. At the time of writing (February 2006), a PIXE analysis, performed by the National Museum of Ireland, has not produced any clear indications of the piece's origins or parallels (Mary Cahill personal communication).

9
Glass

Susan A. Johnston

There were 50 whole and fragmentary artifacts of ancient glass recovered from Dún Ailinne. As many as six others may also have been recovered but are now missing (see Chapter 4). In addition to these, there were four fragments of modern bottle glass, three of them dark green and one olive green, as well as a large number of others noted in the Finds Register but not in the collection for various reasons (see Chapters 4 and 14). These will not be considered further here. The ancient glass included beads, bracelets, toggles, and other unidentified fragments. Table 9-1 shows the numbers of these various categories.

Unlike most other artifacts categories, the majority of these were found in stratified contexts. Of the 50, 17 (34%) were from uncertain or surface contexts, while the remaining 33 (66%) were recovered from known contexts. Just over half of those from known contexts (19 or 58%) came from the occupation deposits. Most of the rest came from trenches associated with Rose and Mauve phase timber structures (four and three respectively) or mound material (five); one bead came from a post-hole and an unidentified glass fragment came from a pit.

While 18 of the glass artifacts represent uncertain or unknown phases, the majority can be identified as to phase. Table 9-2 shows the phases represented. The largest number come from Flame phase contexts, comprising just over half of the known examples. Apart from those recovered from the Rose and Mauve phase trenches, the rest represent the complex levels layering the low mound. Assuming that the glass objects from the Flame phase are not the result of the disturbance of earlier deposits (and they do not appear to be), it is possible to suggest something of the context of these artifacts. Of the 17 from the Flame phase, all but three (two toggles and an unidentified fragment) are personal ornaments, including beads, bracelets, and fragments of these. As argued for copper alloy ornaments, this suggests that they represent what people wore (and presumably lost) when involved in the feasting activities that characterize the Flame phase at Dún Ailinne. In particular, these objects (glass beads and bracelets) may be those typical of more formal occasions, when people might have chosen to wear more elaborate or expensive items in the context of ritual or other activity.

General Characteristics

Table 9-3 shows the distribution of glass colors, broken down into types of artifact. For this table, whole and fragmentary examples have been

Table 9-1. Distribution, Types of Glass Artifacts.

OBJECT	N
bead	16
bead fragment	8
bracelet fragment	11
fragment	4
ring	1
ring bead	2
toggle	8
TOTAL	50

Table 9-2. Distribution, Glass Artifacts by Phase (Where Known).

PHASE	N
Dun	1
Flame	17
Harry	1
Jade	1
Lower Emerald	1
Mauve	3
Rose	4
Upper Emerald	4
TOTAL	32

combined, and ring beads are listed as simply beads. With the exception of the red toggle, all of the other glass colors represented at Dún Ailinne are the ones typical of Irish Iron Age glass (Guido 1978). Over half of the glass artifacts (28 or 56%) are the classic blue color most common in the period (Henderson 1991:128). Next in frequency are amber colored; these appear to be glass (though they could be amber) and are discussed as such here. These are followed by green, colorless, purple, and dark blue. All are translucent. There are also three examples of opaque glass, all toggles; one is the red glass already noted, and the other two are blue. A single translucent blue-green bead (E.79.115) was also recovered from the topsoil. Given its unstratified context, it is worth noting that the most common color for Bronze Age glass is blue-green (Henderson 1988, 1989a), though apparently of a lighter shade than the Dún Ailinne bead. The presence of food vessel sherds in a pit at Dún Ailinne (see Chapter 6) raises the possibility that this bead belongs to an earlier period than the rest of the glass. In the absence of any direct evidence for this, however, it will be treated here with the Iron Age material.

Most of the colors are distributed across all of the types of artifact represented. One exception is blue glass. Of these, 18 (64%) are beads and bead fragments, though bracelets and unidentified fragments are also represented. Put another way, of the 26 beads, ring beads, and bead fragments, 18 (69%) are of blue glass. This underlines the commonness of this type and color of glass artifact in this period.

Two other exceptions are relatively minor ones, and concern toggles. These include the only example of red glass as well as the only opaque glass. Though low numbers prohibit any secure conclusions, this is interesting given the possibility that toggles represent low level manufacturing on the site (see below). If this is the case, then it implies the production of red and opaque beads not recovered from the site, something perhaps worth investigating through further research.

Questions of the possible origins of the glass from which these various artifacts were made cannot be considered here except in the most general way. Chemical analyses of the glass have not yet been done for this assemblage, but would be of interest. In a number of important studies, Henderson (1987a, 1987b, 1988) and others (see Warner and Meighan 1981) have been able to show that many assumptions about glass, commonly based on typological and other visual characteristics, may not be correct. For example, the "Meare" type spiral beads from Loughey, Co. Down (Jope and Wilson 1957), previously thought to have come from the Meare Lake Village in Somerset, have been shown instead to come from some other source, probably

Table 9-3. Distribution, Glass Artifact Types by Glass Color.

	BRACELET	BEAD	TOGGLE	RING	FRAGMENT	TOTAL
Amber	2	2	2	—	—	6
Blue	5	18	—	1	4	28
Blue (opaque)	—	—	2	—	—	2
Dark Blue	1	—	1	—	—	2
Blue-Green	—	1	—	—	—	1
Colorless	1	2	—	—	—	3
Green	1	2	2	—	—	5
Purple	1	1	—	—	—	2
Red (opaque)	—	—	1	—	—	1
TOTAL	11	26	8	1	4	50

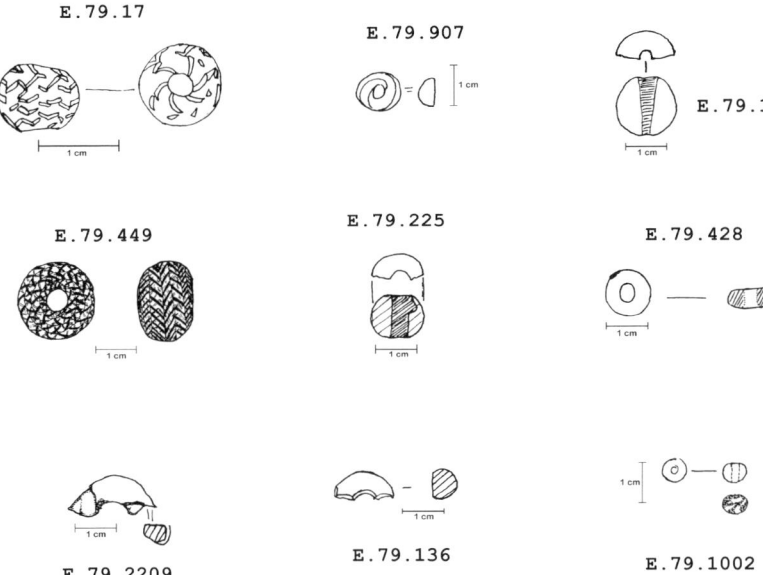

Figure 9-1. Glass beads from Dún Ailinne.

the Continent (Henderson 1987b). A probable Continental origin has also been argued for the purple glass from Hengistbury Head, Dorset (Henderson 1987a), which may have implications for the purple glass from Dún Ailinne. At the same time, the identification of possible/probable glass workshops in England and Scotland (Henderson 1989b) raises the alternative possibility that some of the Dún Ailinne glass could have come from more local sources. This is clearly an area warranting further study, particularly given that glass artifacts from excavated sites like Dún Ailinne still form the distinct minority of known prehistoric glass artifacts.

Description

As Table 9-1 shows, the Dún Ailinne glass artifacts can be broken down into four categories: beads (including rings and ring beads), bracelets, toggles, and unidentified fragments. Each of these categories will be considered separately.

Beads: Description

There are a total of 26 beads and bead fragments among the glass assemblage (Figure 9-1; Plate 9-1 shows a small selection of these). This includes both annular beads and ring beads. An additional artifact, E.79.2101, has been classified as simply a "ring." It is probably also a ring bead, but since it is almost twice the size of the other two complete ring beads (see Plate 9-4), it may have served a different function than that usually assumed for ring beads, perhaps being worn as a bead suspended from a necklace or armlet.

The beads show a range of sizes. Table 9-4 shows the descriptive statistics for the external diameters of the beads. This includes complete beads, ring beads, and all but one of the fragments for which the diameter could not be established (but not including the ring just noted). While a range of diameters is represented, there are some groupings of size which become apparent. Figure 9-2 shows a histogram for bead diameters. The histogram shows several groups of beads of similar size. The smallest are represented by the two at the lower end. These are both blue beads, and presumably belong to the

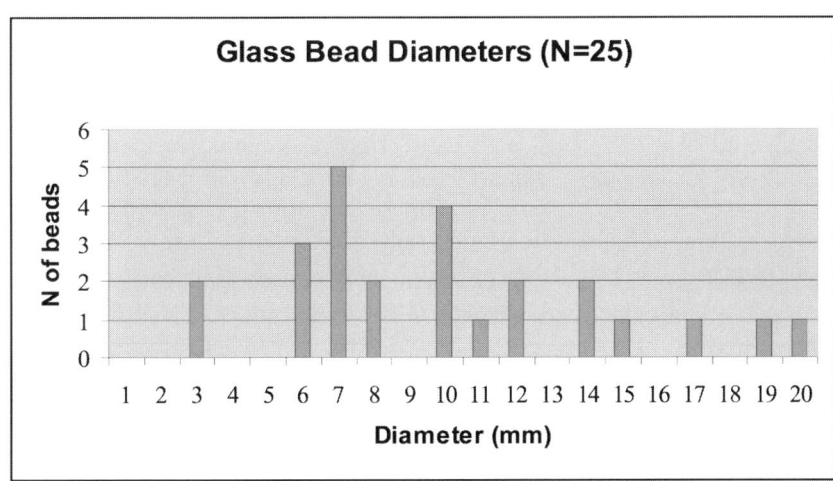

Figure 9-2. Distribution, glass bead diameters.

Table 9-4. Diameter (mm), Glass Beads.

N=25	DIAM.
Mean	9.96
Median	10.0
Mode	7.0
Range	3-20

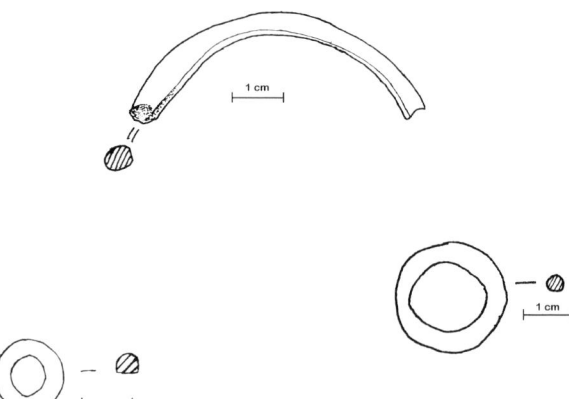

Figure 9-3. Glass ring beads and bracelet fragment from Dún Ailinne.

class of small blue beads seen at sites like Knowth, Co. Meath (Eogan 1974) and Grannagh, Co. Galway (B. Raftery 1981:201; Hughes 1985:24). Since these are said to range in size up to 8 mm (Hughes 1985:29), the group would also include eight beads from the next group on the chart (the other two from this group are blue-green and amber). The remainder of the beads are 10 mm in diameter or greater, ranging in size up to the largest beads: E.79.449 (19 mm), the most elaborately decorated of the Dún Ailinne beads; and E.79.2209 (20 mm), half of a light purple bead which may actually be a ring bead. While sample size makes comparison problematic, decoration and color were each compared to bead diameter. Neither is correlated to a significant degree (though the very smallest beads lack decoration). At least for the Dún Ailinne assemblage, all sizes of beads may be any color and may bear decoration.

Eight of the glass beads from Dún Ailinne have some degree of decoration. The most elaborately decorated bead, E.79.449, is shown in Plate 9-2.

E.79.17. Cable bead, blue glass with white chevron (Figure 9-1). The decoration comes from a 2-ply twist of blue and white. Hughes (1985:20) notes that the chevron pattern has not been completed correctly; the ends of the two cables were carried upwards instead of being laid horizontally to join and complete the chevron. D=10 mm

E.79.241. Small blue glass bead with yellow trail. The surface is somewhat eroded, possibly by heat. D=7 mm

E.79.449. Cable bead, light green glass with white chevrons (Figure 9-1, Plate 9-2). This is the most elaborately decorated bead in the assemblage, and is very well preserved. The cables are 2-ply twists of pale yellowish green and opaque white glass probably laid over a core of light green glass (Hughes 1985:19). D=19 mm

E.79.708. Four fragments of blue glass bead with yellow trail. One fragment is fairly large, and represents ¼ to ⅓ of the bead's circumference. D=ca. 8 mm

E.79.907. Blue glass bead with faint white trail (Figure 9-1). D=10 mm

E.79.1002. Small blue glass bead with white trail (Figure 9-1). D=6 mm

E.79.2815. Fragments (15, plus slivers) of blue glass cable bead with yellow chevrons. The glass is in poor condition and very friable. The surviving pieces suggest that the cables were 3-ply, in opaque white and yellow and translucent blue (Hughes 1985:19).

E.79.2910. Half of a cable bead, blue with smeared white or yellow chevrons. The surface is eroded and appears burned. Hughes describes the cables as blue and yellow, and notes where the yellow glass has deteriorated, leaving empty grooves in places; this is common in yellow glass because of the susceptibility of the lead oxide to weathering (1985:20). D=17 mm

A ninth bead may also be noted in this context. E.79.134 is a small blue bead (7 mm diameter) undecorated, but found with a wire made of copper alloy. The finds register describes the wire as a "bronze ring," though it does not now have this form. As noted in the section on copper alloy, the wire is curved (C-shaped), and thin (1–2 mm) for most of its length (15 mm). At one end, it becomes considerably thicker, almost bulbous, and is pointed on the end. This thicker portion has a small piece of unknown material wrapped around it. There is no specific indication in the finds record that the bead was found strung on the wire, but a photograph from 1968 does show the wire through the bead (Plate 9-3).

Of the remaining undecorated beads, 3–4 may be considered ring beads (Plate 9-4 shows the three certain examples). Two of them seem reasonably interpreted as beads. E.79.111 is amber colored (Figure 9-3). Its external diameter is 14 mm and its internal is 7 mm. E.79.428 is smaller, blue in color, and has external and internal diameters of 11 mm and 5 mm respectively. In both cases, the ratio of external diameter to internal diameter is about 2:1. It is difficult to see these two as being anything other than beads, conventionally assumed to have been worn suspended from a necklace or armlet. A third example, E.79.2209, is a fragment of bead, light purple in color, that appears to have been burned. It represents about ⅓ of the bead's circumference, but is probably also a ring bead. The diameters can only be estimated, but externally it is about 20 mm and about 9 mm internally. This again approaches the 2:1 ratio.

By contrast, E.79.2101 (Figure 9-3; Plate 9-4), also blue glass, is larger externally and has a much larger internal diameter: 23 mm and 16 mm respectively, or a 1.4:1 ratio. While this ring could certainly have been worn as a bead, its larger ratio seems intuitively to suggest it could have been used in more varied ways, perhaps sewn into a garment, as an earring, or as a decoration for some other artifact. Of course, the same might apply to the other ring beads as well. The point is simply that this ring looks significantly different than the others, and so may suggest a corresponding difference in function.

The remaining 14 beads are fairly standard glass beads of the period. Nine of them are blue, ranging in size from 3 mm to 15 mm in diameter. One of these, E.79.1603, is of uncertain date. While it may be modern, the surface is very deteriorated, and surface etching and devitrification features suggest it might be ancient (Sorena Sorensen personal communication). The remaining five beads are amber, blue-green, green, and colorless (two). Of the 14, five are broken, and the rest complete.

Beads: Typology

In an unpublished manuscript, Monica Hughes (1985) makes some typological observations concerning the Dún Ailinne glass finds. The ring beads are said to be comparable to "Haevernick's Group 22, her Taf 17" (Hughes 1985:15); it is unclear from the text which of Haevernick's publications is being referred to here, but this type of ring bead is found relatively commonly on oppida, burials, and other Iron Age sites. Among the specific sites Hughes notes are Manching, Mont Beuvray, Maiden Castle, and the La Tène cemetery at Bad Nauheim. In particular, Hughes notes the close parallel between the blue-green glass ring from Maiden Castle and "the blue ring from Dún Ailinne" (1985:15; she does not specify which blue ring, but the comparative figure provided of the Maiden Castle bead suggests she is referring to E.79.2101, which is a close match in size and type if not in color).

The cable beads from Dún Ailinne seem to fall into Guido's Class 11, which, according to Guido's analysis, would suggest that they have a British origin (Guido 1978:81). Hughes notes that they are "technically similar to the 'Variants' of type a, described by Guido as 'multiple chevrons'" and draws parallels between the Dún Ailinne cable beads and those from the Meare Lake Villages and also from Glastonbury (1985:20). A further bead (E6.639) from Ballinderry 2 Crannog, Co. Offaly, provides a close technological parallel to the green cable bead from Dún Ailinne (E.79.449), which is made in the same fashion (Hughes 1985:21). Finally, the blue and white cable bead (E.79.17) from Dún Ailinne is also well matched with a blue bead with white twists (E14:1556) from Lagore Crannog, Co. Meath (Hughes 1985:23).

Parallels with the undecorated beads are not so readily forthcoming, though Hughes does note a plain, translucent blue globular bead from Moylarg crannog, Co. Antrim, which is "almost identical with specimens from Dún Ailinne" (1985:48). The accompanying figure shows E.79.907 and E.79.3301 as the Dún Ailinne examples. To these may be added possible general parallels to both blue and green beads from Ballydavis, Co. Laois (Keeley 1999:30–31), though there is as yet insufficient published information to be more specific. The general similarity between the small blue beads from Dún Ailinne and those from other sites has already been noted. Finally, it is worth noting at least one possible parallel for the Dún Ailinne bead found with the copper alloy wire (E.79.134). There is no way to be sure of the original shape of the wire, whether a ring or something else. But there is a blue glass bead of a similar type hanging from the spiral head of a bronze loop-headed pin from Lagore crannog, Co. Meath (Hencken 1951:72, fig. 14A). Obviously this is only loosely parallel, but it does suggest a possible context for the Dún Ailinne bead and wire.

Bracelets

None of the glass bracelets from Dún Ailinne were complete, but there are fragments of ten bracelets (Figure 9-3 shows one example and Plate 9-5 shows four) from a variety of contexts at the site (two of the fragments, though having separate numbers, join together, and so there are 11 total fragments).

The colors (all translucent) noted in Table 9-3 may be reiterated here: six blue (one of these dark blue), two amber, and one each in purple, colorless, and green. While the surfaces of some of them are eroded, they are all relatively fine and light in weight; none of them are decorated. They range in length from short segments of 9 mm (E.79.377, blue) to the longest fragment of 60 mm (E.79.1034, purple). In thickness they range from 4–7 mm, and are all D-shaped in section. All but three are short enough to prevent even an estimate of the amount of the circumference they represent. The remaining three (E.79.1034, E.79.1333, and E.79.1020/2274) each represent about ¼ to ⅓ of the bracelet's circumference.

Typologically, Hughes assigns the glass bracelets to Haevernick's Group 3a. These have a shallower D-shape in section, and are lighter than, for example, her Group 1; all the colors found at Dún Ailinne also appear in this group (Hughes 1985:5).

Parallels for glass bracelets appear to be numerous and varied. All of the colors found at Dún Ailinne are common in Iron Age sites, and many sites with glass artifacts seem to include bracelets. The purple bracelet for example is paralleled at Loughey, Co. Down (Jope and Wilson 1957) and also at Hengistbury Head (Henderson 1987a), though some of the latter are decorated. Macalister (1928:202–3) described a possible colorless glass bracelet from the site of Dunadry, Co. Antrim, but this may instead have been a ring bead or other glass artifact. A blue glass bracelet from Freestone Hill, Co. Kilkenny (B. Raftery 1969) is similar to those from Dún Ailinne, as is one from Ó Ríordáin's unpublished excavations at Tara, Co. Meath (Hughes 1985:11). Glass bracelets of various colors were found in the Iron Age buri-

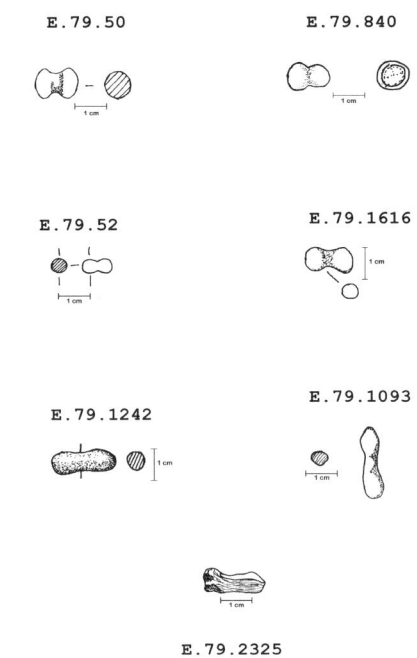

Figure 9-4. Glass toggles from Dún Ailinne.

als at Knowth (Eogan 1974), and Hughes (1985:11) cites in particular a fragment of plain, translucent glass (apparently blue), also from that site.

Toggles

There are eight so-called toggles among the glass artifacts (Figure 9-4; Plate 9-6). The name for this class of artifact is somewhat problematic, as is their function. They are often called "dumbbells" to reflect their shape, and are frequently included with beads in discussions (for example, B. Raftery 1981 refers to them as "dumb-bell beads"). However, they are rarely perforated (Warner and Meighan 1981:54), and their context provides little clue as to their actual function. Here they are referred to as toggles, as suggested by Warner and Meighan (1981) though this too is perhaps somewhat misleading.

As noted in Table 9-3 above, they represent a broad range of colors, including blue (translucent and opaque), amber, green, and opaque red; interestingly, some of the colors, notably the opaque red and blue, are not colors represented among the beads and bracelets found. In general, with the exception of the red toggle, the colors are the ones common in Iron Age contexts (Hughes 1985:43). The red one merits some further discussion. This is a bright "sealing wax" red color, though the surface

Table 9-5. Dimensions (mm), Glass Toggles.

N=8	L	W
Mean	15.6	7.4
Median	14.0	7.0
Mode	14.0	9.0
Range	10–23	5–10

is somewhat deteriorated, and calls to mind the three red glass pieces claimed to have been found near Tara, Co. Meath (Newman 1997:211, 221). While there is some doubt if any of the latter truly came from that context, the rarity of red glass in Ireland at this period suggests the possibility that the two occurrences are somehow related. Perhaps red glass had some significance particularly relevant to ceremonial contexts, or in elite settings. Hughes (1985:42) notes only one other example of red glass from Ireland, Ó Ríordáin's report of several pieces of red glass among those apparently intended for use as enamel from Garranes (Co. Cork). Several sites in Britain have also produced opaque red glass artifacts, including a Bronze Age bead from a barrow in Wiltshire (Guido et al. 1984) and a "pinhead" from Meare, Somerset (Hughes 1985:42). Otherwise, red glass is used primarily as a decoration, and primarily from later periods. Indeed, Hughes suggests that the Dún Ailinne toggle is the first evidence that red glass was being traded into Ireland during the Iron Age, possibly from the Eastern Mediterranean (Hughes 1985:42), though this may have been superceded by more recent evidence.

The toggles from Dún Ailinne vary in size within a relatively narrow range. Table 9-5 shows the statistics for the toggles, and Figure 9-5 shows a comparison of their lengths versus widths. This chart shows that the toggles tend to group into three basic size categories, with most of them centered around 14 mm in length. This may have implications for their manufacture, though the details are still unclear (see below). Their shapes also vary somewhat, from rounder, squatter forms (such as E.79.840) to more elongated examples (such as E.79.1093). None of them are perforated.

This last raises again the question of the function of these pieces. B. Raftery notes that they "seem essentially an Irish form," though they are also known from Britain (1984:202). As noted, they are typically discussed along with beads, though there seems no direct evidence that they were in fact items of personal adornment. In her discussion of the Dún Ailinne glass, Monica Hughes makes the novel suggestion that they are in fact manufacturing debris. This is based on the observation that toggles commonly show a small, twisted projection at one end, which she interprets as the result of the piece having been snipped off while the glass was soft. The narrowed waist, which prompted the name of dumbbell, is then interpreted as resulting from the way the piece was held during this process, by forceps or metal tongs that constricted the middle of the softened glass. Variation in form reflects the different shapes and sizes of implements used. As evidence of this argument, Hughes cites in particular the Dún Ailinne toggles E.79.1093 and E.79.1247, both amber, which seem to her to be "plainly the ends of rods." Thus, rather than decorative objects, toggles can be argued as being manufacturing waste, the leftover ends of glass rods too short to be used further for bead production (Hughes 1985:41).

Unidentified Fragments

Finally, there were four fragments of glass that could not be positively identified (Plate 9-6). All are blue, and one has faint white trails. Two of the pieces (E.79.663 and E.79.2325; see Figure 9-4 for an illustration of the latter) might be bracelet fragments, though not enough of them survives to be sure; each is just under 20 mm in length, and E.79.2325 is somewhat irregular in shape. An alternative is that these are waste remains from glass working, perhaps rejected or broken fragments. E.79.2075 is a

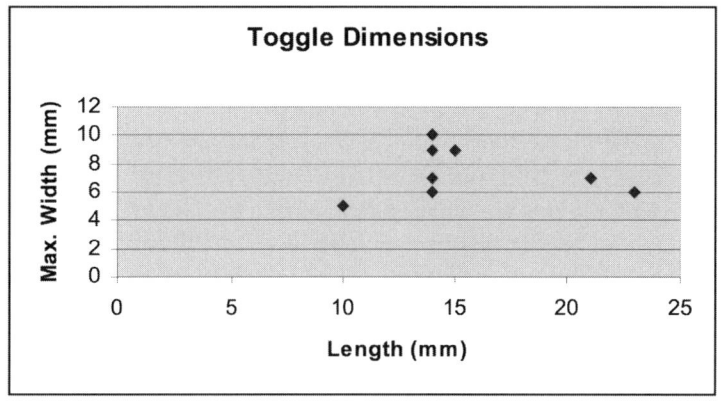

Figure 9-5. Glass toggle length by width.

short glass rod (11 mm in length). It is very thin, only 1 mm in diameter, and slightly curved. Hughes (1985:36) has raised the possibility, given its dimensions, that it is leftover material from making beads like the very small glass beads found at the site. The fourth fragment, E.79.1829, is an unusual shape, irregular and folded over, producing a hollow center. Whether this was its original shape or whether it is the result of damage and/or preservation is unclear. This fragment is also short, 14 mm in length and about 4 mm in thickness, and could also be interpreted as waste material.

Glass Working?

While it is clearly tentative, several strands of evidence suggest that glass working might have been occurring at Dún Ailinne. These include the toggles, the waste glass fragments, and an anomalous piece of slag described in Chapter 12 which may be related to glass working (E.79.3588, which contains fragments of apparently unaltered silica grains). If glass working is implied, then there are several interesting implications, some of which might be followed up in future research. The first is that, if the shapes of the toggles indicate something about both the process of manufacture and the form of at least some of the tools used, then there is the potential for learning more about the details of the manufacture of glass artifacts. For example, do the detailed dimensions of the toggle waists group together in any meaningful way to suggest standardized tool types; or are the dimensions at all associated with types of glass, particular constituent elements, etc. which might affect the manufacturing technique and therefore the particular tools used? Actual manufacturing implements are rare in (or indeed absent from?) the archaeological record, and so this might prove a fruitful means of gaining more information about this technology.

A second implication is that, if toggles give some indication of glass working and its organization, then it may have been more widespread than the archaeological evidence has so far indicated. Certainly toggles are more common than direct evidence of glass manufacture (see Henderson 1989b), and if their presence suggests such an activity, than it may have been more common than previously suspected.

A final implication relates to the manufacture of glass and glass objects in the region. The actual production of glass in Ireland is not attested until the Early Christian period (Henderson and Ivens 1992), and there is no real evidence that glass was being produced at Dún Ailinne. However, the glass could have been imported and then the actual artifacts manufactured locally—glass working as opposed to glass production. A good argument can be made that glass was being worked in Britain, minimally at the Meare Lake Village but possibly elsewhere as well, between the 5th and 2nd centuries BC (Henderson 1989b). Since this is earlier than the period when Dún Ailinne was occupied, such technology could easily have spread. The available evidence is not sufficient to suggest any kind of large-scale production, but along with other evidence of low-level manufacturing such as the copper alloy tracer, slag, and casting jets, it may suggest the production of artifacts at Dún Ailinne. This is considered further in Chapter 18, but Hughes raises the possibility that something on the order of craft fairs, or at least some few craft stalls, were associated with the occasions celebrated at the site. If so, then perhaps glass was one of the commodities on offer.

Parallel Sites and Chronology

It appears that the typical glass assemblages from the Iron Age contain much the same objects, with beads the most common and bracelets less so; other forms, such as toggles, occur in fewer numbers. It has been noted (see B. Raftery 1984:198) that a large proportion of the glass finds from the period, and particularly beads, come from contexts that are either unprovenienced or only broadly provenienced, such as to county or townland. Compounding the problem, many of the more generalized forms (such as undecorated blue beads) were made and used over a long period, so that typological parallels may have little relevance for chronology. This perhaps underlines the importance of conducting further studies on the Dún Ailinne assemblage, since most of the glass artifacts are from relatively secure stratigraphic contexts. In any case, some general observations about the place of Dún Ailinne among other Iron Age glass sites can be made.

Beginning with the other royal sites, the red glass possibly from Tara has already been noted. Other glass objects are reported from excavations at the Rath of the Synods (B. Raftery 1984:200) but these remain unpublished. Navan produced only a few glass finds; four beads of various colors and an unidentified "branching" fragment of blue glass are noted (Waterman 1997:87). Chemical analysis of the glass was carried out, and demonstrated among other things that the blue glass was of high quality

(Henderson 1997:97). Obviously compared to Dún Ailinne, the glass assemblage at Navan is far more limited. Whether this is due to preservation, site dynamics, or some more meaningful difference in behavior at the two sites is open to debate.

Beyond these sites, glass has been recovered from a number of sites in Ireland. Again, the glass is similar in range of types. Specific parallels have already been noted for both beads and bracelets; toggles cannot be precisely paralleled, but have been recovered from sites such as Grannagh, Kiltierney, Knowth, and possibly Loughcrew (B. Raftery 1984:202). It is striking when reading the literature that the same sites tend to recur: Loughey, Kiltierney, Grannagh, Knowth, Loughcrew, Lagore, Rathgall, Freestone Hill, and most recently Ballydavis are the most commonly cited glass assemblages, containing, in varying numbers, beads, bracelets, and sometimes toggles. Hughes in particular notes that the assemblage from Loughcrew, Cairn H, shows close affinities with the Dún Ailinne assemblage (1985:36). What is notable here is that this list of sites covers a range of site types, suggesting that glass artifacts were used in a variety of cultural contexts, and no type of artifact seems associated with any particular type of site. The same has been noted more broadly for Iron Age Europe, where most glass has come from cemeteries and lake villages (Henderson 1991). Instead, glass ornaments were worn in both life and death, with neither state apparently dictating the style of artifact to be worn.

What may be relevant is that glass artifacts may indicate higher levels of wealth among their owners, whether dead or alive. Henderson (1991) argues this based primarily on two lines of evidence. First, glass tends to be associated in cemeteries with other artifacts indicating moderate to high levels of wealth. Further, since glass is the product of specialized artisans, and is made from raw materials whose distribution may be limited, the classic archaeological paradigm can be cited: skilled labor plus spatially limited raw materials allows for the possibility of restricting access, and therefore to control by elites. Applying this to Dún Ailinne, and including copper alloy and iron objects, this indicates the presence of elites at the site. As noted in Chapter 18, there is the possibility that the ceremonies carried out at Dún Ailinne were associated with power, whether religious, political, economic, or all three. The presence of apparently high status materials among the artifact collection clearly supports such an interpretation.

The chronological situation is less clear. B. Raftery notes a variety of potential problems with the glass bead chronology: the fact that so many in Ireland are stray or unstratified finds, the possibility that personal objects such as these would have been passed through generations, and the general continuity of forms over long periods of time (1984:198). Regarding glass bracelets, Hughes observes that, in the archaeological record, the various types and colors of glass bracelets do not have any particular chronological significance, all types and colors being found in graves and settlement sites in a variety of periods (Hughes 1985:3).

Nevertheless, some broad observations regarding the chronological significance of glass artifacts can be made. In Hughes' consideration of the Dún Ailinne glass, she argues that the bracelets belong in the same La Tène C/D horizon as their parallels on the Continent, suggesting a date in the early 1st century BC; this makes them contemporary with the late *oppida*, where the greatest number of plain, undecorated armlets have been found (1985:10).

Toggles are somewhat more complicated. Raftery argues that the material from Kiltierney, Grannagh, and Loughcrew indicate that, by the 1st century AD toggles were being made in Ireland, with a date just before or after the BC/AD transition being supported by other finds from Kiltierney (B. Raftery 1984:202). Hughes, by contrast, would put them earlier, arguing through a complex series of typological parallels that toggles and small blue beads belong to the 3rd and early 2nd centuries BC (1985:37). Inevitably, the simplicity of the forms and the complexity of their various associations mitigates against an easy answer. However, it is worth noting that, if the argument about their function suggested above is accepted, untangling the chronology of toggles would have implications for the development of glass manufacturing in Ireland.

Dún Ailinne's ring beads are assigned to the late La Tène by Hughes (1985:17) based among other considerations on comparisons with examples from Meare and Glastonbury. The same parallels are used to place the Dún Ailinne cable beads in the 3rd to 2nd centuries BC (Hughes 1985:20). Thus overall, the Dún Ailinne glass finds seem to span the middle and late La Tène periods, conforming to what would be expected given the other artifacts and the radiocarbon age determinations from the site.

10
Worked Bone

Pam J. Crabtree and Douglas V. Campana

The excavations at Dún Ailinne produced a large collection of unmodified animal bones that appear to be the remains of periodic ritual feasts. In addition to these food remains, the excavations produced a small number of artifacts that were made of bone and a few pieces of bone that appear to be the remains of bone working. A short report of the more interesting worked bone items appeared in the *MASCA Journal* (Crabtree 1982). This chapter will provide a more complete catalog of the worked bone pieces emphasizing their methods of manufacture and their possible functions. It concludes with a summary of the role of bone working and craft production at Dún Ailinne.

Catalog of Worked Bone Objects

E.79.203. Sawn Cattle Metatarsal Shaft

This bone (Figure 10-1, Plate 10-1) was sawn through on both ends with a metal saw. The bone is sawn around the circumference of the shaft rather than straight across. This is similar to worked bone seen in the Early Medieval period (J. Boyle, personal communication). The exterior of the bone shows occasional transverse scratches which are randomly distributed, but no interpretable wear. There is very little polish or rounding on this specimen; it is most likely at an intermediate stage in the bone-working process, intended for further working into a finished object.

E.79.417. Possible Pig Fibula

This needle (Figure 10-1, Plate 10-2) may have been made from a pig fibula (Crabtree 1982: Plate 10- 2). This anatomical element was commonly used to produce needles throughout antiquity because its narrow shaft can be sharpened to a point and its flat triangular epiphyses can easily be shaped and perforated. Pig fibulae were also frequently used to make pins during the Early Christian period in Ireland (J. Boyle, personal communication). This needle shows some polish on the shaft; the tip has been broken off. The perforation was made from two intersecting drilled holes, the larger 3.6 mm in diameter and the smaller 2.5 mm, producing a perforation that is 5 mm in overall length. Although the relatively slight polish on the shaft argues against prolonged use, the tool did receive some use as the drill lines in the perforation have been obliterated. This object is probably too large to have been used in sewing but may have served as a lacing or weaving needle.

E.79.419. Head of a Cattle Femur

This object (Figure 10-1, Plate 10-3) was made from an unfused proximal epiphysis of a cattle femur. The hourglass shape of the perforation indicates that it was drilled from both sides. The hole was placed near the fovea capitis; this is a natural place to perforate a proximal femur. There is no wear visible on this specimen. This is probably a spindle whorl. Although the form of the object suggests that it might

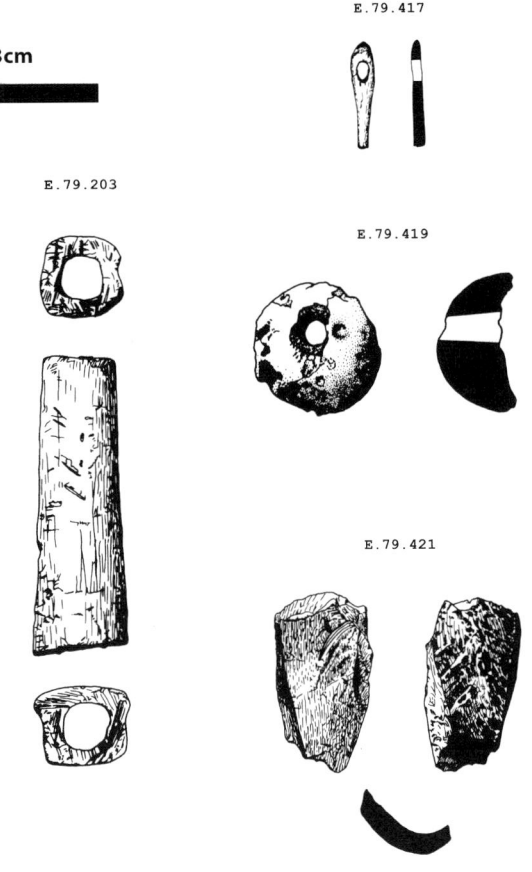

Figure 10-1. Worked bone, Dún Ailinne.

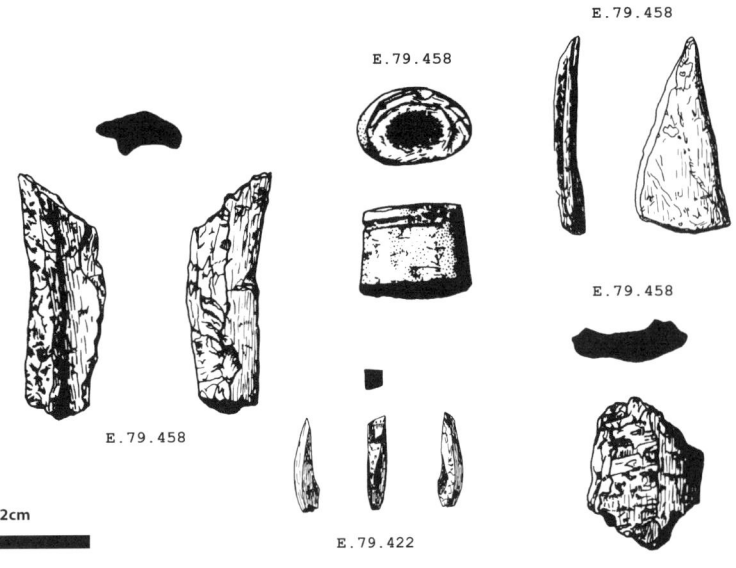

Figure 10-2. Worked bone, Dún Ailinne.

have been used as a button or fastener, there is no wear on the object, particularly within the perforation, that would support this interpretation.

E.79.421. Fragment of a Large Mammal Long Bone

This specimen (Figure 10-1, Plate 10-4) shows heavy polish on its outer face. The polish preceded the break, as the edges of the break are not rounded, and there is no polish along the break.

E.79.422. Mammal Bone Fragment

This small bone object (Figure 10-2, Plate 10-5) is roughly crescent-shaped. The curved side may be unworked, but shave marks on two sides indicate shaping with a sharp blade. One side is perfectly flat, suggesting that this side was abraded, although no manufacture marks are apparent. All the markings are sharp, indicating little or no wear. This object may have served as a decorative inlay.

E.79.424. Mammal Bone Fragment

This object (Plate 10-6) was worked on all six faces and was sawn and filed to shape. There is no obliteration of the marks of manufacture, and the edges of the object are sharp. The partial hole visible on one of the long sides appears to be a remnant of a natural foramen. This object may also have been intended as a decorative inlay. No. 422 and No. 424 were found near one another in the same 1-meter grid square and in the same layer. They may have been part of the same object, or they may have been lost or discarded by a craftsperson producing inlays or inlayed objects at that location.

E.79.458. Horse Metapodial Shaft Fragment, and Three Bone Fragments

This bone (Figure 10-2, Plate 10-7) is probably a fragment of a horse metapodial shaft that has been sawn on either end with a metal saw. The bone shaft was sawn circumferentially and then broken, similar to E.79.203. There is an area on the plantar face of the bone where the manu-

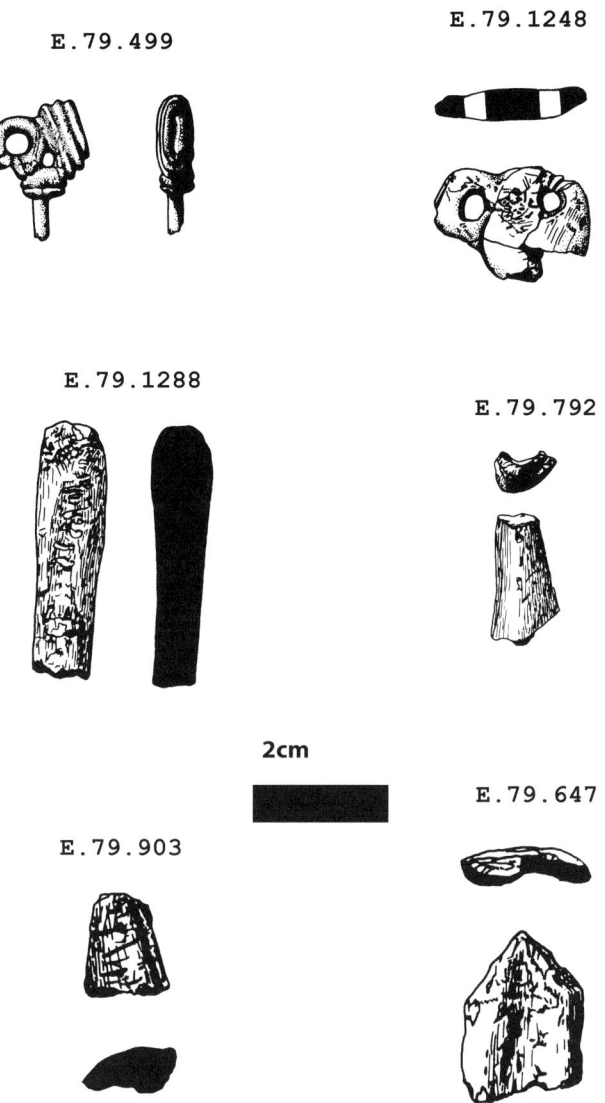

Figure 10-3. Worked bone, Dún Ailinne.

E.79.499. Mammal Bone Fragment

This finished and elaborately decorated bone object (Crabtree 1982: Plate 10-1) appears to be a pin (Figure 10-3, Plate 10-8). It was primarily worked with a small graver. Both holes were made with a drill, although one was subsequently enlarged to match the pattern. The shaft of the object was shaped by transverse grinding, probably against a grindstone or whetstone. The scratches left from the grinding are parallel but irregularly spaced. The object is polished all over. It may have served as a clothing pin. Exquisitely made following La Tène motifs, this object is so far unique in the Irish Iron Age. It is also unlike any bone pin known from Early Medieval Ireland. The shaft of the Dún Ailinne pin is approximately half as wide as the shafts of typical Early Medieval pins from Ireland, and most Early Medieval pins have simple carved heads (James Boyle, personal communication). The closest parallel to the decoration on this pin is seen on some of the metal Type 2 ring-headed pins from Iron Age Scotland and Ireland (see, for example, Raftery 1983: fig. 10-135). The heads of these pins are generally perforated, and they have rather slender shafts. The decoration on these pins, however, is unlike the decoration on the Dún Ailinne artifact.

E.79.647. Large Mammal Long Bone Shaft Fragment

This specimen may have been cut along its sides, possibly with a graver (Figure 10-3, Plate 10-9). The bone is deteriorating, and it is therefore difficult to tell how the sides were cut. This specimen may not have been intentionally worked.

E.79.664. Small Fragment of a Mammal Long Bone Shaft

No manufacture or wear marks are apparent (Plate 10-10). This object may not have been intentionally worked.

E.79.792. Small Fragment of a Mammal Long Bone Shaft

The external surface is highly polished and shows many short, randomly oriented scratches (Figure 10-3, Plate 10-11). The object is gray in color and the external bone surface is covered with a thin

facturer began to saw and then moved the cut over. The width of the saw blade used was 1.7 mm, and the teeth of the saw were straight rather than offset. The cross section of the cut indicates that some saw teeth may have been longer than others. There is no rounding apparent on any of the saw marks, indicating that this object was probably a waster. Associated with this specimen are three additional long bone shaft fragments that show evidence of scraping on their surface with a sharp blade. Several chatter marks are visible on one of these specimens (see discussion of E.79.2706). These objects are too fragmentary for further identification.

layer of calcite. This is clearly a fragment of a larger object and cannot be further identified.

E.79.903. Large Mammal Long Bone Fragment

The surface of this fragment of a bone object shows some score marks on the external surface transverse to the axis of the bone (Figure 10-3, Plate 10-12). A flat-bottomed straight groove has been cut along one side partway through the thickness of the bone, probably with a graver. The surface of the bone is polished, perhaps by extensive handling. This is clearly a fragment of a much larger object.

E.79.1248. Mammal Bone Fragment

This finished bone object was carved from a bone fragment. It is roughly pear-shaped, consisting of two lobes (Figure 10-3, Plate 10-13). The larger, thicker lobe is approximately disc-shaped, with a hole set to one side. There may have been an additional perforation adjacent to the existing hole, but the object is broken, and no trace of this possible hole remains. Attached to the larger lobe is a smaller, thinner sub-rectangular lobe with one central perforation. The two holes were first drilled (a few rotary toolmarks are visible) then enlarged with a small graver pushed through the hole. The hole in the sub-rectangular lobe is strongly elliptical. The diameter of the hole is 2.9 mm in one direction and 4.5 mm in the other. One side of the hole shows some rounding on the inner and outer faces, indicating that a cord probably passed through it. The location of this wear suggests that this object was suspended from the smaller lobe, with the larger lobe hanging downward. The hole in the larger lobe is round, 3.1 mm in diameter, and shows no rounding. The object appears to have been carved with a graver, then polished. This object appears to have been a pendant, or perhaps more likely, a clothing toggle.

E.79.1288. Possible Horse Splint Bone

The large, flat facets visible on this long bone shaft, possibly a horse splint bone, indicate that it was shaped with a metal blade (Figure 10-3, Plate 10-14). The tool was extensively handled; the surface is evenly polished except for the broken end. As the end of the tool has been broken off, it is impossible to determine the implement's function, but it probably an implement handle.

E.79.1601. Cortical Section of a Large Mammal (cattle or horse) Long Bone, Possibly a Radius

This is an elongated rectangular fragment that was made by two nearly parallel, straight saw cuts (Plate 10-15). There is no indication of further use. This object appears to be a waster or unfinished blank intended for further fashioning that was lost or discarded.

E.79.1672. Horse Distal Metapodial

The shaft of this cannon bone was sawn from either side with a metal saw and then broken (Crabtree 1982: pl. 10-3a and b) (Figure 10-4, Plate 10-16). There is an area on the plantar surface of the bone showing saw marks where the manufacturer apparently missed with the saw blade. This object is probably a waster because the edges of the saw marks are sharp and show no wear. The width of the saw mark is 1.6 mm. The cross section of the cut is square and identical to that seen on E.79.458. It is possible that the two bones were cut with the same or very similar saws.

E.79.1864. Cattle-Sized Rib

This implement was shaped from the exterior (dorsal) surface of a cattle-sized rib (Figure 10-4, Plate 10-17). The rib was split lengthwise between its outer and inner surfaces and the cancellous bone removed by shaving against a straight, sharp metal blade. The object is roughly a narrow ellipse in shape with one end broken off. It has been carefully worked to a regular outline and very thin cross-section. A groove has been cut diagonally into the concave surface with a small graver, possibly as an abandoned effort to produce a smaller object, possibly to remove remnant cancellous bone. Axial scratches as well as transverse, regularly spaced undulations and chatter marks, particularly on the concave surface are indicative of shaving with a sharp blade. The edges and tip of the implement are rounded rather than sharp. The entire object's surface is lightly polished, partially obscuring the manufacture marks. The polish is slightly more prominent at the tip. This polish is most likely the result of prolonged usage and handling. The only other wear marks discernable are numerous short, randomly oriented scratches superimposed on the polish. In form and wear pattern this implement most closely resembles a weaving, basketry, or matting needle.

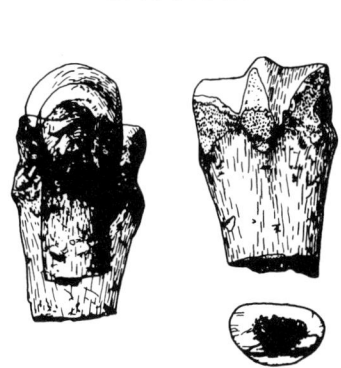

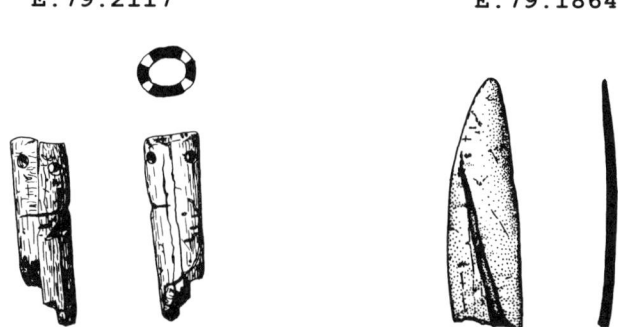

Figure 10-4. Worked bone, Dún Ailinne.

E.79.1872. Cattle Tibia Shaft Fragment

This fragment of a long bone shaft, almost certainly a cattle tibia (Plate 10-18), was sawn near its proximal end. The shaft of the bone has been longitudinally grooved, and the shaft was split lengthwise. The shaft of the bone has been worked with a heavy metal blade, probably a large knife or hatchet. This piece appears to be waste material from bone working.

E.79.2117. Medium Mammal Long Bone Shaft Fragment

This fragmentary object made on a long bone shaft (Figure 10-4, Plate 10-19) was intentionally hollowed at one end of the shaft and the end of the bone has been smoothed both on the outside and inside the lip of the hollowed end. Four holes, approximately 3.3 mm in diameter, have been drilled through the shaft wall about 90° apart and about 6.5 mm from the finished end. The four holes have each been drilled separately, probably with a metal drill. The edges of the holes are fairly sharp; there is no indication that a cord was passed through any of the holes. The object itself has been shaved and filed to shape. A small transverse groove, about 2 cm from the complete end, may also have been made with the edge of a file. The interior cancellous material is very light in color, superficially resembling calcination, but this is likely to be the result of post-depositional chemical processes. The exterior of the shaft appears slightly polished, probably from handing. This object might have served as a haft or handle that was secured in place through the holes with nails or pins.

E.79.2267. Possible Pig Lateral Metapodial

This object appears to have been worked from the proximal end of a possible pig lateral metapodial (Figure 10-5, Plate 10-20). It has been shaved with a sharp blade on the lateral and medial sides. It is polished overall, probably through handling. This is likely to have been the handle of a very small, undetermined implement.

E.79.2307. Two Mammal Bone Fragments

These two dark-colored fragments are so similar in appearance (Figure 10-5, Plate 10-21) that they are almost surely part of the same object, although they do not fit together. The exterior shows a great deal of polishing from handling. The object is covered with manufacture marks and seems to have been shaped by abrasion and shaving. This is apparently the handle end of a small tool. The functional end of the tool has been broken off.

E.79.2650. Mammal Bone Fragment

The entire surface of this bone object has been shaped, and it is so highly polished that most of the manufacture traces are no longer visible (Figure 10-5, Plate 10-22). Only fine file marks are visible run-

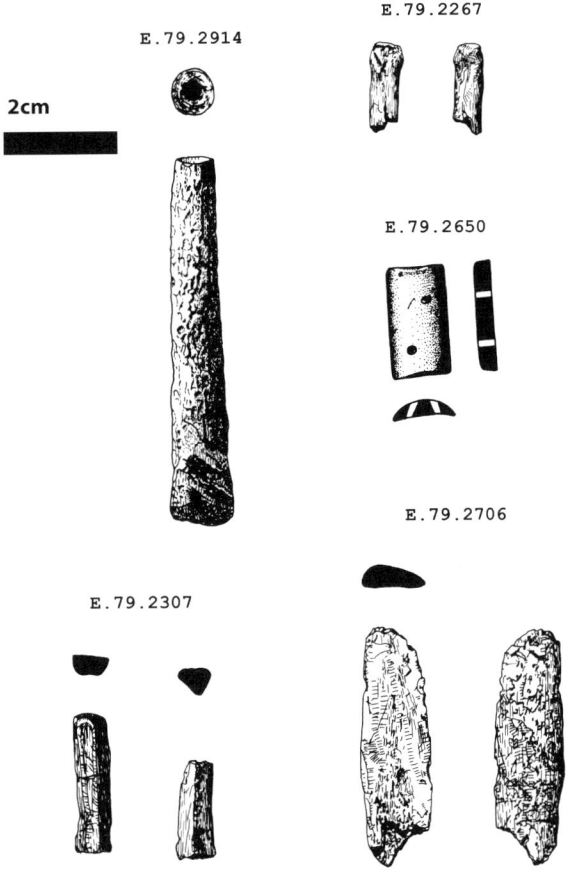

Figure 10-5. Worked bone, Dún Ailinne.

ning diagonally across the ends of the piece. The two perforations angle away from the center of the object. Both holes are 1.4 mm in diameter and were probably made by the same drill. The holes were drilled straight through with a cylindrical bit. The edges of the holes are still sharp on both sides of the object, indicating that no cord passed through them. This item is not likely to have been used as a button. The holes were probably designed to receive small nails. The item, which shows very little wear, was probably used as a decorative piece on a larger object.

E.79.2706. Possible Rib

This object may have been shaped from a portion of a large mammal bone, possibly a rib (Figure 10-5, Plate 10-23). One side has been flattened, probably to produce a sharpened edge. This implement was worked flat by shaving against a straight, sharp, probably stationary blade. This has resulted in shave marks as well as prominent, evenly spaced chatter marks. Similar marks appear on the convex outer surface as well. This pattern can readily be simulated experimentally. There is no polish or evidence of wear on this specimen.

E.79.2810. Medium Mammal Long Bone Shaft

One end of the shaft has been sawn off nearly squarely across (Plate 10-24). A short saw mark is visible adjacent to the cut. This cut end shows considerable polish as well as short scratch marks radial to the curvature of the bone. There is very slight polishing on the shaft, possibly from handling. This object may have been used as a rubber or smoothing implement of some type.

E.79.2914. Red Deer Antler Tine

This specimen (now missing; Figure 10-5) was chopped off at the base with a heavy metal implement such as an axe. The tip of the tine was cut off and intentionally hollowed to form a cup-shaped depression. The interior of the cup is marked by irregularly concentric ridges indicating that the hole was made with a hand-held borer. The shallow hole was cut in the center of the depression to a depth of 10.7 mm below the lip. This object may have served as a haft or handle, although probably not as a knife handle. It is more likely that this antler tine was a handle for an awl or similar tool where the pressure is applied primarily toward the handle during use.

E.79.3088. Medium Mammal Long Bone Shaft

A semicircular notch at one end suggests that this fragment of long bone shaft may have had a hole drilled through it (Figure 10-6, Plate 10-25). However, no clear drill marks are visible. The surface of the bone is in such poor condition that most of the diagnostic features have been lost.

E.79.3657. Horse Metapodial

The distal end of this horse cannon bone (Figure 10-6, Plate 10-26) has been shaped with a hatchet or heavy knife and further smoothed by shaving with a blade. The object is broken in the midshaft area. Although about one-half of the shaft of the bone has been broken off at the shaft end of the object a small rounded segment remains indicating the object retains its full original length. The shaft portion of the specimen has been polished through handling. It fits well in the hand and was almost surely the handle for a large implement such as a knife.

Conclusions

The worked bone items provide additional evidence for some small-scale craft production at Dún Ailinne. While a small number of finished bone objects was recovered from Dún Ailinne, many of the worked bone items appear to be leftovers from bone working. The widespread use of sawing is diagnostic of bone working, since sawing was not used in butchery until the 17th and 18th centuries. James Boyle's ongoing study of bone pin production in Early Christian Ireland suggests that bone pins were produced at a small number of high status sites. Metal pins were also produced at these sites. While there is vociferous debate over whether the Early Christian period can be used as a model for the Iron Age (see Wailes 2004 for a review of these issues), it is certainly possible that bone working took place at high status sites in the Iron Age as well. Cattle and horse bones are often used as raw materials for tools, and higher status individuals most likely had greater access to cattle and horse carcasses during the Iron Age. Regardless of whether or not bone working was a high status activity in Iron Age Ireland, the presence of debris from bone working indicates that activities

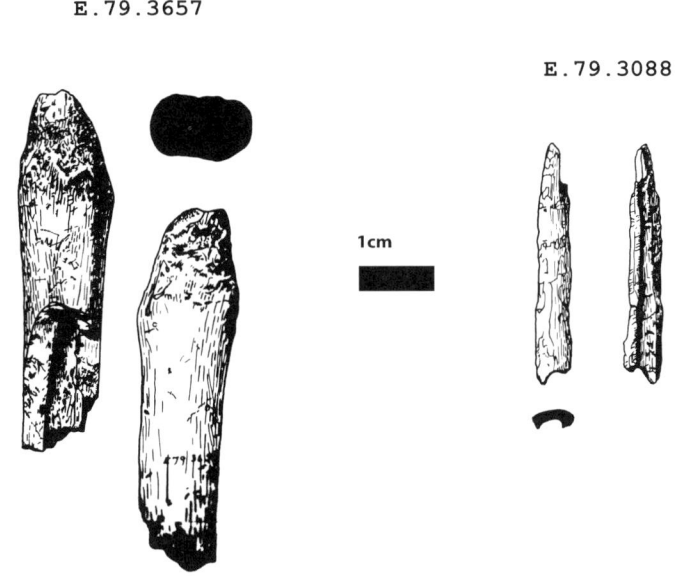

Figure 10-6. Worked bone, Dún Ailinne.

other than feasting and religious ceremonies were taking place at Dún Ailinne.

The finished bone objects also provide evidence for small-scale craft production. Although the spindle whorl may or may not have been used, it may have been intended for spinning wool or flax. The bone needle was probably used for sewing, weaving, or lacing, and a rib fragment may have served as a weaving or basketry tool. These objects indicate that a range of crafts, including the manufacture of items decorated with bone inlays, basketry or mat-making, and textile production may also have been carried out at Dún Ailinne.

11
Miscellaneous Objects

Susan A. Johnston

Cupmarked Stone

A fragment of stone (E.79.2894) with 8-9 pecked cupmarks was recovered from what was thought to have been Mauve phase soils (Plate 11-1). Although a slide of this stone is among the collection, the actual stone cannot now be located; this description is based on the photograph and on information from B. Wailes. When discovered, the stone appeared fresh and unweathered, and had cupmarks on one surface arranged in two rows. Each row had four cupmarks in a line, and an additional cupmark appears to have been appended to the third cupmark in the upper row, which would make a total of nine. It measured approximately 20 cm x 30 cm, and was trapezoidal in shape.

Cupmarks are ubiquitous in Europe throughout both prehistory and early history. They are found in dated contexts ranging from Neolithic long mounds (Piggot 1971-72) through Early Christian souterrains (Wainwright 1963; see his Gazeteer). In Ireland, they are most frequently associated with rock art, typically dated from the later Neolithic through the earlier Bronze Age (Johnston 1989), and passage tomb art (Twohig 1981), dated to the Neolithic. They are also found in some earlier Bronze Age cist burials (Simpson and Thawley 1972), though their contemporaneity with this period is the subject for debate (Burgess 1990; Johnston 1993; Bradley 1997).

At Dún Ailinne, the context of this stone must be considered disturbed. It is possible that it is all that remains of a cist burial, perhaps originally associated with the food vessel (see Chapter 6). However, the stone was found almost 25 m from the food vessel pit, and since there was no trace of the sockets for the stones of a cist's walls in the remains of pit 2790, this seems unlikely. The stone was somewhat closer to trench 281, which is arguably Neolithic in date. This fits better with the frequently Neolithic date of cupmarks in general, but of course there is no compelling reason to associate the two apart from possible chronology. A stone with a cup-and-ring motif was found at Haughey's Fort, near to Navan, and Aitchison (1998) argues that it was intentionally deposited as a votive offering there, the significance of the motifs having been retained into the later Bronze Age. Decorated stones are rare in the Iron Age, with only five known examples (or six if the carving from the portal tomb at Rathkenny is included), plus a few decorated beehive querns (B. Raftery 1994:181-82, 1983:271-73, 1984:291-303), and these do not include cupmarks in their range of motifs. In the end, the stone could therefore date to almost any period, and its origins remain rather enigmatic.

Another possible clue might be provided by the story reported by Hicks (Chapter 16, this volume) in which Fionn Mac Cumhail throws a stone with his footprints from the Hill of Allen to Knockaulin. The person who reported this story (the grandmother of James Coy, in December 1937) said that the stone was still there to be seen. Since cupmarked stones are often associated with footprints in local folklore (Johnston 1989), it may be that the stone was visible at some point, and that its tentative attribution to Mauve phase soils was mistaken.

Lignite Objects

There are three objects made of either lignite or jet (Figure 11-1; Plate 11-2). Their material has not been scientifically identified, but all three could be of either material. As a future project, x-ray fluorescence has been successfully used to differentiate between the two (Sheriden and Davis 1998), and this could certainly be applied here.

One of the objects is a fragment of bracelet, one is a pendant, and the third is somewhat uncertain, but may be either of these two (see below). Unlike many categories of artifacts at Dún Ailinne, all three were found in stratigraphic context. The bracelet fragment and the uncertain object were found in the low mound, in upper and lower parts of the mound respectively; the former was from the Flame phase (and thus the final phase of Iron Age activity at the site) and the latter was from the Upper Emerald phase. The pendant was found in a Mauve phase trench, and so would be associated with the timber structures representing the third major phase of Iron Age activity. However, given the fact that Neolithic and possibly Bronze Age material was also recovered from some of these levels, it is clear that these objects need not date to the Iron Age, but could be earlier.

E.79.1900. Fragment of bracelet, characteristically black. It is fairly thick (11 mm wide and 8 mm thick) and D-shaped in section. Not enough remains of it to determine much of its original shape (the piece is only 58 mm in length), but it does suggest a fairly wide diameter, perhaps as much as 8 cm. It would perhaps be more accurate to call this an "armlet," since with this diameter it seems unlikely to have been worn as a bangle.

E.79.2688. Black, horn-shaped pendant. It is 47 mm long and round in section, with a diameter of 8 mm. The piece comes to point at one end. The opposite end has a perforation (2 mm) surrounded by a shallow hollow on both sides, which extends to opposing edges on opposite sides. If this is from wear, it is an odd pattern, and may suggest that the piece was held flush against wearer's chest, and not allowed to dangle. Whatever passed through the perforation would then have worn against the pendant on opposite sides. Above the perforation is a groove around the circumference at the wide end. Whether this was also intended to fasten the pendant or whether it

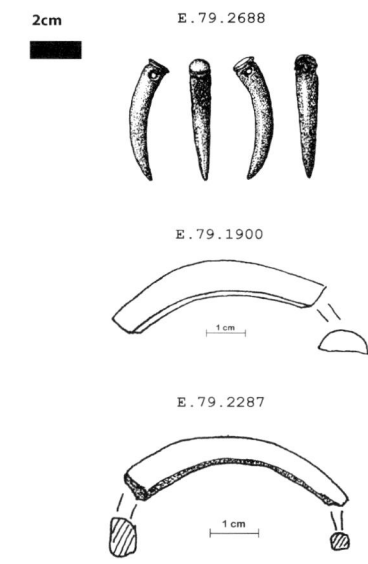

Figure 11-1. Lignite objects from Dún Ailinne.

was decorative is uncertain.

E.79.2287. Fragment of shaped stone, which seems like lignite in terms of its weight and smooth surface, but is brown instead of the characteristic black. The piece is rectangular in section, and has been worked to a rounded point at one end. The opposite end is broken. It is 52 mm in length, and 7 mm wide by 5 mm thick at the broken end; at the other end it is rounded, and is 5 mm in diameter. There are several scenarios to account for this piece. One possibility is that it is a pendant, and broke below the perforation, of which there is now no trace at that end. Alternatively, it was a bracelet, and after it broke it was being worked into something else, perhaps a pendant, which was not yet finished when it was lost or discarded. If a complete circle, it would perhaps have been about 6 cm in diameter (though not enough survives to be certain). A third possibility is that it is some other object that cannot now be identified, perhaps a penannular bracelet or some other decorative object.

Presumably these three pieces arrived at the site as personal possessions, lost in the case of the pendant and perhaps discarded or lost in the case of the other two pieces. Jet or lignite beads and other objects have been recovered from sites dating to the Bronze Age and earlier (for example, a possible lignite toggle in the Linkardstown burial at Baunogenasraid, Co. Carlow; B. Raftery 1974). Bracelets however seem to be more common later in the Bronze Age. They have been recovered from several Dowris phase settlement sites, for example, including Lough Eskragh, Co. Tyrone (Collins and Seaby 1960), Ballinderry, Co. Offaly (Hencken 1942), Knocknalappa, Co. Clare (J. Raftery 1942), and at Rathgall, Co. Wicklow (B. Raftery 1973, 1994:58). Interestingly, amber beads were also recovered from the first two sites, similar in shape to the one from Dún Ailinne (see below, "Stone Beads"). Bracelets of jet or lignite are also occasionally found in the Iron Age, though overall, personal ornaments of clearly Iron Age date are somewhat uncommon (B. Raftery 1994:141). They again become frequent in the Early Christian period, as for example at Lagore, Co. Meath, where 92 fragments of lignite bracelets are reported (Hencken 1951:150).

Lignite was also relatively common at Navan (Waterman 1997:89). A total of 12 pieces are described in the report, all but one the remains of rings of various sizes. The other piece is a fragment of ring with one end tapering to a blunt point and the other perforated for use as a pendant. This broadly resembles both pieces from Dún Ailinne, though there are differences. The Dún Ailinne pendant (E.79.2688) is somewhat more elaborate than the one from Navan, while the other Dún Ailinne piece (E.79.2287), though more like the Navan one, is not perforated. Where their context is assigned to a phase, the Navan pieces are all within phase 3, perhaps spanning the later Bronze Age and the early Iron Age, but earlier than the dendrochronological date of 95 BC. Also very broadly reminiscent of the Dún Ailinne pendant is that apparently made of fossilized wood, recovered from a feature at Haughey's Fort, near Navan (Mallory 1991:23 and Fig 16:9). It is only similar in its curved shape, being far less elaborate than its lignite cousin, but it does suggest some possible stylistic affinity for the general shape.

Obviously the presence of lignite/jet has no significance as a chronological indicator on its own. Stratigraphically, at Dún Ailinne these objects may date to the Iron Age, since they are found associated with Iron Age features. However, given the fact that lignite/jet is relatively common in the later Bronze Age, and knowing the degree of disturbance at Dún Ailinne caused by the successive building of timber structures, it is possible that these objects are in a secondary context. In this case, they could represent a Bronze Age presence at the site.

Rounded Stone and Clay Objects

This section describes 13 artifacts grouped together by virtue of their being possible counters or gaming pieces. All but one are rounded, in some cases artificially. All but two are of stone, and the other two are clay or possibly siltstone (the material of a 13th example has not been identified). While they do appear broadly similar, they may in fact represent different time periods and contexts of use. Following are brief descriptions (for material identifications, Ivor Harkin personal communication). Two of the clay balls (E.79.1203 and E.79.1208) and one stone ball (E.79.2888) are depicted in Plate 6-6 with the ceramic pin.

E.79.1191. Small black pebble, fairly round. The surface appears burnished or perhaps artificially polished. The stone has not been identified, but it is very fine grained. Later Iron Age.

E.79.1203. Small clay (or siltstone?) ball, dark brown and very round. Mauve phase.

E.79.1204. Very small stone (>10 mm in diameter), orange-red in color. The surface may be artificially polished. Mauve phase.

E.79.1208. Small clay (or siltstone?) ball, dark brown and broken in half. It is slightly oval in section, and has a triangular indentation in one end of one half; this is probably natural damage. Topsoil.

E.79.1310. Small back pebble, somewhat irregular in shape. The surface appears polished or burnished, possibly artificially. Upper Emerald phase.

E.79.1804. Small white pebble, oval in shape. The surface may be artificially polished. Topsoil.

E.79.1825. Two round sandstone balls. These are larger than the others in this section, being almost twice their diameter (see below). Both appear water-worn and are artificially worked. Later Iron Age.

E.79.1857. Round stone ball, probably water-worn. It is made of a bedded tuff, brown in color. Mauve phase.

E.79.1982. Rounded stone with a polished surface, possibly artificially. The material is uncertain, but it could be quartz, flint, or some other silicate. Flame phase.

E.79.2047. Small red pebble, somewhat irregular in shape. The surface appears artificially polished. Rose phase.

Table 11-1. Dimensions (mm), Round Stone Objects.

ARTIFACT NUMBER	OBJECT	MATERIAL	L	W	T
E.79.1191	stone	stone	18	15	10
E.79.1203	ball	clay?	19	19	18
E.79.1204	stone	quartz	9	7	8
E.79.1208	ball	clay?	20	18	18
E.79.1310	stone	limestone	23	18	14
E.79.1804	stone	quartz?	14	11	6
E.79.1825	ball	sandstone	41	38	33
E.79.1857	ball	tuff	21	20	17
E.79.1982	stone	quartz?	26	22	15
E.79.2047	stone	silicate?	17	12	9
E.79.2050	stone	chert	13	10	8
E.79.2888	ball	stone	17	15	15
E.79.2919	ball	tuff	22	22	22

E.79.2050. Small square piece of chert. The surface appears polished. Rose phase.

E.79.2888. Small round stone ball. It is unclear if this piece is artificially modified, and instead it may be water-worn.

E.79.2919. Round stone ball, made of a light tan tuff. The surface appears polished and the roundness suggests some artificial working. Unknown phase.

Table 11-1 shows the dimensions of these pieces. With the exception of E.79.1825, which is considerably larger than the others, all of these pieces fall within a relatively narrow and continuous range. For length, while the two ends of the range are almost 2 cm apart, within the range they increase fairly continuously, with no example being more than 3 mm larger or smaller than those on either side. While the width is not quite as limited, it is still relatively narrowly defined. This is demonstrated also by Table 11-2, which shows the descriptive statistics for the stone balls (Table 11-3 shows these statistics without E.79.1825). What is noteworthy is that the mean and median of the length are essentially the same, indicating again the limited nature of the size range. This may support the idea that the artifacts represent some fairly standard size, and therefore some standardized cultural category.

Context and Chronology

There is little about the contexts of these various pieces that suggests that they should be treated as a single class of object. Of the 13, eight have a reasonable chronological context, representing five different phases (Mauve, Rose, Flame, Tan, and Upper Emerald). This makes seven of them generally Iron Age in date; the eighth (E.79.2888) came from the Neolithic trench 281, and so may be Neolithic in date. As always, however, given the disturbance at the site none of these are certain. Two others are probably of later Iron Age date, but their exact phase is uncertain. Of the remaining three, one is from a feature of uncertain date and the other two are from the topsoil.

Given the lack of distinguishing characteristics and stratigraphic context, little can also be said about their chronology. The most common context for stone balls is passage tombs. Stone balls have been reported from the tombs at Newgrange, Carrowkeel, Carrowmore, Fourknocks, and Loughcrew, for example (Waddell 2000:74). This would suggest a Neolithic date, at least for those artifacts that are the most rounded, along with the one found in Trench 281 (E.79.2919, E.79.1825, E.79.1857, E.79.2888), were there in fact any evidence of a megalithic presence at Dún Ailinne. In the absence of this, three scenarios are possible: they represent an example of Neolithic stone balls outside of a passage tomb context, they were collected from a passage tomb (or other Neolithic context) and brought

Table 11-2. Dimensions (mm), Stone Balls.

N=13	L	W	T
Mean	20.0	17.5	14.8
Median	19.0	18.0	15.0
Mode	—	15.0	18.0
Range	9–41	7–38	6–33

Table 11-3. Dimensions (mm), Stone Balls (without E.79.1825).

N=12	L	W	T
Mean	18.3	15.8	13.3
Median	18.5	16.5	14.5
Mode	—	15.0	18.0
Range	9–26	7–22	6–22

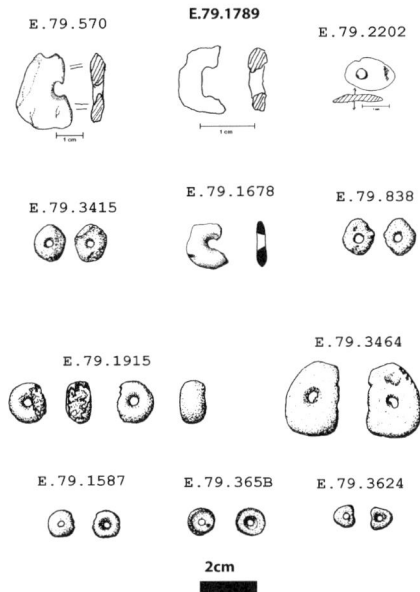

Figure 11-2. Stone, ivory, and amber beads from Dún Ailinne.

resemble both on purely visual terms, and do not provide any details that would allow them to be assigned to either definitively. In terms of function, the Neolithic examples are generally interpreted as symbolic, perhaps pertaining to fertility, or as having a ritual function (they fit, for example, inside the cupmarks found on stone surfaces at Loughcrew; McMann 1994), while the later ones are typically interpreted as gaming pieces or counters (B. Raftery 1984:250). In terms of the latter, the square piece described above (E.79.2050) has more affinities with bone gaming pieces, which are typically rectangular (B. Raftery 1984:248–50), though it lacks any additional decoration. In the case of Dún Ailinne, one might also add to this list of possible functions simple curiosities, good luck charms, or any number of other possibilities. Whatever their specific function (and assuming they are not the result of Neolithic ritual behavior), overall they fit with the pattern of finds from the site, predominantly the personal possessions of those who found themselves involved in the Iron Age activities at Dún Ailinne.

to the site, or they date to a later period as indicated by their stratigraphic context. Rounded, water-worn pebbles have been reported from an Iron Age burial at Knowth, Co. Meath, associated with stone cones; they arguably date to the first half of the first millennium AD (Eogan 1974:76–80). A rounded chalk or bone object was also found with the cremation at Grannagh, Co. Galway, dating to the same period (B. Raftery 1984:250). Flatter examples of polished pebbles, again interpreted as counters because of the association of some of them with objects resembling dice, were recovered from Meare Lake Village (St. George Gray and Cotton 1966:378–79). Finally, clay balls similar in shape and size to those from Dún Ailinne have been reported from Glastonbury (Bulleid and St. George Gray 1917:561–62) but these are either wholly or partially perforated, unlike the Dún Ailinne examples.

Thus they could plausibly be assigned to either the Neolithic or Iron Age based on parallels from other sites. The objects from Dún Ailinne

Stone Beads

A total of 13 beads were found that were not glass (Figure 11-2; Plate 11-3). Ten of them (77%) are stone of various kinds. Of the remaining three, one is amber and the others appear to be ivory. Most were found in unstratified contexts, and so little can be said about them in terms of chronology.

One bead (E.79.1985) is that found in Pit 293, the possible Linkardstown burial. This bead is described with the Neolithic ceramics, and will not

Table 11-4. Stone Beads: Material, Phase, and Context.

ARTIFACT NUMBER	MATERIAL	PHASE	CONTEXT
E.79.838	chlorite schist	Mauve?	slot trench running from Trench 515
E.79.1587	chlorite schist	Unknown	asso. with cleared rock, poss. Iron Age
E.79.1915	amber	Flame	lower mound
E.79.3280	ivory	Jade?	fill of trench, pre-Harry, poss. Jade?
E.79.3464	soapstone	pre-Niamh?	occupation surface
E.79.3624	chlorite schist	Rose?	no information available

Table 11-5. Dimensions (mm), Stone Beads.

N=11	L	W	T
Mean	16.0	12.6	4.0
Median	14.0	12.0	4.0
Mode	28.0	12.0	3.0
Range	9-28	4-21	2-8

be considered further here (see Chapter 6, Figure 6-4 and Plate 6-1). Five of the beads were found on the surface. A seventh bead does not have available provenience or phase information. With the exception of one bead associated with the Flame phase mound, the rest were probably in Iron Age contexts, but are uncertain. Table 11-4 shows the provenience information for these beads.

It is worth noting (in the interest of completeness) that three additional beads of light blue plastic were also recovered from the surface. These were small (4 mm diameter) and presumably (hopefully?) not of ancient provenience. They are rumored to have been introduced into the site by local workers, part joke and part test of the observational powers of the archaeologists. Their dimensions are provided in Chapter 14.

Overall, the beads show a range of sizes. Table 11-5 shows summary statistics on the dimensions of 11 beads. This table excludes the smallest, E.79.3280, which is a tiny yellow bead (see below). As can be seen, the average length and width are close to the middle of a rather large size range. The lengths were largely continuous until 18 mm, after which there is a jump to two beads that were 28 mm long. Widths were less irregular, never increasing more than 4 mm. By contrast, the range of thicknesses is smaller, perhaps indicating a technological or stylistic limit in bead production.

Description

The most common bead materials at Dún Ailinne are a related lithologic suite of schists and soapstones (Sorena Sorensen personal communication). These beads show a range of colors and specific materials. All of them are worn to varying degrees, and three of them are broken and incomplete. Descriptions of this category follow, in numerical order.

E.79.570. Half of a large bead. It is light brown soapstone or serpentine, and has black flecks of magnetite, particularly visible over one surface. Its original shape is somewhat unclear. It could have been a rounded square, or perhaps more oval. However, on one edge, just before the break, there is a notch, perhaps indicating that the bead was not originally symmetrical. The diameter of the surviving perforation is 5 mm.

E.79.838. Small, flattened bead of chlorite schist. It is light brown with black magnetite flecks. Its shape is somewhat irregular. The presence of rounded points at 2 ends may suggest it was originally a lozenge or an elongated oval shape. However, magnification indicates that the shape also could be the result of wear, possibly from having been strung as a single pendant. The perforation is 3 mm in diameter, slightly funneled, and also somewhat oval in shape. The longer axis of the perforation is roughly perpendicular to the longer axis of the bead.

E.79.1587. Small, flattened bead, dark gray in color, a highly polished chlorite schist or serpentine. It is somewhat D-shaped in section, with one side rounded and the other slightly concave, and the bead itself is somewhat flattened on one side. The perforation is 2 mm in diameter, and funnel shaped, having been drilled from the concave side. There is at least one striation within the perforation, visible under magnification.

E.79.1678. An almost complete bead, polished brown soapstone with magnetite inclusions. It is fairly small, with less than a quarter of the circumference missing. The bead's shape is round, but somewhat asymmetrical and uneven. The diameter of the perforation is 4 mm, and it shows a funneled shape, indicating the side from which it was drilled.

E.79.1789. Half of a soapstone or serpentine bead, brown with magnetite inclusions. Parts of the surface show some polish. The surviving half of the bead is irregular in shape. It is somewhat flattened on one side, and the bead is thinner near the flattened side, perhaps from wear. Assuming the perforation was originally round, its diameter is 3 mm.

E.79.2202. Elongated oval stone bead (or possible a pendant). It is a brown mica schist, and the surface is polished. It is D-shaped in section, and the flatter surface is slightly concave. The perforation (3 mm diameter) is funnel shaped, and was drilled from the flatter side. Dr. Sorena Sorenson has suggested the shape might be from its manufacture; the bead could have been held on a dop and one surface ground, leaving the other surface flat (personal communication).

E.79.3415. Small stone bead. It is white, possibly chalcsilicate or marble with black magnetite (or possibly hematite) flecks. There are striations visible within the perforation (3 mm diameter), which is funnel shaped, indicating the side from which it was drilled. The bead is flattened and irregularly oval in shape, and there is a flattened place on one part of the edge, possible from wear.

E.79.3464. Complete soapstone bead. The bead is large and flat, and now D-shaped. The flat surface is somewhat irregular, which may suggest it is broken, and shows some signs of oxidation. The surface is discolored brown and white, with white showing through under the brown. As with several other beads (such as E.79.1678), there are also black magnetite flecks on the surface. The perforation is relatively small (4 mm) and funnel shaped, indicating the side from which it was drilled.

E.79.3624. A small but complete bead, black chlorite schist or serpentine. The bead is now D-shaped, flattened on one side, somewhat irregular but almost triangular. This may be the result of cord wear, in which case the bead may have been strung singly as a pendant. The perforation is now near the flattened side, and the side is very thin in this portion of the bead. Compared to the total diameter of the bead, the perforation is relatively large, 3 mm in diameter.

The remaining beads are of varied materials.

E.79.1915. An amber bead, round and thick, with one side crumbling (Figure 11-2; Plate 11-4). The perforation appears very slightly biconical, suggested it was drilled from both sides (not surprising, given the thickness of the bead). There are distinct striations visible within the perforation under magnification.

E.79.3280. A very tiny yellow bead which appears to be made of ivory (Doug Campana personal communication). It is spherical and 2 mm in diameter. Given its size, it is hard to imagine how it was used, but it is perforated. Perhaps it was part of a larger beaded object rather than being strung per se.

E.79.3656. A small bead which appears to be made of ivory (Doug Campana personal communication). It is D-shaped in section, and is white with brown flecks (possibly signs of weathering) over a surface which appears to have been polished. The perforation (3 mm) is relatively large compared to the bead's diameter (12x13 mm), and is quite markedly funnel shaped. It was drilled from the flatter side. Scattered dark blue marks on the surface may be modern in origin.

In terms of form, the beads show a range of shapes, though most of them are variations on round and flat. Given the scattered contexts in which they were found, it is perhaps stretching interpretation to suggest that any of them are at all related to one another. Yet it is notable that 4-5 of the stone beads are similar in color and material, though arguably weathered to different degrees. The four most convincing matches in this regard (E.79.1789, E.79.3415, E.79.1678, E.79.570) are also graded in size, running, from smallest to largest, 11 mm, 14 mm, 18 mm, and 28 mm respectively (maximum length). Somewhat frustratingly, all four were found in the topsoil, in various locations not particularly near one another. E.79.3464, also possibly part of the series, is also 28 mm in length. Whether these were originally part of the same piece of jewelry is pure speculation, but nonetheless an interesting possibility.

Providing some support for this is the fact that, lithologically, all but the amber and the ivory beads are related, despite being different specific materials. Dr. Sorena Sorenson (personal communication) has indicated that all of these beads could easily have come from a single outcrop or a series of closely related outcrops. Most of these materials are quite soft, and would have been attractive for making beads, being easily worked and holding a polish quite well. Thus, while it cannot be proven, certainly the beads might have resulted from the same bead-making phase, or even from the same piece of jewelry.

Two of the remaining beads are quite small, and not dissimilar in shape to the bead associated with the possible Linkardstown burial. E.79.3624 is particularly notable in the regard, since it also appears to be made of a similar material. Since it was not found near the remains of the burial pit, however, little else can be said.

The amber bead stands out from this collection due to its shape and material. In contrast to the

Table 11-6. Fossil Crinoids by Feature Type and by Phase.

FEATURE TYPE	N	PHASE	N
Baulk	1	Crimson	3
Baulk?	1	Dun	1
Mound	1	Flame	14
Occupation	62	Mauve	11
Pit	1	Mixed	1
Plowsoil	5	Rose	10
Post-hole	1	Uncertain	4
Post-hole?	2	Unknown	70
Topsoil	3	Upper Emerald	1
Trench	23	TOTAL	115
Uncertain	11		
Unknown	4		
TOTAL	115		

overall flat profile of the rest of the beads, it is quite thick, with a relatively small perforation. Although it is broken, it does not show the extensive signs of wear seen on many of the other beads, perhaps indicating it is not as old or was not used as long, or was perhaps in a more protected context. In overall style it resembles many of the beads from Bronze Age sites in Ireland, for example the settlement site at Clonfinlough, Co. Offaly (Moloney 1993), the burials at Kiltierney Deerpark, Co. Fermanagh (Daniells and Williams 1977) and the hoard from Mount Rivers, Co. Co. Cork (Waddell 2000:250-51; fig. 114). Later parallels are provided by amber beads from Lisnacrogher, Co. Antrim (Munro 1890:386; Wakefield 1884:402) and, farther afield, from Meare Lake Village (St. George Gray and Cotton 1966:284-85).

It is worth noting also that a large number of fossil crinoids were recovered from the site. The exact number recovered is unknown, though some 115 were actually counted; one bag contained literally hundreds (if not thousands) of small crinoids, none larger than a pencil point, and these were not counted. They were found in many different phases and features, and also scattered in the topsoil. The distribution of a representative sample by feature type and phase is shown in Table 11-6. Of the total counted, 35 were measured, more or less at random, to get some sense of their dimensions. The statistics on these are presented in Table 11-7.

The potential cultural status of these objects has long been noted, since they are sometimes found in archaeological sites (see Beck and Stone 1935; Daniells and Williams 1977). It has been suggested that they might be placed in burials deliberately, for some symbolic or other reason, and they have also been found in direct association with necklaces, for example, at Upton Pyne in England (Beck and Stone 1935). Unfortunately, given the limestone substrate at Dún Ailinne, it is also quite likely that they would occur naturally. Thus whether they represent accidental associations, deliberate deposits, or in some cases were actually used as beads, or indeed all three, will have to be the subject of future study.

Chronology and Context

To date there is no reliable way to associate particular types of stone beads with particular chronological periods. They are simply too generic in shape. They have been found with portal, passage, and court tombs, and also Linkardstown and other burials, representing both Neolithic and Bronze Age contexts (see Waddell 2000:73, 86, 91, 113, 369 for various descriptions and references). They have also been found at contemporary settlement sites, such as Lough Gur (Ó Ríordáin 1954a). Their use also extends into the Iron Age, as illustrated by the cemetery at Ballydavis (Keeley 1999). Here, 19 stone beads were found, 17 associated with a bronze box and another from the same ring ditch as several glass beads with "Meare spiral" affinities (Keeley personal communication). Stone beads have also been recorded from the possible crannog at Lisnacrogher (Wakeman 1884:402), and a small stone disc from Navan Fort (1997:88, fig. 41:6) might also be a bead, though admittedly a large one. Given the wide chronological range indicated by these potential parallels, and the lack of any clear stratigraphic context for the Dún Ailinne stone beads, they could represent any of these periods.

There are two possible exceptions to this. One is the slate bead from Pit 293, which is arguably a Linkardstown burial and thus dates to the Neolithic. The other is the amber bead. Amber is generally associated with the Bronze Age in Ireland, and became particularly popular in the Dowris phase. Over 30 findspots have been recorded, with num-

Table 11-7. Dimensions (mm), Fossil Crinoids.

N=35	L	W	T
Mean	22.7	14.7	10.7
Median	10.0	9.0	7.0
Mode	10.0	6.0	7.0
Range	0.3-14.3	0.2-9.1	0.1-6.4

bers of beads sometimes running into the hundreds (Waddell 2000:258). As noted above, amber beads that resemble the Dún Ailinne example have been recovered from several Bronze Age sites; amber has also been found at the lakeside settlements at Ballinderry, Co. Offaly (Hencken 1942), Knocknalappa, Co. Clare (J. Raftery 1942), and Moynagh Lough, Co. Meath (Bradley 1991), all generally considered later Bronze Age. At Navan Fort, an amber bead of similar size, though slightly different shape, was also recovered from a phase 3 context at site B (Waterman 1997:87). This stratigraphic designation does not allow it to be narrowed down further than later Bronze Age or early Iron Age, however, and so it fits broadly with the other Bronze Age amber finds. It therefore seems possible, if not likely, that the amber bead represents Bronze Age activity at Dún Ailinne as well, with the possibility that it may overlap with the early Iron Age.

Given this chronological uncertainty, little can be said about the likely cultural context of the beads. While there seems little evidence for stone beads representing higher status elsewhere in Ireland, it is possible to suggest that the amber bead may represent something more. Amber, which has been demonstrated in Ireland to come from Baltic sources, may be considered an exotic material, and thus perhaps something to which not everyone had access. Its frequent association with other more directly high status materials, such as bronze and gold, would support such a suggestion (Waddell 2000:258–59). Who this higher status individual at Dún Ailinne might have been is of course obscure.

As a group, the beads may have been associated with several phases of activity at the site, and so may represent ritual or secular activity, or both. They were presumably the personal possessions of men and women who used the site, but whether the beads arrived at Dún Ailinne accompanying the living or the dead or both remains unknown.

Spindle Whorls

There were two probable spindle whorls recovered from the site. One, E.79.419, is bone, made from the head of an immature cattle femur. This piece is described with the other bone objects (Chapter 10, Figure 10-1 and Plate 10-3). The second, E.79.678 (Figure 11-3, Plate 11-5), is made from stone (type as yet unidentified). It is round and fair-

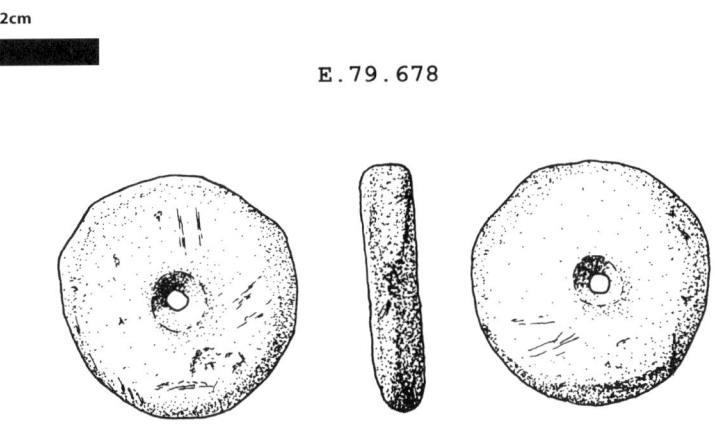

Figure 11-3. Stone spindle whorl from Dún Ailinne.

ly flat, with a well-smoothed surface. The total diameter ranges 55–57 mm and it is 12 mm thick. The perforation is 5 mm in diameter and it is biconical, having been drilled from both sides into the middle. The context of the piece in uncertain; it came from mixed occupation fill of uncertain phase, and could derive from Mauve, Upper or Lower Emerald, Crimson, or Dun. Regardless of which of these phases it belongs to, however, it is likely to have been Iron Age in date.

Two other perforated stones may also be considered in this category (Plate 11-5). E.79.265 is a flat stone, now 91 x 80 mm and 11 mm thick. Its original shape is uncertain as about one quarter (a "corner") is missing. Half of the circumference is rounded while the opposite side is straight; if the broken corner were restored, the piece would look roughly D-shaped. The perforation is oval (13 x 9 mm), drilled from one side, and is off-center. The surface of the piece is rough, possibly partly smoothed but generally seems unfinished. It was found in plowsoil.

The other object is E.79.202, also an incomplete perforated stone. Assuming it was originally round, this one is broken in half and is now 89 x 51 mm and 14 mm thick. It is broken through its biconical perforation, which is 13 mm in diameter and is also positioned off-center. Like E.79.265, the surface of this piece is also either untouched or only partly smoothed. It came from the Flame phase, the final Iron Age use of the site representing episodic feasting.

Neither of these is necessarily a spindle whorl, though both could be incomplete ones in different stages of completion. Either might also be a loom weight (either, when finished, might have looked similar to the example from Cush; Edwards 1996:81), though again their roughened surfaces suggest they are not finished.

Spindle whorls are of course ubiquitous in Irish prehistory and history, and are largely generic in shape and size. They have been recovered from sites ranging from the possible example from the court tomb at Ballyalton, Co. Down (Herity 1987:206, 209, object #50; this may also be a stone bead) to the settlement at Glastonbury (Bulleid and Gray 1911:582); they continued to be used into the early Christian period (Edwards 1996:81) and beyond. Thus these objects cannot be assigned to any particular chronological position.

If they are spindle whorls (and/or possibly loom weights), then they may suggest the presence of women at the site, and that such women were involved in the associated manufacturing activity indicated by other classes of artifact (such as casting debris, glass toggles, and the tracer). In later periods, documentary evidence suggests that women were responsible for spinning both wool and flax, and that the products produced by this labor were a potential source of both status and economic gain (Bitel 1996:126-31). Thus the production of thread, cloth, and/or yarn may have taken its place next to glass working and bronze or copper smelting in the manufacturing context associated with the rituals at the site.

Alternatively, the spindle whorls may not indicate actual production. They may have found their way to the site accidentally, in someone's pocket, or even perhaps have been carried as a kind of symbolic statement. Bitel raises the possibility that cloth making had mythological or ideological overtones in the gender realm in later periods (1996:126-31), and so perhaps on such formal occasions as the rituals carried out at Dún Ailinne gendered statements of identity might have been foregrounded through such a medium.

Whetstones

One, and possibly three, objects can be identified as whetstones. E.79.805 (Figure 11-4, Plate 11-5) is a long, narrow stone, 172 x 43 mm, and 35 mm maximum thickness. It has grooves on both flat surfaces, and these surfaces are significantly smoother than the edges. Both of these characteristics indicate its probable use as a whetstone. It was recovered from trench 515, a Mauve phase palisade trench. A second likely example is E.79.952, recovered from an Upper Emerald context (Plate 11-5). This piece is shorter than the first but is also relatively narrow (though less so). It is 59 mm x 34 mm, and 22 mm thick. The shape and surface characteristics of this object suggest its use in honing. In section it is triangular or chevron shaped, with 2 flat surfaces asymmetrically worn and a ridge running down the middle. This is presumably from use, as is the fact that two of the flat surfaces appear burnished. The piece is limestone and has a dark band of chert running down the middle of the stone. The third piece, E.79.483, is a water-worn piece of tuff, cylindrically shaped and flattened on opposing sides. It is 74 x 17 mm, and 12 mm thick and was recovered from plowsoil. The evidence for its use as a whetstone is less clear, but the shape itself is suggestive.

As with spindle whorls, whetstones are also common, though they are obviously limited to periods where metal tools required re-sharpening. Waddell notes an example from Rathgall, Co. Wicklow (2000:273) and another from Clonfinlough, Co. Offaly, where the find is described as "mundane" (2000:213). At the later site of Cahercommaun, Co. Clare, some 500 were recovered (Edwards 1996:95). As with spindle whorls, these may indicate some type of manufacturing. While ground stone tools also needed sharpening, the contexts of the whetstones just noted suggest their primary association with metal tools. Only tools that are being used need resharpening, and at Dún Ailinne the use of tools would be associated either with the construction of the various timber structures or with the manufacturing activities suggested by other artifacts. These whetstones presumably belong to one or both of these contexts. The use of one of the

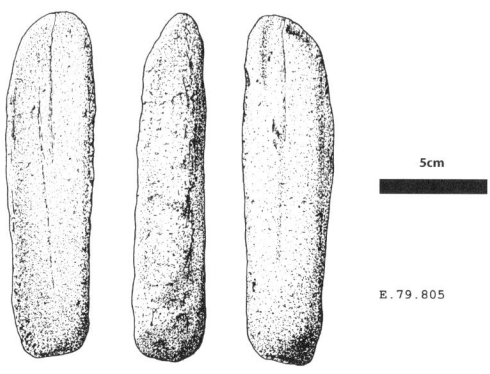

Figure 11-4. Whetstone from Dún Ailinne.

stones, E.79.805, may be suggested by its recovery from one of the Mauve phase trenches that held just such a timber structure.

Uncertain Objects

The objects described here either are or appear artificial, made of various materials. What unites them is that their actual identification and/or function remains elusive.

E.79.646. Small, flat, rectangular piece of fired clay, 20 mm x 11 mm by 3 mm thick. It is very light brown or tan and has possibly been cut, and is similar in material and color to E.79.844. It came from an unknown feature assigned to the Dun phase.

E.79.844. Flat piece of stone, light brown or tan in color. It surfaces are somewhat rough but its edges appear smoothed and the corners are beveled. One end is broken so its original shape and size are unknown, but its current dimensions are 40 mm x 28 mm x 4 mm thick. It was recovered from the fill of a Rose phase trench.

E.79.1171. Flat stone disc, 87 mm x 82 mm x 13 mm thick. One surface is fairly smooth and has what looks like plow scoring on it, while the opposite surface is stepped. It may be natural, but its edge appears deliberately shaped. It came from plowsoil.

E.79.2861. Rectangular fragment of what appears to be ceramic, though it could be clay or a very friable stone. It is 74 mm x 44 mm x 16 mm thick. The long sides are smooth, and possibly cut. One end is flat and less smooth while the opposite end is largely concave and appears broken. There is a perforation 10 mm in diameter about 2/3 along the flat surface. Its provenience is somewhat uncertain, but it appears to have come from a Mauve phase trench.

E.79.3651. Roughly lozenge-shaped stone, 54 mm x 45 mm x 12 mm thick (measurements taken corner to corner). There is a depression in one surface which appears to be a natural solution hollow. The flatness of the opposite surface suggests deliberate cutting and/or smoothing. The context of this piece is unknown.

Probable Natural Objects

All of the following have been determined to be natural objects, though a number of them give the appearance of deliberate manufacture.

E.79.237. A piece of mudstone (four conjoined fragments) which has an uncanny resemblance to a small figurine (Plate 11-6). It is broken, and its orientation is uncertain, but one end appears footed. Several grooves appear on one face, which is concave and has rounded edges. The inside of the hollow is eroded, but the surface appears to have originally projected outward for a slight distance in a shape that resembles a face (particularly in profile). Despite its appearance, however, it is almost certainly natural, with the "face" being the result of dessication cracks (Ivor Harkin personal communication).

E.79.918. Irregular fragment of smooth stone with two roughly parallel grooves on one surface. The piece is 33 m x 25 mm x 17 mm thick. This is probably a natural siltstone.

E.79.1244. Fragment of smooth stone with a pair of roughly parallel grooves on each surface. While the piece is broken at one end, the rest is a rounded oval shape. It is 34 mm x 26 mm x 12 mm thick. This is probably a natural siltstone

E.79.1836. Small, irregular, lumpy stone, 16 mm x 12 mm x 10 mm thick. Its surface is worn smooth. It appears to be iron ore, and as such may have been brought deliberately to the site. However, in the absence of any direct evidence of human working, the piece is considered natural.

E.79.2887. Irregular lump of material 53 mm x 23 mm x 34 mm thick. It is perforated in the middle with an oblong hole, about 9 mm x 6 mm. While it could be clay or mortar, it looks more like natural siltstone or hardened mud.

12
Specialist Analyses

Slag

Susan A. Johnston

Slag was recovered from a variety of locations within Dún Ailinne. While some of it was unstratified, most came from reasonable archaeological contexts. Table 12-1 shows the distribution of 26 fragments of identifiable slag (an additional 16 uncertain pieces were not examined) in terms of context and associated phase.

As can be seen, the largest group (12 or 46%) came from trenches. These were the various slot trenches associated with the Rose and Mauve phase timber structures. Another 6 came from the occupation layers, representing phases such as Flame and Jade. Other contexts were represented by only a few examples. While this is a fairly small sample for firm conclusions, it suggests that the activity which produced the slag took place at the same time as the timber structures were being constructed and/or dismantled. The specialist report included below suggests that this slag represents smithing, and possibly smelting, though the evidence for the latter is problematic. Smithing, however, fits with an emerging pattern of evidence discussed further below, in which small-scale production in a variety of materials seems to have been carried out at Dún Ailinne. The slag recovered suggests that, as far as ironworking was concerned, this activity was predominantly associated with the Rose and Mauve phases, arguably the phases otherwise characterized by ritual activity.

Table 12-1. Distribution, Slag by Phase and Context.

CONTEXT	N	PHASE	N
Mound	2	Dun	1
Occupation	6	Flame	2
Post-hole?	1	Jade	3
Surface	3	Lower Emerald	1
Trench	12	Mauve	7
Uncertain	2	Mauve?	1
TOTAL	26	Rose	5
		Upper Emerald?	1
		White	1
		Uncertain	1
		Unknown	3
		TOTAL	26

Report on the Slag from Dún Ailinne

Elizabeth G. Hamilton

Over thirty pieces of slag, slag/bloom, and ore were found in the excavation of Dún Ailinne. No sieving for hammerscale or spheroids took place and no thin-sectioning or compositional analysis was performed. Since no furnace remains were discovered, the slag is the sole evidence for metalworking. The quantities are not large and do not appear to be localized in any one area. CD Figure 12-1 shows the distribution of the slag; it should be kept in mind that this distribution does not represent a moment in time, but rather a period which spans 7–8 archaeological phases.

Table 12-2. General Characteristics, Slag Finds.

ARTIFACT NUMBER	TYPE	WT GM	N PIECES	COMMENTS
E.79.1008	Fe slag	4.7	1	magnetic
E.79.1094	Fe slag/ bloom	8.0	1	sucker-shaped, magnetic
E.79.1242	Fe slag/ bloom?	15.9	5	light, magnetic
E.79.1706	Fe slag	40.8	1	5.7 cm, very vesicular
E.79.1724	Fe slag	15.0	1	
E.79.2022	Fe slag	15.9	1	too dense to be iron corrosion, not magnetic
E.79.2084	Fe slag and bloom(?) frag	97.8	3	one piece flat patty ~6cm diameter; one surface solidified on dirt; hearth bottom?
E.79.2218	Fe slag	34.6	1	
E.79.2332	Fe slag	430.0	1	large, light brown with large vesicles, 12 cm max dimension, solidified against a flat surface, likely smelting slag
E.79.2824	Fe slag	89.6	1	dense, shiny, vitrified 4.5 cm
E.79.2950	Fe slag	26.9	1	
E.79.2996	Fe slag	45.6	1	dense
E.79.3203	Fe slag	5.4	1	
E.79.3308	Fe slag	78.7	2	light brown
E.79.3315	Fe slag	105.1	1	5 cm, many red-yellow patches
E.79.496	Fe slag	4.5	1	
E.79.534	Fe slag	20.7	1	
E.79.565	Fe slag	28.6	1	dense
E.79.944	Fe slag	1.8	1	slag crust
E.79.3081	Fe ore?	49.5	1	partially reduced ore?
E.79.3588	Fe slag	21.6	10+	several small, light, vesicular pieces; one piece with flow texture
E.79.3733	Fe slag	4.1	1	
E.79.3612	Fe slag?	13.5	1	full of silica grains, possible glass working slag

Most of the slag finds were single pieces. The total weight of the slag found at the site is 1158.7g. The slag probably comes from working or production of iron, since no prills, greenish coats, or other evidence for copper smelting were seen.

There is evidence that some of the slags were produced from smelting and some from smithing. Most of the slag was undiagnostic, and so one cannot positively identify it as either smelting slag or smithing slag. Only one small piece (E.79.3588) exhibits the smooth texture of flow slag, and that one is highly vesicular and contains a large quantity of apparently unaltered silica grains. Though slag of this form can result from smelting, it is unusual, and it may be that this piece came from glass making. One possible smithing hearth bottom (E.79.2084) was identified by its shape—convex on one side, flat on the other. This piece was 6 cm in diameter, too small to result from smelting. Found with it was a small magnetic slag piece that may be a portion of a bloom. Three other pieces from other contexts may also be small portions of a bloom. These pieces could also be gromps, small iron/slag particles that have been knocked off the bloom during forging. One piece (E.79.3081) seems to be partially reduced iron ore, but is far too large (4.5 cm) to have been deliberately added to a smelt. At least four pieces were dense and homogeneous enough to be remains of smelting. Table 12-2 shows the general characteristics of the slag remains.

A sufficient quantity of slag was discovered to suggest that ironworking of some sort, probably smithing, took place somewhere in the vicinity of the site. Most of the slag was undiagnostic. Some of the slag pieces suggest smelting and others smithing, but the slags that may have resulted from smelting were so few in number that no conclusions can be drawn. One piece is probably a partially reduced large (4.6 cm) lump of ore. Four pieces were magnetic and showed signs of iron corrosion. These may be pieces of iron bloom or gromps. One unusual piece may possibly result from glass making.

Metallography of Bronze Artifacts

Katherine Moreau

This analysis is based on metallography of 11 bronze artifacts out of a total of 55 whole and fragmentary artifacts. The conclusions drawn are significant given the scarcity of metallographic studies of bronze for Iron Age Ireland and the firm archaeological context of the objects sampled. Because of the small size and corroded nature of the samples, only five artifacts were considered suitable for compositional analysis by proton-induced x-ray emission spectroscopy (PIXE) (Table 12-3). We speak of these artifacts as bronzes because tin is clearly the major alloying ingredient in all five of the copper-base samples analyzed by PIXE.

Sample Preparation at MASCA

Records from the University of Pennsylvania's Museum Applied Science Center for Archaeology (MASCA) indicate that the bronze artifacts from Dún Ailinne, Co. Kildare, were sampled in the early 1980s. Later, the bronze samples were processed using standard metallographic procedures on three occasions—1990, 1991, and 1999. They proved particularly difficult to etch when the commonly applied etchants $K_2Cr_2O_7$, $FeCl_3$, and $NH_4OH + H_2O_2$ were used, either individually or sequentially, owing to compositional heterogeneity. In many instances what was revealed was possible evidence of prior dendritic segregation not completely homogenized by a subsequent annealing process. These remnants of the casting process obscured the recrystallized structure, which was lying beneath the segregated areas. In 1999, Dr. Samuel Nash, a research scientist at MASCA, suggested trying Klemm's III reagent, which we used with some success, and in some cases Dr. Nash applied the other previously mentioned etchants directly over the Klemm's reagent to improve the contrast or even in some cases completely reveal the structure. He also gave valuable advice on the microstructure (Samuel Nash, Helen Schenck, and Vincent Piggot personal communication). It is the author's opinion that element segregation may be responsible for the difficulties encountered etching the samples. The results of the metallography are presented below.

Casting

Artifacts can be made by pouring molten metal into a mold designed to produce an artifact's intended shape or its close approximation, as was probably the case with the button-like object (or possible weight), E.79.3017. Bronze can also be cast in a mold to produce bars or some other desired preform from which to create wrought artifacts. Under typical nonequilibrium cooling conditions, (see discussion of equilibrium conditions below and in connection with artifact E.79.3017), solidification starts with nuclei forming initially at, for example, the cool sides of the mold wall, the growth of which is dependent on a number of factors such as temperature of the melt, and the size, material, and form of the mold (affecting the heat flow), which determine the form, shape, and amount of the liquid and resulting solid metal. These variables also affect casting soundness, or freedom from defects: shrinkage voids that form when liquid metal flow is restricted; porosity formed by gas released as liquid metal solidifies.

Table 12-3. Values for Artifacts Subject to PIXE Analysis.

	ARTIFACT NUMBER	Cu	As	Sn	Fe	S	Pb	Ag	Sb	Ni	Cl
1	79.416	93.8	.403	3.53	.131	$\leq$ .011	.097	.72	.61	.26	$\leq$ .012
2	79.3017	90.5	.212	7.16	.086	.044	.241	.43	.43	.38	$\leq$ .014
3	79.911	92.1	.174	5.39	.205	.016	.329	.52	.46	.43	$\leq$ .014
4	79.1951	91.9	.082	6.14	.062	.016	.178	.54	.39	.35	$\leq$ .014
5	79.2836	91.7	$\leq$ .020	7.49	.095	.025	.027	.046	$\leq$ .04	.15	$\leq$ .010

Microstructures

Most of the samples taken from this small corpus of excavated artifacts exhibit similarities in structure: they are characterized by small to very small recrystallized grains—some with strain markings (intersecting lines within each crystal or grain indicative of localized plastic deformation) and others without. These markings may result from the conditions of casting, or from the working imposed by the metalworker: cold working a metal, which refers to a deformation process carried out at a temperature that renders the metal progressively harder and more brittle, and annealing, a heat treatment intended to soften by removing the effects of cold working. The stress applied by the metalworker to fashion the artifact results in microstructures that appear in the metal and are visible under the microscope after the metal sample has been appropriately prepared and chemically etched.

The etchant reveals microstructures that are known to result from cold working and annealing that affect the crystalline structure in different ways: either the crystalline planes are plastically moved to the point where the planes are sheared (a mechanism known as slip [Brick, Pense, and Gordon 1977:71]), thereby producing visible slip lines in the grains, or an individual grain's orientation is changed to produce twins (which look like bands within each crystal) by a combination of working and annealing.

Under modern conditions of deformation, when the temperature, method of deformation, and amount of stress can be somewhat controlled, the aforementioned changes in the microstructure from its undeformed state to its state after deformation (Brick, Pense, and Gordon 1977:69-91) become accessible for interpretation and analysis. These structures give us a fair approximation of what the ancient metalworker did to fashion artifacts, even those that were produced under what we now recognize as nonequilibrium conditions, that is, rapid cooling.

Interpretation of the microstructures and crystallography of artifacts is based on what is graphically presented by an equilibrium phrase diagram that displays the range of stability of the phases of metal alloys in relation to their temperature and composition. Modern diagrams include crystallographic information as well. Using the diagram as a reference point (in this instance, the Cu-Sn diagram) we see what ideally would happen to metal when its alloys solidify (Brick, Pense, and Gordon 1977:50-51).

It should be noted that solidification and the formation of phases often do not take place under the specific conditions predicted by the phase diagram (Bailey 1966:15). Nonequilibrium conditions often prevail.

Metallography

The cast artifact E.79.3017 will be discussed first as the presence of segregation (concentration gradients) of elements in its microstructure might shed light on the microstructures of the bronze rings and fragment.

E.79.3017

Copper alloy domed object (counter or weight?) with round outline and flat underside; described on tag as "button-like object"; whole artifact mounted for PIXE analysis
Grid Ref.: 46900/47800
Phase: Harry
Feature #: 1023
Feature Type: Pit
Micrograph 1:200x. Etchant: $K_2Cr_2O_7$ + HCL (Plate 12-1)
Micrograph 2:600x. Etchant: $K_2Cr_2O_7$ + HCL (Plate 12-2)
PIXE Analysis: Cu: 90.5%; Sn: 7.16%

Etching this sample revealed a cored dendritic structure (an indication of element segregation that normally appears with cast structures) and a two-phase $\alpha + \delta$ eutectoid between the arms of the dendrites (Micrograph 1).

Important for the Dún Ailinne artifacts are the differences in composition between liquid and solid that ensue to permit the growth of dendrites. The alloying element (solute), in this case tin, often remains in the liquid, lowering the freezing temperature; however, some of the liquid will have a higher freezing point, dependent on the amount of solute, and create a situation where the copper-rich dendrites are able to propagate, as they grow in a direction away from the hotter areas of the liquid and toward the cooler areas (Brick, Pense, and Gordon 1977:44-48).

Because the freezing temperatures of both liquid and the emerging solid are different (and indeed there is a freezing-temperature gradient in the liquid phase itself in relation to the forming solid, allowing the dendrites to continue to grow), the base metal and the alloying elements do not solidify as a homogenous solid. Instead, the initial solidification of the copper-rich dendrites into an undercooled liquid with a higher percentage of solute results in a heterogeneous composition, manifested as the cored dendrites and the eventual emergence of a eutectoid (a two-phase structure) in between the arms of the dendrites. If the composition was uniform, equiaxed grains would form from the liquid (Brick, Pense, and Gordon 1977:46-47; Bailey 1966:7).

Instead, under nonequilibrium conditions, the initial "spike" of the dendrite emerges into the liquid cooled to a point under the freezing temperature and "may send out side branches" (Brick, Pense, and Gordon 1977:46-47), giving the structure the fir tree-like appearance. Dendritic segregation on a microscopic scale, where there are "continuous differences in composition from the interdendritic spaces to the cores" (Brick, Pense, and Gordon 1977:55), is called coring (Brick, Pense, and Gordon 1977:54-55). Since cooling under nonequilibrium conditions occurs too fast to allow for the elements of the solid to be evenly dispersed, the phase composition and microstructure of tin bronze such as the ones in this corpus will undergo a series of changes (ideally charted on an equilibrium diagram) at precise temperatures and compositions. The liquid remaining between the arms of the dendrites solidifies and eventually from solid metal forms two different compositional and physical components in association with each other: a two-phase $\alpha + \delta$ eutectoid (the δ phase, being tin-rich, can be brittle) (Brick, Pense, and Gordon 1977:54-55; 180-81).

The structure in artifact 3017 is typically fir tree-like, however, amid branchlike formations there appear globular, almost equiaxed, predominantly copper grains, an indication that perhaps there were differences in temperature in the liquid that caused the "branches" to "break" or "melt off" and "float" in the liquid, becoming "broken dendrites" (Brick, Pense, and Gordon 1977: 48) (Micrograph 2).

This dendritic cast structure exhibits much shrinkage porosity. At the perimeter of the sample, corrosion preserves the dendritic structure.

E.79.667
Copper alloy ring, overlapping ends (partial spiral?); one end stepped, other end rounded; circular in section; worn
Grid Ref.: 46915/49520
Phase: Flame
Feature #: 9999
Feature Type: Uncertain
Micrograph: 400x. Etchants: Klemm's III, $K_2Cr_2O_7$, and $FeCl_3$ (Plate 12-3).

As mentioned above, after casting, an artifact may be cold worked to achieve the desired form; the metal will become harder and stronger up to a point, at which it will become brittle. Hardness and strength are possible because the deformation imposed on the metal causes the planes of atoms in individual crystals to move or slip, sometimes across each other, creating a situation where further movement or deformation can occur only if the metalworker keeps raising the applied force of the cold working—the result of this action is strain hardening (Brick, Pense, and Gordon 1977: 71).

A drawback of cold working is that eventually an artifact will lose its ductility, that is, the ability to undergo further deformation without fracturing. This certainly could have been a concern for this ring, as working the metal into a long thin shape would be necessary to create the spiral form, perhaps by rolling or extruding it through a die, and then twisting or rolling the metal into a spiral shape.

If the metal needs further working, it must be annealed, that is, given a heat treatment that results in recrystallization. This permits (1) the removal of the strain imposed on the metal by working, (2) the formation of equiaxed grains from the elongated grains, and (3) grain growth—the latter two stages occurring simultaneously in different areas of the metal. At this point annealing twins are apparent in the microstructure, indicating that the metal was subjected to cold working and annealing after casting (Brick, Pense, and Gordon 1977:80-86).

Because recrystallization grain size is a function of (1) degree of deformation; (2) temperature of heating; and (3) time of heating, the tiny size of the recrystallized grains in E.79.667 indicates several things may have happened during cold working and annealing. The stress applied may have been great; the temperature of annealing may have been the lowest possible for recrystallization to occur; and recrystallization may have occurred and become complete in a short time (see Brick, Pense, and Gordon 1977: 84). That this artifact may have been subjected to great stress is likely, given the processes, as described above, that may have been employed to shape it. Temperature and length of time of annealing may have been factors as well. (Indeed, as will become apparent, these may have been factors for all the rings.) The strain markings that appear within the grains indicate that some hardness was desired after annealing or perhaps just that the shape had been attained and no further work and annealing to accomplish it was necessary beyond a final cold working.

To sum up, it is clear this sample was annealed: small recrystallized grains are visible under 100x. At higher magnification one can see that the grains are equiaxed with annealing twins that are somewhat obscured by strain markings—an indication that the metal in this part of the artifact was cold worked after the final annealing treatment. A further indication is the presence of short fragmented inclusions—perhaps broken up by cold working. Corrosion surrounds the entire sample.

E.79.514
Spiral ring, copper alloy; one smaller fragment, with this attached would have made 2 complete turns; oval in section; both ends tapering and intact; fragment polished for analysis
Grid Ref.: 47950/48500
Phase: Flame
Feature #: 8888
Feature Type: Occupation
Micrograph: 200x. Etchants: $FeCl_3 + K_2Cr_2O_7$ (Plate 12-4)

Large areas of corrosion are present throughout the matrix of this sample. The structure, like that of E.79.667, was annealed; however, etching revealed larger recrystallized grains. Although the cold working may have been just as extensive and the annealing temperature as relatively low as postulated for E.79.667, if the annealing temperature was higher and the annealing time was longer these conditions would have allowed for sustained grain growth. Strain markings appear only at the edges of this very corroded sample. Also in the corroded edges of the sample possible relict structures are found showing recrystallized grains with annealing twins (better seen in this sample than E.79.667), another indication of cold working before annealing.

E.79.2271
Spiral ring, copper alloy, about 1 1/2 turns; one end polished for analysis, other end appears broken; oval in section
Grid Ref.: 47499/48090
Phase: Emerald
Feature #: 9999
Feature Type: Mound
Micrograph: 600x. Etchant: Klemm's III (Plate 12-5)

Half the sample is corroded, making resolution of the structure, as well as the etching of the sample, very difficult. Equiaxed recrystallized grains are so tiny that they could be seen clearly only at 600x. At least several annealing twins are present. Numerous elongated inclusions are oriented in the direction of working. As in sample E.79.667, inclusions are short and perhaps are the fragmented remains of long stringers.

E.79.1951
Small flat copper alloy strip; one end polished for analysis; irregular shape, though slightly curved and tapers to blunted point at one end
Grid Ref.: 46200/47600
Phase: Flame
Feature #: 9999
Feature Type: Mound
Micrograph: 100x. Etchant: Al. $FeCl_3 + K_2Cr_2O_7$ (Plate 12-6)
PIXE Analysis: Cu: 91.9%; Sn: 6.14%

A recrystallized fine-grained structure, indicating heavy cold working and a low recrystallization temperature, was revealed with great difficulty because of the presence of corrosion products. The annealing twins present indicate cold working and annealing after casting. Slate gray inclusions are globular in shape. Unlike E.76.2836 the percentage of tin at about 6% did not preclude a uniform composition after annealing.

E.79.1881
Penannular ring, copper alloy; one end polished for analysis; other end appears intact, and is blunted; circular in section
Grid Ref.: 47900/47700
Phase: Flame
Feature #: 9999
Feature Type: Mound
Micrograph 1: 100x. Etchant: Klemm's III (Plate 12-7)
Micrograph 2: 100x. Unetched (Plate 12-8)
Micrograph 3: 600x. Etchant: $NH_4OH + H_2O_2$ (Plate 12-9)
Micrograph 4: 100x. Etchant: $NH_4OH + H_2O_2$ (Plate 12-10)

This recrystallized sample exhibits very coarse grains in the center and very fine grains at the edges, an indication of non-uniform deformation. Annealing twins are present and some appear slightly bent—perhaps a sign of slight cold working after annealing (Micrograph 1).

The difference in grain size may also be attributed to segregation of elements still present in the annealed metal—segregation that remained because the annealing temperature was not high enough or the time of annealing was not long enough to allow the sample to become homogenized. Another possible explanation may be that this sample experienced differences in temperature at the time of annealing, though with a small artifact such as this that explanation seems unlikely.

There was some evidence for cold working in the 1990 and 1991 metallography as strain markings are present in both large and small grains. In 1999, Klemm's reagent revealed slightly bent twins. The elongated inclusions indicate a work gradient when hot working (Micrograph 2). Perhaps there is intergranular corrosion or another intergranular phase more clearly seen (as are the strain markings) in the 1991 processing with $NH_4OH + H_2O_2$ (Micrograph 3).

This was another sample which when initially processed with $NH_4OH + H_2O_2$ did not etch well: it showed very faint traces of the bands of large recrystallized grains (Micrograph 4).

E.79.1986
Penannular ring, copper alloy; one end polished for analysis, other end appears intact, tapers to rounded point; band is worn, and circular in section
Grid Ref.: 46670/48000
Phase: Mauve
Feature #: 9999
Feature Type: Mound
Micrograph: 100x. Etchants: $K_2Cr_2O_7 + FeCl_3$ (Plate 12-11)

This sample is corroded around the edges; however, uncorroded areas exhibit a very fine-grained structure at 100x. At higher magnification, annealing twins and strain markings are apparent, and perhaps some slight banding indicating element segregation, which may indicate that the annealing time or temperature was not sufficient to permit homogenization of the elements. It may be possible to see the banding better at 100x as the bands did not etch as well as the matrix of the sample. Inclusions are globular in shape.

E.79.2836
Curved fragment of copper alloy, probably part of ring (about 1/2 of circumference); circular in section; one end polished for analysis, other end appears intact and comes to point; L is total length
Grid Ref.: 47700/48200
Phase: Lower Emerald
Feature #: 472
Feature Type: Pit
Micrograph 1: 100x. Etchant: $FeCl_3$ (Plate 12-12)
Micrograph 2: 100x. Etchant: $FeCl_3$ (Plate 12-13)
Micrograph 3: 400x. Etchant: $FeCl_3$ (Plate 12-14)
Micrograph 4: 200x. Etchant: $FeCl_3$ (Plate 12-15)

PIXE Analysis: Cu: 91.7%; Sn: 7.49%

This sample exhibits casting stress (perhaps due to the shape of the mold and shrinkage) and then corrosion resulting from an aggressive environment. The "stress corrosion cracks" (Micrograph 1) and a long corrosion crack on one side of the sample that widens toward the edge are evidence of this. Either corrosion or inclusions appear as streaks in a wave pattern across the sample in a transverse direction (Micrograph 2). The metal shows a fine-grained recrystallized structure with annealing twins and strain markings present (Micrograph 3). This sample is notable for segregation of elements, as bands of grains appear in the matrix (Micrograph 4). The sample probably was not annealed at a sufficient temperature or for the time necessary to allow for homogenization of the elements in the solid, as is postulated also for E.79.1986. Perhaps the percentage of tin of approximately 7% affected the metalworker's ability to fully anneal this artifact in a reasonable amount of time at temperature.

E.79.911
Long, thin bar, possible ingot, copper alloy; square in section with slightly tapered ends
Grid Ref.: 47640/48940
Phase: Upper Emerald
Feature #: 9999
Feature Type: Uncertain
Micrograph 1: 100x. Etchant: $FeCl_3$ (Plate 12-16)
Micrograph 2: 100x. Etchant: $NH_4OH + H_2O_2$ (Plate 12-17)
PIXE Analysis: Cu: 92.1%; Sn: 5.39%

This recrystallized fine-grained structure is notable for an ill-defined eutectoid structure (or perhaps structures) in the matrix of the sample, which is another sign of segregation of elements and inadequate time of annealing for homogenization to take place (Micrograph 1). An interesting point: when etched with $NH_4OH + H_2O_2$, flow lines appeared that did not etch and showed no structure amid the recrystallized structure. The flow lines curved along the shape of the artifact (Micrograph 2). The percentage of tin was at about 5%—lower than that of E.79.1951; a uniform composition was not attained after annealing. Inclusions are mainly globular in shape. Strain markings are not present.

E.79.416
Copper alloy bar, possible ingot, one end removed for analysis; this end almost square in section, opposite end tapers to flattened rectangle

Grid Ref.: 47180/49170
Phase: Flame
Feature #: 8888
Feature Type: Occupation
Micrograph: 100x. Etchant: $NH_4OH + H_2O_2$ (Plate 12-18)
PIXE Analysis: Cu: 93.8%; Sn: 3.53%

This sample is notable for a segregated structure resulting from the casting process that still obscures the recrystallized structure (Micrograph 1). Initial applications of $NH_4OH + H_2O_2$ and $K_2Cr_2O_7$ etchants, followed by application of $FeCl_3$, revealed areas that did not etch; these unetched areas might be described as having an elongated dendritic shape. Application of $NH_4OH + H_2O_2$ showed this microstructural feature best.

The recrystallized structure is fine grained with annealing twins. An indication of segregation is the flow pattern in one direction of areas of the sample that did not etch—these areas are remnant cast structures that have been cold worked.

This artifact had the lowest percentage of tin, about 3%; segregation of the elements occurred even after annealing.

E.79.902
Spiral ring, copper alloy, almost two complete turns; one end polished for analysis, other end intact, comes to rounded point; oval in section
Grid Ref.: 47220/48745
Phase: Unknown
Feature #: 9999
Feature Type: Pit
Micrograph: 600x. Etchant: Klemm's III (Plate 12-19)

A very fine-grained recrystallized structure characterizes this sample; grains are so minute that structure was resolvable only under 600x. Annealing twins appear slightly bent, indicating some amount of working after annealing. There is a stress corrosion crack running through the matrix of the sample.

Summary

The cored dendritic structure of E.79.3107 and the appearance of the two-phase $\alpha + \delta$ eutectoid are indicative of elemental segregation as well as signifying nonequilibrium conditions. Under equilibrium cooling conditions a 5% tin bronze will be only a single-phase solid solution (Brick, Pense, and Gordon 1977: 180–81); however, Hamilton reports, citing materials scientist Michael R. Notis, that "in reality [a eutectoid] can appear in alloys with as little as 5% tin, provided the cooling is rapid" (Hamilton 1996:22, n.3). Therefore nonequilibrium conditions account for the appearance of the eutectoid in this approximately 7% tin bronze. Segregation is also indicated by the variance in grain size of E.79.1881. And perhaps the difficulty in etching all of the samples, even the cast structure's eutectoid (not visible using the $NH_4OH + H_2O_2$), may indicate preferential etching, the result of elemental segregation.

Another interesting point, in view of the appearance of segregation of elements, is that one artifact, E.79.1951, appears to be of uniform composition, while the other artifacts (E.79.3017; E.79.416; E.79.911; E.79.2836), with higher and lower tin compositions than E.79.1951, were not of uniform composition after what seems to be an inadequate time of annealing. E.79.1951 may have been reduced to its final shape by a series of hot and cold working and annealing operations to produce its final uniform microstructure.

The very small size of the recrystallized grains of most of these artifacts indicates heavy cold working and a low recrystallization annealing temperature. This is exactly what one would expect would result from fashioning rings of the sort mentioned here. That the other artifacts (strips or bars of metal) exhibit this type of working as well is perhaps indicative of the accustomed practice of the metalworkers and may mean that the type of working had nothing to do with the shape or function of the object. That a low annealing temperature was probably applied to these artifacts is interesting in view of what sort of artifact was being made—a spiral ring in most cases—and may have something to do with the type of alloy.

PIXE results indicate tin (an element that would harden the metal) as an alloying element in percentages to a maximum of 7.49%; however other elements are present in much lower percentages. Phosphorus and zinc are not documented in the analysis done in 1989 because either these elements were not looked for or amounts fell below detection limits.

Metallography of Iron Artifacts

Katherine Moreau

Three iron artifacts from a corpus of just over 400 iron artifacts from Dún Ailinne were analyzed at MASCA in 1988. The results were published by B. G. Scott (1990). Three additional iron artifacts were subsequently selected for analysis and were processed at MASCA in 1990 using standard metallographic procedures, including being etched with 3% Nital solution. In comparison to the "Dún Ailinne double-edged knife" (E.79.407), the "Dún Ailinne round-sectioned rod" (E.79.1926), and the "Dún Ailinne spearhead" (E.79.2305) examined by B. G. Scott (1990:88–91; 78–80), the microstructures of the artifacts presented below are much simpler. It is useful to include them here as an indication of the range of iron microstructures found at Dún Ailinne.

The Bloomery Process

In the Early Iron Age, iron artifacts were produced by their own distinctive process, different in many ways from that of bronze. The direct or bloomery process (a single-stage process) of smelting iron ore produces in the furnace a "spongy mass" (Scott 1990:16), called a bloom, with slag impurities embedded throughout. The iron does not melt and cannot be poured into a mold as bronze can. Therefore the bloom must be hot forged to consolidate the iron and rid the bloom of the slag. Some slag does remain, with amounts depending on the skill of the worker; however, there does not to appear to be a correlation between artifact type and concentration of slag (Ehrenrich 1985:60).

The metal that these artifacts are composed of was probably carburized to some extent during the smelting process (primary carburization), a process that was, in most instances, unintentional. As the ore was subjected to a reducing atmosphere in the furnace, the resulting bloom took up carbon as carbon monoxide from the charcoal used as fuel. That the carbon in the artifacts made from that bloom was unevenly dispersed may be due to the way the bloom was consolidated or the presence of phosphorus (presumably from the ore smelted)—phosphorus prevents carburization of ferrite grains (Tylecote and Thomsen 1973:197) and "promotes" grain growth (B. G. Scott 1990:12, 20).

Forging

The artifacts are simple shapes and the bloom was probably simply held in place on an anvil with a pair of tongs and then hammered to shape. The bloom would have to have been heated or annealed to render it workable. The temperature that the bloom was subjected to and the rate of cooling can affect the microstructure, as will be seen below.

Microstructures

The equilibrium diagram for iron and iron carbide (Fe_3C) charts the phase changes that the alloy undergoes as it solidifies, takes up carbon, and reaches room temperature. Iron takes on different forms depending on its carbon concentration and temperature: at 1147°C austenite forms from delta iron—austenite capable of taking up 2.06% carbon. Carbon that cannot be absorbed by austenite appears at its grain boundaries and may eventually form Widmanstätten plates if enough carbide is present (Brick, Pense, and Gordon 1977:128). As the temperature lowers to 723°C the austenite with a composition of 0.8% carbon changes into ferrite, which can take up 0.025% carbon, and iron carbide (Fe_3C), also called cementite. Pearlite, plates (lamellae) of alternating iron and cementite, forms in a eutectoid reaction when the carbon content of the austenite is at 0.8% and the alloy is slow cooled, for example, air cooled.

If the carbon concentration is below 0.8% then the alloy is known as hypoeutectoid steel (Brick, Pense, and Gordon 1977:127–129, 131). Based on the microstructures seen, the samples here probably range between 0.007–0.025% carbon—a concentration that does not allow a eutectoid reaction so the carbon forms a precipitate of Fe_3C within the grains, or more often, at the grain boundaries—and 0.025–0.8%, which results in a combination of ferrite grains and pearlite (see Brick, Pense, and Gordon 1977:135). The pearlite in these samples is so finely dispersed, that is, divorced, that low concentrations not even approaching 0.8% carbon are estimated here and therefore such samples cannot be described as true steel. There are instances of carbide or cementite at the grain boundaries in artifacts E.79.2233 and E.79.2700.

Metallography

E.79.2233
Flat piece of iron, rectangular in section, now bent into L shape; one end removed for analysis, other end appears broken; two other fragments in bag
Grid Ref.: 47095/48250
Feature #: 9999
Feature Type: Mound
Phase: Dun/Emerald
Sample taken at the top of the longer side
Micrograph 1: 100x. Etchant: 3% Nital (Plate 12-20)
Micrograph 2: 100x. Etchant: 3% Nital (Plate 12-21)

The sample exhibits ferrite bands—large ferrite grains alternate with bands of smaller grains, the latter having iron carbide at the grain boundaries (Micrograph 1). In some areas of the sample, bands appear parallel to each other; however, in other areas of the sample areas of large and small grains appear. Slag is dispersed throughout the sample; some stringers are evident.

The random alignment of bands and ill-defined areas of clusters of grains (Micrograph 2), along with the differences in grain size and the lack of pearlite or carbide in the areas with large grains, may indicate that this artifact was made from a bloom that was heterogeneously carburized in the furnace. Alternatively, the alternating bands may simply reflect compositional inhomogeneity in the hot worked metal.

The size of the smaller ferrite grains may be a reflection of the annealing temperature (higher temperatures resulting in smaller grains) and the time at the annealing temperature. The extent of forging (the greater the deformation, the smaller the grain size) and the temperature of the bloom while forging are also factors in grain size.

That this artifact is nearly completely ferrite without any evidence of pearlite and the lack of cold working to render it hard may mean that this metal was either not meant to be an object, or, if an object, was malleable at room temperature.

E.79.661

Iron shaft fragment, possibly nail; one end removed for analysis, other end broken; roughly square in section; 11+ additional smaller fragments
Grid Ref: 46750/49400
Feature #: 8888
Feature Type: Occupation
Phase: Flame
Sample taken before a protrusion in the pin
Micrograph 1: 100x. 3% Nital (Plate 12-22)
Micrograph 2: 400x. 3% Nital (Plate 12-23)

This sample is characterized by low carbon areas and a higher carbon area (Micrograph 1). In the lower carbon areas, small ferrite grains are surrounded by areas of spheroidized carbide, indicating that this section was heated and held for some hours just below the eutectoid temperature (Micrograph 2). Arranged in curvilinear bands lengthwise down the sample are large ferrite grains without pearlite—however, there is what may well be cementite at the boundaries of some of the grains.

One thin slag inclusion and several smaller chains appear lengthwise along the sample. The appearance of the slag suggests that it was plastic or ductile when worked. There are some smaller slag inclusions but no larger aggregations.

Like artifact E.79.2233 the differences in grain size and carbon content in the bands indicate that the artifact was made from a bloom that was heterogeneously carburized in the furnace. The lack of large amounts of slag shows that the slag was expelled to some degree.

That this artifact is nearly completely ferrite with only some evidence of eutectoid pearlite—but only spheroidized carbide that would make the metal soft—and no cold working to render it hard may indicate that this metal was not meant to be an object.

E.79.2700

Long iron shaft; one end removed for analysis, rounded rectangle in section at this end; tapers to other end which is flattened and appears broken
Grid Ref: 48150/48090
Feature #: 515?
Feature Type: Trench?
Phase: Mauve?
Sample taken at the thin end of the shaft
Micrograph 1: 100x. 3% Nital (Plate 12-24)
Micrograph 2: 100x. 3% Nital (Plate 12-25)

The structure of this sample is very heterogeneous: there are no bands of ferrite and carburized iron. Instead, part of the sample is composed of large ferrite grains without carbon. In addition there is some porosity or texturing that may be the result of a fine precipitate forming. In these areas appear small particles of slag (Micrograph 1). Porosity can also be a result of age hardening—a result of heating the metal well into the austenitic range, then cooling it quickly and then working at low temperatures (B. G. Scott 1990:19), which was seen in the Dún Ailinne spearhead (E.79.2305) (B. G. Scott 1990:78–80).

Adjacent to this area are smaller elongated grains with carbide surrounding the grain boundaries. It is possible that the elongated grains in a jagged platelike pattern may be Widmanstätten side-plates, indicating that the bloom was heated for a prolonged period at a temperature when the ferrite transforms into austenite; or that the bloom was heated to that transformation point and then slowly cooled (B. G. Scott 1990:13–14) (Micrograph 2). Other areas of the sample reveal tiny grains with a small amount of pearlite or carbide around the grain boundaries, although it is difficult to state this with certainty.

This artifact was probably made from a bloom that was heterogeneously carburized in the furnace. If the Widmanstätten side-plates are in fact as described, this structure would render this artifact somewhat brittle (B. G. Scott 1990:14).

Summary

These artifacts were made from blooms that were probably heterogeneously caburized during smelting or possibly during subsequent working. The previously published Dún Ailinne artifacts—the spearhead (E.79.2305), the knife (E.79.407), and the rod (E.79.1926)—are different in significant ways from the artifacts analyzed here. The most obvious difference is that two of them (the knife and the spearhead) are finished objects with an identifiable function, unlike the three pieces discussed here, which are rectangular shafts or a flat strip with no apparent function. They may simply be pieces of scrap metal. Since they were subjected to less manipulation, their microstructures are correspondingly simpler.

In addition, the three artifacts analyzed here lack significant carburization, whereas the previously published knife and the rod show more than mild carburization. The spearhead, however, is similar to the artifacts discussed here, and different from the knife and rod, by its lack of carburization.

A structure similar to the Widmanstätten-like structure seen in E.79.2700 was perhaps apparent in the Dún Ailinne knife when it was initially processed in MASCA in 1988. The spearhead is also set apart from the other five artifacts by virtue of the presence of Neumann bands, as noted by Reed Knox in 1988 at MASCA. This structure results from the application of about 10 kilobars of pressure at room temperature.

The knife and the rod were also described by B. G. Scott as having concentrations of phosphorus (0.101% and 0.132%, respectively) (Scott 1991:88–91; his table 4.2.2). The ferritic spearhead is listed in the same table as having a similar concentration of phosphorus, amounting to 0.093%, although this is not explicitly mentioned in the description of the piece (Scott 1991:79–80; his table 4.2.2). The differences in grain size and the lack of pearlite or carbide in the areas of large grains that are seen in the three artifacts discussed here would certainly not be surprising in samples with concentrations of phosphorus, in view of phosphorus's role in preventing carburization and encouraging grain growth. The knife and rod examined by the author and B. G. Scott all show a differential of grain size and carbon content due to the distribution of phosphorus, as posed by Scott in view of their elemental analysis. However, since there has been no elemental analysis performed of the three artifacts presented in this report, the possibility that these three pieces of possible iron scrap might have similar levels of phosphorus must remain as speculation.

Arsenic also had an impact: concentrations of arsenic possibly produce characteristic "white lines" arising from the forging of the bloom (see Plate 4.2.21c of the knife as seen in B. G. Scott who refers to this artifact as a possible example of the white lines [1990:20]). This feature, although *not* seen in the artifacts in this report is mentioned as Scott refers to the banding of the knife and the rod as a result of phosphorus/arsenic concentrations—and not simply of phosphorus. His caveat is that although the concentrations of phosphorus and arsenic are "coincident" they may be perhaps "mutually exclusive" and so white lines should be viewed with some "suspicion" (1990:20)

Floral Remains from Dún Ailinne

Pam J. Crabtree

In the late 1960s, flotation or, more properly, water separation techniques were developed in order to recover botanical remains from archaeological sites. At Dún Ailinne, flotation was carried out on selected archaeological samples during the 1972 field season. As such, Dún Ailinne was one of the first sites in Ireland where flotation techniques were used. The results of the analysis of the botanical remains recovered from Dún Ailinne have been described in detail elsewhere (Crabtree 1982a). This section will summarize the methods used to recover plant remains from Dún Ailinne and the results of the analysis of these floral remains.

Methods

All the plant remains from Dún Ailinne, with the exception of the nutshell fragments, were recovered using water separation and chemical flotation techniques similar to those described by Streuver (1968). Water separation was conducted on site during the 1972 field season, using a four-gallon (16 l) bucket with 1/16th inch (about 1.5 mm) wire-mesh screening at the bottom. The bucket was filled with water and stirred with a wooden spoon to create a swirling action. When the soil was added to the bucket, the light organic remains were held in suspension momentarily, and they could be recovered from the moving water using a fine-mesh tea strainer (Munson 1981). This method was particularly useful for the recovery of seeds and small charcoal fragments.

The resulting light fraction was then floated in a zinc chloride solution (with a specific gravity of 1.62) in an attempt to separate the floral and faunal remains. Both seeds and charcoal "floated" in the $ZnCl_2$ solution, while the small bone fragments did not. The seed remains were separated from the charcoal under a low-power microscope. The seed remains were then examined under a binocular stereoscopic microscope at a magnification of about 15X.

Results

Four different kinds of plant material were recovered from Dún Ailinne, including non-carbonized seeds of common agricultural weeds, charred cereal remains, charred fruit pits, and carbonized nutshells. The non-carbonized seeds represent eight species of common agricultural weeds. Since these remains are not charred, it is reasonable to assume that they are modern, rather than prehistoric, in date (following Minnis 1981). The charred cereal remains include 13 caryopses of barley, many of which had been heavily distorted during carbonization. The presence of barley in the Dún Ailinne flotation samples is not surprising, as barley is the most common cereal crop in the British Isles from the beginnings of agriculture until the Viking Period. Additional plant materials recovered from Dún Ailinne include the remains of the stones of sloes (*Prunus spinosa*). These plants flower in the spring, and the fruits (a form of small plum) are available in the autumn. Finally, burned hazelnut shells were recovered from two separate archaeological contexts at Dún Ailinne. Hazelnuts are useful wild plant foods because they are storable and contain high quantities of protein, fat, and carbohydrates (Renfrew 1993:194). They are commonly found on archaeological sites from the early Mesolithic onward. For example, charred hazelnut shell fragments were recovered from hearths at Mount Sandel in Northern Ireland dating to about 8000 Cal-BC (Woodman 2004:153). Hazelnuts are available in the fall, but they can be stored for consumption throughout the year. In short, the plant remains recovered from Dún Ailinne are consistent with its function as a site of ritual feasting. There is no evidence for plant processing at the site. Barley and hazelnuts may well have formed part of the feasts that were held periodically at Dún Ailinne. While sloes are generally too sharp to be eaten as raw fruits, they can be used to make a wide range of foods and medicines.

Implications for Seasonality

Can the botanical data provide any evidence for the season or seasons in which these ritual feasts were held? Both the hazelnuts and the sloes would have been available in September and October. These data alone probably do not prove that Dún Ailinne was occupied during the fall, since hazelnuts can be stored for use throughout the year. However, the faunal assemblage included many young calves, ranging in age from neonates to calves of about 6 months of age. Since calves are traditionally born in the spring, most of the calves killed at Dún Ailinne would have been killed between the late spring and fall. When combined with the botanical data, the evidence from the faunal remains suggests that the feasting activities at Dún Ailinne may have taken place primarily during the warmer months between April and October.

13
Biological Remains

Pam J. Crabtree

The eight excavation seasons at Dún Ailinne yielded over 18,000 mammal bones and fragments, as well as a small amount of plant remains and 1–2 fragments of human skull. The last is the most easily dispensed with. One fragment of human skull (E.79.722) was recovered from the Flame phase occupation layer (Plate 13-1). The fragment is now missing, but an informal examination of the piece when it was found as well as a subsequent assessment based solely on a photograph, both agree that it is likely to have been a human parietal, probably the right side (Rachel Scott, personal communication). A second fragment, E.79.5, is also in the collection. It is 15 mm x 12 mm x 4 mm thick, and came from the topsoil, so its archaeological relevance is unclear. It is certainly bone, but it is uncertain whether or not it is human (Rachel Scott, personal communication).

Mammal Remains

The Dún Ailinne faunal collection is by far the largest faunal assemblage to have been systematically collected and analyzed from a pre-Christian Iron Age site in Ireland. The size and quality of the Dún Ailinne faunal collection alone make it one of the most important late prehistoric faunal assemblages in the British Isles. This collection also has the potential to provide new information about the kinds of livestock kept by the pre-Christian inhabitants of Ireland.

The faunal remains from Dún Ailinne have been studied by a number of different analysts over the past three decades, but the first comprehensive analysis was prepared in 1984 by the present author. This chapter was substantially revised between 2002 and 2005, but the revisions are based on 1983 identifications that formed the basis of the 1984 analysis.

It is worth noting here that early publications on the Dún Ailinne fauna (notably Crabtree 1985, 1986, 1990; see also McCormick 1991) were written from an essentially paleoeconomic perspective, which was the standard at the time. However, since Dún Ailinne is a ritual site, the fauna can also provide a unique opportunity to study late Iron Age ritual feasting practices. This report will describe the fauna recovered from each phase of the Iron Age occupation at Dún Ailinne, including the animal species and body parts identified, estimates of the relative importance of the various species, the ages at which the Dún Ailinne animals were killed, bone measurements, and butchery practices. These data will be used to examine the practice of ritual feasting in late pre-Christian Ireland.

Materials and Methods

The faunal collection from Dún Ailinne included 18,755 animal bones and fragments. The animal bones were identified using comparative specimens in the collections of the Anthropology Department and the University Museum, University of Pennsylvania. The Department of Vertebrate Biology of the Academy of Natural Sciences in Philadelphia provided additional comparative materials. Bone fragments were identified to species whenever possible. When this was not possible, the bones

Table 13-1. Animal Bones Identified from Dún Ailinne.

	CATTLE	SHEEP	S/G	PIG	HORSE	DOG	RED DEER	L UNG.	S. AR.	UNIDENTIFIED	TOTAL
Flame	1,075	11	162	711	46		2	773	446	2,378	5,604
Dun	91		9	72	3			35	65	119	394
Upper Emerald	205	1	27	123	5			122	161	328	972
Crimson	54	1	5	29	2			17	40	179	327
Lower Emerald	84		12	62	9	1		90	140	296	694
Later Iron Age	228	2	17	166	15			117	149	1,232	1,926
Harry	101		18	77	4		1	41	56	1,309	1,607
Jade	6		1	7	1			1	4	81	101
Niamh	3			18				2	5	55	83
Mauve	283	1	25	132	21			102	69	538	1,171
Rose	491	3	44	355	17	2		165	190	2,394	3,504
White	27		8	23	1			12	53	135	259
Iron Age Gen.	32	1	7	45	1			16	47	73	222
Total Iron Age	2,680	20	335	1,820	125	3	3	1,493	1,425	9,117	16,864
Pre-Iron Age	10			21	1				3	101	136
Unphased	127		19	92	4			73	92	1,348	1,755

were identified to higher order categories. The categories used included small artiodactyl (sheep, goat, or pig), large ungulate (cattle, horse, or red deer), and unidentified mammal. As only a small portion of the heavily fragmented vertebrae and ribs could be identified to the species level, all costal and vertebral fragments, except atlas, axis, and sacrum, were assigned to the small artiodactyl or the large ungulate category. The Dún Ailinne faunal sample also included a few poorly preserved bones of small mammals, apparently the remains of the intrusive rabbit, *Oryctolagus cunniculus*. These bones were not examined in great detail and are not included in this report.

Once the faunal remains were identified, body-part distributions were examined, and species ratios (measures of taxonomic abundance) were calculated for each chronological phase. Species ratios were calculated using both minimum numbers of individuals (MNI) and fragment counts (NISP or the Number of Identified Specimens Per taxon). The advantages and limitations of both methods have been well described in the literature (see, for example, Gautier 1984, Klein and Cruz-Uribe 1984, Grayson 1984, Reitz and Wing 1999) and need not be discussed here. In addition to estimates of taxonomic abundance, the zooarchaeological analysis of the Dún Ailinne assemblage focused on butchery practices, estimates of ages at death, and bone measurements. Butchery studies emphasized the identification of cut and chop marks on identified animal bone fragments. Ages at death were estimated on the basis of epiphyseal fusion of the long bones and dental eruption and wear (following Grant 1975, 1982). Measurements were taken following the recommendations of von den Driesch (1976).

Composition of the Faunal Sample

The Dún Ailinne faunal assemblage has been subdivided on archaeological grounds into a series of stratigraphic and structural phases. The stratigraphic phases reflect the complex layering of the mound area that appears to represent a palimpsest of discrete feasting episodes. The structural phases include animal bones that were recovered from trenches and post-holes associated with the main architecture at the site. The structural and stratigraphic details have been described in an earlier portion of this volume (see also Wailes 1990). However, it is important to note here that the fauna from the various structural and stratigraphic phases were analyzed separately (see Table 13-1). The fauna from the Iron Age stratigraphic phases are listed in chronological order from youngest to oldest. The later Iron Age category includes material that can be assigned to

Table 13-2. Minimum Numbers of Individuals for the Main Structural and Stratigraphic Phases at Dún Ailinne.

N=201	CATTLE	S/G	PIG	HORSE
Flame	23	9	23	1
Dun	3	1	4	1
Upper Emerald	7	4	4	1
Crimson	3	2	2	1
Lower Emerald	5	1	6	1
Later Iron Age	8	1	3	1
Harry	3	2	2	1
Jade	6	1	7	1
Niamh	1	0	2	1
Mauve	10	2	5	1
Rose	12	3	8	2
White	2	1	2	1
Iron Age General	1	1	2	1
Pre Iron Age	1	0	3	1

the Flame through Lower Emerald phases, but cannot be dated more closely. These data are followed by the fauna from the structural phases, listed from youngest to oldest. The Iron Age General category includes a small number of bones which could not be assigned to a specific structural or stratigraphic phase. Only 136 animal bones and fragments were recovered from pre-Iron Age contexts at Dún Ailinne. These contexts produced a small number of cattle, pig, and horse bones. The faunal assemblage from the pre-Iron Age contexts is so small that it will not be discussed further in this report.

Species Ratios

As can be seen from Table 13-1, the Dún Ailinne excavations produced over 18,000 animal bones and fragments that could be reliably dated to the Iron Age, making this the largest Iron Age faunal collection in Ireland. With the exception of the small samples recovered from the Jade and Niamh phases, all the Iron Age structural and stratigraphic phases show a consistent pattern of faunal representation. Cattle (*Bos taurus*) are the most commonly represented animals, followed by pigs (*Sus scrofa*), sheep/goat, and a few horses (*Equus caballus*). Sheep bones were distinguished from goat remains following the recommendations of Boessneck et al. (1964). Twenty bones from the Iron Age features could confidently be identified as sheep (*Ovis aries*), but no goat (*Capra hircus*) bones were identified. It is therefore likely that most, if not all, the sheep/goat bones come from sheep rather than goats. A small number of dog (*Canus familiaris*) and red deer (*Cervus elaphus*) bones were also identified. The deer bones consist of two pieces of antler and a fragment of a frontal bone (the portion of the skull to which the antlers are attached). It is therefore likely that the red deer antlers were collected for craft purposes. There are no post-cranial elements, and there is no evidence for actual hunting of red deer.

The Dún Ailinne faunal assemblage included a large number of fragments that were not identified to species. Many of these were small, calcined fragments of mammal bone. Historically documented parallels (for example, 18th century Valley Forge; Campana and Crabtree 2003), where food bones were burned as garbage, suggest it is also likely that many of the bones at Dún Ailinne used in feasting may have been tossed in the fire at the end of the feast.

Minimum Numbers of Individuals (MNIs) were calculated for the main structural and stratigraphic phases at the site (Table 13-2). These data should be seen as minimum MNIs. They are based on the most frequent skeletal element, taking right and left sides into consideration, but the bones have not been matched for age and size. Complete and partial mandibles and maxillae were included in the MNI calculations, but loose teeth were excluded. Including the loose teeth from the Flame Phase deposits would raise the MNI for cattle to 41 (12 mature and 29 immature cattle).

That said, these MNI figures have not been used for quantitative comparisons for two reasons. First, MNI data are subject to aggregation effects. As McCormick (2002:103) and others have noted, it is risky to add together MNIs calculated for a series of small samples, since the sum of the MNIs for the small samples is generally not equal to the MNI for the pooled sample. This is a particular problem for the Dún Ailinne data since there is some overlap in the chronological categories; the later Iron Age material could be from several different chronological phases, and there is some overlap between the structural and stratigraphic phases. Second, comparable data for other late prehistoric sites in Ireland have been presented as NISPs. McCormick (2002) has summarized most of the comparanda in his report on the recently excavated faunal assemblage from Tara, Co. Meath.

Table 13-3. Species Ratios Based on NISP.

	N	%
Cattle	2,680	53.8
Sheep/goat	355	7.1
Pig	1,820	36.5
Horse	125	2.5
Dog	3	0.1
Red Deer	3	0.1
TOTAL	4,986	100.1

Table 13-4. Body Part Frequencies for the Main Domestic Mammals from Flame Phase.

	CATTLE	SHEEP/GOAT	PIG	HORSE
Skull/skull fragments	43	1	53	0
Horncore	7	0	0	0
Maxilla	3	1	16	0
Upper Teeth	143	18	66	9
Mandible	45	11	72	1
Lower teeth	226	50	165	13
Tooth fragments	121	3	22	4
Hyoid	1	2	0	0
Atlas	5	4	12	0
Axis	5	0	2	0
Scapula	32	4	30	1
Humerus	18	9	15	0
Radius	22	12	13	1
Ulna	11	2	15	1
Carpals	25	1	5	1
Metacarpus	31	8	8	1
Innominate	38	13	34	1
Sacrum	8	0	5	0
Femur	17	1	17	0
Patella	6	0	0	1
Tibia	23	11	17	1
Fibula	0	0	14	0
Astragalus	16	5	12	0
Calcaleus	23	4	12	0
Tarsals	15	2	4	1
Metatarsus	34	7	9	1
Metapodials	14	0	44	0
First Phalanx	62	4	31	4
Second Phalanx	40	0	12	3
Third Phalanx	36	0	6	1
Sesamoid	5	0	0	1
TOTAL	1075	173	711	46

The species ratios based on NISP for all Iron Age features at Dún Ailinne are presented in Table 13-3. The data clearly show that cattle were the most common species at Dún Ailinne during the Iron Age; cattle make up over half of the identified specimens. Pigs are second in importance, followed by much smaller numbers of sheep and horses.

The Dún Ailinne species ratios show some interesting differences from other early Iron Age royal sites (Wailes 2004). The faunal collection from the Ráith na Ríg at Tara, Co. Meath (McCormick 2002:104) is also dominated by cattle (48.1% of NISP), but the Tara faunal collection includes a much higher proportion of horse (6.2%) and dog (9.4%) bones. The Early Iron Age faunal collection from Navan, Co. Armagh, another Irish royal site, is dominated by pigs (60.2% NISP), and cattle make up only 30.4% of the Navan faunal collection. McCormick (1997:188) notes that the high proportions of pig bones at Navan Fort cannot be explained on environmental grounds, and he attributes the large number of swine to social and/or economic factors. Navan produced no dog remains and somewhat fewer horses (0.8% of NISP) than Dún Ailinne. These data indicate that there is no consistent pattern of faunal utilization at Iron Age high status, royal sites in eastern Ireland. While cattle and pigs are clearly the most important domestic animals at all the royal sites, the relative importance of all the domestic animals varies markedly from site to site. In contrast, the Dún Ailinne faunal data show very little variability from phase to phase, indicating that the pattern of feasting that was established at Dún Ailinne in the early Iron Age continued unchanged throughout the history of the site.

Body Part Distributions

The analysis of body part frequencies has played an important role in many modern zooarchaeological studies. At a very basic level, body part frequencies can reveal whether whole animals were driven to Dún Ailinne for slaughter or whether only selected parts of animal carcasses were brought to the site for consumption. In addition, body part frequencies can shed light on some of the taphonomic processes that may have affected the faunal collection.

The body part distribution for the main domestic mammals from Flame phase is shown in Table 13-4. The body frequencies from the other stratigraphic and structural phases show similar patterns and are not illustrated here. They are available, on request, from the author.

The Flame phase body part frequencies clearly illustrate that all parts of the animals' skeletons were represented in the faunal collection. Thus, it is likely that cattle, sheep, pigs, and horses were driven to the site and slaughtered there. Although all body parts are represented in the faunal assemblage, some anatomical elements are clearly more common than others. Very small body parts, such as sheep/goat incisors and sesamoids, are underrepresented in the assemblage. Fine screening is needed to recover these small faunal elements. Although all the Dún Ailinne soils were screened, fine screening was not common at the time the site was excavated; for the same reason, only a small portion of the soil from the site was floated.

Most of the Dún Ailinne animal bones were heavily fragmented, and this fragmentation is apparent in the body part distribution. Complete tooth rows are relatively rare, while loose teeth are quite common. Many of the long bones showed signs of weathering, suggesting that they had lain on the surface for some time prior to burial. The fragmentation and weathering limited the number of measurements that could be taken on the Dún Ailinne bones, and the small number of complete mandibles made the analysis of ages at death more difficult.

Kill Patterns

Analysis of kill patterns and ages at death have played a central role in faunal analyses since the early 1970s. As Payne (1973) ably demonstrated, mortality profiles can often be used to determine whether livestock were kept for meat, milk, wool, or traction. Two methods have been traditionally used to determine age at death for archaeological mammal bones: (1) dental eruption and wear (Payne 1973; Grant 1975, 1982), and (2) epiphyseal fusion of the long bones (Silver 1969). Age assessments based on dental eruption and wear are generally preferred because an animal's teeth continue to wear throughout its lifetime. Epiphyseal fusion ceases when an animal reaches bodily maturity, so these data cannot be used to distinguish adult from elderly animals. Ageing analyses based on dental eruption and wear generally require large numbers of complete or nearly complete mandibles. Unfortunately, few complete mandibles with teeth were recovered from Dún Ailinne. Mortality profiles were therefore based on a combination of an analysis of the small number of complete and near complete mandibles, epiphyseal fusion of the limb bones, and wear patterns seen on some individual teeth.

Table 13-5. Complete Cattle Mandibles from Dún Ailinne (Estimated MWS Appear in Brackets).

PHASE	dp4	M1	M2	M3	MWS
Upper Emerald		L	K	K	46
Later Iron Age	5				[1-5]
Later Iron Age			K	K	[42-45]
Harry		K	K	G	42
Mauve			L	K	[46]
Rose		K	K	J	44
Rose		G	E	A	28
White	5				[1-5]
Unphased			L	L	[47]
Unphased	F	5			5

Cattle

The complete cattle mandibles from Dún Ailinne are shown in Table 13-5. The state of eruption or degree of wear on each mandibular molar and the deciduous 4th premolar was recorded, following Grant (1982). Mandible Wear Stages (MWS) were calculated for the complete and nearly complete mandibles. Estimated Mandible Wear States are shown in brackets. Although the sample of complete mandibles is small, the data clearly indicate that the Dún Ailinne faunal assemblage includes both a number of very young cattle (MWS less than or equal to 6) and many elderly cattle with well-worn lower third molars (MWS greater than or equal to 42). Only one prime age adult (MWS = 28) is present.

Since the number of complete mandibles from Dún Ailinne was so small, we also examined the degree of wear on the individual cattle teeth from the Flame phase deposits. These deposits yielded the largest animal bone assemblage from the site, and the Flame phase fauna are most clearly connected

Table 13-6. Wear Stages in Isolated Teeth from Flame Phase Deposits at Dún Ailinne.

WEAR STAGE	dlp4	LM3
unworn	16	1
A	13	0
B	9	0
C	3	1
D	1	1
E	3	1
F	4	2
G	1	6
H	5	3
J	0	4
K	2	4
L	0	1
TOTAL	57	24

Table 13-7. Epiphyseal Fusion Data for Cattle from Flame Phase.

EARLY FUSING (BY 1.5 YEARS)	NO. UNFUSED	NO. FUSED
Distal Humerus	2	6
Proximal Radius	2	2
Proximal First Phalanx	9	39
Proximal Second Phalanx	3	36
TOTAL	16	83
Middle Fusing (by 3 years)		
Distal Metacarpus	2	5
Distal Metatarsus	4	11
Distal Metapodia	4	4
Distal Tibia	3	6
TOTAL	13	26
Late Fusing (by 4 years)		
Proximal Humerus	3	1
Distal Radius	2	8
Proximal Ulna	2	1
Distal Ulna	0	0
Proximal Femur	1	4
Distal Femur	0	1
Proximal Tibia	3	1
Calcaneus	3	6
TOTAL	14	22

with feasting. Wear on the deciduous lower 4th premolar (dlp4) and the lower third molar (LM3) was examined, since the dlp4 is shed at about the time that the LM3 comes into wear. The wear stages in the individual teeth are shown in Table 13-6.

The ageing data indicate that the majority of the cattle from Dún Ailinne were immature and that many showed little or no wear on the deciduous 4th premolar. Most of these calves appear to have been 6 months of age or younger at the time that they were slaughtered. Approximately half the dlp4s (29 out of 57) came from calves that were one month of age or less (dlp4 unworn or wear stage A, following Mulville et al. [2005:171]). Since milk residues have recently been identified on Neolithic, Bronze Age, and Iron Age ceramics from the British Isles (Copley et al. 2003, Mulvilleet al. 2005), it seems reasonable to suggest that the cattle slaughtered at Dún Ailinne may have been kept, *at least in part*, for milk products. As McCormick (1991, see also McCormick 1983) has suggested, the slaughter of these young calves may have caused their mothers to cease lactating. The slaughter and consumption of these calves would have been quite costly, as it would have entailed the sacrifice of the calf and the possible loss of valuable milk products. Under what circumstances might these costly sacrifices be made? These questions lead to broader issues of political economy which will be addressed at the end of this chapter.

The rest of the cattle were mainly older adults with heavily worn third molars. Most of these animals would have been more than 5 years old at the time of their death. Few prime age adults were slaughtered at Dún Ailinne.

The ageing data based on epiphyseal fusion present a somewhat different picture (Table 13-7). The epiphyseal data indicate that fewer cattle were killed during the first six months of life and that nearly two-thirds of the cattle survived to more than three years of age. The differences between the age profile based on dental eruption and wear and the one based on epiphyseal fusion are probably the result of taphonomic processes that affected the animal bones after they were discarded. As noted above, many of the Dún Ailinne bones were heavily calcined and fragmented. In addition, trampling and weathering may have destroyed many of the fragile unfused epiphyses of young cattle. Since teeth are denser and more durable than limb bones, the age profile based on dentition is probably a more accurate reflection of the ages of the cattle that were consumed at Dún Ailinne.

Table 13-8. Dental Eruption and Wear Data for Complete Pig Mandibles from Dún Ailinne (Estimated MWS in Brackets).

PHASE	M1	M2	M3	MWS
Flame		C	5	[28]
Flame	A			6
Flame	J	C	5	27
Flame	C	5		13
Flame	G		3	[21]
Upper Emerald	J	E		[30]
Crimson		C	5	[27]
Lower Emerald	B	3		10
Later Iron Age		E	A	[30]
Harry	D	5		14
Mauve	5			5
Mauve	J	C		[27]
Rose	C	A	1-2	15-16
Rose		F	B	[33]
Rose		L	D	[43]
Rose	M	G		[37]
White	B	2		9
Iron Age General	G	D	B	28
Unphased	B	3		10
Unphased	G	B	2	21

Pigs

While cattle can be used for a variety of second products such as milk and traction, pigs are primarily raised for their meat. An examination of the kill patterns for the Dún Ailinne pigs should reveal the ages of the pigs that were chosen for feasting. Twenty complete or nearly complete mandibles were recovered from Dún Ailinne (Table 13-8). The data indicate that pigs of all ages were slaughtered. The youngest animals show minimal wear on the first molar and were probably about 6 months old when they were slaughtered; the oldest animals have worn third molars and would have been at least 3 years of age when they were killed.

The epiphyseal fusion data for pigs (Table 13-9) generally mirror the ageing data based on dental eruption and wear. The epiphyseal data indicate that about two-thirds of the pigs were killed by the age of two and one-half years, and that a very small number survived to more than 3.5 years.

Table 13-9. Epiphyseal Fusion Data for Pigs from Flame Phase.

EARLY FUSING (BY 1.5 YEARS)	NO. UNFUSED	NO. FUSED
Distal Humerus	0	5
Proximal Radius	0	7
Proximal Second Phalanx	2	9
TOTAL	2	21
Middle Fusing (by 2.5 years)		
Distal Metacarpus	6	1
Proximal First Phalanx	16	9
Distal Tibia	5	4
Calcaneus	5	2
Distal Metatarsus	6	1
Distal Metapodia	25	6
TOTAL	63	23
Late Fusing (by 3.5 years)		
Proximal Humerus	2	0
Distal Radius	3	0
Proximal Ulna	3	0
Distal Ulna	3	0
Proximal Femur	4	0
Distal Femur	6	2
Proximal Tibia	3	0
TOTAL	24	2

Sheep

Since sheep make up a small part of the Dún Ailinne faunal assemblage, complete mandibles and ageable limb bones are relatively rare. Although only 6 complete or nearly complete mandibles were recovered from Dún Ailinne, the faunal assemblage includes both very young animals with

Table 13-10. Sheep/Goat Mandibles from Dún Ailinne (Estimated MWS in Brackets).

PHASE	dp4	M1	M2	M3	MWS
Flame		E	3		13
Flame		G	D		[23]
Upper Emerald		M	G		[41]
Crimson		J	G	F+	[38]
Rose		G	C		[32]
Unphased	4				[1–4]

Table 13-11. Epiphyseal Fusion Data for Sheep from Flame Phase.

EARLY FUSING (BY 1.5 YEARS)	NO. UNFUSED	NO. FUSED
Distal Humerus	0	6
Proximal Radius	1	5
Proximal First Phalanx	1	3
TOTAL	2	14
MIDDLE FUSING (BY 2.5 YEARS)		
Proximal Ulna	1	0
Distal Metacarpus	1	0
Distal Metatarsus	1	0
Distal Tibia	1	4
TOTAL	4	4
LATE FUSING (BY 3.5 YEARS)		
Distal Radius	1	0
Proximal Tibia	1	0
Calcaneus	0	2
TOTAL	2	2

unworn deciduous teeth and adult animals with worn third molars. The ageable sheep/goat mandibles are listed in Table 13-10. Since the analysis of the Dún Ailinne fauna was completed, criteria have been established for distinguishing the deciduous (Payne 1985) and adult (Halstead and Collins 2002) teeth of sheep and goats.

The limited epiphyseal fusion data for sheep from Flame Phase are presented in Table 13-11. The data are so limited that firm conclusions about slaughter patterns for sheep cannot be drawn from them.

Horses

While the number of horse limb bones and teeth from Dún Ailinne is far too small for the construction of a detailed age profile, it is important to note that all the Dún Ailinne horses appear to be mature. No deciduous or unworn teeth and no unfused limb bones were recovered from the site.

Measurement

Animal bone measurements can provide useful information on the sizes of prehistoric animals and on changes in animal size through both time and space. As few faunal collections have been recovered from Iron Age sites in Ireland, the Dún Ailinne animal bone assemblage provides a unique opportunity to study the sizes of Irish Iron Age livestock. This analysis follows the recommendations of von den Driesch (1976), so that only the fully fused epiphyses of adult animals were measured. This limited the number of measurable specimens, since, as described above, many of the cattle and

Table 13-12. Summary of Measurements Taken on Cattle, Pig, and Sheep Bones from Dún Ailinne.

SPECIES	BONE	MEAS.	MEAN	MIN.	MAX.	S.D.	C.V.	N
Cattle	Humerus	BT	65.1	60.0	68.9	3.25	0.05	5
Cattle	Metacarpus	Bp	54.8	51.9	58.7	2.2	0.04	7
Cattle	Metacarpus	Bd	52.6	50.8	54.0	1.2	0.02	7
Cattle	Astragalus	GLl	60.9	50.4	64.6	3.8	0.06	13
Cattle	Astragalus	GLm	56.4	54.1	59.8	1.7	0.03	14
Cattle	Astragalus	Bd	38.2	32.3	47.3	3.7	0.10	12
Cattle	Metatarsus	Bd	52.6	49.0	61.3	3.9	0.07	8
Pig	Humerus	Bd	35.7	29.5	38.7	2.5	0.07	11
Pig	Radius	Bp	264.0	25.2	29.0	1.0	0.04	11
Pig	Astragalus	GLl	38.5	36.2	40.9	1.5	0.04	9
Pig	Astragalus	Glm	35.3	33.6	37.5	1.3	0.04	10
Pig	Tibia	Bd	29.2	27.3	34.3	2.1	0.07	9
Pig	Upper M3	Length	31.1	28.5	34.2	1.9	0.06	20
Pig	Lower M3	Length	34.2	29.3	39.0	2.7	0.08	23
Sheep	Tibia	Bd	24.2	22.3	26.0	1.5	0.06	5

Table 13-13: Withers Height Estimates (mm) for Cattle and Horses from Dún Ailinne.

SPECIES	MEASUREMENT	LENGTH	W.H.
Cattle	Metacarpus GL	182.0	111.5
Cattle	Metatarsus GL	211.0	115.0
Cattle	Femur (GLC)	311.0	107.0
Horse	Metatarsus LL	232.0	123.7

Note: All measurements based on von den Driesch (1976); withers heights calculated following von den Driesch and Boessneck (1974).

pigs from Dún Ailinne were immature. In addition, many of the mature bones were extensively weathered or burnt, making accurate measurement impossible. As a result, the number of measurable specimens from Dún Ailinne is much smaller than one might expect from an assemblage of this size. However, since the publication of von den Driesch's (1976) measurement manual and the completion of the identification of the Dún Ailinne fauna, Zeder and Hesse (2000) have shown that measurements of immature specimens can be useful in distinguishing male from female animals, especially goats which show a high degree of sexual dimorphism.

Table 13-12 presents a summary of the measurements taken on cattle, pig, and sheep bones from Dún Ailinne. The measurements included in the table could be taken on 5 or more individual bones. The mean, range, standard deviation (s.d.), and co-efficient of variation (c.v.) for these measurements are shown in the table. Individual measurements for these bones can be obtained from the author.

A small number of complete long bones were recovered from Dún Ailinne, and these bones can be used to estimate withers heights for the domestic animals. Withers' heights were calculated following the recommendations of von den Driesch and Boessneck (1974). A single complete horse metatarsus yielded a withers' height of 123.7 cm. This animal would have been a small pony, just over 12 hands in stature (see Table 13-13). The Dún Ailinne horse is considerably smaller than the Iron Age horse from Tara (McCormick 2002:107), which is estimated at about 13–14 hands. The withers' heights for cattle range from 107.9 to 115 cm., with a mean of 111.5 cm. The Dún Ailinne cattle appear generally comparable in size to the early Anglo-Saxon cattle from West Stow (Crabtree 1989:29–38), but they are somewhat larger than the pre-Roman Iron Age cattle from West Stow.

Butchery

All the identified bones from Dún Ailinne were examined for the presence of butchery marks. Three types of butchery traces were apparent: (1)

Table 13-14. Distribution of Butchery Traces on Cattle, Sheep, Pig, and Horse Bones from Dún Ailinne.

	CATTLE	SHEEP/GOAT	PIG	HORSE
Skull/skull fragments	1		3	
Horncore				
Maxilla				
Upper Teeth				
Mandible	11		1	
Lower teeth				
Tooth fragments				
Hyoid	2			
Atlas	3	1	3	
Axis				
Scapula	3		2	
Humerus	2		6	
Radius	1	1		
Ulna			1	
Carpals				
Metacarpus	13		2	
Innominate	6		3	1
Sacrum				
Femur	2			
Patella				
Tibia	3		2	1
Fibula				
Astragalus	9		2	1
Calcaleus	5		1	
Tarsals			1	
Metatarsus	6		1	
Metapodials	3			
First Phalanx	17			1
Second Phalanx				1
Third Phalanx				
Sesamoid				1
TOTAL	87	5	26	5

fine knife cuts, (2) heavy chop marks, probably made with a heavy knife, axe, or cleaver-like implement, and (3) axial splitting of the long bones and first phalanges, possibly for marrow extraction.

Butchery marks were seen on 123 Iron Age bones from Dún Ailinne. The distribution of these marks is shown in Table 13-14. As can be seen from the table, the vast majority of the butchery marks appear on cattle bones, and marks are relatively more common on large mammal (cattle and horse) bones than on the bones of smaller animals.

Cattle

Head
The mandible is the most commonly butchered cranial element. Four mandibles show cut marks on the medial side that may have resulted from the removal of the tongue. The cut marks seen on two hyoid bones were also probably produced in this way. Chop marks on the back of the mandible may have been produced during the removal of the jaw, while cut marks on the lateral side of the mandible could have resulted from the massive masseter muscle. A single chop mark on a temporal bone may also have been produced during the separation of the lower jaw. The chop marks seen on three atlases were probably the result of decapitation.

Forelimb
Few butchery marks are evident on cattle forelimb bones. One radius and one distal humerus have been axially split, probably for marrow extraction. Knife cuts on the scapula undoubtedly resulted from meat removal, as did the transverse knife cuts seen on a single humeral shaft.

Hindlimb
The chop marks seen on the ilium, ischium, pubis, and acetabulum clearly resulted from the disarticulation of the pelvis. A single chopped-off femoral head was probably produced in the same way. Two tibiae have been axially split, presumably for marrow removal. Knife cuts seen on a single proximal tibia must have resulted from the disarticulation of the stiffle (knee) joint.

Feet
Butchery marks are most common on cattle foot bones. The disarticulation of the hock joint produced transverse knife cuts on nine astragali and four calcanei. Metapodia bear very little meat but are excellent marrow bones. Thirteen metapodia have been axially split for marrow extraction. In addition, six first phalanges have been axially split. Transverse knife cuts are seen across the plantar surfaces of two metacarpals, two metatarsals, and six first phalanges. While the function of these cuts is not entirely clear, they may have been produced when the digital flexor tendons were severed.

Pig

Analysis of the butchery on the Dún Ailinne pig bones presents some difficulties due to small sample size. While many different pig anatomical elements show butchery marks, in most cases there are only one or two examples for each anatomical element. It is therefore very difficult to generalize about butchery *patterns* from a sample size this small.

Head
Two pig frontals have been chopped through. These butchery marks may have been produced when the pig was stunned or pole-axed. A third skull fragment shows a chop mark on the temporal, possibly as a result of the removal of the mandible. Chop and cut marks on the ventral portion of the atlas probably resulted from decapitation.

Forelimb
Knife cuts seen on the lateral face of the scapula probably resulted from meat removal. The chop marks seen on a second scapula are more difficult to explain, as the shoulder joint can be easily disarticulated without the necessity of chopping through bone. This may represent the work of an individual who does not butcher meat on a regular basis. Knife cuts on three distal humeri were probably produced in the disarticulation of the elbow joint. Those on the midshaft of the humerus probably represent meat removal, while a single example of knife cutting on the proximal humerus was probably produced during the disarticulation of the shoulder joint.

Hindlimb
The knife cuts and superficial chop marks seen on three pig ilia probably resulted from meat removal. Knife cuts on the distal tibia resulted from the disarticulation of the hock joint, while chop marks on the proximal tibia probably resulted from the separation of the stiffle joint.

Feet
It is difficult to see any pattern in the butchery

of the feet. A larger sample of butchered bones is needed before any conclusions can be drawn.

Sheep

Only five sheep/goat bones preserved butchery traces, but these few marks suggest that caprines and cattle were butchered in similar ways. The fine knife cuts seen on two astragali and a single calcaneus clearly resulted from the disarticulation of the hock joint. The single butchered atlas may have been split during decapitation. The knife cuts seen on a distal radius may have been produced by the removal of the feet at the carpal joint.

Horse

With the exception of the knife cuts seen on a single horse ischium, all the butchery marks preserved on horse bones are seen on foot and lower limb elements. The cuts on a tibial midshaft resulted from meat removal, while those on a sesamoid and second phalanx may have been produced during the removal of the feet and hooves. A first phalanx had been split and a second phalanx chopped through, possibly for marrow extraction.

Dog

Only three dog bones were identified from the Dún Ailinne faunal assemblage (0.1% of the NISP), and none of them showed traces of butchery. In contrast, the faunal remains from the Ráith na Ríg at Tara included substantial numbers of dog bones (9.4% of NISP), and one of the pelves included cut marks associated with the disarticulation of the hip joint (McCormick 2002). The data from Tara indicate that dogs formed a part of the Irish Iron Age diet, at least on occasion. The data from Dún Ailinne, on the other hand, suggest that dogs played no more than a minimal role in feasting at the site. Give the small numbers of dog bones and the absence of traces of butchery, we cannot say for certain whether dogs were eaten at Dún Ailinne.

Bone Working

The worked bone from Dún Ailinne has been described in detail elsewhere (Crabtree 1982b; Chapter 10) and will be discussed only briefly here. Most of the worked bones were finished objects which have been described as artifacts. The species and body part used in the production of these objects is unknown. However, it was possible to identify the anatomical elements used in the production of six worked bone objects. They included a bone needle that was probably made from a pig fibula and a spindle whorl made from a perforated femoral head of a cow. In addition, three ungulate metapodia (two horse, one cow) were sawn into sections. Saw marks also appear on a split fragment of a cow's tibia. These sawn bones probably represent an early stage in the production of bone objects, since sawing was not regularly used in butchery until post-medieval times. James Boyle (2004) reports that cattle metapodia were used as raw materials for the production of bone pins in Early Christian Ireland, so both cattle and horse metapodia may also have been used for such a purpose in the Iron Age.

The worked bone from Dún Ailinne may indicate that some craft production was taking place at the site. Both the spindle whorl and the bone needle could have been used in textile production. The sawn metapodia also suggest that some limited amount of bone working may have taken place at Dún Ailinne. The evidence for bone working is interesting because Boyle's (2004) study of bone pins from Early Christian Ireland indicates that bone pin production took place at a limited number of Irish sites in the Early Middle Ages. Most Early Christian sites produced only finished bone pins, but bone production debris was recovered from a few of the larger, high status sites. These sites also had evidence for metalworking. Since Dún Ailinne has also yielded some evidence for metalworking, it is possible to suggest that the association between metalworking and bone working may have its roots in the Iron Age. Moreover, the evidence for bone working and metallurgy at Dún Ailinne suggest that a variety of different non-residential activities may have taken place at the site. While Dún Ailinne is traditionally identified as the seat of the kings of Leinster (Grabowski 1990), it is possible that craft fairs and periodic markets may have taken place at the site as well. If this is the case, then it may be possible to see Dún Ailinne as a forerunner to the Type A emporia described by Hodges (1982).

Dairying in the Iron Age: An Alternative Approach

The role of dairying in the economy of the Irish Iron Age has been subject to intensive debate in the zooarchaeological literature. The historical record clearly shows that a dairying economy was established in Ireland by the Early Medieval (Early Christian) Period (McCormick 1991; Lucas 1958). Since we lack historical records for the Irish Iron Age, the question of dairying must be addressed on the basis of archaeological evidence. Zooarchaeologists have often assumed that dairying economies will include a high proportion of young juveniles (see, for example, Legge 1981). Since the effective lactation period for early medieval cattle would have been about 6 months (McCormick 1991:57), we would expect to find a large number of calves slaughtered at about 6 months of age. The ageing data for the Flame Phase cattle from Dún Ailinne indicate that 18% of the cattle were killed about 6 months of age (Crabtree 1990:24). This pattern would certainly be consistent with a dairying economy.

The problem is that a high proportion of the Flame Phase cattle were slaughtered before they reached the age of about 6 months. McCormick (1991, 1992) suggests that these cattle could not have been used for dairying, because an unimproved cow that is deprived of its calf will stop lactating. Ethnographic and historical data indicate that several methods can be used to stimulate a cow to lactate in the absence of her calf. These include the use of surrogate offspring and blowing air into the cow's vagina to stimulate its let-down reflex (Russell 2004). It is certainly possible that these methods could have been used in Iron Age Ireland. If they were, we might expect some of the calves to have been slaughtered before 6 months to minimize the competition between the calves and the human milk-consumers. However, without documentary evidence, we cannot prove that these methods for stimulating lactation were used in Iron Age Ireland.

An alternative approach is to use archaeological, chemical, and historical evidence for dairy economies from the North Atlantic to develop models of mortality profiles that can be identified with a dairy economy. Mulville et al. (2005) describe a number of Bronze Age and Iron Age sites in the Northern and Western Isles of Scotland that have produced high numbers of very young cattle bones. Analyses of residues on pottery from Bronze Age and Iron Age sites in the Western Isles have revealed traces of bovine milk. Mulville and her colleagues (2005) conclude that high calf mortality in the Scottish Isles may be a result of active cattle management, including management for the production of milk, butter, and cheese.

The North Atlantic Biocultural Organization (NABO) has excavated a wide range of Viking Age, medieval, and post-medieval sites in Iceland, Greenland, and northern Scotland. Historical records indicate that the Norse raised their cattle primarily for dairying from the initial Viking settlement until modern times. Archaeological data appear to support that conclusion. For example, age profiles from the 9th–11th century site of Sveigakot in northern Iceland indicate that the majority of the cattle were killed at or before 6 months of age. The remaining cattle were killed as mature adults. The excavators (McGovern et al. 2005) interpret this pattern as a dairying strategy.

While the debate over the archaeological signatures for dairying continues, the increasing body of evidence from Bronze Age, Iron Age, and Viking-Period sites in the North Atlantic suggests that a high proportion of neonates and young juvenile cattle, combined with a smaller number of mature adults, may represent a valid signature for dairying in the archaeological record. It is therefore reasonable to suggest that the cattle that were used for ritual feasting at Dún Ailinne may have been drawn from dairying herds from the surrounding Leinster countryside.

Conclusions

What can the fauna from Dún Ailinne tell us about life in the Irish Iron Age and specifically about ritual feasting at this royal site? When I first analyzed the Dún Ailinne animal bones in the early 1980s, my primary interest was in paleoeconomic reconstruction. I suggested (Crabtree 1985, 1986, 1990) that the animals slaughtered at Dún Ailinne represented the surplus from a dairying economy. McCormick (1991, 1992) challenged this interpretation on paleoeconomic grounds. McCormick argued that the presence of a young calf was needed to maintain lactation in dairy cattle, so killing these young calves would have caused the dairy production to cease. The question of whether high numbers of neonatal and young juvenile cattle can be seen as a signature of a dairying economy is addressed in greater detail in the preceding section. McCormick's criticism, however, fails to address the unique, non-residential nature of Dún Ailinne as a royal and ritual site.

Unlike many of the early medieval sites in Ireland, Dún Ailinne (as well as the other Irish royal sites) was not permanently occupied. Extensive archaeological survey and excavation at Dún Ailinne has failed to uncover any structure that could have served as an Iron Age residence. In addition, the complex stratigraphy of the mound includes a series of thin, but discrete, bone-bearing layers, suggesting that Dún Ailinne was the site of ritual feasting on a periodic basis. The faunal remains contained in these layers result from the political economy of feasting. As Dietler and Hayden (2001:3) note, "It is crucial to recognize and understand feasting as a particular form of *ritual* activity" (emphasis original). The faunal remains from Dún Ailinne tell us about Iron Age ritual; they are, at best, an indirect reflection of the pastoral economy of pre-Christian Ireland.

When we view the Dún Ailinne faunal assemblage as a ritual assemblage, several important conclusions emerge. First, beef and pork played a major role in ritual feasting. Mutton, lamb, and horseflesh were of secondary importance, and dog and red deer do not appear to have been eaten. Cattle and pigs were the animals of choice at the other Irish royal sites. The faunal assemblage from the Ráith na Ríg at Tara is also dominated by cattle bones, and pig bones form the majority of the faunal assemblage at Navan. As described above, the predominance of pig is not a reflection of the local ecology. These data suggest that beef and pork played a major role in Irish Iron Age ritual; they are clearly the preferred meats. Second, the butchery and body part data indicate that the animals were driven to Dún Ailinne and slaughtered on site. Third, spit marks (charring marks near the ends of bones) are conspicuously absent from the Dún Ailinne animal remains. This absence suggests that meat was not roasted over an open fire. Boiling or possibly pit roasting are more likely alternatives. Fourth, the ageing data indicate that both young calves and older cattle formed part of the feast. Since calves are born in the spring, the presence of neonatal and young juvenile cattle (6 months of age or less) indicates that many of the feasts must have been held during the warmer months of the year (late spring to fall). If McCormick (1991) is correct, these young calves would have been expensive to procure, as their slaughter may have caused some of their mothers to cease lactation. Moreover, the meat yield from these young calves is low. From a purely economic perspective, it might have been less expensive to slaughter these calves at about 18 months of age when their meat yields would have been considerably higher. The expense involved in these ritual feasts forces us to address important questions of political economy.

Historical sources indicate that Dún Ailinne is associated with the kings of Leinster (Grabowski 1990). If we assume that the kings of Leinster/lords of Dún Ailinne were responsible both for constructing the architecture at the site and for sponsoring the feasts that were held there, then the kings are clearly persons of substantial social status, political power, and material wealth. In order to construct the elaborate timber architecture, the lords of Dún Ailinne must have had control over both labor and timber. Many laborers would have been needed to construct the elaborate Mauve, Rose, and White Phase structures, and the construction would have required access to mature oak trees. Similarly, many mature cattle and young calves were required for the Flame Phase feasts. These cattle were probably not procured from a single large herd, since the slaughter of both young calves and older adult cattle from a single herd would have rendered it non-viable. It is more reasonable to assume that these cattle were drawn from a number of different herds throughout Leinster. If this is the case, then the kings of Leinster must have been powerful patrons who were able to call on their clients and allies for contributions to the feasts. The elaborate feasts would therefore have been a visible testament to the power and wealth of the lords of Dún Ailinne/kings of Leinster.

The recovery and analysis of animal remains from Dún Ailinne were important and pioneering attempts to apply the new techniques for the study of biological materials to an Irish Iron Age site. Significantly, all faunal remains from Dún Ailinne were carefully recovered and catalogued. While this is now standard practice, forty years ago, when Dún Ailinne was being excavated, many archaeologists kept only complete or "identifiable" animal bones. The care with which the faunal samples were recovered from Dún Ailinne guarantees that this collection will continue to serve as an important resource for archaeologists who are interested in the economy of Iron Age Ireland.

14
Medieval and Modern Objects
Susan A. Johnston

A total of 30 objects in the collection were post-Iron Age, including both a medieval cresset lamp (an open lamp intended to hold oil and a floating wick) and a number of later objects designated loosely as modern. These are described more fully below. A further 192 objects listed in the finds register are missing, but were probably (183) or possibly (nine) modern. Missing objects were recorded verbatim from the finds register, and so vary in terms of detail (see Chapter 4 for a fuller discussion of the issues involved with this process). In some cases these were clearly modern (such as bullet casings) while others (such as "bottle glass" and "green glass") were assumed to be modern, though some uncertainty must remain. Those objects categorized as possibly modern were typically those, such as "glass fragment" or "metal tube," which were found in surface contexts and whose descriptions were sufficiently vague that they could not be identified clearly.

Table 14-1 shows the distribution of materials among modern objects, both likely and possible, recorded as missing. Combining these two groups for the purpose of discussion, glass was by far the largest category, with 116 examples recorded. This represents 60% of the modern missing objects. Most (114) were simply listed as fragments, but there were two bottles noted, both labeled "Savage Smyth." The rest of the materials can be combined into four larger groups: metals, ceramics, kaolin, and a miscellaneous group which includes 1 example each of leather, paper, plastic, and a button of unspecified material (listed in Table 14-1 as "unknown"). The leather is described only as a "fragment," while the paper is several pieces of brown paper bag; the plastic object is described, somewhat intriguingly, as a "tiger head." No doubt a story in that object remains to be told.

All of the fragments of kaolin are pipe fragments. Some were identified clearly as kaolin and

Table 14-1. Distribution, Modern Artifacts Recorded as Missing, by Material.

MODERN (N=183)		MODERN? (N=9)	
MATERIAL	N	MATERIAL	N
decorated ceramic	1	copper alloy	1
decorated ceramic?	2	glass	3
glass	113	metal	3
iron	1	undecorated ceramic?	2
kaolin	5		
kaolin?	14		
lead	1		
leather	1		
metal	18		
metal?	2		
paper	1		
plastic	1		
undecorated ceramic	1		
undecorated ceramic?	21		
unknown	1		

Table 14-2. Metal Artifacts Considered Modern, Listed as Missing.

OBJECT	N
bullets and fragments	12
coin	1
cufflink	1
fragment	1
insignia	1
musket ball	4
ring	1
scissor handle	1
screw	1
tube	3
TOTAL	26

Table 14-3. Types of Modern Artifacts.

OBJECT	N
bead	3
body sherd	2
cap badge	1
coin	4
cresset lamp	1
crucifix	1
fragment	7
horseshoe	1
horseshoe?	2
medal	1
nail	1
plowshare?	1
spike	1
uncertain	4
TOTAL	30

were entered accordingly. Those with a question mark were either listed in the register as "kaolin?" or were described as "clay pipe." Ceramics were also classified according to the description. If there was some indication that the sherd was decorated, such as "willow pattern china" or "Delft," it was listed as such; otherwise it was designated as undecorated, with question marks where appropriate.

As for the metal category, this is somewhat more complex. Table 14-2 shows the list of metal objects designated modern. In addition to objects whose description indicated that they were modern, others were designated as such based on their context. Much of the metal can be attributed to the use of the hill by the British Army, probably during the period 1916–21. The brass badges and probably the insignia, discussed below, as well as the bullets and bullet fragments, can be assigned to this period (as perhaps can some of the pipe fragments noted above). Somewhat earlier, 18th–19th century, use is indicated by the musket balls, and probably some of the glass. Local knowledge indicates that the hill was supposed to have been occupied by rebels during the 1798 uprising. The remaining material is either more recent (such as the scissors handle) or too generic for further identification (such as the three "tubes").

It is unclear what happened to this missing material. At one time some of the modern material may have been stored separately from the rest of the collection, but inquiries have failed to turn up any verification that there is material stored elsewhere. Since there are several places in the finds register where material labeled "modern" was indicated as discarded (and, as noted, was never numbered), it is possible that some of this numbered material was also discarded. In the absence of further information, they are simply noted here as "missing."

Modern/Medieval Objects

Most of the objects still in the collection and discussed here (such as coins and plastic beads) were obviously modern, but a few were not so certain. All are described below, grouped according to type of object. Table 14-3 summarizes the categories. As would be expected, the majority (16, or 53%) of these objects were found in surface layers, while an additional seven (23%) were from uncertain or unknown contexts. The remainder came from features. Table 14-4 shows this distribution.

The six objects which came from archaeological contexts are a mixed bag. The object from the baulk was a coin, and its position was uncertain. Another coin came from the embankment, whose actual age is uncertain, and may well be disturbed. The age of the spike is also uncertain, though it does appear modern based on its metal content and overall good preservation; its context in the mound may suggest the spike is in fact older, or it may indicate disturbance, the mound having been sometimes stratigraphically problematic. Two objects came from the occupation layers, themselves often complex. Both objects illustrate its stratigraphic uncertainty: one is a fragment of what appears to be cement while the other is a small, copper alloy "knob," also fairly certainly modern. Finally, there is the coin which was described as coming from the

Table 14-4. Distribution, Modern Artifacts by Type of Feature.

FEATURE TYPE	N
Baulk	1
Embankment	1
Mound	1
Occupation	2
Surface	16
Trench?	1
Uncertain	4
Unknown	4
TOTAL	30

top fill of Trench 514, but which was noted as possibly coming from the baulk as well. Its context is probably better described as uncertain.

The medieval and modern objects are described here along with their measurements. As with the iron objects, "fragment" indicates something whose shape suggests no obvious, known object, while "uncertain" indicates a definite but illusive shape.

Cresset Lamp

E.79.3014 appears to be a medieval cresset lamp (Plate 14-1). It is large and goblet-shaped, 112 mm long, and lacks any decoration. The narrower middle section is 97 mm x 62 mm. The wider end is concave and footed, while the other end appears broken; this end is also flared, though not as much as the opposite end. A shaft runs for a short way down the center from the narrower end. The wider end is reddened around the rim and also in the center of the hollow, suggesting burning. While it has not been subjected to expert scrutiny, it appears to be made of sandstone. Because of the broken end it is difficult to determine its original profile, and so to assign it to a type. Based on the drawings provided by Moore (1984), it may belong to Class 1, since the surviving cup is not strongly differentiated from the stem. However, if it is Class 1 it would be an outlier in the distribution, which is primarily in Munster (Moore 1984:107).

While this piece is almost certainly a cresset lamp, there are some anomalies about it. To begin with, since one end is broken, it is difficult to know which end was the primary one used to hold oil. On the one hand, the reddening in and around the wider end suggests burning, and thus that this was the "business end." On other hand, the hole in the center may be something akin to those described by Moore (1984), which he argues, were used to hold the wick. If so, since the hole does not go through the wider end, then this suggests that the broken end was the end used. It is difficult to chose given the incomplete state of the piece, though on purely subjective grounds the wider end seems more likely to be the primary one.

Its context is also problematic (it was classed as "uncertain" in the table above). It is described as coming from "old sod—under quarry (292)." However, feature 292 in the feature log is a post-hole, so this number may be incorrect. Lacking any other provenience information, it is difficult to say more about its relationship to the use of the site. Moore (1984, 1997) indicates that Irish cressets are likely to date between the 10th and 12th centuries AD, which would suggest it comes from a time after the site's primary Iron Age use. The association with the quarry may also suggest it is in a secondary position and so its late date may not pose any chronological difficulties.

Interestingly, cressets have also been recovered from both Tara and Rathcroghan (Moore 1984; Newman 1997:350; Waddell 1983:44). In neither case is there any useful information about the find circumstances, with each only being known generally to have come from its respective site. However, given the fact that there are relatively few cressets known from Ireland (Moore lists 46, to which can be added the four reported from Waterford; 1984, 1997), and that the one from Rathcroghan appears to be an outlier in the overall distribution (Moore 1984:106, fig. 40), it is an interesting coincidence that three of them would be found at three of the royal sites.

Modern Beads

E.79.1553, E.79.1626, E.79.1641. Each is a small turquoise plastic bead, unperforated, and each is 4 mm in length, width, and thickness.

These beads are also noted in Chapter 11 and are probably rosary beads, introduced by workers at the site to test archaeological perspicacity, or perhaps gullibility.

Body Sherds

E.79.5003. Modern body sherd. Its exterior surface has a dark orange slip and 2-3 parallel grooves running across it; its interior surface is blackened, and has what looks like "186" stamped on it. The fabric suggests stoneware. L=31 mm W=30 mm T=8 mm

E.79.263. Probable sherd, possibly modern. It is extremely light and aerated, and possibly burned. There are traces of red and pale pink on both surfaces that may be the remains of glaze, but the piece is very eroded. L=19 mm W=17 mm T=8 mm

Cap Badge

E.79.1123. Copper alloy cap badge. It has the inscription "SOUTH LANCASHIRE" at the top. Along the opposite edge the inscription is worn smooth on the front surface, but from the back the letters "---ING OF WALES'S VO--" can be read. There are leaves on both sides, with an insignia (a plant?) in the middle. L=51 mm W=42 mm T=1 mm

Coins

E.79.14. Coin, both faces completely worn smooth. The slight glints of what appears to be copper suggest a penny or halfpenny. L=28 mm W=28 mm T=2 mm

E.79.1003. Coin, apparently copper, with some green oxidation. It is probably a penny or halfpenny. There are traces of an Irish harp on one side and faint letters on the other. L=27 mm W=27 mm T=2 mm

E.79.1216. Copper coin (penny or halfpenny), with one surface worn smooth. The other side has an Irish harp surmounted by a crown. It is probably 18th-19th century. L=26 mm W=26 mm T=1 mm

E.79.1925. Copper halfpenny. One face has a profile head and faint traces of letters ("GEOR-"), presumably George I. The opposite face has a figure holding a scepter, letters which appear to say "BRITANNIA" around the top, and the date "1720" at the bottom. L=27 mm W=27 mm T=2 mm

Crucifix

E.79.999. Silver metal crucifix, fairly worn, and subrectangular in section. L=93 mm W=41 mm T=5 mm

Fragments

E.79.5016. Two fragments of modern bottle glass, 1 dark green, 1 more olive green. L=60 mm W=29 mm T=10 mm (larger fragment)

E.79.154. Two fragments of modern bottle glass, 1 dark green, 1 more olive green. L=54 mm W=43 mm T=9 mm (larger fragment)

E.79.1099. Two fragments of modern bottle glass, both dark green. L=32 mm W=22 mm T=5 mm (larger fragment)

E.79.2889 Flat, irregular fragment of what appears to be cement. L=38 mm W=35 mm T=11 mm

Horseshoes

E.79.3185. Fragment (almost half) of an iron horseshoe. One end is largely intact; a small nail protrudes from one surface, the head visible on the opposite surface. There are also numerous fragments presumably also belonging to it. L=110 mm W=30 mm T=8 mm

E.79.5008. Part of what appears to be an iron horseshoe, as well as numerous fragments presumably belonging to it. There appears to be a small nail protruding from one surface, and there are nail heads visible at various other places along the surface. L=105 mm W=24 mm T=10 mm

E.79.3027. Curved fragment of iron, thick and heavy, which appears to be a horseshoe. A small nail is protruding from one side, and the head is visible on the opposite side. There are also numerous fragments that presumably belong to it. L=85 mm W=26 mm T=13 mm

Medal

E.79.998. Oval religious medal made from silver metal. There is a broken loop at the top, and the opposite end comes to a rounded point. One side has an angel and a child, with the inscription "DEAR ANGEL EVER AT MY SIDE PRAY FOR ME". The other side has a seated male figure and child and the inscription "S. JOSEPH EXAMPLE OF HUMILITY AND OBEDIENCE PRAY FOR US". The surface shows oxidation on both sides. L=47 mm W=32 mm T=4 mm

Nail

E.79.38. Iron nail; its relatively good condition and shape suggest a modern wire nail. L=53 mm W=5 mm T=4 mm

Medieval and Modern Objects

Plowshare?

E.79.3602. Fragments of iron, identified as a possible plowshare in the finds register. It is fragmented into 15+ pieces, and the largest is curved and somewhat flat. Whether it was a plowshare is uncertain. L=81 mm W=16 mm T=12 mm

Spike

E.79.2258. Long iron spike, probably a harrow tooth. There are also numerous fragments that belong to it. L=266 mm W=16 mm T=15 mm

Uncertain

E.79.16. "Keyhole" shaped object, copper alloy (Figure 14-1). It has an oval ring at one end; at the other end, a strip projects outward, and is scored at the end with parallel lines across the width of the flat surface. The piece is flat in section. L=24 mm W=11 mm T=1 mm

E.79.23. Iron implement, probably of modern agricultural origin. It is shaped like a spike but curved, narrowing to a point at one end. The opposite end is threaded. There are also several fragments belonging to it. L=164 mm W=23 mm T=17 mm

E.79.566. A flat, copper alloy object, possibly a brace (Figure 14-1). It is rectangular with rounded ends, and has four threaded holes

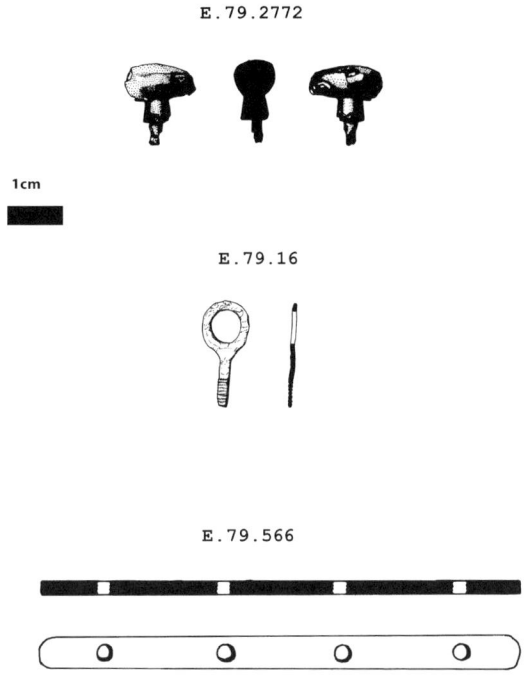

Figure 14-1. Modern copper alloy objects from Dún Ailinne.

through it, distributed equally along the surface. L=125 mm W=9 mm T=3 mm

E.79.2772. Small ovoid knob, probably bronze (Figure 14-1; see also Plate 8-6). There is a stepped shank off center on one side, and it is broken at the bottom. L=17 mm W=16 mm T=9 mm

15
Chronology

Susan A. Johnston

Dates for the site could be derived from stylistic characteristics of the artifacts and from a series of absolute dates (C^{14} and a single thermoluminescence date). To anticipate the conclusion, it can be said here that this evidence, taken together indicates activity at the site in the Neolithic, the Bronze Age, and the latter part of the pre-Christian Iron Age, the bulk being in the last period.

Artifact Dates

While the artifacts from Dún Ailinne were not numerous, many of them provide stylistic dates to varying degrees of specificity. At the most general end of the continuum, there are a number of artifacts (such as iron blades, spindle whorls, stone balls) which are too generic to narrow down further than a span of several millennia. Equally unsatisfying were those general categories of material which can be bracketed by a period, but which cannot be narrowed down further. This includes examples like the iron spearhead, since iron does not appear for the most part before the eponymous period, or flint and chert debris, which is most likely to belong to the Neolithic or Bronze Age. While these general chronological observations can be broadly helpful in circumstances such as determining the degree of disturbance in a feature, they are not very helpful in pinpointing the chronology of the site. As such, these artifacts do not need to be considered further.

More helpful were those artifacts whose typology could be used to assign them to periods of varying spans of time. These can be considered in more detail, beginning with the more narrow time frames and working through increasingly general categories.

Neolithic

Typologically, the ceramics provide the narrowest chronological window for this period. The Linkardstown vessel (E.79.1980) and the associated slate bead (E.79.1985) have been assigned to the middle of the Neolithic, 2850–2650 Cal-BC (Chapter 6). The rest of the diagnostic ceramics, while not a perfect fit, also seem to belong to this part of the Neolithic.

Less easy to place are the lithics. Of the recognizable tool types, the leaf-shaped and *petit tranchet* derivative projectile points both belong to the Neolithic in general, as does the "javelin" or lance head; it is not possible to narrow these further. The other lithic objects, including the hollow scrapers, round and other types of scrapers, the stone axes, and the cupmarked stone all were typical for the Neolithic and earlier Bronze Age, and probably belong to one of these periods. However, at least some of them may have come from later periods (see Chapters 5 and 11).

Bronze Age

As noted in Chapter 4, the only definitive Bronze Age artifact was the food vessel (E.79.905). A C^{14} age determination (SI-982) of 3220 ± 55 BP (1623–1400 Cal-BC) came from charcoal in the pit where the sherds were recovered (see also below). While this relatively late date is somewhat anomalous for a bowl type vessel, it is not entirely unique (see Chapter 6), and indicates a presence at Dún Ailinne in the later Bronze Age.

Other artifacts were also suggested as possibly Bronze Age. These are an amber bead (E.79.1915; Ch. 11), a projectile point with asymmetrical barbs (E.79.1832; Ch. 5), and a turquoise glass bead (E.79.115; Chapter 9). None of these are certainly Bronze Age, however, and in any case, even if they are, they cannot be narrowed down to any particular part of the period.

Iron Age

For the Iron Age, the typological situation is somewhat better than for the Neolithic. The style of a small number of artifacts allows them to be assigned to a relatively narrow date range, in some cases a matter of a few centuries. Being based on more qualitative assessments they are of course always debatable, but they do provide a chronological context for the Iron Age phases with which they are associated.

The earliest of the stylistically datable artifacts are the sword (E.79.630), the glass cable beads, and possibly the glass toggles. The first two can be assigned to the 3rd-2nd centuries BC on morphological grounds. Regarding the toggles, the chronological situation is less clear; Hughes (1985:37) would place them in the 3rd-2nd centuries BC, making them contemporary with the sword and the cable beads, while B. Raftery (1984:202) would put them much later, in the 1st century AD. (see Chapter 9 for further discussion). Thus they may belong here or with other, later artifacts noted below.

Also relatively narrowly dated is the Nauheim fibula, E.79.743, which is assigned to the 3rd quarter of the 1st century AD, perhaps AD 50-75. If Raftery's dating of the toggles is correct, then they would be broadly contemporary with this.

Other artifacts can only be placed in a much larger chronological range. Spiral rings, for example, are found from the last centuries BC through the first centuries AD while the fragment of copper alloy ribbed bracelet has been placed in a similarly broad period, 100 BC through AD 500 (see Chapter 8). Hughes assigns the glass bracelets to "La Tène C/D," and the copper alloy fastener and the glass ring beads belong to the "late La Tène," but she attaches no calendar date to these designations.

While not terribly satisfying, the stylistic data do prompt a few observations. Allowing for the possibility that some of the artifacts represent the extremes of their date ranges, much of the pre-Christian Iron Age is potentially represented. However, given the size of most of the date ranges, it is impossible to determine whether many of these artifacts are contemporary or represent entirely separate periods. It should also be pointed out that the date of potentially early artifacts does not necessarily date the arrival of that artifact at the site. The possibility of some of these artifacts having been kept for some time, as heirlooms for example, before they were deposited is only increased by the arguably ritual nature of the site. The deposition or wearing of an ancient family heirloom might have greater ritual significance, for example, then one newly acquired. Thus the earlier of the dates provide only a *terminus post quem* for Dún Ailinne.

Absolute Dates

I assume your crew understand the principle of stratigraphic succession, but apparently the former occupants [of Dún Ailinne] hadn't given it a thought. (Robert Stuckenrath to Bernard Wailes, letter dated July 25, 1973 concerning the Dún Ailinne radiocarbon samples).

As the preceding quote indicates, absolute dates should be the more definitive of the dating evidence, but in reality, the absolute dates were just as difficult to interpret. This is likely to be the result of the repeated disturbance produced by the sequential construction and destruction of the various Iron Age timber structures. While samples were collected with care to represent the various stages of the site's use, the sequence that was returned does not always seem to follow logically. The single TL date is noted first, followed by a discussion of the radiocarbon chronology.

Thermoluminescence

A single TL date was obtained on a sample of burned soil. As described in the published report (Carpenter and Ryan 1975), the sample was taken from what was then designated as "Iron Age 4" sediments; this correlates broadly with what has since been described in published accounts as the Mauve phase. Having established that the sample was amenable to TL dating, a date of AD 477 ± 190 was obtained. While the later half of this range seems somewhat out of sync with the artifacts (and perhaps the C^{14} dates; see below), the earlier half, though more recent than the C^{14} dates would indicate, matches reasonably well.

Chronology

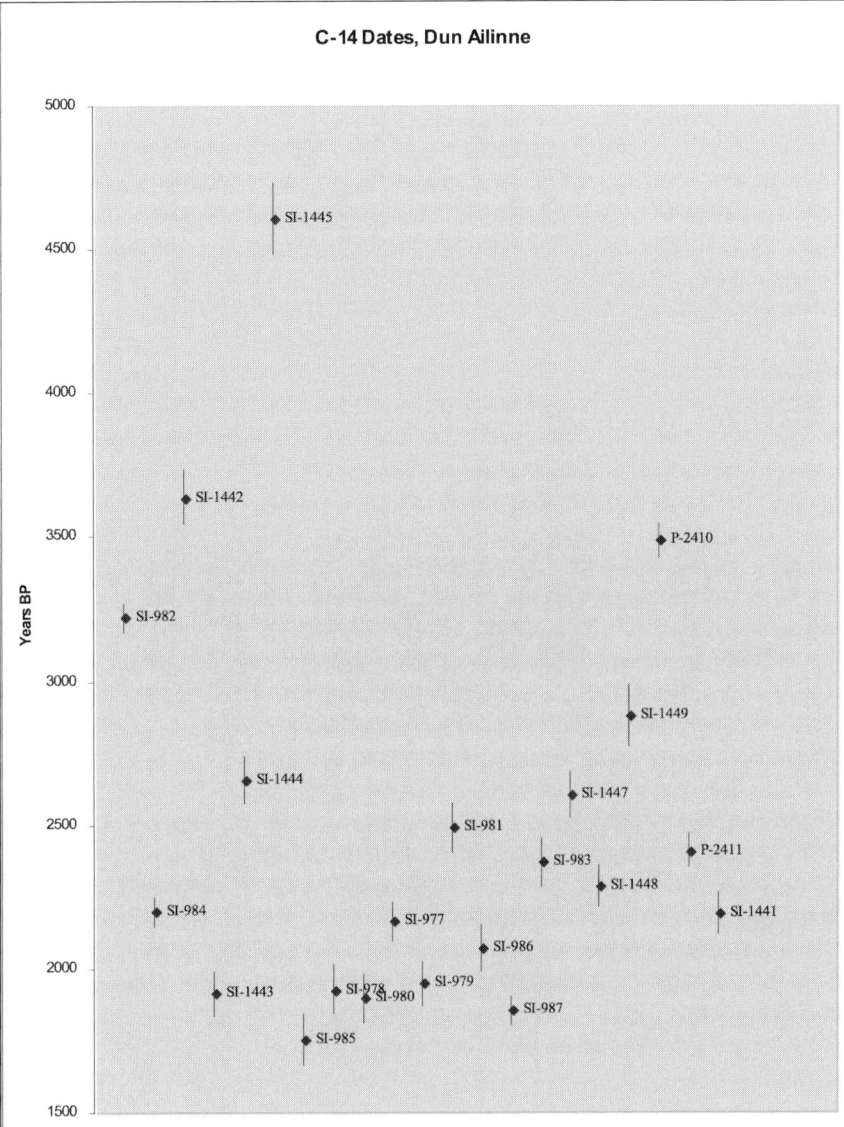

Figure 15-1. Distribution, uncalibrated radiocarbon age.

Radiocarbon Age Determinations

The finds register records a large number of samples collected for radiocarbon dating. In several cases, multiple samples from the same context were combined into a single sample; of these six were not submitted for stratigraphic reasons, and another (SI-1446) was too small to produce an age determination. This left 21 age determinations from Dún Ailinne. These are shown in Table 15-1, grouped according to the phase they were believed to represent and in what should be roughly chronological order. The dates are shown in BP format (based on the conventional "present" of 1950), as uncalibrated dates BC, and as calibrated ranges of two standard deviations (Stuiver, Reimer, and Reimer 2005). Figure 15-1 shows the uncalibrated dates in a graphic form, with one standard deviation indicated by the error bar. Since the samples were generally not identified as to species, no "old wood" corrections have been applied.

Obviously there are some problems with this apparent sequence. There is no obvious patterning to the dates that would suggest a consistent stratigraphic progression. While it is not terribly satisfying, however, there are some useful observations to be made from it. First, SI-982, the food vessel date, while late, is not entirely out of line. As noted

179

Table 15-1. Radiocarbon Age-Determinations.

LAB #	DATE BP	DATE AD/BC UNCALIBRATED	DATE CALIBRATED (STUIVER, REIMER AND REIMER 2005)	PHASE	SAMPLE DESCRIPTION
SI-982*	3220 ± 55	1270 BC	1623–1400 Cal-BC	Tan/Khaki	Charcoal, Pit 2790, asso. with food vessel sherds
SI-984*	2200 ± 50	250 BC	390–116 Cal-BC	Rose	Charcoal, fill of Feature 60, Iron Age phases 2, 3
SI-1442	3640 ± 95	1690 BC	2286–1749 Cal-BC	Rose	Charcoal, fill of Feature 314, slot trench forming structure entrance
SI-1443	1915 ± 80	AD 35	107 Cal-BC–322 Cal-AD	Rose	Charcoal, fill of Feature 316, slot trench in entrance
SI-1444	2660 ± 80	710 BC	1011–543 Cal-BC	Rose	Charcoal, secondary fill, Feature 316, marks extraction of posts
SI-1445	4605 ± 125	2655 BC	3639–2943 Cal-BC	Rose	Nut shells, Trench Y (Feature 514)
SI-985*	1755 ± 90	AD 195	68–532 Cal-AD	Mauve	Charcoal, fill of Trench A (Feature 515), Iron Age phases 3, 4
SI-978*	1930 ± 85	AD 20	163 Cal-BC–316 Cal-AD	Mauve	Charcoal, fill of Trench B (Feature 516), Iron Age phases 3, 4
SI-980*	1900 ± 85	AD 50	93 Cal-BC–336 Cal-AD	Mauve	Charcoal, fill of Trench A (Feature 515), Iron Age phases 3, 4
SI-977*	2165 ± 70	215 BC	384–50 Cal-BC	Emerald/Crimson	Charcoal, 1 of last 3 Iron age levels
SI-979*	1950 ± 80	0 BC/AD	164 Cal-BC–238 Cal-AD	Emerald/Crimson	Charcoal, occupation material from 1 of last 3 Iron Age levels
SI-981*	2490 ± 85	540 BC	792–409 Cal-BC	Emerald/Crimson	Charcoal, occupation material from 1 of last 3 Iron Age levels
SI-986*	2075 ± 80	125 BC	358 Cal-BC–76 Cal-AD	Crimson	Charcoal, fill of Feature 36, Iron Age phases 4, 5, 6
SI-987*	1855 ± 50	AD 95	31–19 Cal-AD	Crimson	Charcoal, fill of Feature 33, Iron Age phases 4, 5, 6
SI-983*	2370 ± 85	420 BC	768–210 Cal-BC	Uncertain	Charcoal, occupation contemporary with Iron Age phases 2, 3, 4
SI-1447	2605 ± 85	655 BC	923–416 Cal-BC	Emerald	Charcoal, low mound
SI-1448	2290 ± 75	340 BC	734–120 Cal-BC	Emerald	Charcoal, burned patch, Feature 449
SI-1449	2880 ± 105	930 BC	1373–832 Cal-BC	Flame	Charcoal, dark stoney W balk K, last Iron Age phase
P-2410*	3490 ± 60	1540 BC	1964–1643 Cal-BC	Site entrance	Old sod covered by small bank at original entrance
P-2411*	2410 ± 60	460 BC	756–394 Cal-BC	Site entrance	Grey soil and iron pan from old sod covered by enclosure bank
SI-1441	2195 ± 75	245 BC	395–55 Cal-BC	"Latrine pit"	Charcoal, burned area under hill wash

*Date published in *Radiocarbon* 15(1973):399–400 and 19(1977):222–23.

in Chapter 6, there is at least one other example reported from an even later time period, so this would not be the latest by any means. Thus while the sample might have been misattributed, the date may well be an accurate reflection of the date of the pit containing the food vessel.

Since its context is somewhat anomalous, SI-1441 can also be noted here. While digging a pit in relation to the physical needs of the site's work force, a small burned area was uncovered. This feature (#388) produced no finds, and no stratigraphic relationships were available to place it in the context of the larger site. A sample was taken for C^{14} age determination, and it produced a date of 2195 $\pm$ 75 BP (395–55 Cal-BC). This date is quite a bit earlier than others which are considered more reliable (see below), so it is unclear how it might relate to the site's overall sequence of use.

As for the remainder, all should be Iron Age dates, and based on stratigraphy and soil characteristics they should also be relatively close in time. Clearly, they are not. A number of the dates (5–6 depending on where the lines are drawn) are not even Iron Age, but instead apparently represent earlier material. These dates are probably the result of samples being taken inadvertently from earlier materials dredged up during the construction and destruction of the various timber structures. That this is likely may be suggested by the fact that all these age determinations are *earlier* than expected, rather than later (which might be more likely to suggest modern contamination). Also, in the case of several samples (SI-1447, SI-1441, SI-1443) there was heavy root contamination requiring pretreatment, while the sample for SI-1445 was noted as "small" (though not too small for a date). These factors might also have affected the dates produced.

The most convincing group of age determinations is the three that came from features 515 and 516, SI-985, SI-978, and SI-980. These date two of the trenches of the Mauve phase timber structure. Stratigraphically, this is the last phase of large-scale building at the site; when calibrated, these dates place it during the last few centuries of the pre-Christian Iron Age, or the first few centuries AD. While this is significantly later than some of the more narrowly dated artifacts (such as the sword and the cable beads), it accords well with objects such as the Nauheim fibulae, as well as being accommodated by the broader artifact date ranges. Given the possibility of the presence of heirlooms, as noted, the contradiction with the former is perhaps less significant than the correlation with the latter. It is worth noting that these three dates are also not too far out of line with the TL date noted, considering the size of both ranges.

The rest of the C^{14} dates seem to present no particular patterns; they do not make sense for the phases they should have represented, and they do not make sense in terms of each other. For example, the five samples which should date the Rose phase are not only internally inconsistent, they are also (mostly) at odds with the Mauve series and with the artifact evidence. Of those dates, if the three Mauve phase dates are accepted, then SI-1443 may be relatively accurate. The sample came from Feature 316, the trench that forms the terminus connecting the inner and middle trenches of the Rose phase timber structure (see Chapter 2). This feature lies in the middle of the entrance area, between those framing the V-shaped approach. Stratigraphically there is no certain evidence of the time that passed between the Mauve and Rose phases, but there is also no evidence to suggest that the site was left unused for long periods. Allowing for the 160-year date range (or more, if doubled for two standard deviations), this date places the Rose phase reasonably well into the time prior to the Mauve building phase.

Using similar logic, SI-979 and SI-987 may also be acceptable. SI-979 was a sample of occupation material, while SI-987 came from one of the myriad post-holes not associated with the main timber structures. Both provide dates for the low mound, including Upper and Lower Emerald and Crimson. Due to the complexity of the stratigraphy in that area, it was impossible to determine which of the individual phases each sample represented. However, stratigraphically, Emerald and Crimson should both post-date Mauve, though apparently not by much. While the earlier part of SI-979 seems too early to be accurate, the latter part and the bulk of the range of SI-987 seem to match reasonably well.

It is also worth noting P-2410 and P-2411. The fact that Dún Ailinne and the other royal sites have an internal ditch and external bank has frequently led to a comparison with earlier henge and hengiform monuments (see Mallory 2000:21–23 for a useful summary). In come cases, the possibility has been raised that these sites could represent re-use of earlier monuments (see D.D.A. Simpson 1989; Robertson 1992:30; Weir 1989). As a way to address the date of the enclosure bank at Dún Ailinne, P-2410 and P-2411 were collected from the "old sod" under the bank at the entrance (see Chapter 3). P-2410 (3490 $\pm$ 60 BP, 1964–1643 Cal-BC) came from the sod layer under a short spur (feature 3130) that extends from the site's enclosing bank toward the outer roadway; P-2411 (2410 ± 60, 756–394 Cal-BC) came from iron pan and gray soil within the old sod layer covered by the enclosure bank. While these dates are quite early compared to those just discussed (P-2410 particularly so), they at least demonstrate that the bank at the entrance (and by extension, the bank as a whole) is not a survivor of some monument from earlier prehistory. Along with the dendrochronology date from the timber in the Navan enclosure ditch (91 BC; Mallory 2000), the idea that these sites represent re-use (as opposed to reinvention, renaissance, or re-creation; see Chapter 17, 18) can be reasonably well laid to rest.

Using the most reliable dates, then, calibrated and reported with two standard deviations, the C14 chronology stretches from about 165 Cal-BC to as late as Cal-AD 530, with the bulk in the early centuries AD. While it is impossible to know whether this represents an actual range of use or if the main site use was only a short period within the range, it seems somewhat later overall than the date range from Navan (the only other well-dated royal site). This may mean that Dún Ailinne was constructed rather later, and perhaps used later, than its cousin in the north. If so, it raises the possibility that there was some influence from Navan on the construction of Dún Ailinne. While such relationships must remain speculation for the time being, further work at the other royal sites may allow us to determine whether some sites are earlier than others, and perhaps which ones might have provided the original model(s) for those that came later. While the uncertainties of the chronological evidence make any conclusions tentative, the patterns which can be teased out suggest that Dún Ailinne may have been one of the later, and indeed possibly the latest, of the royal sites to be used in a purely pagan context (see Chapter 17).

Finally, in one of those moments where you read something that makes you wonder about possibilities, Warner (1994b) cites a reference to Dún Ailinne in one of the genealogies contained in the Rawlinson B.502 manuscript (see O'Brien 1962:20). In this text, an ancestor figure of the Laigin built and then ruled from the "Wall of Ailinn," undoubtedly a reference to Dún Ailinne. This figure, Més Delmann, is situated by various of the Irish pseudo-histories somewhere between 100 BC and the first couple of centuries AD (Warner 1994b:21). While this is likely a coincidence, it is interesting that this corresponds extremely closely to the radiocarbon date range just discussed.

16
Dún Ailinne's Role in Folklore, Myth, and the Sacred Landscape

Ronald Hicks

Excavations of sites like Dún Ailinne provide us with various kinds of data that allow us to reconstruct the nature of the site and some of the activities that took place there. However, these can seldom provide us with much in the way of an understanding of the meaning of the site within the culture that created it. In recent years, it has become increasingly clear that such monuments can only be fully understood if one realizes that they are part of a larger cultural landscape. Their continued existence down through the centuries as features within that landscape tends to ensure that they have an ongoing role in those cultures, one that to one extent or another reflects their original meaning (Darvill 1999; Bender et al. 1997, Marcus and Flannery 1993).

Several types of evidence are available that may help us to gain some insight into the belief system that led to the construction of Dún Ailinne and other such monuments. Vestiges of the meaning of such sites may be glimpsed today in folk beliefs concerning them. In the case of Irish sites such as Dún Ailinne we also have sources of information much closer in time to that in which the site was part of everyday life, namely the manuscripts of medieval Ireland. This chapter will examine the information from these and other sources and analyze the relationship of Dún Ailinne to the larger landscape in hopes of gaining some understanding of Dún Ailinne's place in the thinking and life of its builders and those who followed them.

Folklore

I was part of the excavation crew at Dún Ailinne during the 1971 field season, and visited the site numerous times in subsequent years while doing my PhD research. During the excavation at Dún Ailinne the local workmen on the excavation crew often commented on the belief that there was treasure there and a tunnel leading from Dún Ailinne either to the Curragh some 3 km to the northwest or under the Liffey 3 km to the northeast. Also, on the slope of Knockaulin Hill itself, within the enclosing embankment of Dún Ailinne, lay an intermittent spring known locally as "St. John's Well." All of these may help us to understand the role of the site.

The available materials in the National Folklore Collection at University College Dublin, add surprisingly little additional folklore concerning Dún Ailinne. In one tale, a troop of Irish soldiers who were surrounded there by the English in 1798 prayed for help to save them from hunger and thirst, and after three days water sprang up out of the ground, perhaps a reference to the well (National Folklore Collection, Schools Manuscripts [NFCS] 777:9–10).

There was also some interesting comparative material. Two other hills within sight of Knockaulin—the Hill of Allen (Almu, legendary stronghold of Fionn MacCumhail) and Grange Hill—are also said to contain treasures. The same is true of Carbury Hill, hidden from Dún Ailinne by the Hill of

Allen (NFCS 774:5; 776:328, 455-56; 779:32, 101). Each, like Knockaulin, can be considered to be a *síd*, a dwelling places of the old gods, because of its association with characters in the myths or, in the case of Grange Hill, because on its southern slope lies the "Chair of Kildare," traditional inauguration place of the local kings. The treasure in Grange Hill is said to be guarded by a man on horseback who appears on only one night each year. In the case of the Hill of Allen, we are told that those who seek the treasure will be frightened off by Fionn's dog, Bran. As we will see later, a dog is associated with Dún Ailinne as well, although there the treasure is said to be guarded by a ghost.

Fionn Mac Cumhail is associated with Knockaulin as well as with the Hill of Allen. It is said that one day he "jumped from the top of the hill [of Allen] to the bottom and…landed on a great big stone. With the force of the jump his feet were planted in the stone. He picked up the stone and threw it from the Hill of Allen to Knockaulin. If you go over to Knockaulin you will see the stone with the footprints on it. Every night he is seen sitting on it about midnight." — James Coy, Dec. 1937, from his grandmother, about 80 (NFCS 777:10-11, 21).

Tunnels also figure in these beliefs. One is said to run between "the old church and the rath" in Furness (NFCS 776:396). The rath referred to is Longstone Rath, a henge-like earthwork near Naas whose entrance faces toward the Curragh and the three hills (Red Hills, Dunmurry Hill, and Grange Hill) on its western edge.

Myth

According to Hogan (1910), Dún Ailinne is mentioned in nearly two dozen of the Irish manuscripts. In the *Book of Ballymote* and *H.2.7*, we are told that it was built by Sétna, while in *MacFirbis's Book of Genealogies* it is said to have been built by Seudna Siothbhac. Other mentions—in the *Annals of Ulster*, Lynch's *Cambrensis Eversus*, Muirchertach's *Circuit of Ireland*, the *Annals of the Four Masters*, and Keating's *History of Ireland*—refer to the apparently historical Battle of Aillinn (Grabowski 1990). Just as Tara, Emain Macha, and Ráth Crúachan are associated with the kingship of Mide, Ulster, and Connacht, Dún Ailinne is linked with that of Leinster. In Muirchertach's *Circuit of Ireland*, the *Book of Rights (Leabhar na gCeart)*, and the *Book of Leinster (Leabhar na Núachongbála)*, it is listed as a seat of the kings of Leinster. As is the case with the other royal sites, this does not appear to mean Dún Ailinne was a place actually occupied by the king but rather that it was a sacred/ritual site linked with the kingship and with the goddess of sovereignty of the territory. Thus, what is of interest here are references that link Dún Ailinne to Irish myth.

The most relevant documents for an understanding of the place of Dún Ailinne in the myths are undoubtedly those containing the *dindshenchas* tales. These tales, compiled between the tenth and twelfth centuries, purport to explain the origins of sites' names. The prose version of that pertaining to Dún Ailinne (Alend), in the Rennes dindshenchas translated by Whitley Stokes (1895:310), reads as follows:

> Crem Marda abducted a daughter of Lugaid king of Leinster. Aillenn was her name and Ailbe the name of her lapdog. And Aillenn, being in Crem's possession, died of shame, and through her grave grew an appletree which is called "Aillenn's Appletree". And after her died her lapdog, and up through him a yewtree grew. Of this is said "the Yewtree of *Baile*" that is *Ailbe* by transposition of letters, as is said "The Appletree of lofty Ailleen, the Yewtree of Baile—little profit. Though their lays are uttered rude men understand them not."
>
> Art Mes-delmand son of Setna was the first who excavated the rampart of Aillenn. Fiach then, and Buirech and Ururus dug it finally. 'T was Buirech too, that out of the ditch cast the stone that is (still) at Aillenn, and said: *Ail and* "a rock there", and this is the name it shall have. Many names besides it has, as some one said:
>
> "Aillend an assembly for our warriors, etc."

Gwynn's (1903 [I]:80-85) translation of the metrical portion of the tale is much longer but adds little (for more detailed discussion, see http://rhicks.iweb.bsu.edu). As Gwynn pointed out in his notes (1903 [I]:107-8), it provides us primarily with "a string of titles by which the place might be described, in memory of various chieftains who had possessed it."

Gwynn tells us that in the *Leabhar na gCeart*, the legendary 2nd century king Cathair Mór (called in the dindshenchas "high king of Érenn from Alend" (Gwynn 1913 [III]:178-79) leaves Dún Ailinne to his youngest son, Fiachu Baicid. *Timna Chatháir Máir*, the "Testament of Cathair Mór," is indeed incorporated into or attached to some manuscripts of *Leabhar na gCeart* (Dillon 1962:167). In it Cathair says that Fiachu will *seize* pleasant Aillenn, hold famous Carman, rule venerable Almain (the Hill of Allen), and strengthen Naas with splendor. This listing of sites has implications for the extent of the sacred landscape presided over by Dún Ailinne, as we shall see a bit later.

Significant Characters

An inevitable question concerning those mentioned is whether they are indeed historical figures or rather aspects of the old gods. The answer most likely is that they are a mixture of the two. Some of the names certainly seem to be from myth, and those few who are central to the tale require comment.

Those said to have been involved with the construction of the earthwork may be historical. Setna Sithbacc ("Long-Staff"), also identified as Seudna Siothbhac, is credited by some of Hogan's sources with the construction of Dún Ailinne. However, according to both the prose and metrical dindshenchas, his son Art Mes-Delmond is the builder. And, as noted in the dindshenchas, three others are said to have excavated it—Fiach, Buirech, and Ururus (Aururas). For comparison, Emain Macha (Navan Fort) is said to have been dug by the five sons of Díthorba.

Of the others mentioned, Crem Marda, kidnapper of Aillenn is quickly disposed of since there seems to be no other reference to this character, who may be the result of an error in copying. It is conceivable that Crem is a miscopying of Crom, as in Crom Dubh, who is certainly an important character in regards to Lughnasa, the festival at the beginning of harvest (MacNeill 1962).

The most obvious of the possible links to myth is Aillenn's father, Lugaid. His name is, of course, a form of that of the god said to have founded Lughnasa to honor the memory of his foster mother, Tailtiu (Stokes 1895:61; Gwynn 1924 [IV]:147), or to honor his two wives, the sisters Bói and Nás (Stokes 1894:318). Lugh's name means "light" or "brightness," which also suggests a connection with the sky.

Finally, we come to Aillenn herself. We know little of Aillenn beyond what we are told here and in the story of Báile Mac Buain, where we have an alternative tale of her death (O'Curry 1861:465). In that case, she is to meet her lover, Báilé, at Ros-na-righ (Rosnaree) on the Boyne. Báilé, however, is told that she had been killed on the way to meet him, whereupon he drops dead. Aillenn, in the meantime, is sitting in her "sunny chamber." The same fierce-looking man who had misled Báilé brings her word of his death, as a result of which she, too, falls dead. Here, as in the dindshenchas tale, an apple tree grows from her grave, in this case bearing the form of her head at its top. Likewise, a yew tree grows from that of Báilé with his likeness. After seven years the trees are cut down and "poet's tablets" made from them, upon which are written, respectively, the visions, espousals, loves, and courtships of Leinster and of Ulster. Much later, in the time of Art Mac Conn, the two tablets are brought together at Tara at Samhain, whereupon they sprang together and intertwined so that they could not be pulled apart.

It is unquestionably significant that those for whom the royal sites are named are all women who have been carried off, held hostage, or died—Macha, who died after giving birth at the end of a race against Conchobar's horses; Cruachu, who was carried off with her mistress Étaíne; Tea, in memory of whom Tara was built; and Aillenn (Hicks and Elder 2003). It is tempting to see here echoes of an ancient pan-European myth that also finds expression as the tale of Demeter (Ceres) and her daughter Persephone. In other words, at the time of harvest, that aspect of the goddess of the land associated with the grain dies or is carried away, and her death is honored with funeral games. Emain Macha—which in an aerial view appears a virtual twin to Dún Ailinne—and Ráth Crúachan are both said to have had associated Lughnasa festivals (MacNeill 1962:348). The site at Tailtiu is within the royal desmesne of Tara, whose associations are with Samhain rather than Lughnasa. There are good reasons to believe that Dún Ailinne overlooks the site of another such Lughnasa festival, that of Carman.

When we consider the other royal sites and the female figures associated with them, we notice that of the four major royal sites—Emain Macha, Ráth Crúachan, Temair (Tara), and Dún Ailinne—only Emain Macha is named for a figure that plays a prominent role in myth. In the case of Ráth Crúachan, Medb is a far more important figure than Cruachu (who is, however, said to be Medb's mother—Gwynn 1913 [III]:355). In the area around Dún Ailinne, the most prominent figure is that of Brigit, who receives only passing mention in the dindshenchas, although many other tales concern her. This scarcity of references to Aillenn and Cruachu may be simply a matter of historical accident or may indicate that they were invented for purposes of explaining the names. In either case, it seems likely to be more productive for our quest to understand related myth if we look at those figures who are more prominently mentioned, as we will do in considering the wider sacred landscape.

Aillend is mentioned in two other tales of the metrical dindshenchas, the first being that of Cell Chorbbáin, where a listing of those said to be buried at that place includes "Aillend and Aine in one tomb, Ailbe and full-modest Aife," (Gwynn 1924 [IV]:343). Hogan (1910:184) and Gwynn (1931 [V]:185) would place Cell Chorbbáin near Naas. Though Ailbe is here said to refer to a queen, the linking of the name once again with Aillend is interesting. And in Hogan's discussion of Cell Chorbbáin, he points out a reference to the burial of Cerball there that links it with Naas, the Liffey, Cnoc Almaine (the Hill of Allen), and Cnoc Aillenn.

The last dindshenchas tale mentioning Dún Ailinne is that for Acall (the Hill of Skreen, just to the east of Tara). Here the character involved is Fionn MacCumhail (Gwynn 1903 [I]:49): "Brothers were Finn from cold Alend, and Ailell from stern Cruachan, of Cairpre Nia from Temair in that country, whose noble daughter Achall was."

Three of the royal sites are mentioned in this verse, Dún Ailinne, Ráth Crúachan, and Tara. Ailill is the consort of Medb, while Cairpre gives his name to Carbury Hill, which was also mentioned earlier. Cairpre, too, can be either father or grandfather of Lugh (Stokes 1894/95:39, 320, 322).

We have been discussing the human characters mentioned in the dindshenchas, but what about Aillenn's lapdog, Ailbe? Ó Corráin and Maguire (1981:16) suggest that the name may be "connected with the old root *albho-* 'white' and with Gaulish *Albiorix* 'world-king.'" There are a number of Ailbes mentioned in the early literature, some of them human. These include the daughters of Midir and of Cormac mac Airt. The latter was, like her sister Gráinne, married to Fionn mac Cumhaill (NFCS 779:32). There are also male Ailbes, including 12 warriors of the Fianna. But perhaps most interestingly, there is a much more famous dog, the hound of Mac Dá Tho, the quest for whose ownership led to war between Ulster and Connacht. That Ailbe, like this one, is associated with Leinster, the whole of which he is said to have defended (as a human hound, Cú Chulainn, defended Ulster). It is possible the Ailbes are the same.

Assembly Sites

To gain some further understanding of Dún Ailinne's role, it is necessary to move beyond the characters mentioned to the nature of the site itself. At various places in other early documents we find it referred to not only as a *dún* but also as a *rath* and as a *múr*. Each of these obviously refers to the enclosing earthwork. In the first line of verse, however, we find another term applied to it. The actual passage reads: "Alend óenach diar n-ócaib." The term *oenach* (pl. *oinage*) most often refers not just to any gathering but rather to gatherings of a quasi-ritual nature or to the place where those are held.

When we compile a list of oinage mentioned in the dindshenchas, what is most notable is that we have a single site mentioned in Ulster at Ard Macha, in Mide at Tailtiu, at Loch Rí (between Dún Ailinne and Ráth Crúachan), and at Ráth Crúachan in Connacht. But there are four in the area near Dún Ailinne, in Leinster: Alend, Carman, Nás, and Maistiu. Maistiu refers to an area about 13 km to the south-southwest of Dún Ailinne, between Athy and Ballitore, where one finds, at Mullaghmast, Rath Maistiu. While this particular enclosure does not appear henge-like, it is intriguing that it lies approximately the same distance from Dún Ailinne as Nás and very nearly on the same alignment.

We are not told explicitly of the time of most of the oinage. Certainly we are not told when the assembly at Dún Ailinne was held. Nor do we know if the assemblies in its vicinity were held at the same time. However, when we are told a time of year, as in the tales for Carman and Tailtiu, it is at Lughnasa. Indirectly that date is implied for the oenach at Ráth Crúachan, as it is by the horse race involving Macha, since in the dindshenchas tale for Ráth Crúachan we are told Eochaid Airem ("ploughman"—Eochaid, or Eochu, in his various forms being the god commonly referred to as the Dagda, "the good god") was holding an assembly for horseracing when Étaíne and Cruachu were carried off (Gwynn 1913 [III]:351). As MacNeill pointed out (1962:349), there is good reason to believe that all oinage named for women of the otherworld were Lughnasa assemblies. This conclusion is supported by the references in the dindshenchas (Hicks and Elder 2003).

The identification of Dún Ailinne as an *óenach* has implications for the extent of the sacred landscape associated with it. According to Hogan (1910), eight ancient assembly sites mentioned in the manuscripts seem to lie in the immediate vicinity of Dún Ailinne—Alend, Ailbi, Colmáin, Carman, Clochair, Lethchraich, Life, and Sengormain.

Hogan suggests that most of the names may refer to a single site; in particular, he considers Colmáin, Clochair, Life, and Lethcraich to be identical.

However, it is certain that there are at least two, and it is not impossible that each may be distinct. Alend and Carman have separate listings in the dindshenchas, and in two listings of the burial places of the kings, Carman and Ailbe appear to be alternative names for that of the kings of Laigin (Leinster). In his discussion of the probable location of Carman, Ó Murchadha (2002) has argued for a location in the area to the north and east of the bridge across the River Liffey into Kilcullen, about 3 km north of Dún Ailinne, where one finds the parish of Carnalway, which he shows was originally called Carn Ailbe.

Colmáin, also described as the burial place of the Leinster princes, is in one case referred to as Circus Colmáin, suggesting it may be a rather large area suitable for horse races. This would seem to point to the Curragh, whose name appears to be derived from the Early Irish word for a racecourse. Óenach Sengormain, which Hogan considers an alias for Óenach Carman, is listed as having been in Mag Mesca. This also suggests a large open area like the Curragh. His equation of the two comes from the dindshenchas tale for Carman, where Mesca is described as having been carried off from a síd and dying of shame there. Carman, too, was a hostage (Stokes 1894:313ff).

The Curragh is marked with an accumulation of what appear to be ritual enclosures of the sort known as henges—circular earthworks with internal ditches interrupted by one or more causewayed entrances, named for the penannular bank and ditch that constitutes the first construction phase at Stonehenge. At least ten survive, their mean diameter (crest-to-crest) being 28.5 m. Dún Ailinne and Emain Macha are, of course, much larger examples of this sort of enclosure, whose bank and ditch are generally taken to mark the boundaries of a sacred space. Ráth Crúachan, too, is known from aerial photos to have once had a surrounding ditch (Waddell 1988b, Condit and Simpson 1998:58, Barton and Fenwick 2005) and probably an embankment. It would be tempting to assume that the enclosures on the Curragh are the sites of the oinage referred to as being in this area, but they appear too small to have served as gathering places. However, clusters of such henge-like earthworks do tend to be found in the same vicinities as Hogan's oenach sites elsewhere (Hicks 2004). To the suggestion that they might instead be ring barrows, the royal gravesites mentioned, we can offer the evidence of excavations that appear to refute this. Of the three excavated during the spring and summer of 1944 by Seán P. Ó Ríordáin (1950), just one, site 4, the single double-entranced enclosure, had a burial at its center. This burial is of particular interest because, in the opinion of the excavator and of medical experts consulted by him, the individual, a female in her twenties, was buried alive. This suggests a voluntary ritual sacrifice, perhaps in dedication of the site. The closest of the ten henge-like enclosures to Dún Ailinne lies some 3.2 km to its northwest. From there they stretch on to the northwest in an uneven line for an additional 6.4 km.

The dindshenchas speaks of 21 raths at Carman (Gwynn 1913 [III]:25), which might be a reference to these enclosures, if Carman incorporates the Curragh. The report on the excavations by Ó Riordain offers some additional suggestive information. His report (1950:272) refers to a passage in Geoffrey Keating's *Trí Bior-Ghaoithe an Bhiás* "describing the custom of ancient Irish burial in which the body is interred within a small rath…A single entrance was prescribed for the grave…of a man of learning, two entrances to that of a woman and none for the grave of a child." Keating was apparently drawing on a passage in the metrical dindshenchas (Gwynn 1924 [IV]:153), which Gwynn translates as specifying a "man of art" rather than "learning" and "young men and maidens" rather than merely "child." This passage occurs in a discussion of the periodic gatherings at the site of Tailtiu, where there were said to have been at the time nine "royal raths," one or more of which may have been like the royal sites already discussed though now none resembling a henge survives there. One of those raths, interestingly, was named Rath Cú, or "enclosure of the hound." Hounds and horses do both seem to have a connection to the oinage.

There are two other possibly relevant passages here. The first (Gwynn 1924 [IV]:151) states "No man going into the seats of the women, nor woman into the seats of the men." The term translated as "seats" is forad, which refers to a mound or platform which "may in some cases have been circular" (Quin 1998:327). It has been suggested in various places that the embankments of henges may have served as seating, and in one or two cases in Britain that seems definitely to have been the case in later use of the monuments. There is a similar passage in the dindshenchas of Carman, where we are told "No men to go into an assembly [airecht] of women, no women into an assembly of fair, pure, men" (Gwynn 1913 [III]:19). A bit further along in the Tailtiu description it says "On the wall of Eochu [Eochaid]…

twenty seats of the kings of Tara; and on the smooth wall of his wife twenty seats of their queens" (Gwynn 1924 [IV]:155). The term Gwynn translates as "wall" is múr, which is usually interpreted as an earthen rampart enclosing an area (Quin 1998:472). The term was applied to Dún Ailinne and is also used in the dindshenchas of Temair (Tara). These comments may have a bearing on the purpose and nature of the henge-like enclosures, including Dún Ailinne, which has one entrance and is linked in the dindshenchas with assemblies of the young or of warriors (Stokes 1895:310, Gwynn 1903 [I]:880).

The Larger Ritual Landscape

Both the oinage material and Dún Ailinne's relationship to the Curragh sites suggest it was part of a larger sacred landscape. Analysis of other royal sites has shown that they, too, do not exist in isolation but rather as part of larger sacred or ritual landscapes, in each case as part of a complex of monuments that may cover several square kilometers (also see discussion in Chapter 17). Certain characteristics tend to be shared by such complexes.

First, they can be identified by the presence of clusters of monuments recognized as being of a ritual or ceremonial nature—passage tumuli, henge-like earthen enclosures, stone circles, parallel banks of a sort known as "cursuses" (again named for an example in the Stonehenge complex), or other such monuments. Tara, for example, has not only the "Mound of the Hostages" but also henge-like earthworks as well as standing stones, the cursus-like "Banqueting Hall," and a considerable number of other monuments.

Second, they often include monuments or other archaeological evidence belonging to more than one period. This is indicative of their continuing importance as sacred places, as can clearly be seen in the Bend of the Boyne complex, where we find the central monument of Newgrange—reliably dated to over 5000 years ago—serving as a place for the deposit of apparently ritual offerings of coins and other objects dating to the immediate pre-Christian period, some 60 objects, most dating from the late third to early fifth centuries AD, according to Raghnall Ó Floinn of the National Museum (2003). In the case of Newgrange (Brúg na Boinne), as with Tara and Emain Macha, this continuing importance is emphasized by its role in Irish myth. And in a number of cases—e.g., Tara, Dún Ailinne, and Emain Macha—there is an Early Christian site, often attributed to a founding by St. Patrick, close to the complex.

Third, while these complexes often focus on one or more hilltops or other high points of land, they normally extend well beyond these. The Stonehenge complex, as defined by Darvill (1999), measures some 3.0 km east-west by 1.6 km north-south. In Ireland, the Boyne complex provides a good comparative example. It extends at least from the Dowth Hall henge on the east to Knowth passage tumulus on the west, a distance of over 4 km, and may originally have extended as far as the Hill of Slane, if the tumulus there is also Neolithic, which seems very possible. The north-south extent of the complex is also over 4 km, from the henge and tumuli of Monknewtown and Townley Hall to the enclosures below Newgrange along the Boyne. Thus the extent of the complex is 16 km^2 at a minimum.

A considerable number of such complexes exist besides those centered on the royal sites—for example, around Fourknocks, Knockainy/Lough Gur, Loughcrew/Slieve na Calliagh, Magh Adair, near Sligo, Boyle, Tralee, and just to the south of (and probably including) Cashel. The complexes typically cover several square kilometers, as is evident when we consider those surrounding the other royal sites of Emain Macha and Ráth Crúachan. Although much has undoubtedly been destroyed in the vicinity during recent centuries, the Emain Macha complex (Lynn 2003) must at a minimum have included the enclosure itself, the plain neighboring it where the Lughnasa festival was held, and two nearby sites, namely Ard Macha (the hill upon which the Armagh cathedral stands, where excavation revealed traces of a surrounding ditch of uncertain date) and the "ritual pond" known as the King's Stables. That would encompass an area extending at least 3.7 km east-west and an indeterminate distance north-south. At Ráth Crúachan, a wide variety of monuments are spread across an area measuring approximately 3.0 km east-west by 3.3 km north-south (Waddell 1983; Herity 1984, 1985, 1988, 1989).

What, then, is the extent of the ritual landscape associated with Dún Ailinne? Dún Ailinne and the Curragh sites may form a single complex because they do appear to represent a coherent whole. Survey work by Clancy (forthcoming) will augment this picture considerably. There is a pattern here, with Dún Ailinne anchoring the southeast end of a ragged alignment of monuments. The clustering of oenach names in the vicinity contributes to this sense of a pattern. If we accept Ó Murchadha's (2002) argument that Oenach Ailbe lay about 3 km to the north of Dún Ailinne at Kilcullen, the complex might have extended that far.

Oenach Colmáin, with its associated horse races, is more likely to have lain to the west, on the Curragh. And, of course, the Curragh is readily visible from Dún Ailinne, and vice versa.

If Dún Ailinne and the Curragh earthworks (and perhaps Carn Ailbe) do belong to the same complex, it would constitute a district some 3 km in width but nearly 10 km long. Knockaulin Hill is a much more prominent feature of the landscape than the relatively small elevations at Emain Macha and Ráth Crúachan. But if we were to include all within the viewshed of Dún Ailinne, we could argue for the inclusion of the three hills on the far side of the Curragh, the Hill of Allen somewhat further to the north, and more. This seems unlikely. The difficulty, of course, is that there are so many apparently ritual monuments spread across the Irish countryside. The entire Irish landscape was seen as in some sense sacred. One clue to the extent of the complex may be offered by the dindshenchas. It appears that what we are provided with in the dindshenchas is primarily a listing of sacred places and that we can separate the sacred places to some degree by the way they are divided in that listing.

In the metrical version (Gwynn 1906 [II]:72ff], Alend is preceded by the tale of Almu, the Hill of Allen. In the prose, however, we find that Alend is preceded by that of Adarca Hua Failgi (Stokes 1894:308-9), which incorporates the tale of Almu. Adarca Hua Failgi itself is not clearly explained, the name seeming to mean "the horns of Offaly," and the tale telling of the cattle of Iuchna Horsemouth (who is elsewhere identified as Iuchna Eachach Echbeoil—identifying him with Eochaid Horsemouth—Stokes 1894:449), who lives at Machad Brigte, "Brigit's Milking-Yard." Upon his death, the cattle shed their horns, which formed mounds or hillocks (*dumae*). The most obvious things in the vicinity that could plausibly be considered the "horns" are the hills of Dunmurry and Grange a little to the south of the Hill of Allen, the dip between which has a significance that will be discussed in a later section.

The dindshenchas tale for Alend is followed by the long poem describing the Lughnasa assembly at Carmun (Stokes 1894:311-15; Gwynn 1913 [III]:1-25). This would seem to suggest not only that Carman is in the vicinity but that it is in some way separate from Dún Ailinne itself. If it is indeed around Carn Ailbe as Ó Murchadha (2002) suggests, that would seem to exclude that area from the Dún Ailinne complex.

Next comes the tale of Bóand, describing the origin of the River Boyne at Síd Nechtáin (Stokes 1894:315-16; Gwynn 1913 [III]: 26-39) . Síd Nechtáin is Carbury Hill, which was also mentioned earlier. Thus Carbury Hill appears to be the focus of another neighboring complex. The hill has on its top two enclosures, the smaller of them henge-like with a single entrance, the larger entranceless (Willmot 1938). In the folklore, Carbury Hill is linked with two others nearby that form a line with it, Green Hill (Donadea) and Rourke's Hill. Here again we see a clustering of three hills in connection with sacred sites, as we did with the three on the west of the Curragh (and as well also with the three of Slieve na Calliagh); these groupings are something that would seem to warrant further investigation.

Finally come the tales for Cnogba and Nás. The prose version (Stokes 1894:316-18) mentions only Nás and is completely different from the metrical, identifying Nás as a man who shirked his part of the task of clearing the forest from Tailtiu's plain and was forced by Eochaid the Rough to build a rath as punishment. In the metrical (Gwynn 1913 [III]:40-53) the verses concerning Cnogba (Knowth) precede those for Nás and seem out of place in this list until one reads the tale, which identifies it as the burial place of Lugh's wife Bói, sister of Nás, as mentioned earlier. Nás, of course, gives her name to Naas. Naas and Longstone Rath were also mentioned earlier. Lying as they do some 13 to 15 km to the northeast, they may seem too far away to be relevant to the study of Dún Ailinne, but there are reasons for believing they are related even though belonging to a subsidiary or neighboring complex. As mentioned earlier, Dún Ailinne, Carman, the Hill of Allen, and Naas were linked in the passage from *Timna Chathaír Máir* (Dillon 1962:167). The Lughnasa connection is certainly there. Also, we find some of the same motifs in folk belief there as at Dún Ailinne (as well as at the Hill of Allen and Carbury Hill). The motte in Naas, too, is supposed to have a treasure buried within (NFCS 776:328), and a black dog is said to guard a treasure in a tunnel running under the nearby canal. The entrance of Longstone Rath also looks toward the hills across the Curragh from Dún Ailinne.

The Ritual Year

I have made a number of references to the festival of Lughnasa, which seems to have some link to the royal sites. This festival is one component in the "ritual year," which is to say the sequence of festivals based on the annual agricultural cycle. In any culture in a temperate environment dependent on agriculture for its food supply and thus on the annual cycle of seasons, it is reasonable to assume that this would be a primary focus of the belief system.

The festivals divide the year into four parts and fall in time midway between the solstices and equinoxes, at times referred to as the cross-quarter days. Today they are said to fall on the first days of February, May, August, and November. Before the introduction of Christianity and the Julian calendar, the date would most likely have been determined by a phase of the moon falling near the solstice/equinox midpoints. This would place them a week or two either side of a date in the first week of the months mentioned. MacNeill (1962:16, 657-58) found Lughnasa celebrations falling at various dates between 21 July and 12 August.

The first festival, called Imbolc or Oimelg, is today associated with Saint Brigit, who seems to have replaced an earlier goddess of that name (Ó Catháin 1995:ix). It falls at the beginning of February. The first name, Imbolc, seems to refer to the belly or swelling and may imply the earth is pregnant and about to give birth; the second means "ewe's milk," apparently referring to the beginning of the lambing season. Either name would mark this as the beginning of the agricultural year, when the earth begins to bear new life.

The second festival is Beltaine, "Bel's fire," at the beginning of May (Danaher 1972:86-127). At this time two fires were traditionally built and the herds and flocks were driven between them (to confer protection from disease and injury) and off to the summer pastures.

As noted, the third festival, Lughnasa ("games of Lugh") was celebrated near the beginning of August with a week—some sources say two—of horse races and other contests (MacNeill 1962).

Finally, we have the festival that ended the Irish year, Samhain (Danaher 1972:200-32), Johnson 1968), whose meaning there seems to be some disagreement about. It can be interpreted simply as "end of summer," though that would appear to work only if you assume the year has just two seasons, summer and winter. It can also be interpreted as coming from an Indo-European root meaning "coming together," thus giving it a meaning of "reassembly" (Powell 1958:117; Watkins 2000:75), and it was certainly the time when the herds and flocks were brought back from the summer pastures. It marked the end of the harvest and a time of feasting, particularly the time of the Feast of Tara (Gwynn 1924 [IV]:297ff) to which the high king expected all lower kings to come and contribute. This festival has come down to us as Halloween, or more accurately its characteristics have been spread among Halloween, All Saint's Day, and All Soul's Day.

It is probably significant that the only two seasonal festivals described in detail in the dindshenchas are the Lughnasa assemblies at Tailtiu and Carman. The Tailtiu festival, being linked to Tara not far to its southeast as well as being the site associated with the founding of the festival, was important for both those reasons. The area surrounding Dún Ailinne was also important because of an especially strong link with Lughnasa. The tale of Carman (Stokes 1894:311-15; Gwynn 1913 [III]: 2-25) is our best source for what the festival overlooked by Dún Ailinne was like.

Lughnasa at Carman

The prose version tells us that the Leinstermen held this fair during the first eight days of August down to the time of Cathair Mór. There were seven horseraces during a week also devoted to promulgating the judgments and laws of the province for a year (rightly three years, since it was held every third year, the preceding two being used for preparations). For holding it, the Leinstermen were assured grain and milk and freedom from conquest. They were assured heroic royal men, tender women, good cheer in every house, good fruit, nets full of fish. If they failed to hold it, they could expect decay and early grayness and short-lived kings.

The metrical dindshenchas tells us of those things that would be threatened if disputes prevented celebration of the fair (Gwynn 1913 [III]:11, 15). The earth, the heavens, people, and all their possessions were hostage to its proper celebration. We are told that the site of the fair had a level area for races and a burial-ground of kings. There is also mention of special areas being set aside for markets, pasturing of horses, cooking, and the use of the women. Each day had a race and a different dedication: the first of the saints, the second of the high kings, the third of the women, the fourth that of the Laigsi and the Fothairt, the fifth of the princes, the multitudes of Erin for the sixth, and the Clann Condla the last. Other things to be found at the fair were music and storytelling.

In both versions, we are told a date for the founding of the fair—580 BC. This date is not inconsistent with a number of the radiocarbon dates for the Iron Age phases at Dún Ailinne—e.g., dates of 540 ± 85 BC/792-409 BC (SI-981) and 420 ± 85 BC/768-210 BC (SI-983) (Chapter 15, this volume).

Thus the Lughnasa assembly at Carman was most importantly a gathering to ensure the prosperity and safety of the land and to promulgate laws. It was a religious event, but also a social and economic one. As has been pointed out by Crabtree (Chapter 13), the evidence for boneworking and metallurgy at Dún Ailinne suggest that it, too, may have been the site of fairs and periodic markets for crafts. While the botanical and faunal remains from Dún Ailinne cannot pin down the timing of the feasts held there precisely, Crabtree does conclude that they most likely occurred some time between April and October, which would be consistent with Beltaine or, more likely, with the summer solstice or Lughnasa.

Female Figures at the Assembly Sites and Their Festival Roles

To better understand the sites we have been discussing and their place in the belief system, we must consider the role each of the female characters associated with them plays in the agricultural cycle. While we know little of Ailenn, Brigit is firmly associated not only with the festival of Imbolc/Oimelg but also with the Curragh, which is said to have been given to her. In the beliefs surrounding her, she is closely associated with the cattle and particularly with their role in supplying milk.

Macha is less clearly associated with one of the festivals, but there was certainly a Lughnasa festival held on Mag Macha in early August. The Lughnasa connection is bolstered by the famous tale associated with the names of Emain Macha and Ard Macha, in which she is said to have been forced into a race against the horses of Conchobar while heavily pregnant (Stokes 1895:45–46). The outcome of this race is that she wins, gives birth to twins, and curses the Ulstermen. Horse races, with some indication that they may have held some ritual significance, are very much a feature of the Lughnasa celebrations.

Medb is also closely associated with one of the festivals, but in her case that at the end of the harvest, Samhain. *Táin Bó Cúalnge*, "The Cooley Cattle Raid," in which she is a central character, states that the raid began on the Monday after Samhain and, later, that Cú Chulainn fought the armies of Medb from Samhain until the Wednesday after Imbolc (Stokes 1894:467). The lesser cattle raid tales also are focused on Ráth Crúachan and Samhain. Thus Medb's domain is clearly the winter and particularly its start.

The only festival missing from this list is that of Beltaine, at the beginning of May. It differs from the other three in that it has to do not with the crops but primarily with the movement of the herds and flocks to their summer pastures. The most prominent role played by that festival in the myths is in the arrival of various groups in *Lebor Gabála Érenn* ("The Book of the Takings"), where we find Cessair, Partholon, and the Tuatha Dé all arriving at this time of year.

The presence of a well dedicated to St. John within the enclosing rampart of Dún Ailinne calls our attention to another celebration, this one held at the time of the summer solstice.

Astronomical Aspects of the Sites and Landscape

The cycles of seasons with their accompanying festivals presuppose an interest in and concern with the calendar and thus with astronomy. And what we know of astronomy in prehistoric Ireland, as in Britain, focuses on the horizon and specifically on the rising and setting of the sun and moon at significant times in their cycles—the solstices in the case of the sun and the so-called lunar standstill positions in the case of the moon. The sun's cycle is one we are all familiar with—with sunrises slowly progressing from the southeast at winter solstice toward the northeast where, at summer solstice, the path reverses.

The moon has a similar cycle, but considerably more complex. It makes the journey from south to north and back again each month. But how far north and south it travels changes from month to month, from a maximum swing wider than that of the sun at each end of an 18.6-year cycle to one that is narrower than the sun's 9.3 years later. The rising full moon is always roughly diametrically opposite the setting sun—in the northeast near the winter solstice and in the southeast near the summer.

It is also possible, of course, to mark in-between positions such as the rising and setting places of the sun and full moon midway between the solstices and equinoxes, at the time of the festivals. What one must also remember in this case is that just as both the vernal and autumnal equinoxes are marked by the same east-west alignment, so too are those for Imbolc and Samhain (with sunrise in the southeast) and Beltaine and Lughnasa (northeast sunrise). It has been stated that Beltaine and

Samhain were seen as being the beginning and end of summer, thus linking these two festivals which were considered to mark the transitions between the light and dark halves of the year. Astronomically, assuming the horizon were near the same height in each direction, sunrise at Beltaine—to the northeast—would be diametrically opposite sunset at Samhain, to the southwest (or vice versa, with Samhain sunrise being in the southeast and Beltaine sunset in the northwest). One could make a similar linkage between the other two festivals, Imbolc and Lughnasa. Here, of course, the Imbolc sunrise would be in the southeast and Lughnasa sunset in the northwest or Lughnasa sunrise in the northeast and Imbolc sunset in the southwest.

The important point is that one can show similar linkages for both sets of festivals. To find Brigit, who is so strongly associated with the beginning of spring, also associated with an area that appears to be so strongly associated with Lughnasa is likely to be significant. They form a natural opposition, marking the times of birth and death of the crops.

Together, the two associations and the proliferation of Lughnasa sites in the vicinity of Dún Ailinne suggest that this area is strongly associated with the growing season, thus encompassing also Beltaine, in its middle.

To see if these astronomical considerations play a role in helping us understand Dún Ailinne and its surroundings, we must examine the alignments that are to be found there. In doing so, it is important to bear in mind that "the alignments are likely to have been rough and symbolic, intended for ritual purposes rather than for precise observations" (Hicks 1984:204).

Dún Ailinne and most of the henge-like enclosures on the Curragh have entrance alignments that fall near those for equinox sunrise or sunset (Hicks 1975). From the center of Dún Ailinne, at the southeast end of the complex, the enclosure's entrance faces east, while at Raheenanairy at the northwest end, it faces west. Only Curragh 4, with its sacrificial burial, adjacent to Raheenanairy has entrances facing both east and west. Based on sur-

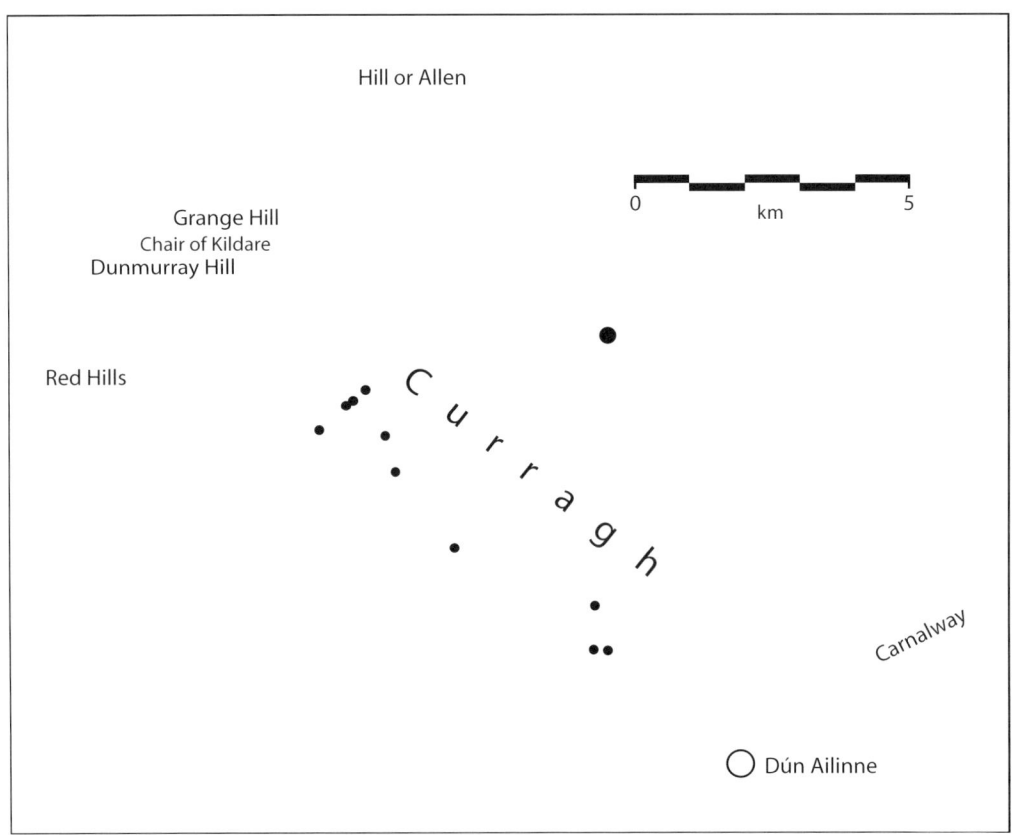

Figure 16-1. Dún Ailinne and the henge-like enclosures of the Curragh in relation to Carnalway and the hills on the western edge of the Curragh.

veys carried out in 1977 (Hicks 1981), of the ten henge-like Curragh sites, seven have entrances oriented to rising and setting positions within a lunar month of the equinoxes—Curragh 4 plus two others to the east and four to the west. One site seems oriented outside the sun's range, one near Beltaine/Lughnasa sunrise, and two have been so disturbed that it is impossible to identify their entrances. All of the henge-like enclosures on the Curragh fall within 800 m of a line from Dún Ailinne to the site labeled on the Ordnance Survey maps as the "Chair of Kildare." Most are less than half that. If one looks at the distribution, it very much looks as though it marks this alignment (Figure 16-1).

If one shifts from the center of the Dún Ailinne enclosure to the large timber structures found during excavation, one finds that their orientations are to the north of east. Since precise orientations were not recorded in terms of true north at the time of the excavations, one cannot be certain, but it appears from the published plans that the Iron Age Rose phase structure has an orientation also falling within a lunar month of the equinox while that of Iron Age Mauve phase falls near the orientation for Beltaine/Lughnasa sunrise.

"Chair of Kildare" and Adarca Hui Failgi

The most significant alignment, however, appears to be that involving the entire complex. Recalling the earlier mention of St. John's Well, we note that the feast of St. John the Baptist is 24 June, nicely linking it with the summer solstice (as John the Evangelist is honored near the winter solstice on 27 December). If one observes the summer solstice sunset from Dún Ailinne, or from sites along the line on the Curragh such as Raheenanairy or Site 4, the sun appears to set in the gap between Dunmurry and Grange Hills, near the Chair of Kildare. An examination of the surveyor's field notes in the Ordnance Survey reveals that there is a mound at that location (Killanin and Duignan [1967:320] say a limestone outcrop) that was identified as the inauguration place of the Earls of Kildare (and thus, presumably, the kings before them).

If indeed the two hills of Dunmurry and Grange can be identified with the Adarca Hui Failgi, named for the horns of Eochaid's cattle, this would be an indication of why that place was considered of enough ritual significance to be mentioned in the dindshenchas. It is quite likely that the naming of the hill as Grange is itself an indicator of its part in this alignment rather than a reference to a granary.

Grange, in other words, is likely a Anglicization of *grían* or *gréine*, referring to the sun. There is another Grange Hill in the ritual complex around Lough Gur in Co. Limerick, not to mention the hilltop site of Grianan of Ailech in Co. Donegal. Ó Ríordáin and Daniel (1964:16) also referred to the possibility that Newgrange is a corruption of *An Uamh Gréine*, which would mean "the cave of the sun," although in this case the suggestion was that Gréine was derived from Gráinne (a misconception perhaps resulting from the fact that Professor Daniel finished the book from Ó Ríordáin's notes after his death).

If one extends the solstice alignment from Dún Ailinne further to the northwest, it leads one eventually not only very close to Eochaid's home on Uisneach, which lies at the midpoint of a line ending just south of Ráth Crúachan.

It is said that from atop Uisneach it is possible to see 20 of Ireland's 32 counties (Killanin and Duignan 1967:101). Given the elevation of both Uisneach and Dún Ailinne relative to the surrounding countryside, one should certainly be able to see from one to the other, if my calculations are correct. At least one should be able to on a clear day; I have so far failed to do so. However, for a long-distance alignment to be significant symbolically, it is not essential that sites along it always be intervisible. Uisneach is associated not only with Eochaid and Lugh but is also a site traditionally visited on Beltaine. It is also the only site in Ireland associated with a gathering of the druids, and the dindshenchas for Mide seems to suggest it was the seat of the chief druid (Gwynn 1906 [II]:45).

Summary and Conclusions

References to treasures and tunnels in Knockaulin, the Hill of Allen, Grange Hill, and Carbury Hill make it clear that these were considered *sídhe*, dwelling places of the old gods and thus components of a sacred landscape. This status is also evident from their place in myth.

The primary themes in myth regarding Dún Ailinne are that it is linked with the kingship of Leinster and that it was named for a woman who was abducted and died of shame. This motif clearly links it with the other royal sites as well as with the festival of Lughnasa. We are also told that it is a oenach, an assembly site, which likewise appears to indicate links with Lughnasa.

Several names of assembly sites are mentioned as being in the vicinity of Dún Ailinne. How many of these are alternative names for single sites is unclear, but there were certainly at least two—Dún Ailinne and Carman. Dún Ailinne appears to be the southeastern anchor of a complex of earthworks extending to the northwest across the Curragh toward the hills of Adarca Hui Failgi and Almu. And for Carman, we have an extended description of a Lughnasa assembly that shows the social and economic as well as ritual nature of such gatherings.

The distribution of the oinage mentioned in the dindshenchas hints at the existence of a larger sacred landscape, linking the royal sites of Dún Ailinne, Ráth Crúachan, and Emain Macha, as well as others. The female figures most prominently associated with the vicinities of these sites also appear to be associated with different seasonal festivals. In the case of Dún Ailinne and its vicinity, these—with Brigit and the festival of Lughnasa—are to the beginning and end of the growing season for the crops. And the alignments linking the sites also appear to be significant, with the sites lying to the northwest of Dún Ailinne falling along the line to summer solstice sunset.

What I have attempted to do in this chapter is to push the available evidence for the belief system of which Dún Ailinne was a part, and the place of Dún Aililnne within that system, as far as I was able in an attempt to gain some understanding of the role of the site and its surroundings. Inevitably the results are very speculative. Nonetheless, I believe at least some of what I have suggested is near or on the road to a true explanation. I hope that I have in any case provided some approaches and hypotheses that may prove useful in fully interpreting this and other parts of the ancient Irish landscape.

17
The Larger Archaeological Context

Susan A. Johnston

It has long been clear from both artifacts and Classical documentary sources that, during the main period of activity at Dún Ailinne, Ireland was connected to the larger British and European world and also to the Classical cultures of the Mediterranean. This connection was mediated largely through trade, which provided both material goods and a potential conduit for less tangible things such as attitudes, ideologies, and world views (Freeman 2001; Cunliffe 2001). For example, Newman has argued that, rather than representing smaller political entities (see below), sites like Raffin Fort which mimic the form of the royal sites but on a smaller scale, indicate the appearance of a new means of achieving social status. This was made possible after the conquest by the ready availability in Britain of Roman goods that were used to create elite status (Newman 1998).

That Dún Ailinne participated in this trade network is made clear by the presence of such objects as the bronze fibulae (Chapter 8) and the glass beads and bracelets (Chapter 9), the latter originating as whole artifacts or as raw materials outside of Ireland. This connection is further indicated by the fact that there are parallels to Dún Ailinne itself not only in Ireland, but also in Britain and on the continent. If these parallels can be taken to indicate similarly shared ideologies, then a consideration of them can help in the analysis of the meaning of the site.

It is possible to draw parallels for Dún Ailinne in a variety of different ways depending on which aspects of the site are emphasized. It is first a royal site, the category which forms the main comparative group of sites. Beyond this, a number of different functions have been attributed to it—ritual, assembly, inauguration—and so it can also be compared to other sites that share these various functions. Alternatively, breaking the site down into its components, it was comprised of a series of structural elements—an internally ditched enclosure, a series of timber structures, a figure-of-eight structure—and these all provide additional possibilities for comparison.

The Royal Sites of Ireland

Dún Ailinne is most commonly grouped with those sites conventionally known as "royal." This grouping is based on both historical documents and archaeological data, and has come to include, minimally, Dún Ailinne, Tara, Emhain Macha, and Cruachain (others have been proposed, such as Cashel, by Newman 1998). While royal sites would have been defined as a group by the accumulation of archaeological evidence, documents first placed them together and suggested that they be compared archaeologically. The historical references to Dún Ailinne are discussed in more detail elsewhere (Chapter 18 and Grabowski 1990), but several main points can be reiterated here. First, the royal sites are consistently grouped in ancient sources, suggesting that they were remembered as sharing the same general character. Second, their memory remained important enough that they could provide an effective symbol of the pagan past. Third, they were powerful, but were ultimately defeated by Christianity. Finally, alone among the royal sites, Dún Ailinne does not appear in the epic, literary sources but rather as a real, historical place.

A number of authors (see Wailes 1982; Newman 1998; Warner 1988) have discussed the archaeological characteristics of this group, while others (see Lynn 1991; Warner 1994b) have made more detailed comparisons. All of the various archaeological work at the royal sites (for Navan, Waterman 1997; Lynn 2000, 2002; Larsen and Ambos 1997; Ambos et al. 1996; Kvamme 1996; Ambos and Larson 2002; for Tara, Ó Ríordáin 1955; Newman 1997; Fenwick and Newman 2002; Roche 1999, 2002; for Rathcroghan, Waddell 1983, 1988a; Fenwick et al. 1999; Fenwick, Brennan and Delaney 1997; Waddell and Barton 1997; Barton and Fenwick 2005; Herity 1984, 1985, 1988, 1989) shows that this class of sites forms a coherent category, mirroring the groupings which appear in the documentary record.

This impressive amount of data allows a discussion of what the Irish royal sites have in common, as well as how they differ. Chronologically, their main periods of use can be shown to be approximately contemporary (see Johnston, In press for a more detailed discussion of the dating evidence for the royal sites). For Dún Ailinne (see Chapter 15), the dates range from the final century and a half BC through the first few centuries AD. Navan overlaps broadly but appears slightly earlier, with the bulk of activity at the site from the 4th century BC through the 1st century AD (Warner, in Waterman 1997:101-4; Baillie 1988; Mallory 2000; Mallory, Brown and Baillie 1999; Lynn 2000). There is comparatively less dating evidence available for the other two royal sites, but recent work at Tara suggests a broad range of use from the 4th century BC through the 5th century AD (Roche 2002), while more limited work at Rathcroghan produced dates from the 3rd century BC to the 3rd-4th centuries AD (Waddell 1988a; Warner, Mallory and Baillie 1990). Figure 17-1 shows a summary of this, based primarily on the radiocarbon data.

While the sites are broadly contemporary, however, there are variations in periods of use. Navan is somewhat earlier, Rathcroghan lies in the middle, and Tara and Dún Ailinne are somewhat later. While these are ranges, and so lack precision, this figure may still show something of the order in which the sites were constructed and used: Navan seems to be the earliest with the other sites somewhat later, and Tara and Dún Ailinne would be the last survivors of the pagan royal site context. If this is so, then it may suggest possible directions of influences between sites.

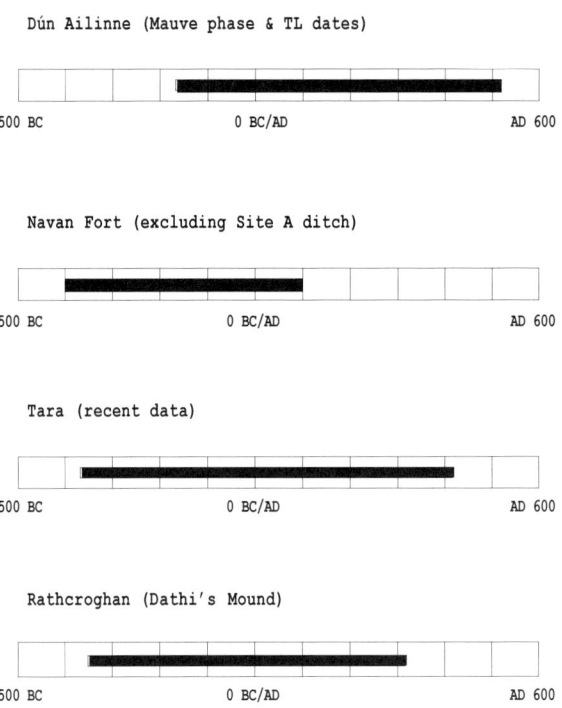

Figure 17-1. Chronology, royal sites in Ireland.

Similarities and Differences

To begin with similarities, all of the sites are located on hilltops, and all have enclosures surrounding the main area of activity. The enclosures at three of the sites are composed of an outer bank and an internal ditch (that at Rathcroghan remains uncertain). The internal ditch/external bank is something which the royal sites share with ceremonial monuments, notably henges (see below) and which differentiates them from more obviously defensive structures, like hillforts (see B. Raftery 1994). The significance of this has been the subject of speculation, but it is typically argued that an inner ditch is not effective in defense since attackers would be able to surmount the bank more quickly and have the advantage of height. However, Mallory (2000) has argued quite convincingly that this may be an over-simplification, and depends largely on how contemporary weaponry and battle tactics are envisioned. This leaves the configuration of the bank and ditch a somewhat open question.

In terms of lifespan, all three excavated sites have evidence of multi-period use beginning in the

Neolithic and ending in the Iron Age. Neolithic evidence ranges from the passage tomb at Tara (Duma na nGiall, or Mound of the Hostages; Newman 1997) and the Linkardstown burial at Dún Ailinne through the more ephemeral remains at Navan (Waterman 1997) and Dún Ailinne (Chapters 4-6). Site use continued into the Bronze Age at Tara (Newman 1997) and Dún Ailinne (Chapters 4-6), while at Navan such continuity is indicated by a sequence of construction that begins in the latter part of the Bronze Age (Waterman 1997). For all four royal sites, however, the apogee of their use lay in the Iron Age.

All four royal sites also lie in larger archaeological landscapes which are characterized by a high proportion of ritual monuments. Tara is surrounded by almost 100 monuments (Newman 1997), while an archaeological survey in the area of Rathcroghan lists 53 (Waddell 1983, 1988b). Dún Ailinne's landscape is similarly populated, with over 180 recorded monuments (Ó Ríordáin 1950; Clancy, Forthcoming), and the monuments surrounding Navan are also numerous (Waterman 1997; Warner 1986, 1994c; Hartwell 1987, 1991). Thus all four royal sites were placed in a landscape already populated by markers of ritual significance.

The impression of internal similarities among the royal sites is also great, but in fact they vary quite a bit in detail. Some features are shared by only some of the sites and even shared features might vary in specific aspect. For example, timber structures are common, but not all are exactly the same. This is significant because it allows the definition, on the one hand, of the essential components of a royal site and, on the other, where the site may have been "tailored" to local needs and/or expectations.

The first characteristic that all the sites appear to share is the construction of large, circular, timber structures. There are at least three at Dún Ailinne (see Chapter 2, 18), constructed in sequence, with each having been dismantled before the next began. At Navan, they include the series of timber buildings comprising Sites A and B and the 40 m structure (Waterman 1997), while at Tara, an enclosure comprised of two concentric circles of pits (which likely held posts) with a ditch in between was revealed in a recent geophysical survey (Fenwick and Newman 2002). Rathcroghan needs further evaluation, but recent geophysical work has provided evidence of a number of circular features which may be the remains of timber structures (Barton and Fenwick 2005).

A second shared feature is seen in the presence of what have been dubbed "figure-of-eight" structures. Lynn (1991) has already drawn a detailed comparison between the figure-of-eights at Dún Ailinne and Navan, and in his Figure 1A (1991:52) the resemblance is really quite remarkable. A second figure-of-eight structure uncovered at Navan also seems to shares the same features (Lynn 2002). The two enclosures within the Ráith na Ríg at Tara, while structurally quite different from those at Dún Ailinne and Navan, form a similar pattern overall, and it is likely that this was intended (Newman 1997:86). Other possibilities are the newly discovered timber structure noted above, which overlaps the Ráith na Ríg on its northern edge (Fenwick and Newman 2002), and the small southern enclosure under the Rath of the Synods, situated between two larger enclosures (Cooney and Grogan 1991:37). Further examples at Tara are suggested by Newman (1998). The significance of this feature is uncertain, but may been intended to echo domestic architecture, since this configuration is seen in surviving houses from several periods. There is, for example, a figure-of-eight structure from the Early Christian period at Deer Park Farms, Co. Armagh (Lynn 1988) and another from the Bronze Age at Crossreagh East, Co. Derry (McSparron, www.northarch.supanet.com/CRE%20Report.htm).

Beyond the overall similarities of the timber structures and figure-of-eight patterns, however, the details vary considerably. For example, what are glossed here as "timber structures" in fact include:

- palisaded and walled figure-of-eight structures and the walled palisade surrounding a more open timber ring of the 40 m structure at Navan, which was arguably roofed;
- the post pits at Tara and possibly Rathcroghan;
- three versions of timber structures at Dún Ailinne, none of them apparently roofed: the relatively simple palisade of the White phase (with a possible open ring at the center), the more complex palisaded figure-of-eight of the Rose phase, and the palisade of the Mauve phase which encloses an open timber ring.

The placement of the timber structures also varies. While the timber structures at Dún Ailinne and Navan are within enclosures, the post pit ring at Tara is not (though it overlaps the Ráith na Rig). Tara, Rathcroghan, and Navan all had a variety of structures simultaneously on their hilltops, while there appears to have been only one at Dún Ailinne at any given time. The figure-of-eight structures

Table 17-1. Comparison, Royal Site Sizes.

SITE	ENCLOSURE AREA	MAX. DIAM., ENCLOSURE	MAX. DIAM., TIMBER CIRCLE	MAX DIAM., FIGURE-OF-EIGHT
Dún Ailinne	13 ha	460m	42m	36m
Navan	6 ha	250m	40m	30m
Tara (Ráith na Ríg)	7 ha	380m	210m	—
Rathcroghan	(10.7 ha)*	370m	32m	—

*Based on diameter of 370 m and assuming enclosure is circular.

at Navan produced occupation material, while no such material was recovered from Dún Ailinne. Tara and Navan both have a central mound within their enclosures, while Dún Ailinne lacks such a mound (though Feature 42 at the center of the Mauve phase complex might have been functionally similar; the steep rise of the hill towards the summit at Dún Ailinne might also serve the same visual purpose).

There is also a great disparity in size among the various sites, as shown in Table 17-1. The most obvious difference is the truly massive timber structure at Tara, five times larger than the next largest at Dún Ailinne. The sizes of the timber structures at Navan and Dún Ailinne are closely comparable. For the other structures, Dún Ailinne is the largest, though not always by much. The Rose phase figure-of-eight structure and the diameter and area of Dún Ailinne's enclosure are each about 20% larger than the next largest examples (respectively Navan Site C, Tara, and Rathcroghan). What the size differences mean is unclear. Obviously larger structures are more imposing, more visible, attest to the greater power of their builders, etc. It might also have something to do with the number of people available to work on construction. In addition, it might be suggested that the larger size was deemed necessary to accommodate the activities held within, whether it be the enclosure itself or the structures within it.

It is interesting that Warner, citing 7th century legal documents, describes the requisite shape and size of the king's fort (*dún*) as being circular and about 40 m (Warner 1988:59). This is the size of the timber structure at Navan, and is close to the diameter of the Mauve structure at Dún Ailinne. While the documents are much later and describe residences, it may be that the 40 m measurement was in some way based on the idea, prevalent when the documents were written, that sites like Navan and Dún Ailinne were ancient royal residences. Far be it for later rulers to have houses smaller than their legendary predecessors! Alternatively, the reverse could be the case—that the ceremonial structures were in some fashion echoing an older notion of a ruler's proper residence, which in turn was codified much later in written sources. While speculative, it does fit the idea noted earlier of a connection between figure-of-eight structures in domestic versus ritual settings.

The available evidence for activity which occurred on these sites also suggests some variety. While the periodic dismantling of structures and the construction of new ones happened at all four sites, the dramatic destruction of the 40 m structure at Navan (Waterman 1997) is unique. Similarly, the industrial activity at Tara (Roche 2002) does not appear elsewhere, though there is evidence of low-level manufacture in a variety of materials at Dún Ailinne (Chapter 18). This would suggest the likelihood that the rituals associated with the royal sites were also variable, though they may well have contained some core rites shared by all.

Taken together, this comparison suggests that, at minimum, a royal site was a large hilltop enclosure with an exterior bank and an interior ditch. Within this there would have been a timber structure, which presumably formed the central focus of the site. The importance of the timber structures may be measured by the recent suggestion that the etymology of the name "Dún Ailinne" lies in an Insular Celtic common noun **alesjā* meaning "fence, palisade, or pen" (Schrijver, In press). Choosing the more poetic of the three meanings, this would make the translation of the place name "hill of the palisades," indicating not only that this was the most striking feature on the hill but also that its presence was retained for a very long time in popular memory.

Further elaborations on this basic pattern must be assumed to be on the level of local preference. Whether the central structure was roofed or not, walled or not, large or small, alone or in a group, may have been more in the way of a regional pattern, perhaps reflecting local religious beliefs, local histories, stylistic fashion, political whims, or some combination of all of these.

Other Royal Sites?

While the four sites just discussed form the generally accepted royal sites, others have been suggested (see Wailes 1982; Newman 1998) based on the documentary association between the known royal sites and the provinces in which they were located. Three are worth noting here. Cashel, Co. Tipperary, has been suggested as the royal site for ancient Munster, which otherwise lacks one (Newman 1998). However, this evidence is debatable on a variety of points (Byrne 2001:177-78; Wailes 1982:6-7). Another candidate is Uisneach, Co. Westmeath, traditionally considered the geographic centre of Ireland (Macalister and Praeger 1928). Although it is not mentioned in texts with the other royal sites, it is sometimes considered one because (1) its function is uncertain and it could be a ritual site and (2) its date is unclear and it could be later Iron Age (Wailes 1982:18-19). To this might be added the fact that the internal arrangement of one of its structures is a figure-of-eight (see Macalister and Praeger 1928).

Raffin Fort, Co. Meath, may represent a different kind of royal site (Newman 1993a, 1993b, 1995, 1998). If the Iron Age provinces are themselves the top of a hierarchy, there may be smaller subdivisions also represented by proportionately smaller sites. Later documents indicate that Ireland was organized along a number of different hierarchies, including the various levels of kings, groups within the *tuatha*, etc. (Byrne 2001; Patterson 1994; MacNiocaill 1972; Ó Corráin 1972). Such a hierarchy may have had earlier roots, with similar subdivisions within the Iron Age provinces represented by proportionately smaller sites that were similar to their larger siblings. Raffin Fort may be such a site. Although the surviving texts are silent on its identity as a royal site, it has all the relevant archaeological characteristics of a royal site, though on a much smaller scale. This has been taken to indicate that it represented a proportionately smaller political entity (Newman 1995).

Other Parallels

Beyond the royal sites, Dún Ailinne may be compared with a host of other kinds of sites, depending on which aspects are emphasized. Gibson, for example, notes the royal sites as the extreme end of a distribution of timber structures, lying mostly in the Neolithic but stretching through the remainder of the prehistoric period (Gibson 1995, 1998a, 1998b, 2001). Based purely on morphology, all are circular timber structures, all have an arguably ritual function, and so all may, in some sense, be connected as a single phenomenon (though this may be a matter of convergence or copying rather than continuity). In a similar vein, the form of the enclosure suggests parallels to a variety of earlier monuments, including henges and other enclosures (Condit and Simpson 1998; Clare 1986, 1987; Stout 1991; Hicks 1975), identifying the ancestry of the royal site enclosure and perhaps something about its ideological underpinnings (see Chapter 18). This feature also ties the royal sites to the larger, contemporary Iron Age world, where it has been argued on the basis of both archaeology (Brunaux 1987; Wait 1985) and Classical references (Webster 1995) that an enclosure is a defining characteristic of European Iron Age ritual sites.

The combination of hilltop location and enclosure (and probably the documentary association with status and politics) has also prompted comparisons with hillforts. While they are typically cited in terms of differences (see Wailes 1976), recent work has suggested that hillforts may have a more ritual character (see Hill 1995, 1996; Haselgrove 1994). This is in opposition to the more traditional view (see Cunliffe 1991), which sees them as high status occupation sites.

The Irish royal sites may belong to the larger group of assembly places known from a variety of locations throughout Europe. In its broadest sense, Dún Ailinne is obviously a place of assembly, and the possibility that it was the site of an *óenach* was noted above (see Chapter 16). More typically, "assembly place" implies a political function, such as inauguration, the handing down of legal decisions, etc., functions which can often be verified in other places by textual references (see Pantos and Semple 2004; Driscoll 1998). At Dún Ailinne, such a political function remains a reasonable hypothesis (see Chapter 16, 18).

Obviously, Dún Ailinne shares with assembly sites the need to accommodate large numbers of people. In addition, assembly sites are also characterized by the incorporation of older sites into later monuments (see Driscoll 1998; Pantos and Semple 2004). While Dún Ailinne did not incorporate an earlier monument per se in its construction, the fact that some aspects (the internally ditched enclosure and the timber structures) echo earlier forms may suggest the same concept. While the sites known to be places of assembly are typically of later periods than the royal sites, there is a striking resonance between, for example, the reconstructed timber structures of the Rose and Mauve phases at Dún Ailinne (Chapter 2, 18) and something like Building E at Yeavering, in Northumbria (Hope-Taylor 1977). While this may be a simple case of similar solutions to similar problems, the parallel still remains.

Moving even further outwards, Dún Ailinne can also be considered in the context of the ritual sites of the larger British and European Iron Age. Here the comparison becomes less exact, though again Dún Ailinne clearly belongs in the same general class. The majority of Iron Age ritual enclosures outside Ireland are rectangular, but as Wait points out (1985:156-58, 177), it is likely that there were more circular enclosures during the Iron Age that have not been recognized due to the tendency to assume that temples of the period are rectangular while houses are round. At Frilford, in Oxfordshire, there is a ditched enclosure with a post-hole setting and also a timber circle, either or both of which may have had a ritual function, though this is uncertain (Harding 1987); and at Maiden Castle, Dorset, a circular enclosure was constructed of stone (Cunliffe 1991:511-12). One of the most commonly cited parallels is the Goloring in Germany (see Wailes 1976; B. Raftery, in Waterman 1997:221-23). Here, a central post raised on an artificially constructed earthen platform was surrounded by an enclosure composed of a bank and internal ditch (Röder 1948). No other structures inside the enclosure were reported, but the presence of a central post at the centre of the enclosure recalls the similar post within the 40 m structure at Navan (B. Raftery, in Waterman 1997:221-23).

British Iron Age religious structures also are comparatively small, suggesting that they were not intended for large group activities (Wait 1985:171-72). This is in contrast to Dún Ailinne, which seems specifically designed for such use. In addition, both British and European sites are also characterized by offerings of artifacts, sometimes in large quantities (Wait 1985; Brunaux 1987). While some of the artifacts from Dún Ailinne are arguably foundational offerings, for example, the sword (see Chapter 7), most of the artifacts are not easily interpreted in this way.

Timber arrangements associated with Iron Age temples are not common, but are known. There was a palisade of unknown shape around the temple at Harlow, Essex, and also a palisade around the Iron Age phase at Hayling Island, West Sussex; the latter was rectangular, but enclosed a circular structure (Cunliffe 1991:512-14). A circular post structure is also reported at Trisov, near Prague (Brunaux 1987:39). Such exceptions notwithstanding, it does seem that sites like Dún Ailinne are unusual when compared to ritual sites of the European Iron Age. Indeed, B. Raftery notes that the Goloring appears to be unique on the Continent, and the excavator looked to Britain and Ireland for parallels (in Waterman 1997:223).

Thus in summary it can be said that the best parallels for Dún Ailinne are those that are closest, and they become less exact as they move farther away. The other royal sites obviously provide the best matches. Beyond this, specific aspects of Dún Ailinne can be paralleled with other classes of site (enclosures, timber structures, hillforts, assembly places), while other Iron Age ritual sites in Britain and elsewhere provide general parallels but also specific differences. In the end, it is logical that both the details of the structures and, presumably, the beliefs that were enacted through ritual within them, would become less similar as they diverge in time and space. No doubt Dún Ailinne shared some general features of ritual and the buildings that housed it with many places and times. It is likely that only among the Irish royal sites, however, was there true similarity in both the ideologies and the spaces that were structured to contain them.

18

The Social and Cultural Context of Dún Ailinne

Susan A. Johnston

With all the evidence described, it is now possible to discuss what was happening at Dún Ailinne during the various periods in which it was occupied. During all of the phases of use at Dún Ailinne the dominant theme is one of ritual. There is some reason to suggest that some aspects during the Neolithic may have had a more secular character, but overall, the story of Dún Ailinne is the story of the ritual life of those who used the hill in the prehistoric period.

Neolithic

As can be seen from the discussions in Chapters 4–6, no clear picture emerges from an analysis of the Neolithic artifacts and features. The artifacts (chipped and ground stone and ceramics) are sufficiently generic in number, type, and relative proportion that they could belong to a secular or a ritual context. Exceptions are the Linkardstown pot and the associated bead, arguably part of a burial, and the cupmarked stone (if it was Neolithic), arguably indicative of ritual (Johnston 1989). But these cannot be taken to indicate a ritual nature for other Neolithic activity; the cupmarked stone lacks any context and so its original position and location are unknown, and since there is no evidence of any above-ground feature that would have indicated the presence of a burial, it cannot be assumed that other Neolithic visitors would have known it was there.

Similarly, the features attributable to the Neolithic are also of uncertain character. Only the largest of the features, Trench 281, is something more than a simple pit. It forms the better part of a ditched enclosure, but whether sacred, secular, or both is uncertain. Ritual enclosures are well documented from the Irish Neolithic, and while domestic enclosures are less numerous, they are also known (Sheridan 2001).

In an earlier publication (Johnston 1990) it was suggested that the nature of the Neolithic remains, if they were domestic, indicated a relatively impoverished settlement. This was based primarily on very intensive use of relatively poor quality flint and perhaps limited access to good quality ceramic technology. On further analysis, there may be other possibilities for interpretation. While the Neolithic remains still suggest limited access to good quality materials and technologies, economic impoverishment may not be the only possible explanation. Ritual concerns, such as being restricted to the use of certain materials or technologies or not being allowed to leave the site for a certain period of time, might also have constrained access to good quality materials. Alternatively, they may have been there for only short periods of time (for sacred or secular reasons), and were simply content to use whatever materials were close at hand and therefore expedient.

It is difficult to choose from many possible interpretations given the disturbed context and generalized character of most of the Neolithic artifacts. They do not even allow us to know whether they represent activity over a single period of relatively long duration or a series of visits, none lasting more than a very short time. All we can say is that people have been using the hill since at least the middle of the Neolithic, making the ultimate span of use during prehistory more than three millennia.

Bronze Age

Compared to the Neolithic, even less can be said about the Bronze Age at Dún Ailinne. The presence of a bowl food vessel probably means that there was a burial from this period (though a domestic context cannot be discounted; see Chapter 6), and so again indicates ritual use in the Bronze Age. The C^{14} date of 1623-1400 Cal-BC (SI-982, 3220 ± 55 BP) suggests it was in the middle part of the period, and the nature of the remains that it was a single episode of use. Some of the artifacts might also date to the Bronze Age (such as one the projectile points and one of the glass beads; see Chapter 5 and Chapter 9), and also some of the pits and stakeholes of unknown date. In the absence of clear evidence, all that can be said is that people were on the hill during the Bronze Age, burying one of their own and possibly engaging in other activities.

Iron Age

> I gather this is simply confirmation of your comments that that the site was beginning to look like the glass-ringed table following an exceptional party? (Robert Stuckenrath to Bernard Wailes, letter dated July 25, 1973).

Despite earlier use, it was the later Iron Age that saw the major focus of activity at Dún Ailinne. This period produced the vast majority of archaeological remains at the site and is the one remembered in later historical texts. In order to construct an interpretation of Dún Ailinne, both of these sources of evidence can be considered.

Textual Sources

The applicability of early medieval textual evidence to the Iron Age has been the subject of considerable discussion over the last several decades. Since Jackson (1964) declared optimistically that it could be used directly as a window on the period, all of the many drawbacks to this optimism have been spelled out with inexorable clarity (for example, McCone 1990; Aitchison 1987, 1994; Mallory 1981, 1993; Koch 1994; Ó hUiginn 1988; Mackey 1992; Ó Riain 1995). Chief among these is the amount of time that passed between the later Iron Age and the spread of literacy. Bradley (2003), citing ethnographic sources, has estimated that the accuracy of historical details would not survive via oral transmission beyond about 200 years, a time frame more than exceeded by the 300-400 years between the final abandonment of Dún Ailinne and any textual references to the royal sites. Thus the details that describe Dún Ailinne are unlikely to be usefully applied to the site's interpretation.

That said, their appearance in those texts indicates that the royal sites still had some resonance in memory, and so while the details are not useful the general sense of the sites is relevant. The textual references that refer to Dún Ailinne have been outlined previously (Grabowski 1990 and Chapter 16), but in the earliest ("Félire nÓengusso" and "Hail Brigit"; Greene and O'Connor 1967; CELT 2005) the royal sites are identified implicitly as significant political centers that have been superceded by religious ones. While three different words are used (*borg* for Tara and Dún Ailinne, *ráith* for Crúachain, and *dún* for Emain Macha), a three words refer to defensive sites, all imply residence, and two, *dún* and *ráith*, have an additional association with royalty (Mallory 1994; Royal Irish Academy 1983). While archaeological investigation shows that Dún Ailinne was not a residence, the general association of the site with power and elites remains. This is supported by the triumphant tone of the texts, since there would be little point in crowing about the downfall of insignificant sites (a point made in a slightly different context by Schneiders 1995).

Archaeology and Ritual

In contrast to the historical sources, the excavations at Dún Ailinne indicate that it was a ritual site. The use of the term "ritual" in archaeology is somewhat problematic; it has been used in a wide variety of ways (see Hodder 1982: 164; 1995:222-23), often as a gloss for "religion" (see discussion in Insoll 2004). In fact, ritual can be both secular and religious, sometimes simultaneously. This is reflected in the definition suggested by Santino in his study of the use of public symbols in Northern Ireland. In this work ritual is defined as "social dramatic enactments that the participants believe to have some transformational or confirmatory agency and to derive this power from an overarching parahuman authority such as a deity, the state, an institution such as a university, and so on" (2004:29). This definition seems appropriate for a site such as Dún Ailinne, where there are any number of possible contexts in which ritual behavior could have occurred.

At Dún Ailinne, there are a number of sources of archaeological evidence which support its identification as a ritual site during the Iron Age. These include the structures recovered through excavation and their likely character; elements from earlier periods that were incorporated into Dún Ailinne; the larger landscape in which the site is situated; and, paradoxically, the lack of evidence for a domestic focus.

The last can be dealt with first. While it is somewhat of an archaeological joke to suggest that anything that lacks a utilitarian function must be a ritual object, there is a kind of logic to it. Ritual, by its nature, is not everyday behavior, but is instead special, a context set apart (Turner 1969 is the classic discussion of this idea). While it is not always easy to distinguish the everyday from the unusual in archaeological contexts, this approach to identifying ritual has merit. Together with Santino's definition, an argument for Dún Ailinne as a ritual site can be made.

First, the structures that formed the focus for each of the main Iron Age phases (White, Rose, and Mauve) are too large to have been roofed, and so would not have provided adequate shelter in the Irish climate (in any period, past or present). The Mauve phase structure had, at its center, an open timber setting surrounding a smaller, enclosed structure with no apparent entrance. The final phase of use, the Flame phase, produced quantities of animal bone, indicative of periodic feasting on a scale exceeding any kind of domestic needs.

The site also produced no artifact evidence for occupation. A significant proportion of the artifacts were items of personal dress, of a kind suggesting special occasions and not everyday wear; where the artifacts are arguably utilitarian (apart from the traces of manufacturing debris), they can be considered personal possessions or part of the waste left behind from the construction of the site. Some of the artifacts, too, may indicate ritual behavior. The best evidence is the sword, found in one of the Mauve phase palisade trenches, which almost certainly should be seen as a kind of votive deposit.

In addition, a number of elements appear in the construction of Dún Ailinne that echo forms characteristic of earlier Irish ritual sites. The enclosure, with its internal ditch and external bank, follows the "hengiform" pattern (Condit and Simpson 1998; Clare 1986, 1987; Stout 1991; Hicks 1975), while the timber structures recall those from earlier periods found alone and with hengiform enclosures (Gibson 1995, 1998a, 1998b, 2001). Other parallels with explicitly religious sites (for example, temples; Wait 1985; Brunaux 1987) were noted in Chapter 17. It is possible that Dún Ailinne could retain these forms without retaining their ritual character, but together with the previous evidence it seems more likely that ritual continuity is indicated.

The landscape in which Dún Ailinne is set also contains numerous ritual sites, some visible from the hill itself. Clancy (Forthcoming) noted 179 of these, the vast majority of them burial mounds of various types. This suggests that the choice of this particular hill for the construction of Dún Ailinne may have been influenced by the nearness of these reminders of ancient ritual life. Thus the evidence seems to point away from an everyday use of the site and towards ritual as the primary cultural context of activity at Dún Ailinne.

What Kind of Ritual?

If Dún Ailinne is a ritual site, then this raises the question—what kind of ritual took place at the site? There is little direct evidence for this, apart from the Flame phase feasting. However, considering all of the available evidence, it is possible to offer informed speculation.

The first aspect to consider is the simple size of Dún Ailinne. Even among royal sites it is large (see Chapter 17). The timber structures are also large and would have been visually impressive. The constituent elements, including elaborated entrances, roadways, palisades, timber circles, and other kinds of elaborations would have required considerable labor input. Together, these suggest that those who commissioned Dún Ailinne had a large community of people on which they could draw, and that the construction was therefore construed as legitimate—those who commissioned it had the power, the right, the authority, or the persuasiveness to get the site built. Force may have been a factor but those who did the actual labor may have seen some benefit to the construction, presumably in the ritual context in which Dún Ailinne was used.

The size of Dún Ailinne also suggests the possibility of large groups, at least on some occasions, and the number of personal ornaments, though small, speaks to the presence of more than a few people. Size can mean many things—displays of power, symbolic intimidation, or religious or ideological dimensions that can only be guessed at (for example, the idea that deities require lots of room when they appear). But size can also be necessary to accommodate large numbers of people, so the size of the site may indicate that large numbers were involved. In addition, if the interpretation of the Rose and Mauve phase structures as a kind of viewing stand is accepted, then this too indicates that groups of people were involved in ceremonies at Dún Ailinne.

The specific cultural context of these rituals could be numerous, but three can be examined in more detail—religious rituals, political rituals, and economic rituals. While such categories may have been meaningless to those who built and used Dún Ailinne, it is easier for analytical purposes to consider them individually.

Religious Rituals

It is likely that one framework for ritual behavior at Dún Ailinne was religion. One possible indicator of this is the references to the royal sites in sources like "Hail Brigit" and "Félire nÓengusso." The Christian church had considerable political power in the 9th century (Bitel 1990), and yet the royal sites are mentioned in the context of the triumph of Christianity. Is this because it was in the religious arena that the sites were perceived as threatening? The placement of St. Patrick's church at Armagh near Navan Fort may have been deliberate (see Sharpe 1982; Lambkin 1987, Aitchison 1994), and the same could be true for St. Brigit's monastery at Kildare and Dún Ailinne. The texts do not describe the royal sites as religious, but the juxtaposition of the royal sites and Christianity may reflect the survival of some very general memory.

The nature of Iron Age religious belief is largely unknown, but presumably they revolved around the invocation of deities, the renewal of natural and/or social power, the celebration of calendrical cycles, the movement of people through life-cycle stages, and a host of other possibilities too numerous to list (see Chapter 16 for further discussion). One possible religious context for religious activity at Dún Ailinne is suggested by the astronomical correlations noted by Hicks (1975 and Chapter 16).

Another is suggested by Warner (2000), who argues that the internal ditch/external bank configuration of the royal sites' enclosures was designed to keep deities from leaving the interior space. It is usually argued that this is not a defensive configuration, since potential attackers could surmount the bank and rain down all sorts of mayhem on the defenders within, even across a large and deep ditch. Warner argues instead that the ditch was intended to keep something in, rather than to repel those outside. Given a religious context, those who needed to be kept in are likely to have been of a spiritual nature rather than a corporeal one. If those inside the enclosure were summoning deities, then it follows that they would presumably want those deities to remain for a time, while simultaneously wanting to protect the uninitiated from their potentially destructive power.

The idea that an internal ditch is not effective in terms of protection has been effectively questioned by Mallory (2000), who points out that this interpretation depends on how warfare is envisioned. From some tactical perspectives, an internal ditch could be quite effective. Indeed, the two are not mutually exclusive; perhaps an internal ditch, while not as effective in defense as an external one, was still reasonably effective, and thus provided a compromise between the need for defense and some religious need as considered by Warner.

Political Rituals

Based on documentary sources the royal sites have often been seen as a kind of political center, implicit in the label "royal." They are often included with assembly sites (see Warner 1988; Driscoll 1998; Wailes 1982), and have been interpreted as sites for inauguration (see Binchy 1970; Swift 1997; Lynn 2003:122-29). The later use of Tara in such a political context (Newman 1997; Bhreathnach 1995a, 1995b; Aitchison 1994) may support this kind of interpretation for the royal sites in general. However, terms like "royalty" and "inauguration" probably have too many modern associations to be used in the Iron Age, implying a kind of political organization not evidenced in the archaeological record.

For example, the fact that the four primary royal sites map fairly neatly onto four of the five *cóiceda*, defined in later periods as political territories, may be one reason why the royal sites were traditionally seen as political "capitals." However, whether these territories had any reality in the later Iron Age and, if they did, whether they necessarily represented political entities are both uncertain (Ó Cróinín 1995; Aitchison 1994; Mallory 1997). What archaeology can contribute is evidence that there were elites in this period; this is evidenced by the distribution of La Tène artifacts (B. Raftery 1984) and larger sites associated with elites which may be residential, such as Haughey's Fort (Mallory 1991, 1996). The size and location of Dún Ailinne and the other royal sites may also indicate that they were "central places," perhaps in the political sense (Wailes 1982).

Beyond this, the exact nature of political power in this period remains elusive. In later periods, kings in Ireland came from a group of men eligible to succeed on the basis of factors such as kinship and other personal relationships to the previous king (Patterson 1990; Ó Cróinín 1995; Jaski 2000). This would often have produced multiple potential rivals for the position on the death of the current ruler. A successor would then have to claim his position on the basis of kinship, alliances, and the force of his personality, thereby perhaps needing public ceremonies to create and consolidate that position (see Cherry 1978 for an analogous argument for Minoan Crete).

While this pertains to a later period, political succession in earlier periods is unlikely to have been more secure, and so the need for ritual to consolidate political power is likely to have been felt in the later Iron Age as well. This may have been accelerated by contacts between Ireland, Britain, and the Continent, the latter two increasingly impacted by Roman expansion. The earliest dates for the royal sites are too early to suggest an origin analogous to the "tribalization" described for cultures on the fringes of the Roman empire (see Wells 2001; Ferguson and Whitehead 1992; see also (Cunliffe 1997:154; 2001: 359). But with the "heyday" of the royal sites being contemporary with an increasing Roman presence on the Continent and in Britain, a similar process may have accelerated political centralization in Ireland. Being therefore relatively new and so potentially unstable, ritual at the royal sites designed to consolidate political status would be expected.

Economic Rituals

There is evidence in the form of materials, waste products, and tools suggesting that economic activities were carried out at Dún Ailinne. Table 18-1 shows the numbers and kind of objects which fall into this category, while Table 18-2 shows the phases represented.

The objects in Table 18-1 can be broken down into two major categories. The first comprises various kinds of materials which are left over from the production of other objects. This would include slag, bone waste fragments, and copper alloy casting jets. The glass toggles are arguably the result of glass working (see Chapter 9), as are the four frag-

Table 18-1. Artifacts Possibly Associated with Manufacturing.

OBJECT	MATERIAL	N
weaving tool?	bone	1
casting jet	copper alloy	2
waste fragment	bone	7
ingot?	copper alloy	2
needle	bone	1
needle	iron	8
slag	slag	52
spindle whorl	bone	1
spindle whorl	stone	1
toggle	glass	8
tracer	copper alloy	1
TOTAL		84

ments of glass waste. The copper alloy ingot may also be leftover raw material. In the second category are objects which are used to produce other goods. This includes the spindle whorls, the weaving tool, the needles, and the tracer (and possibly the various iron chisels and blades, but these cannot be tied directly to manufacture). While these latter may have been personal possessions, carried into the site inadvertently or as part of personal attire, the other evidence makes it is likely that they too resulted from manufacturing at Dún Ailinne.

Table 18-2 shows that, although this material is scattered through most phases, those with the largest numbers (apart from Uncertain and Unknown)

Table 18-2. Artifacts Possibly Associated with Manufacturing by Phase.

PHASE	N
Dun	1
Flame	18
Harry	1
Jade	3
Lower Emerald	1
Mauve	19
Rose	8
Uncertain	19
Unknown	11
Upper Emerald	2
White	1
TOTAL	84

are Mauve and Flame. This would suggest the primary contexts for manufacturing as (1) the last of the timber structures and (2) the final phase of site use associated with periodic feasting. The level of site disturbance also allows for the possibility that some of this material was dredged up from earlier phases.

Objects associated with manufacturing are not numerous, which may mean that this activity was also at a fairly low level. However, since most of the material came from the summit, the low numbers may instead reflect depositional factors. The actual location of manufacturing activity is currently unknown. On the one hand, while the image of craftspeople hawking their wares literally in the middle of serious, cosmically meaningful religious ritual may seem incongruous, it might not have been perceived that way in the early centuries AD. Alternatively, this material may have been left inadvertently in the summit area, an accidental byproduct of manufacturing occurring elsewhere on the site. This would mean that there are denser deposits of material elsewhere at Dún Ailinne that would indicate more definitively where manufacturing occurred.

Chronologically, manufacturing could have been associated with either the construction of the timber structures or the ceremonies carried out in them, or indeed both. If it was associated with the construction phases then it is likely to have been the somewhat opportunistic appearance of entrepreneurs trying to benefit from the unusual concentration of people on the hill. This may then have diminished once the primary focus shifted to ceremonial activities. However, if such economic venues were also appropriate to ceremonial occasions, then this raises a number of possibilities for interpretation.

One such possibility is something analogous to the *óenaige* which are known from later periods. These are discussed in Chapter 16, but could feature a range of activities, including markets, and at least one (Carman) might have been held near Dún Ailinne (MacNeill 1962:339-44; Byrne 2001:121-23; Smyth 1982:34-35; Aitchison 1994:61-66). If *óenaige* are descendants of similar, earlier versions then they could easily have been accommodated in a space like Dún Ailinne, even if the timber structures were present. If the space between the enclosure and the summit was mostly empty, it could easily have been filled with temporary stalls, shelters, lean-tos, etc. where economic activities could be carried out.

At least some of the stake-holes and post-holes at Dún Ailinne may represent this kind of activity, although their interpretation is difficult. Many could not be assigned to a chronological phase, and few of them formed obvious patterns. Since it was the focus of excavation, most were also found in the summit area, the very place where the actual manufacturing seems unlikely to have taken place. Nevertheless, stake-holes and post-holes were also noted in the recent excavations at Tara, where definitive evidence for metal working and some suggestion of glass working were recovered (Crew and Rehern, in Roche 2002:95-96). There, they were interpreted as possible workshop shelters.

Manufacturing activity at Dún Ailinne could fit comfortably within a political or a religious context, or indeed both. One could envision different uses for the site on different occasions, or different parts of the site being reserved for particular types of activity, or all of it happening at once in a glorious jumble of human interaction. Spaces need not be dedicated, but instead can be defined by the cultural needs of the moment. The size of Dún Ailinne, with permanent structures concentrated on the summit, surrounded by a space reserved for various uses, may have been specifically intended to retain that very flexibility, allowing for religious, political, and economic activity all to take place within the enclosure.

Relations of Power?

The re-use at Dún Ailinne of forms found in earlier periods (principally the hengiform bank and ditch and the timber structures) may also have significance for the site's interpretation. In earlier archaeological research, this type of re-use was taken as evidence of continuity in the associated ideology. More recently, with the tendency to interpret human interactions as redolent with unequal power relations, such re-use has been seen in terms of co-opting important architectural and other forms in an attempt to legitimate the needs of the current power structure. Since early work in this regard (see Wailes 1974; Bradley 1984, 1987), this has become the norm for interpreting this kind of re-use (see Driscoll 1998; Pantos and Semple 2004; Mallory 2000; Hingley 1999).

At Dún Ailinne, the inclusion of earlier forms may have been designed to invoke those who lived before, perhaps to imply ancestral approval of current reality or to demonstrate power over ancestors. This would have had particular ideological resonance in the context of political or religious ritual, where ancestors commonly loom large. However, the notion that this was somehow manipulative, the creation of a kind of false reality, is still an assumption. It is equally likely that those currently in charge genuinely believed themselves to be the latest in a long line of ancestral power brokers. In this sense, the use of earlier forms may also be seen as a kind of continuity, albeit not an objectively "real" kind.

In the same vein, the structure of Dún Ailinne may also be interpreted as either inclusive or exclusive, depending on how the relations of power at the site were envisioned (this analysis follows some of the ideas applied to Stonehenge by Bradley 1998a; another possible scenario is offered in Chapter 2). Beginning at the outer edge of the site, the enclosure bank and ditch differentiate "inside" from "outside," which may have been about controlling access to the interior. The single entrance into the enclosure may have achieved the same end. People might have been allowed to stand on the bank and look inside the enclosure (though their view of the center would have been blocked by the timber palisades in some phases), but as long as the entrance was monitored, actual entry could be limited.

Once inside, there are several ways in which people could be further segregated. The palisades (as opposed to free-standing timbers) would block the view of the interior, and, since there were multiple palisades, perhaps facilitate multiple levels of access. In the Rose phase the figure-of-eight structure adds an additional spatial division, with each of the two conjoined enclosures encircled by palisades. The Mauve phase has what is perhaps the most exclusive space: a triple palisade surrounding a free-standing timber circle, within which is an enclosure with no entrance, providing for the ultimate in limited access and, perhaps, reflecting the final stage in a progressive "internalizing" of focus at the site (see Chapter 2).

Space may also have been regulated via less imposing structures, perhaps indicated by the large number of stake-holes and post-holes (see Chapter 4). A total of 2042 stake-holes and post-holes were recorded, 147 from the Mauve phase and 471 from Harry (a phase interpreted as contemporary with Mauve). Together these represent about 30% of the total. An additional 101 are from the Rose phase, 343 came from the Jade phase (likely to be broadly contemporary with Rose), and 37 came from Niamh (which may represent activity correlated with an earlier period within Rose). CD Figure 18-1 shows the distribution of these stake-holes and post-holes in two groups, Mauve and Harry on one map and Rose, Jade, and Niamh on the other.

As the first map shows, the Rose phase stake-holes and post-holes not found in the actual palisade trenches form two clusters. One is in the northern circle of the figure-of-eight structure, close to the gap between the two circles; the other is in the southern circle, again close to the gap but hugging the northwest interior side of the inner palisade. The stakes and posts from Jade and Niamh were clustered in the approximate center of the northern circle. In the Mauve phase, the stakes and posts not associated with the palisade trenches are in two small clusters, one roughly between Feature 42 and the palisade opposite the entrance and the other just outside the palisade on the southeast side. Those from Harry, by contrast, cluster clearly in the entrance area inside the innermost palisade.

It is unclear what exactly these various cluster mean, since the functions of the stakes and posts cannot be determined—they could have been parts of structures, or instrumental in the construction of the palisades, or something else. Interestingly, there is a significant difference in the average depth of the stake-holes and post-holes from the various phases. Table 18-3 shows the summary statistics for the depths of the stake-holes and post-holes from Harry, Jade, and Niamh (only those features where the depth was recorded are included). For both stake-holes and

Table 18-3. Stake-hole and Post-hole Depths.

STAKE-HOLES

PHASE	MEAN (cm)	ST. DEV.	MEDIAN	MODE	RANGE	N
Harry	24.9	8.5	25.0	32.0	5–48	294
Jade	18.2	7.0	17.5	12.0	3–43	303
Niamh	10.4	4.9	11.0	6.0	3–24	27

POST-HOLES

PHASE	MEAN (cm)	ST. DEV.	MEDIAN	MODE	RANGE	N
Harry	33.0	10.9	30.0	46.0	12–60	64
Jade	28.2	10.4	27.0	33.0	14–62.5	34
Niamh	21.8	16.6	19.5	6.0	6–50	6

Table 18-4. *Average Depth of Stake-holes and Post-holes by Phase, with Statistical Comparison.*

STAKE-HOLES

PHASE	N	MEAN	VARIANCE
Harry	294	24.9	73.0
Jade	303	18.2	49.5
Niamh	27	10.4	24.0

Source of Variation	df	F	P-value
Between Groups	2	82.3511	>0.001
Within Groups	621		
TOTAL	623		

POST-HOLES

PHASE	N	MEAN	VARIANCE
Harry	294	33.0	118.0
Jade	303	28.2	109.0
Niamh	27	21.8	274.6

Source of Variation	df	F	P-value
Between Groups	2	4.20089	0.01768
Within Groups	101		
TOTAL	103		

post-holes, the average depth increases with time. An analysis of variance (Table 18-4) shows that, for each, the difference is significant to a degree greater than 0.05 (and the difference between the stake-hole mean depths is highly significant, to a degree far greater than 0.01).

Since this is the average depth, not all stake-holes and post-holes got deeper with time. But given that the ranges and standard deviations of the two groups are very similar, it suggests that the pattern is real. So why did this happen? One possibility, particularly for the post-holes, is that the corresponding stakes and posts were getting longer, requiring them to be sunk more deeply into the ground. With stakes this is more complicated because it cannot be assumed that part of the stake always remained above ground. That said, there are various possible explanations for why the stakes and posts might be getting longer with time—different kinds of structures were being built, the stakes and posts were being used in different kinds of ways, or the builders were using different sources of wood.

In studying structures composed of free-standing posts, Gibson (1988a:106-7) calculates post height using the depth of the surviving post-hole. He suggests a ratio of 1:3–1:4 would provide an optimum range for the amount of post that must be below ground to provide stability for the post above ground. Thus a 1 m post-hole would provide a sufficient anchor for a post standing between 2–3 m above ground.

Using this idea, the numbers in Table 18-5 suggest a range for the average height of the corresponding posts at Dún Ailinne (stake height cannot be measured this way because it cannot be assumed that part of the stake remained above ground). The formula suggests that the posts on average were quite short, in all cases a meter or less in height. This in turn indicates that whatever the posts were being used for, it was not for large, robust structures, but for something smaller, perhaps analogous to tent stakes or poles, or lean-tos, or screens, or covers over something low to the ground, or indeed something that we can no longer envision. Or perhaps they were not parts of structures at all but markers of some kind, with each stake or post carrying a flag or pennant or some other marker (such as a carving or color) of group identity.

If they do represent structures then they were small ones, perhaps meaning they were for short term use. But since they got progressively larger over time, they may have changed function, or may have become more stable, and perhaps more permanent. This might indicate that the associated activities were in turn more standard, had a more permanent context, or were larger in scale. Or there may have been a competitive element, with size increases being the basis for claims of increased status and/or role.

On the other hand, the stakes and posts may have had something to do with the construction of the timber palisades. If so, then the increasing depth may have had something to do with technological needs associated with the changes in the palisades and other structures from Rose to Mauve. Alternatively, they may indicate short-term structures associated

Table 18-5. *Possible Post Heights (cm) as a Function of Post-hole Depth by Phase.*

PHASE	MEAN DEPTH	MEAN HEIGHT (1:3)	MEAN HEIGHT (1:4)
Harry	33.0	66.0	99.0
Jade	28.2	56.4	84.6
Niamh	21.8	43.6	65.4

with economic activity. One scenario is that they developed while the structures were being built, before any formal or official ceremonial context had been established. Another is that the space could have been defined differently at different times. In that case, while the area would have been reserved for ceremonial activity in some periods, at others it was permissible to set up craft fairs or other market-like venues. This would be analogous to church sanctuaries being used for services most of the time, but occasionally being co-opted for bake sales or craft fairs.

Many of the stake-holes and post-holes retained some humic material, indicating that those stakes or posts had rotted in place (see Chapter 2). For the stakes this might not be a problem since they might have been flush with the ground, but posts left standing in the central area might have been rather a nuisance given their central location. Thus another interpretation is that some of them may have been used to manage access to space, perhaps the remains of screens, aisles, or other spatial divisions that managed how people moved within the summit area. The most elaborate parallel for this is the 40 m structure at Navan (Waterman 1997), which arguably provided the framework for various kind of movement within the enclosure there (Lynn 2003).

There is no evidence for anything as formal or elaborate as this at Dún Ailinne, but there still may have been ways in which movement through the summit area could have been manipulated. Many stakes and posts in the Mauve phase were clustered near the entrance to the palisade, where, if they supported screens etc., they would have effectively blocked the view to the interior. If the space was sometimes used in different ways, then the need to put up or take down such features might explain why they were not made permanent (and perhaps account for the large number of them). For the Rose phase, while they are not in the entrance, some stakes do cluster roughly in the center of the northernmost palisade enclosure, while others seem associated with the gap between the northern and southern sections of the figure-of-eight structure. Since there was no evidence of other features inside this circle, perhaps the stakes and posts supported something that screened activity in various parts of the palisaded enclosures. A similar argument might be made for feature 2302 (see Chapter 2), a cluster of post-holes that may be assigned to the White phase. This might be the first version of a central marked or limited area of some kind, indicated by the stake-holes and post-holes in the succeeding Rose phase and made more permanent in the Mauve phase in Feature 42.

Incorporating the feasting aspect of the Flame phase into this interpretation is more difficult. Features from this phase were not recovered, and so the way in which activities in this phase were carried out is more elusive. Perhaps it was done in open air settings, or perhaps some of the features whose phases are unknown belong to this phase. At least one level of potential spatial restriction would have been provided by the enclosure, but beyond that there is simply no evidence. Having taken place after the timber structures were dismantled, however, it does suggest some kind of major shift in the way Dún Ailinne was used, and perhaps therefore in the way that its cultural context was envisioned.

Whether this is manipulation by those in power or a way of satisfying more democratic ceremonial or ritual needs is unknown. These spatial divisions might be the result of those in power providing the illusion of access while in fact maintaining tight control over those areas that mattered. Alternatively, those areas most closely controlled might ultimately have been accessible to large numbers of people, depending on such factors such as age, gender, or initiatory status. This is another kind of power but perhaps one which is slightly more democratic, as formerly forbidden places and knowledge become available as individuals move through their own lives.

Either way, the internal complexity that characterized Dún Ailinne had an enormous potential for ritual and ceremonial use. In this sense, it was *the* premier site in Leinster, the central place for this region in later Iron Age Ireland. So while the later textual sources may have been wrong in details, they were right in their characterization of the royal sites as centers of power. There was reason to be concerned about the influence that sites like Dún Ailinne had; after all, they had played their part for centuries, if not millennia, and as such could not have been easily overthrown.

Directions for Future Research

The various interpretations offered here suggest a number of future research possibilities. An important first step is to characterize the site outside the summit area. A 13 hectare site is large indeed, and it is important to know if this area was largely empty or if it was filled with structures. This kind of research can be done, first, through geophysical survey, followed by excavation in which particular areas of interest could then be targeted.

Other parts of the summit area should also be explored including the areas suggested here.

- The angled approaches of the Rose entrance. These were excavated to the eastern limit of the area as permitted by the landowner, but presumably continue down the hill away from the summit. How far do they continue and do they change character over their length?
- The inner roadway, from the point where it peters out as a feature visible on the surface up to the excavated Rose antennae trenches. Similar to the Rose phase entrance, the mid-line of the inner roadway, when extended uphill, runs right through the middle of the Rose entrance structures. Does it continue, what is its character, and is it related to the various ways movement and/or access may have been controlled?
- The outer roadway, downhill from the entrance through the bank and ditch on the eastern perimeter of the site. There is a fairly short, slightly sinuous, stretch of outer roadway that is visible as a surface feature, but it is unclear where it might go from there, and for how long. How does this impact ideas about the site? Is the site actually larger than the area within the enclosure itself, including perhaps a long approach area? Does this imply some kind of ceremonial procession, and if so, how did it fit with the ceremonies conducted inside the enclosure?

In addition to these larger questions about the site, there are several kinds of materials analysis that could be carried out on the artifacts from Dún Ailinne. The analysis of glass has proved fruitful in gaining important information (Henderson (1987a, 1987b, 1988, 1989; Warner and Meighan 1981) and the glass from Dún Ailinne is reasonably well preserved and relatively plentiful. Its analysis would provide data significant for understanding the production and use of glass in later Iron Age Ireland. Similarly, recent analyses of pottery fabric (see Boreland 1996) can help in identifying the uses to which the pottery was put. Similar analysis of the ceramics at Dún Ailinne might help clarify the character of the Neolithic occupation.

Finally, there is the relatively unexplored area of the larger landscape of Dún Ailinne. As noted by Hicks (Chapter 16), there are many areas to explore in terms of the patterning in the landscape, the inter-relationship between sites, and other kinds of connections between them and the larger environment. Clancy (Forthcoming) has begun to identify this landscape, and further research in this area will contribute significantly to the understanding of how Dún Ailinne was situated with regard to the larger community on which it drew.

References Cited

Addyman, Peter V. 1965. Coney Island, Lough Neagh: Prehistoric Settlement, Anglo-Norman Castle and Elizabethan Fortress. *Ulster Journal of Archaeology* 28:78-101.

Adkins, Lesley, and Roy Adkins 1985. Neolithic Axes from Roman Sites in Britain. *Oxford Journal of Archaeology* 4(1):69-75.

Aitchison, Nicholas B. 1987. The Ulster Cycle: Heroic Image and Historical Reality. *Journal of Medieval History* 13:87-116.

——— 1994. *Armagh and the Royal Centres in Early Medieval Ireland*. Rochester, NY: Boydell and Brewer.

——— 1998. Late Bronze Age Ritual at Haughey's Fort: The Evidence of the Deposited Cup-and-Ring Marked Stone. *Emania* 17:31-39.

Alcock, Leslie 1972. *Was This Camelot? Excavations at Cadbury Castle 1966-1970*. New York: Stein and Day.

Ambos, Elizabeth L., and Daniel O. Larson 2002. Verification of Virtual Excavation Using Multiple Geophysical Methods. *SAA Archaeological Record* (January):32-38.

Ambos, E. L., D. O. Larson, K. Kvamme, M. Conway, and S. Cibbarelli 1996. Remote Sensing Surveys of Navan Fort. *Emania* 15:15-32.

Anger, S. 1890. Das Gräberfeld zu Rondsen im Kreise Graudenz. *Abhandlungen zur Landeskundes der Provinz Westpreussen* 1:1-70.

ApSimon, A. M. 1969a. An Early Neolithic House in Co. Tyrone. *Journal of the Royal Society of Antiquaries of Ireland* 99:165-68.

——— 1969b. The Earlier Bronze Age in the North of Ireland. *Ulster Journal of Archaeology* 32:28-72.

Armstrong, E. C. R. 1911. A Bronze Bracelet of Hallstatt Type, Said to Have Been Found Near the Town of Antrim. *Journal of the Royal Society of Antiquaries of Ireland* 41:58-60.

——— 1920. *Guide to the Collection of Irish Antiquities. Catalogue of Irish Gold Ornaments in the Collection of the Royal Irish Academy*. Dublin: Stationery Office.

——— 1924. The Early Iron Age, or Hallstatt Period in Ireland. *Journal of the Royal Society of Antiquaries of Ireland* 54:1-14, 109-27.

Bailey, A. R. 1966. *The Role of Microstructure in Metals*. Surrey, England: Metallurgical Services.

Baillie, M. G. L. 1988. The Dating of the Timbers from Navan Fort and the Dorsey, Co. Armagh. *Emania* 4:37-40.

Baring, C. 1907. Contributions to the Natural History of Lambay, County Dublin: Historical Notes. *Irish Naturalist* 16:17-19.

Barton, Kevin, and Joe Fenwick 2005. Geophysical Investigations at the Ancient Royal Site of Rathcroghan, County Roscommon, Ireland. *Archaeological Prospection* 12:3-18.

Beck, H. C., and J. F. S. Stone 1935. Faience Beads of the British Bronze Age. *Archaeologia* 85:203-52.

Bender, Barbara, Sue Hamilton, and Christopher Tilley 1997. Stone Worlds, Alternative Narratives, Nested Landscapes. *Proceedings of the Prehis-*

toric Society 63:147-78.

Bhreathnach, Edel 1995a. *The Topography of Tara: The Documentary Evidence.* Discovery Programme Reports 2. Dublin: Royal Irish Academy.

———— 1995b. *Tara: A Select Bibliography.* Discovery Programme Reports No. 3. Dublin: Royal Irish Academy.

Binchy, D. A. 1970. *Celtic and Anglo-Saxon Kingship.* Oxford: Clarendon Press.

Bitel, Lisa M. 1990. *Isle of the Saints: Monastic Settlement and Christian Community in Early Ireland.* Ithaca, NY: Cornell University Press.

———— 1996. *Land of Women.* Ithaca, NY: Cornell University Press.

Boessneck, J. A., H.-H Müller, and M. Teichert 1964. Osteologische Unterschneidungsmerkmale zwichen Schaf (Ovis aries L.) und Ziege (Capra hircus L.). *Kühn-Archiv* 78:1-129.

Boreland, Dorcas 1996. Late Bronze Age Pottery from Haughey's Fort. *Emania* 14:21-28.

Boyle, J. 2004. Pins, Combs and Metapodia: The Organization of Bone and Antler Working in Ireland and Britain. Paper presented at the 69th Annual Meeting of the Society for American Archaeology, Montreal, Canada, March 31-April 4.

Bradley, John 1991. Excavations at Moynagh Lough, County Meath. *Journal of the Royal Society of Antiquaries of Ireland* 121:5-26.

Bradley, Richard 1970. The Excavation of a Beaker Settlement at Belle Tout, East Sussex, England. *Proceedings of the Prehistoric Society* 36:312-79.

———— 1984. *Consumption, Change and the Archaeological Record.* Edinburgh: University of Edinburgh Dept. of Archaeology.

———— 1987. Time Regained: The Creation of Continuity. *Journal of the British Archaeological Association* 140: 1-17.

———— 1990. *The Passage of Arms.* New York: Cambridge University Press.

———— 1991. Monuments and Places. In *Sacred and Profane*, ed. P. Garwood et al., pp. 135-40. Oxford: Oxford Committee for Archaeology.

———— 1997. *Rock Art and the Prehistory of Atlantic Europe: Signing the Land.* New York: Routledge.

———— 1998a. *The Significance of Monuments.* New York: Routledge.

———— 1998b. Stone Circles and Passage Graves—A Contested Relationship. In *Prehistoric Ritual and Religion*, ed. Alex Gibson and Derek Simpson, pp. 2-13. Phoenix Mill, England: Sutton.

———— 2003. The Translation of Time. In *Archaeologies of Memory*, ed. Ruth M. Van Dyke and Susan E. Alcock, pp. 221-27. Malden, MA: Blackwell.

Brailsford, J. W. 1962. *Hod Hill: Volume I. Antiquities from Hod Hill in the Durden Collection.* London: Trustees of the British Museum.

Brick, Robert M., Alan W. Pense, and Robert B. Gordon 1977. *Structure and Properties of Engineering Materials.* New York: McGraw Hill.

Brindley, A. L., and J. N. Lanting. 1989-90. Radiocarbon Dates for Neolithic Single Burials. *Journal of Irish Archaeology* 5:1-7.

Brodribb, A. C. C., A. R. Hands, and D. R. Walker 1971. *Excavations at Shakenoak Farm, Near Wilcote, Oxfordshire.* Part 3. Oxford: Omega Press.

Brunaux, Jean Louis 1987. *The Celtic Gauls: Gods, Rites and Sanctuaries.* London: Seaby.

Bulleid, Arthur, and Harold St. George Gray 1911. *The Glastonbury Lake Village,* Vol. 1. Taunton: Wessex Press.

———— 1917. *The Glastonbury Lake Village,* Vol. 2. Taunton: Wessex Press.

———— 1948. *The Meare Lake Village, Vol. I.* Taunton Castle: private printing.

Bushe-Fox, J. P. 1915. *Excavations at Hengistbury Head, Hampshire.* Reports of the Research Committee of the Society of Antiquaries of London, No. III. Oxford: Society of Antiquaries.

Byrne, Francis John 2001. *Irish Kings and High-Kings.* Dublin: Four Courts Press.

Callander, J. G. 1920-21. A Bronze Age Hoard from Glen Trool, Stewartry of Kircudbright. *Proceedings of the Society of Antiquaries of Scotland* 55:29-37.

Camden, W. 1789. *Descriptions of Ireland.* 3 vols. Vol. 3, *Britannia.* Trans. 1607 edition by R. Gough.

Campana, D. V., and P. J. Crabtree. 1987. ANIMALS-A C Language Computer Program for the Analysis of Faunal Remains and Its Use in the Study of Early Iron Age Fauna from Dún Ailinne. *Archaeozoologia* 1(1): 57-68.

———— 2003. Soldiers' Diet at Valley Forge: An Analysis of the Faunal Remains from the 2000 Excavation Season. *Bulletin Florida Museum Natural History* 44(1): 199-204.

Carew, Mairéad 2003. *Tara and the Ark of the Covenant: A Search for the Ark of the Covenant by British-Israelites on the Hill of Tara (1899-1902)*. Dublin: Wordwell.

Carey, John. 1995. Native Elements in Irish Pseudohistory. In *Cultural Identity and Cultural Integration: Ireland and Europe in the Early Middle Ages*, ed. Doris Edel, pp. 45-60. Dublin: Four Courts Press.

Carpenter, R. J., and K. Ryan. 1975. TL Dating of Burnt Soil. *MASCA Newsletter* 11(2).

Carson, R. A. G., and Claire O'Kelly 1977. A Catalogue of the Roman Coins from Newgrange, Co. Meath, and Notes on the Coins and Related Finds. *Proceedings of the Royal Irish Academy* 77C:35-56.

Case, Humphrey J. 1953. The Neolithic Site at Goodland, Co. Antrim. *Ulster Journal of Archaeology* 16:24.

——— 1973. A Ritual Site in North-East Ireland. In *Megalithic Graves and Ritual*, eds. G. Daniel and P. Kjaerum, pp. 173-96. Moesgard: Jutland Archaeological Society.

——— 1961. Irish Neolithic Pottery: Distribution and Sequence. *Proceedings of the Prehistoric Society* 27:174-233.

——— 1963. Foreign Connections in the Irish Neolithic. *Ulster Journal of Archaeology* 26:3-18.

CELT 2005. CELT: Corpus of Electronic Texts. http://www.ucc.ie/celt/index.html.

Challis, A. J., and D. W. Harding 1975. *Later Prehistory from the Trent to the Tyne*. Oxford: BAR.

Cherry, John F. 1978. *Generalization and the Archaeology of the State. Social Organization and Settlement*. Oxford: BAR.

Clancy, Padraig In press. The Curragh Barrow: A Preliminary Investigation of the Barrow Clusters on the Curragh, Co. Kildare. *Kildare History and Society*.

Clare, T. 1986. Towards a Reappraisal of Henge Monuments. *Proceedings of the Prehistoric Society* 52:281-316.

——— 1987. Towards a Reappraisal of Henge Monuments: Origins, Evolution and Hierarchies. *Proceedings of the Prehistoric Society* 53:457-77.

Clarke, D. V. 1971. Small Finds in the Atlantic Province: Problems of Approach. *Scottish Archaeological Forum* 3:22-54.

Coffey, G. 1897. Notes on the Prehistoric Cemetery of Loughcrew with Fasciculus of Photographic Illustrations of the Sepulchral Cairns. *Transactions of the Royal Irish Academy* 31:23-38.

Collins, A. E. P. 1952. Excavations in the Sandhills at Dundrum, Co. Down, 1950-51. *Ulster Journal of Archaeology* 15:2-26.

——— 1957a. Trial Excavations in a Round Cairn on Knockiveagh, Co. Down. *Ulster Journal of Archaeology* 20:8-28.

——— 1957b. A Destroyed Burial Chamber at 'Edenville,' Ballygraffan, Co. Down. *Ulster Journal of Archaeology* 20:35-36.

——— 1966a. Barnes Lower Court Cairn, Co. Tyrone. *Ulster Journal of Archaeology* 29:43-75.

——— 1966b. Excavations at Dressogagh Rath, Co. Armagh. *Ulster Journal of Archaeology* 29:117-29.

——— 1978. Excavations on Ballygalley Hill, County Antrim. *Ulster Journal of Archaeology* 41:15-32.

——— 1981. Flint Javelin Heads. In *Irish Antiquity*, ed. Donnchadh Ó Corráin, pp. 111-33. Dublin: Four Courts Press.

Collins, A. E. P., and W. A. Seaby 1960. Structures and Small Finds Discovered at Lough Eskragh, Co. Tyrone. *Ulster Journal of Archaeology* 23:25-37.

Collis, John R. 1968. Excavations at Owslebury, Hants: An Interim Report. *Antiquaries Journal* 48:18-31.

——— 1973. Burials with Weapons in Iron Age Britain. *Germania* 51:121-33.

——— 1984. *Oppida: Earliest Towns North of the Alps*. Sheffield: University of Sheffield.

——— 1996. Hill-forts, Enclosures and Boundaries. In *The Iron Age in Britain and Ireland: Recent Trends*, ed. T. C. Champion and J. R. Collis, pp. 87-94. Sheffield: J. R. Collis.

Condit, Tom, and Derek Simpson 1998. Irish Hengiform Enclosures and Related Monuments: A Review. In *Prehistoric Ritual and Religion*, ed. Alex Gibson and Derek Simpson, pp. 45-61. Phoenix Mill, England: Sutton.

Coombs, D., and J. Bradshaw 1979. A Carp's Tongue Hoard from Stourmouth, Kent. In *Bronze Age Hoards: Some Finds Old and New*, ed. C. Burgess and D. Coombs, pp. 181-96. Oxford: BAR.

Cooney, Gabriel 1998. Breaking Stones, Making

Places: The Social Landscape of Axe-Production Sites. In *Prehistoric Ritual and Religion*, ed. Alex Gibson and Derek Simpson, pp. 108–18. Phoenix Mill, England: Sutton.

Cooney, Gabriel, and Eoin Grogan 1991. An Archaeological Solution to the 'Irish' Problem? *Emania* 9: 33–43.

——— 1994. *Irish Prehistory: A Social Perspective*. Dublin: Wordwell.

Cooney, Gabriel, and Stephen Mandal 1998. *The Irish Stone Axe Project*. Bray: Wordwell.

Copley, M. S., R. Berstan, S. N. Dudd, G. Docherty, A. J. Mukherjee, V. Straker, S. Payne, and R. P. Evershed 2003. The Earliest Direct Evidence for Widespread Dairying in Prehistoric Britain. *Proceedings National Academy Sciences* 100(4): 1524–29.

Crabtree, Pam J. 1982a. Paleoethnobotany at Dún Ailinne, Co. Kildare, Ireland. *MASCA Journal* 2(1): 3–5.

——— 1982b. Worked Bone from Dún Ailinne, Co. Kildare, Ireland. *MASCA Journal* 2(1): 6–7.

——— 1985. The Mammalian Fauna from Dún Ailinne, Co. Kildare, Ireland. *MASCA Journal* 3(6): 179–81.

——— 1986. Dairying in Irish Prehistory. *Expedition* 28(2): 59–62.

——— 1989. *West Stow: Early Anglo-Saxon Animal Husbandry. East Anglian Archaeology, Report No. 47*. Ipswich: Suffolk County Planning Department.

——— 1990. Subsistence and Ritual: The Faunal Remains from Dún Ailinne, Co. Kildare, Ireland. *Emania* 7: 22–25.

——— 2003. Ritual Feasting in the Irish Iron Age: Re-examining the Fauna from Dun Ailinne in Light of Contemporary Archaeological Theory. In *Proceedings of the 9th ICAZ conference, Durham 2002. Vol. 1, Behavior Behind Bones: The Zooarchaeology of Ritual, Religion, Status and Identity*, ed. Sharyn Jones O'Day, Win Van Neer, and Anton Ervynck, pp. 62–65. Oxford: Oxbow.

Cunliffe, Barry 1991. *Iron Age Communities in Britain*. New York: Routledge.

——— 2001. *Facing the Ocean: The Atlantic and Its Peoples 8000 BC–AD 1500*. New York: Oxford University Press.

Curle, A. O. 1919–20. Report on the Excavation on Traprain Law in the Summer of 1919. *Proceedings of the Society of Antiquaries of Scotland* 54: 54–124.

Danaher, Kevin 1972. *The Year in Ireland*. Cork: Mercier Press.

Daniells, M. J., and B. B. Williams 1977. Excavations at Kiltierney Deerpark, County Fermanagh. *Ulster Journal of Archaeology* 40: 32–41.

Darvill, Timothy 1999. The Historic Environment, Historic Landscapes, and Space-Time-Action Models in Landscape Archaeology. In *The Archaeology and Anthropology of Landscape*, ed. Peter J. Ucko and Robert Layton, pp. 104–18. London: Routledge.

Davies, Oliver 1935–36. Excavations at Dun Ruadh. *Proceedings and Reports of the Belfast Natural History and Philosophical Society*, 2nd Series 1: 50–75.

——— 1939. Excavations at the Giant's Grave, Loughash. *Ulster Journal of Archaeology* 2: 254–68.

——— 1950. *Excavations at Island MacHugh*. Belfast: Supplement to Proceedings Belfast Natural History and Philosophical Society.

Day, R. 1899. Gold Plates and Discs Found near Cloyne, County Cork. *Journal of the Royal Society of Antiquaries of Ireland* 29: 413–16.

Déchelette, J. 1914. *Manuel D'archéologie: Prehistorique, Celtique et Gallo-Romaine. Volume 2, Part III*. Paris: Auguste Picard.

Dibble, Harold L. 1985. Technical Aspects of Flake Variation: A Comparison of Experimental and Prehistoric Flake Production. *American Archaeology* 5: 236–40.

Dibble, Harold L., and John C. Whittaker 1981. New Experimental Evidence on the Relation Between Percussion Flaking and Flake Variation. *Journal of Archaeological Science* 8: 283–96.

Dietler, M., and B. Hayden 2001. Digesting the Feast: Good to Eat, Good to Drink, Good to Think. In *Feasts: Archaeological and Ethnographic Perspectives on Food, Politics, and Power*, ed. M. Dietler and B. Hayden, pp. 1–20. Washington, DC: Smithsonian Institution Press.

——— 1962. *Lebor na Cert: The Book of Rights*. Dublin: Irish Texts Society.

Driesch, A. von den 1976. *A Guide to the Measurement of Animal Bones from Archaeological Sites*. Cambridge, MA: Peabody Museum of Harvard University.

Driesch, A. von den, and J. Boessneck 1974. Kritische

Anmerkungen zur Widerristhöhenberechnung aus Längenmassen vor- und frühgeschichtlicher Tierknocken. *Säugetierkundliche Mitteilungen* 22: 325–48.

Driscoll, Stephen T. 1998. Picts and Prehistory: Cultural Resource Management in Early Medieval Scotland. *World Archaeology* 30:142–58.

Edwards, Nancy 1996. *The Archaeology of Early Medieval Ireland*. London: Routledge.

Ehrenreich, Robert 1985. *Trade, Technology, and the Ironworking Community in the Iron Age of Southern Britain*. Oxford: BAR.

Ehrenreich, Robert M., Elizabeth Hamilton, and Samuel K. Nash 2005. Far from Barbaric: Reassessing the Sophistication of Merovingian Metalworking. *Journal Minerals, Metals & Materials Society* 57(8): 51–55.

Eichhorn, G. 1927. Der Urnenfriedhof auf der Schanze bei Groß-Romstedt. *Mannus-Bibliothek* 41.

Eogan, George 1963. A Neolithic Habitation Site and Megalithic Tomb in Townleyhall Townland, Co. Louth. *Journal of the Royal Society of Antiquaries of Ireland* 93:37–81.

——— 1964. The Later Bronze Age in Ireland in Light of Recent Research. *Proceedings of the Prehistoric Society* 14:268–351.

——— 1974. Report on the Excavation of Some Passage Graves, Unprotected Inhumation Burials and a Settlement Site at Knowth, Co. Meath. *Proceedings of the Royal Irish Academy* 74C:11–112.

——— 1981. The Gold Vessels of the Bronze Age in Ireland and Beyond. *Proceedings of the Royal Irish Academy* 81C:345–82.

——— 1986. *Knowth and the Passage-Tombs of Ireland*. New York: Thames & Hudson.

Eogan, George, and Helen Roche 1994. A Grooved Ware Wooden Structure at Knowth, Boyne Valley, Ireland. *Antiquity* 68:322–30.

Evans, E. E. 1939. Excavations at Carnanbane, County Londonderry: A Double Horned Cairn. *Proceedings of the Royal Irish Academy* 45C:1–12.

——— 1953. *Lyles Hill. A Late Neolithic Site in County Antrim*. Belfast: Stationery Office.

——— 1966. *Prehistoric and Early Christian Ireland*. London: Batsford.

Evans, J. 1881. *The Ancient Bronze Implements, Weapons, and Ornaments of Great Britain and Ireland*. London: Longmans, Green.

Fenwick, Joe, Yvonne Brennan, and Finn Delaney 1997. The Anatomy of a Mound: Geophysical Images of Rathcroghan. *Archaeology Ireland* 10(3): 20–23.

Fenwick, Joe, and Conor Newman 2002. *Geomagnetic Survey on the Hill of Tara, Co. Meath, 1998–9*. Discovery Programme Reports No. 6. Dublin: Royal Irish Academy.

Fenwick, Joe, Yvonne Brennan, Kevin Barton, and John Waddell 1999. The Magnetic Presence of Queen Medb. *Archaeology Ireland* 13(1):8–11.

Ferguson, R. B., and N. L. Whitehead, ed. 1992. *War in the Tribal Zone: Expanding States and Indigenous Warfare*. Santa Fe, NM: SAR.

Flanagan, Laurence N. W. 1965. Flint Hollow Scrapers and the Irish Neolithic. *Atti del VI Congresso Internazionale delle Scienze Preistoriche e Protostoriche*, ed. Massimo Pallottino, Luigi Cardini, and Delia Brusadin. Florence: Sansoni.

——— 1966. The Petit-Tranchet Derivative Arrowhead and the Irish Neolithic. *Actes du VII Congrès International des Sciences Préhistoriques et Protohistoriques I,* ed. Jan Filip. Prague: Academia.

——— 1966. An Unpublished Flint Hoard from the Braid Valley, Co. Antrim. *Ulster Journal of Archaeology* 29:82–90.

Flannery, Kent V., and Joyce Marcus 1993. Cognitive Archaeology. *Cambridge Archaeological Journal* 3:260–70.

Frazer, William 1879. Description of a Sepulchral Mound at Donnybrook, Containing Human and Other Remains Referable to the Tenth or Eleventh Centuries. *Proceedings of the Royal Irish Academy* Ser. 2, 2, 88:29–55.

——— 1899. On "Patrick's Crosses"—Stone, Bronze, and Gold. *Journal of the Royal Society of Antiquaries of Ireland* 29:35–43.

Freeman, Philip 2001. *Ireland and the Classical World*. Austin, TX: University of Texas Press.

Gautier, A. 1984. How Do I Count You, Let Me Count the Ways? Problems of Archaeozoological Quantification. In *Animals and Archaeology: 4. Husbandry in Europe*, ed. C. Grigson and J. Clutton-Brock, pp. 237–51. Oxford: BAR.

Gibson, Alex 1995. The Dating of Timber Circles: New Thoughts in the Light of Recent Irish and

British Discoveries. In *Ireland in the Bronze Age*, ed. J. Waddell and E. Shee Twohig, pp. 87-89. Dublin: Stationery Office.

——— 1998a. *Stonehenge and Timber Circles*. Charleston, SC: Tempus.

——— 1998b. Hindwell and the Neolithic Palisaded Sites of Britain and Ireland. In *Prehistoric Ritual and Religion*, ed. Alex Gibson and Derek Simpson, pp. 68-79. Phoenix Mill, England: Sutton.

Gibson, Alex, Helmut Becker, Eoin Grogan, Nigel Jones, and Barry Masterson 2001. Survey at Hindwell Enclosure, Walton, Powys, Wales. In *Neolithic Enclosures in Atlantic Northwest Europe*, ed. Timothy Darvill and Julian Thomas, pp. 101-10. Oxford: Oxbow.

Gillam, J. P. 1958. Roman and Native, A.D. 122-197. In *Roman and Native in Northern Britain*, ed. I. A. Richmond, pp. 79-85. Edinburgh: Nelson.

Goodway, Martha, and Robert M. Fisher 1988. Phosphorus in Low-Carbon Iron: Its Beneficial Properties. *Journal of the Historical Metallurgy Society* 22(1): 21-24.

Grabowski, Kathryn 1990. The Historical Overview of Dún Ailinne. *Emania* 7:32-36.

Grant, A. 1975. Appendix B: The Use of Tooth Wear as a Guide to Ageing the Domestic Animals—A Brief Explanation. In *Excavations at Portchester Castle. Volume 1: Roman*, ed. B. Cunliffe, pp. 437-50. London: Society of Antiquaries of London, Research Report No. 32.

——— 1982. The Use of Tooth Wear as a Guide to the Age of Domestic Ungulates. In *Ageing and Sexing Animal Bones from Archaeological Sites*, ed. B. Wilson, C. Grigson, and S. Payne, pp. 91-108. Oxford: BAR.

Graue, J. 1974. Die Gräberfeld von Ornavasso. *Hamburger Beiträge zur Archäologie*, Beiheft 1.

Grayson, Donald K. 1984. *Quantitative Zooarchaeology: Topics in the Analysis of Archaeological Faunas*. Orlando, FL: Academic.

Green, H. Stephen 1980. *The Flint Arrowheads of the British Isles I*. Oxford: BAR.

Greene, David, and Frank O'Connor 1967. *A Golden Treasury of Irish Poetry A.D. 600-1200*. Dingle, Co. Kerry: Brandon.

Greenwell, W. 1877. *British Barrows*. Oxford: Clarendon Press.

Guido, Margaret 1978. *The Glass Beads of the Prehistoric and Roman Periods in Britain and Ireland*. London: Society Antiquaries.

Guido, Margaret, J. Henderson, M. Cable, J. Bayley, and Leo Biek 1984. A Bronze Age Glass Bead from Wilsford, Wiltshire: Barrow G.42 in the Lake Group. *Proceedings of the Prehistoric Society* 50:245-54.

Gwynn, Edward 1903-35. *The Metrical Dindshenchas [in Five Parts]*. Royal Irish Academy Todd Lecture Series 8-12. Dublin: Hodges Figgis.

Haley, Gene 2003. The Way They Went: The Táin Itinerary List, Its Provenance, Structure, and Topography. Paper presented at 12th International Congress of Celtic Studies, Aberystwyth, 28 August.

Halstead, P., and P. Collins 2002. Sorting the Sheep from the Goats: Morphological Distinctions between the Mandibles and Mandibular Teeth of Adult Ovis and Capra. *Journal of Archaeological Science* 29: 545-53.

Hamilton, Elizabeth 1996. *Technology and Social Change in Belgic Gaul: Copper Working and the Titelberg, Luxembourg, 125 B.C.-A.D. 300*. MASCA Monograph Series. Philadelphia, PA: University of Pennsylvania Museum of Archaeology and Anthropology.

Harbison, Peter 1967. Some Minor Metal Products of the Early Bronze Age in Ireland. *Journal of the Cork Historical and Archaeological Society* 72:93-100.

——— 1969. The Relative Chronology of Irish Early Bronze Age Pottery. *Journal of the Royal Society of Antiquaries of Ireland* 99:63-82.

——— 1973. The Earlier Bronze Age in Ireland. *Journal of the Royal Society of Antiquaries of Ireland* 103:93-152.

——— 1988. *Pre-Christian Ireland*. New York: Thames & Hudson.

Harding, A., and R. Young 1979. Reconstruction of the Hafting Methods and Function of Stone Implements. In *Stone Axe Studies*, ed. T. H. McK. Clough and W. A. Cummins, pp. 102-5. Research Reports No. 23. London: Council for British Archaeology.

Harding, D. W. 1987. *Excavations in Oxfordshire, 1964-66*. Occasional Paper 15. Edinburgh: University of Edinburgh Dept. of Archaeology.

Hartmann, A. 1970. *Prähistorische Goldfunde aus Europa*. Berlin: Mann.

Hartnett, P. J. 1951. A Neolithic Burial from Martinstown, Kiltale, Co. Meath. *Journal of the Royal Society of Antiquaries of Ireland* 81:19-23.

Hartnett, P. J., and G. Eogan 1964. Feltrim Hill, Co. Dublin: A Neolithic and Early Christian Site. *Journal of the Royal Society of Antiquaries of Ireland* 94:1-37.

Hartwell, Barrie 1987. An Air Photographic Survey of the Navan Area. *Emania* 2:5-11.

——— 1991. Recent Air Survey Results from Navan. *Emania* 8:5-9.

Haselgrove, Colin 1994. Social Organization in Iron Age Wessex. In *The Iron Age in Wessex*, ed. A. P. Fitzpatrick and Elaine L. Morris, pp. 1-3. Salisbury: Trust for Wessex Archaeology.

——— 1997. Iron Age Brooch Deposition and Chronology. In *Reconstructing Iron Age Societies*, ed. Adam Gwilt and Colin Haselgrove, pp. 51-72. Oxford: Oxbow.

——— 1981. The Wearing of the Brooch: Early Iron Age Dress among the Irish. In *Studies on Early Ireland*, ed. B. G. Scott, pp. 51-73. Dublin: Association Young Irish Archaeologists.

Hawkes, C. F. C., and M. R. Hull 1947. *Camulodunum: First Report on the Excavations at Colchester 1930-1939*. London: Research Committee Society of Antiquaries.

Hencken, Hugh 1942. Ballinderry Crannog No. 2. *Proceedings of the Royal Irish Academy* 47C:1-76.

——— 1951. Lagore Crannog: An Irish Royal Residence of the 7th to 10th Centuries A.D. *Proceedings of the Royal Irish Academy* 53C:1-247.

Henderson, Julian 1987a. Glass. In *Hengistbury Head, Dorset*, ed. Barry Cunliffe, pp. 160-63. Oxford: Oxford University Committee for Archaeology.

——— 1987b. The Iron Age of 'Loughey' and Meare: Some Inferences from Glass Analysis. *Antiquaries Journal* 67:29-42.

——— 1988. Glass Production and Bronze Age Europe. *Antiquity* 62:435-51.

——— 1989a. The Earliest Glass in Britain and Ireland. In *Le Verre Prèromain en Europe Occidentale*, ed. M. Feugère. Montagnac: M. Mergoil.

——— 1989b. The Evidence for Regional Production of Iron Age Glass in Britain. In *Le Verre Prèromain en Europe Occidentale*, ed. M. Feugère. Montagnac: M. Mergoil.

——— 1991. Industrial Specialization in Late Iron Age Britain and Europe. *Archaeological Journal* 148:104-48.

——— 1997. The Glass Objects from Navan Site B, Composition and Archaeological Implications. In *Excavations at Navan Fort 1961-71, D. M. Waterman*, ed. C. J. Lynn, pp. 95-100. Belfast: Stationery Office.

Henderson, Julian, and Richard Ivens 1992. Dunmisk and Glass-making in Early Christian Ireland. *Antiquity* 66:52-64.

Herity, M., and George Eogan 1977. *Ireland in Prehistory*. Boston: Routledge and Kegan Paul.

Herity, Michael 1974. *Irish Passage Graves*. Dublin: Irish University Press.

——— 1982. Irish Decorated Neolithic Pottery. *Proceedings of the Royal Irish Academy* 82C:247-404.

——— 1984. A Survey of the Royal Site of Cruchain in Connacht: Introduction, the Monuments and Topography. *Journal of the Royal Society of Antiquaries of Ireland* 113:121-42.

——— 1985. A Survey of the Royal Site of Cruchain in Connacht: Prehistoric Monuments. *Journal of the Royal Society of Antiquaries of Ireland* 114:125-38.

——— 1987. The Finds from Irish Court Tombs. *Proceedings of the Royal Irish Academy* 87C:103-281.

——— 1988. A Survey of the Royal Site of Cruchain in Connacht: Ringforts and Ecclesiastical Sites. *Journal of the Royal Society of Antiquaries of Ireland* 117:125-41.

——— 1989. A Survey of the Royal Site of Cruchain in Connacht: Ancient Field Systems at Rathcrogan and Carnfree. *Journal of the Royal Society of Antiquaries of Ireland* 118:67-84.

Hicks, Ronald 1975. *Some Henges and Hengiform Earthworks in Ireland*. Ann Arbor, MI: University Microfilms.

——— 1981. Irish Henge Orientations: Preliminary Results and Some Problems. In *Archaeoastronomy in the Americas*, ed. Ray A. Williamson, pp. 343-50. Los Altos, CA: Ballena.

——— 1984. Stones and Henges: Megalithic Astronomy Reviewed. In *Archaeoastronomy and the Roots of Science*, ed. E. C. Krupp, pp. 169-210. Boulder, CO: Westview.

——— 2004. Using Archaeological Reconnaissance Data to Identify Oenach Sites. Paper presented at the 39th International Congress of Medieval Studies, Kalamazoo, MI, May 6.

Hicks, Ronald, and Laura Ward Elder 2003. Festivals, Deaths, and the Sacred Landscape of Ancient Ireland. *Journal of Indo-European Studies* 31:307–35.

Hill, J. D. 1995. How Should We Understand Iron Age Societies and Hillforts? A Contextual Study from Southern Britain. In *Different Iron Ages: Studies on the Iron Age in Temperate Europe*, ed. J. D. Hill and C. G. Cumberpatch, pp. 45–66. Oxford: Tempus Reparatum/BAR.

——— 1996. Hill-Forts and the Iron Age of Wessex. In *The Iron Age in Britain and Ireland: Recent Trends*, ed. T. C. Champion and J. R. Collis, pp. 95–116. Sheffield: J. R. Collis.

Hingley, Richard 1997. Iron, Ironworking, and Regeneration: A Study of the Symbolic Meaning of Metalworking in Iron Age Britain. In *Reconstructing Iron Age Societies*, ed. Adam Gwilt and Colin Haselgrove, pp. 9–18. Oxford: Oxbow.

——— 1999. The Creation of Later Prehistoric Landscapes and the Context of the Reuse of Neolithic and Earlier Bronze Age Monuments in Britain and Ireland. In *Northern Exposure: Interpretative Devolution and the Iron Ages in Britain*, ed. Bill Bevan, pp. 233–51. Leicester: University of Leicester.

Hodder, Ian 1982. *The Present Past: An Introduction to Anthropology for Archaeologists*. New York: Pica Press.

——— 1995. *Theory and Practice in Archaeology*. New York: Routledge.

Hodges, Richard 1982. *Dark Age Economics: The Origins of Towns and Trade A.D. 600–1000*. London: Duckworth.

Hogan, Edmund 1910. *Onomasticon Goedelicum*. Dublin: Hodges, Figgis.

Hope-Taylor, Brian 1977. *Yeavering: An Anglo-British Centre of Early Northumbria*. London: Stationery Office.

Hughes, Monica M. 1985. The Dún Ailinne Glass Finds and Their Importance for Irish Chronology. Unpublished manuscript.

Inventaria Archaeologica 1956. *An Illustrated Card-Inventory of Important Associated Finds on Archaeology*. International Congress of Prehistoric and Protohistoric Sciences. Great Britain, Third Set, ed. M. A. Smith. London: Garraway.

Insoll, Timothy 2004. *Archaeology, Ritual, Religion*. New York: Routledge.

Jackson, Kenneth H. 1964. *The Oldest Irish Tradition: A Window on the Iron Age*. Cambridge: Cambridge University Press.

Jaski, Bart 2000. *Early Irish Kingship and Succession*. Dublin: Four Courts Press.

Johns, Catherine 1997. *The Snettisham Roman Jeweller's Hoard*. London: British Museum Press.

Johnson, Helen Sewell 1968. November Eve Beliefs and Customs in Irish Life and Literature. *Journal of American Folklore* 81:133–42.

Johnston, Susan A. 1989. *Prehistoric Irish Petroglyphs: Their Analysis and Interpretation in Anthropological Context*. Ann Arbor, MI: University Microfilms.

——— 1990. The Neolithic and Bronze Age Activity at Dún Ailinne, Co. Kildare. *Emania* 7:26–31.

——— In press. Revisiting the Irish Royal Sites. *Emania* 20.

Jope, E. M. 1961–62. Iron Age Brooches in Ireland: A Summary. *Ulster Journal of Archaeology* 24–25:25–38.

Jope, E. M., and B. C. S. Wilson 1957. A Burial Group of the First Century A.D. near Donaghadee, Co. Down. *Ulster Journal of Archaeology* 20:96–102.

Keeley, Valerie 1999. Iron Age Discoveries at Ballydavis. In *Laois: History and Society,* ed. Padraig G. Lane and William Nolan, pp. 25–34. Dublin: Geography Publications.

Kenyon, K. M. 1953. Excavations at Sutton Walls, Herefordshire, 1948–1951. *Archaeological Journal* 110: 1–87.

Killanin, Lord, and Michael Duignan 1967. *The Shell Guide to Ireland*. London: Ebury Press & Rainbird.

Klein, Richard G., and Kathryn Cruz-Uribe 1984. *The Analysis of Animal Bones from Archaeological Sites*. Chicago, IL: University of Chicago Press.

Koch, John T. 1994. Windows on the Iron Age: 1964–1994. In *Ulidia*, ed. J. P. Mallory and Gerard Stockman, pp. 229–37. Belfast: December Publications.

Kostrzewski, J. 1919. *Die Ostgermanische Kultur der Spätlatenezeit*. Mannus-Bibliothek 18.

Kromer, K. 1959. *Das Gräberfeld von Hallstatt*.

Florence: Sansoni.

Kvamme, K. 1996. A Proton Magnetometry Survey at Navan Fort. *Emania* 14:65-88.

Lambkin, B. K. 1987. Patrick, Armagh, and Emain Macha. *Emania* 2:29-31.

Larson, Daniel O., and Elizabeth L. Ambos 1997. New Developments in Geophysical Prospecting and Archaeological Research: An Example from the Navan Complex, County Armagh, Northern Ireland. *SAA Bulletin* 15(1): 10-30.

Legge, A. J. 1981. The Agricultural Economy. In *Grimes Graves Excavations 1971-72*, ed. R. Mercer, pp. 79-103. London: Stationery Office.

Liversage, G. D. 1968. Excavations at Dalkey Island, Co. Dublin, 1956-1959. *Proceedings of the Royal Irish Academy* 60C:53-233.

Lowery, P. R., R. D. A. Savage, and R. L. Wilkins 1971. Scriber, Graver, Scorper, Tracer: Notes on Experiments in Bronze-Working Technique. *Proceedings of the Prehistoric Society* 37:167-82.

Lucas, A. T. 1958. Cattle in Ancient Ireland. *O'Connell School Union Record 1938-1958*, pp. 75-86. Dublin: O'Connell School.

——— 1967. National Museum of Ireland: Archaeological Acquisitions in 1964. *Journal of the Royal Society of Antiquaries of Ireland* 97:1-28.

Lynn, Chris J. 1988. Ulster's Oldest Wooden Houses. In *Pieces of the Past*, ed. Anne Hamlin and Chris Lynn, pp. 44-47. Belfast: Stationery Office.

——— 1991. Knockaulin (Dún Ailinne) and Navan: Some Architectural Comparisons. *Emania* 8:51-56.

——— 2000. Navan Fort Site C Excavations, June 1999: Interim Report. *Emania* 18:5-16.

——— 2002. Navan Fort Site C Excavations, May 2000. *Emania* 19:5-18.

——— 2003. *Navan Fort: Archaeology and Myth*. Bray: Wordwell.

Macalister, R. A. S. 1928. *The Archaeology of Ireland*. London: Methuen.

——— 1931. *Tara: A Pagan Sanctuary of Ancient Ireland*. London: Scribner's.

Macalister, R. A. S., and R. Lloyd Praeger 1928. Report on the Excavations of Uisneach. *Proceedings of the Royal Irish Academy* 38C:69-127.

Mackey, J. P. 1992. Christian Past and Primal Present. *Études Celtique* 29:285-97.

MacKie, E. W. 1974. *Dun Mor Vaul: An Iron Age Broch on Tiree*. Glasgow: Glasgow University Press.

MacNeill, Máire 1962. *The Festival of Lughnasa*. London: Oxford University Press.

MacNiocaill, Gearóid 1972. *Ireland Before the Vikings*. Dublin: Gill and Macmillan.

Mallory, J. P. 1981. The Sword of the Ulster Cycle. In *Studies in Early Ireland*, ed. B.G. Scott, pp. 99-114. Dublin: Association of Young Irish Archaeologists.

——— 1988. Trial Excavations at Haughey's Fort. *Emania* 4:5-20.

——— 1991a. Excavations at Haughey's Fort: 1989-1990. *Emania* 8:10-26.

——— 1991b. Further Dates from Haughey's Fort. *Emania* 9:64-65.

——— 1993. The Archaeology of the Irish Dreamtime. *Proceedings of the Harvard Celtic Colloquium* 13:1-24.

——— 1994. The Fort of the Ulster Tales. *Emania* 12:28-38.

——— 1995. Haughey's Fort and the Navan complex in the Late Bronze Age. In *Ireland in the Bronze Age*, ed. J. Waddell and E. Shee Twohig, pp. 73-86. Dublin: Stationery Office.

——— 1997. Review: Armagh and the Royal Centres in Early Medieval Ireland. Monuments, Cosmology and the Past. *Speculum* 72:777-78.

——— 2000. Excavations of the Navan Ditch. *Emania* 18:21-35.

Mallory, J. P., D. M. Brown, and M. G. L. Baillie 1999. Dating Navan Fort. *Antiquity* 73:427-31.

Mallory, J. P., and B. Hartwell 1984. Donegore. *Current Archaeology* 8:271-75.

Mallory, J. P., and C. J. Lynn 2002. Recent Excavations and Speculations on the Navan Complex. *Antiquity* 76:532-41.

Mallory, J. P., D. G. Moore, and L. J. Canning 1996. Excavations at Haughey's Fort 1991 and 1995. *Emania* 14:5-20.

Maryon, H. 1955. *Metalwork and Enamelling: A Practical Treatise on Gold and Silversmith's Work and Their Allied Crafts*. 3rd rev. ed. New York: Dover.

McCone, Kim 1990. *Pagan Past and Christian Present in Early Irish Literature*. Maynooth: An Sagart.

McCormick, Finbar 1983. Dairying and Beef Production in Early Christian Ireland: The Faunal Evidence. In *Landscape Archaeology in Ireland*, ed. F. Hamond and T. Reeves-Smyth, pp. 253-67. Oxford: BAR.

——— 1988. The Animal Bones from Haughey's Fort. *Emania* 4:24-27.

——— 1991. Evidence of Dairying at Dún Ailinne? *Emania* 8:57-59.

——— 1992. Early Faunal Evidence for Dairying. *Oxford Journal of Archaeology* 11(2): 201-9.

——— 1994. Faunal Remains from Navan and Other Late Prehistoric Sites in Ireland. In *Ulidia*, ed. J. P. Mallory and Gerard Stockman, pp. 181-86. Belfast: December Publications.

——— 1997. The Animal Bones from Site B. In *Excavations at Navan Fort 1961-1971 by D. M. Waterman*, ed. C. J. Lynn, pp. 117-20. Belfast: Stationery Office.

——— 2002. Appendix 2: The Animal Bones from Tara. *Discovery Programme Reports, No. 6*, pp. 103-16. Dublin: Royal Irish Academy/Discovery Programme.

McGovern, T. H., et al. 2005. *Zooarchaeology at Landnám: 9th-11th C. Midden Deposits at Sveigakot, N. Iceland*. Norsec 18.

McSparron, Cormac n.d. Excavations at Crossreagh East, Portstewart, Co. Derry. www.northarch.supanet.com/CRE%20Report.htm.

Meduna, J. 1970. Das Keltische Oppidum Staré Hradisko in Mähren. *Germania* 48:34-59.

Meighan, I. G., D. D. A. Simpson, and B. N. Hartwell 2003. Sourcing the Quartz at Newgrange, Brú na Bóinne, Ireland. In *Stones and Bones*, ed. G. Burenhult and S. Westergaard, pp. 247-51. Oxford: Archaeopress.

Minnis, P. E. 1981. Seeds in Archaeological Sites: Sources and Some Interpretive Problems. *American Antiquity* 46:143-52.

Moloney, A. 1993. *Excavations at Clonfinlough, Co. Offaly*. Dublin: Irish Archaeological Wetland Unit Transactions 2.

Moore, Michael J. 1984. Irish Cresset-Stones. *Journal of the Royal Society of Antiquaries of Ireland* 114:98-116.

——— 1997. The Stone and Pottery Lamps. In *Late Viking Age and Medieval Waterford*, ed. M. F. Hurley and O. M. B. Scully, pp. 432-36. Waterford: Waterford Corporation.

Mortimer, J. R. 1905. *Forty Years' Researches in British and Saxon Burial Mounds of East Yorkshire*. London: A. Brown.

Mount, Charles 1995. New Research on Irish Early Bronze Age Cemeteries. In *Ireland in the Bronze Age*, ed. John Waddell and Elizabeth Shee Twohig, pp. 97-112. Dublin: Stationery Office.

Mulhall, Isabella 1998. Irish Early Christian Metal Finger Rings. Master's thesis, Department of Archaeology, University College Dublin.

Mulville, J., J. Bond, and O. Craig 2005. The White Stuff; Milking in the Outer Scottish Isles. In *The Zooarchaeology of Fats, Oils, Milk and Dairying*, ed. J. Mulville and A. K. Outram, pp. 167-82. Oxford: Oxbow.

Munro, Robert 1890. *The Lake-Dwellings of Europe*. London: Cassell.

Munson, Patrick J. 1981. Note on the Use and Misuse of Water-Separation ("Flotation") for the Recovery of Small-Scale Botanical Remains. *Mid-Continental Journal of Archaeology* 6:123-30.

Nagy, Joseph Falaky 1997. *Conversing with Angels and Ancients*. Ithaca, NY: Cornell University Press.

National Folklore Collection, Schools Manuscripts n.d. Schools' Manuscript Collection. On file at Delargy Centre for Irish Folklore, University College Dublin.

Newman, Conor 1993a. Sleeping in Elysium. *Archaeology Ireland* 7(3): 20-23.

——— 1993b. The Show's Not Over until the Fat Lady Sings. *Archaeology Ireland* 7(4): 8-9.

——— 1995. Raffin Fort, Co. Meath: Neolithic and Bronze age Activity. In *Annus Archaeologiae:1992*, ed. E. Grogan and C. Mount, pp. 55-65. Dublin: Organisation Irish Archaeologists.

——— 1997. *Tara: An Archaeological Survey*. Dublin: Discovery Programme.

——— 1998. Reflections on the Making of a 'Royal Site' in Early Ireland. *World Archaeology* 30:127-41.

Ó Catháin, Séamas 1995. *The Festival of Brigit*. Blackrock: DBA.

Ó Corráin, Donnchadh 1972. *Ireland Before the Normans*. Dublin: Gill and Macmillan.

Ó Corráin, Donnchadh, and Fidelma Maguire 1981. *Gaelic Personal Names*. Dublin: Academy Press.

Ó Cróinín, Dáibhí 1995. *Early Medieval Ireland, 400-1200*. New York: Longman.

Ó Floinn, Raghnall 2003. The Newgrange, Co. Meath, 'Shrine' Re-visited. Paper presented at 12th International Congress Celtic Studies, Aberystwyth, August 27.

Ó hUiginn, Ruairí 1988. Crúachu, Connachta, and the Ulster Cycle. *Emania* 5:19-23.

Ó Murchadha, Diarmuid 2002. Carman, Site of Óenach Carmain: A Proposed Location. *Éigse* 33:57-70.

Ó Nualláin, Sean 1972. A Neolithic House at Ballyglass, near Ballycastle, Co. Mayo. *Journal of the Royal Society of Antiquaries of Ireland* 102:49-57.

Ó Riain, Pádraig 1995. Pagan Example and Christian Practice: A Reconsideration. In *Cultural Identity and Cultural Integration: Ireland and Europe in the Early Middle Ages*, ed. Doris Edel, pp. 45-60. Dublin: Four Courts Press.

Ó Ríordáin, Breandán, and John Waddell 1993. *The Funerary Bowls and Vases of the Irish Bronze Age*. Galway: Galway University Press.

Ó Ríordáin, Séan P. 1942. The Excavation of a Large Earth Ring-Fort at Garranes, Co. Cork. *Proceedings of the Royal Irish Academy* 47C:77-150.

—— 1946. Prehistory in Ireland, 1937-1946. *Proceedings of the Prehistoric Society* 6:142-71.

—— 1948. Lough Gur Excavations: Carraig Aille and the "Spectacles." *Proceedings of the Royal Irish Academy* 52C:39-111.

—— 1950. Excavation of Some Earthworks on the Curragh, Co. Kildare. *Proceedings of the Royal Irish Academy* 53C:249-77.

—— 1951. Lough Gur Excavations: The Great Stone Circle (B) in Grange Townland. *Proceedings of the Royal Irish Academy* 554C:37-74.

—— 1953. *Antiquities of the Irish Countryside*. London: Methuen.

—— 1954a. Lough Gur Excavations: Neolithic and Bronze Age Houses on Knockadoon. *Proceedings of the Royal Irish Academy* 56C:297-459.

—— 1954b [1969]. *Tara: The Monuments on the Hill.* Rev. ed. Dundalk: Dundalgan Press.

—— 1955. A Burial with Faience Beads at Tara. *Proceedings of the Prehistoric Society* 21:163-73.

Ó Ríordáin, Seán P., and Glyn Daniel 1964. *New Grange and the Bend of the Boyne*. London: Thames & Hudson.

O'Brien, M. A. 1962. *Corpus Genealogiarum, Hiberniae 1*. Dublin: Dublin Institute for Advanced Studies.

O'Curry, Eugene 1861. *Lectures on the Manuscript Materials of Ancient Irish History*. Dublin: Catholic University.

O'Donovan, John 1837. *Ordnance Survey Letters, Kildare vol. II* (references cited with pagination from original ms.).

O'Kelly, Michael J. 1951. An Early Bronze Age Ring-Fort at Carrigillihy, Co. Cork. *Journal of the Cork Historical and Archaeological Society* 56:69-86.

—— 1989. *Early Ireland: An Introduction to Irish Prehistory*. Cambridge: Cambridge University Press.

O'Kelly, Michael J., R. M. Cleary, and Daragh Lehane 1983. *Newgrange, Co. Meath, Ireland: The Late Neolithic/Beaker Period Settlement*. Oxford: BAR.

Olmstead, Garrett S. 1979. A Contemporary View on Irish 'Hill-Top Enclosures.' *Études Celtiques* 16:171-85.

Pantos, Aliki, and Sarah Semple, eds. 2004. *Assembly Places and Practices in Medieval Europe*. Dublin: Four Courts Press.

Patterson, Nerys 1994. *Cattle Lords and Clansmen: The Social Structure of Early Ireland*. Notre Dame, IN: University of Notre Dame Press.

Payne, S. 1973. Kill-off Patterns in Sheep and Goats: The Mandibles from Aşvan Kale. *Anatolian Studies* 23: 281-303.

—— 1985. Morphological Distinctions between the Mandibular Teeth of Young Sheep, Ovis, and Goats, Capra. *Journal of Archaeological Science* 12: 139-47.

Pič, J. L. 1906. *Le Hradischt de Stradonitz en Bohême*. Leipzig: Karl H. Hiersemann.

Piggott, Stuart 1971-72. Exavation of the Dalladies Long Barrow, Federcairn, Kincardineshire. *Proceedings of the Society of Antiquaries of Scotland* 104:23-47.

Pleiner, Radomír 1993. *The Celtic Sword*. Oxford: Clarendon Press.

Plunkett, T., and G. Coffey 1898. Report on the Excavation of Topped Mountain Cairn. *Proceedings of the Royal Irish Academy* 4C:651-58.

Powell, T. G. E. 1958. *The Celts*. London: Thames & Hudson.

Quilling, F. 1903. *Die Nauheimer Funde der Hallstatt—und Latène—Periods in der Museen zu Frankfurt a. M. und Darmstadt*. Frankfurt: Schirmer & Mahlau.

Quin, E. G., ed. 1998. *Dictionary of the Irish Language: Based Mainly on Old and Middle Irish Materials*. Compact ed. Dublin: Royal Irish Academy.

Raftery, Barry 1969. Freestone Hill: An Iron Age Hillfort and Bronze Age Cairn. *Proceedings of the Royal Irish Academy* 68C:1-108.

——— 1973. Rathgall: A Late Bronze Age Burial in Ireland. *Antiquity* 47:293-95.

——— 1974. A Prehistoric Burial Mound at Baunogenasraid, Co. Carlow. *Proceedings of the Royal Irish Academy* 74C:277-312.

——— 1981. Iron Age Burials in Ireland. In *Irish Antiquity*, ed. Donnchadh Ó Corráin, pp. 173-204. Dublin: Four Courts Press.

——— 1983. *A Catalogue of Irish Iron Age Antiquities*. Marburg: Veröffentlichung des Vorgeschichtlichen Seminars Marburg.

——— 1984. *La Tène in Ireland: Problems of Origin and Chronology*. Marburg: Veröffentlichung des Vorgeschichtlichen Seminars Marburg, Sonderband 2.

——— 1994. *Pagan Celtic Ireland*. New York: Thames & Hudson.

——— 1997. Discussion of Diagnostic Finds. *Excavations at Navan Fort 1961-71, by D. M. Waterman*, ed. Chris Lynn, pp. 90-95. Belfast: Stationery Office.

Raftery, Joseph 1942. Knocknalappa Crannóg, Co. Clare. *North Munster Antiquarian Journal* 3:53-72.

——— 1944. The Turoe Stone and the Rath of Feerwore. *Journal of the Royal Society of Antiquaries of Ireland* 74: 23-52.

——— 1951. *Prehistoric Ireland*. London: Batsford.

——— 1960. A Hoard of the Early Iron Age. *Journal of the Royal Society of Antiquaries of Ireland* 90:2-5.

——— 1961. The Derrinboy Hoard, Co. Offaly. *Journal of the Royal Society of Antiquaries of Ireland* 91:55-58.

——— 1973. National Museum of Ireland: Archaeological Acquisitions in the Year 1970. *Journal of the Royal Society of Antiquaries of Ireland* 103: 177-213.

Ralph, Elizabeth K. 1968. Archaeological Prospecting. *MASCA Newsletter* 4(2): 1-2.

Rangs-Borchling, A. 1963. Das Urnengräberfeld von Hornbeck in Holstein. *Offa-Bücher* 18.

Reitz, E. J., and E. S. Wing 1999. *Zooarchaeology*. Cambridge: Cambridge University Press.

Renfrew, Jane 1973. *Palaeoethnobotany*. New York: Columbia University Press.

Ritchie, J. N. G. 1970-71. Iron Age Finds from Dun an Fheurain Gallanach, Argyll. *Proceedings of the Society of Antiquaries of Scotland* 103:100-12.

Roche, Helen 1999. Late Iron Age Activity at Tara, Co. Meath. *Ríocht na Midhe* 10:18-30.

——— 2002. Excavations at Raith na Ríg, Tara, Co. Meath, 1997. *Discovery Programme Reports No. 6*. Dublin: Royal Irish Academy.

Röder, J. 1948. Der Goloring, ein eisenzeitliches Heiligtum vom Henge-Character im Koberner Wald (Landkreis Koblenz). *Bonner Jahrbücher* 148:81-132.

Royal Irish Academy 1983. *Dictionary of the Irish Language*. Dublin: Royal Irish Academy.

Russell, N. 2004. Milk, Wool, and Traction: Secondary Animal Products. In *Ancient Europe 8000 B.C.-A.D. 1000: Encyclopedia of the Barbarian World*, ed. P. Bogucki and P. Crabtree, pp. 325-33. New York: Scribner's.

Rynne, Etienne 1960. La Tène Sword from Near Lough Gara. *Journal of the Royal Society of Antiquaries of Ireland* 90:12-13.

——— 1976. The La Tène and Roman Finds from Lambay, Co. Dublin: A Reassessment. *Proceedings of the Royal Irish Academy* 76C:231-44.

——— 1981. A Classification of Pre-Viking Irish Iron Swords. In *Studies on Early Ireland*, ed. B. G. Scott, pp. 93-97. Dublin: Association of Young Irish Archaeologists.

——— 1983. Some Early Iron Age Sword-Hilts from Ireland and Scotland. *From the Stone Age to the 'Forty-Five*, ed. A. O'Connor amd D. V. Clarke, pp. 188-96. Edinburgh: John Donald.

Santino, Jack 2004. *Signs of War and Peace: Social Conflict and the Uses of Symbols in Public in Northern Ireland*. New York: Palgrave Macmillan.

Schneiders, Marc 1995. 'Pagan Past and Christian Present' in 'Félire Óengusso.' In *Cultural Identity and Cultural Integration: Ireland and Europe in the Early Middle Ages*, ed. Doris Edel, pp. 157-69. Dublin: Four Courts Press.

Schrijver, Peter In press. Early Irish Ailenn: An Etymology. *Emania*.

Scott, B. G. 1990. *Early Irish Iron Working*. Belfast: Ulster Museum.

Scott, David 1991. *Metallography and Microstructures of Ancient and Historic Metals*. Malibu, CA: Getty Museum.

Selkirk, A., and W. Selkirk 1970. Navan Fort. *Current Archaeology* 22:304-8.

Semple, Sarah 1998. A Fear of the Past: The Place of the Prehistoric Burial Mound in the Ideology of Middle and Later Anglo-Saxon England. *World Archaeology* 30:109-26.

Sharpe, Richard 1982. St. Patrick and the See of Armagh. *Cambridge Medieval Celtic Studies* 4:33-59.

Sheridan, Alison 1993. The Manufacture, Production and Use of Irish Bowls and Vases. In *The Funerary Bowls and Vases of the Irish Bronze Age,* ed. Breandán Ó Ríordáin and John Waddell. pp. 45-75. Galway: Galway University Press.

——— 1995. Irish Neolithic Pottery: The Story in 1995. In *Unbaked Urns of Rudely Shape,* ed. I. Kinnes and G. Varndell, pp. 3-21. Oxford: Oxbow.

——— 2001. Donegore Hill and Other Irish Neolithic Enclosures: A View from Outside. In *Neolithic Enclosures in Altantic Northwest Europe,* ed. Timothy Darvill and Julian Thomas, pp. 171-89. Oxford: Oxbow.

Sheridan, Alison, Gabriel Cooney, and Eoin Grogan 1992. Stone Axe Studies in Ireland. *Proceedings of the Prehistoric Society* 58:389-416.

Sheridan, Alison, and Mary Davis 1998. The Welsh "Jet Set" in Prehistory: A Case of Keeping up with the Joneses? In *Prehistoric Ritual and Religion,* ed. Alex Gibson and Derek Simpson, pp. 148-62. Sutton, England: Phoenix Mills.

Silver, I. A. 1969. The Ageing of Domestic Animals. In *Science in Archaeology,* 2nd ed., ed. Don Brothwell and Eric Higgs, pp. 283-302. London: Thames & Hudson.

Simpson, D. D. A. 1968. Food Vessels: Associations and Chronology. In *Studies in Ancient Europe,* ed. J.M. Coles and D. D.A. Simpson, pp. 197-211. Bristol: Leicester University Press.

——— 1989. Neolithic Navan? *Emania* 6:31-33.

Simpson, D. D. A., and J. E. Thawley 1972. Single Grave Art in Britain. *Scottish Archaeological Forum* 4:81-104.

Simpson, M. 1968. Massive Armlets in the North British Iron Age. In *Studies in Ancient Europe,* ed. J.M. Coles and D. D.A. Simpson, pp. 233-54. Leicester: University Leicester Press.

Smith, R. A. 1927. Pre-Roman Remains at Scarborough. *Archaeologia* 77:179-200.

Smyth, Alfred P. 1982. *Celtic Leinster*. Dublin: Irish Academic Press.

St. George Gray, Harold, and Arthur Bulleid 1953. *The Meare Lake Village, Vol. II*. Taunton Castle: Private printing.

St. George Gray, Harold, and M. Aylwin Cotton 1966. *The Meare Lake Village, Vol. III*. Taunton Castle: Private printing.

Stead, I. 1979. *The Arras Culture*. York: Yorkshire Philosophical Society.

Stokes, Whitley 1894-95. The Prose Tales in the Rennes Dindsenchas. *Revue Celtique* 15:272-336, 418-84; 16:31-83, 135-67, 269-312.

Stout, Geraldine 1991. Embanked Enclosures of the Boyne Region. *Proceedings of the Royal Irish Academy* 91C:245-84.

Streuver, S. 1968. Flotation Techniques for the Recovery of Small-Scale Archaeological Remains. *American Antiquity* 33(3): 353-62.

Stuckenrath, R., and J. E. Mielke 1973. Smithsonian Institute Radiocarbon Measurements 8. *Radiocarbon* 15 (2388): 424.

Stuiver, M., P. J. Reimer, and R. W. Reimer 2005. CALIB 5.0 http://radiocarbon.pa.qub.ac.uk/calib/.

Sweetman, P. David 1987. Excavation of a Late Neolithic/Early Bronze Age Site at Newgrange, Co. Meath. *Proceedings of the Royal Irish Academy* 87C: 283-98.

Sweetman, P. D. 1976. An Earthen Enclosure at Monknewtown, Slane. *Proceedings of the Royal Irish Academy* 76C:25-73.

Swift, Cathy J. 1997. Review Article, Tara: A Select Bibliography. *Riocht na Midhe* 9(3): 12-27.

Taylor, J. J. 1980. *Bronze Age Goldwork of the British Isles*. Cambridge: Cambridge University Press.

Turner, Victor W. 1969. *The Ritual Process*. Chicago, IL: Aldine.

Twohig, Elizabeth Shee 1981. *The Megalithic Art of Western Europe*. Oxford: Clarendon Press.

Tylecote, R. F., and R. Thomsen 1973. The Segregation and Surface-Enrichment of Arsenic and Phosphorus in Early Iron Artifacts. *Archaeom-*

etry 15(2): 193-98.

Von den Driesch, Angela 1976. *A Guide to the Measurement of Animal Bones from Archaeological Sites.* Cambridge, MA: Peabody Museum of Harvard University.

Von den Driesch, Angela, and J. Boessneck 1974. Kritische Anmerkungen zur Widderisthöhenberechnung aus Längenmassen vor- und frühgeschichtlicher Tierknocken. *Säugetierkundliche Mitteilungen* 22:325-48.

Waddell, John 1983. Rathcrogan—A Royal Site in Connacht. *Journal of Irish Archaeology* 1:21-46.

——— 1988a. Excavation at 'Dathi's Mound', Rathcrogan, Co. Roscommon. *Journal of Irish Archaeology* 1:21-46.

——— 1988b. Rathcroghan in Connacht. *Emania* 5:5-18.

——— 1990. *The Bronze Age Burials of Ireland.* Galway: Galway University Press.

——— 2000. *The Prehistoric Archaeology of Ireland.* Dublin: Wordwell.

Waddell, John, and Kevin Barton 1997. Seeing Beneath Rathcroghan. *Archaeology Ireland* 9(1): 38-40.

Wailes, Bernard 1970. Excavations at Dún Ailinne, Co. Kildare. *Journal of the Royal Society of Antiquaries of Ireland* 100:79-90.

——— 1971. Excavation at Dún Ailinne, near Kilcullen, 1971. *Journal of the County Kildare Archaeological Society* 15(1): 5-11.

——— 1973. Excavation at Dún Ailinne, near Kilcullen, 1973. *Journal of the County Kildare Archaeological Society* 15(3): 234-42.

——— 1974. Excavation at Dún Ailinne, near Kilcullen, 1974. *Journal of the County Kildare Archaeological Society* 15(4): 345-58.

——— 1976. Dún Ailinne: An Interim Report. In *Hillforts: Later Prehistoric Earthworks in Britain and Ireland,* ed. D. W. Harding, pp. 319-38. New York: Academic Press.

——— 1982. The Irish 'Royal Sites' in History and Archaeology. *Cambridge Medieval Celtic Studies* 3:1-29.

——— 1990. Dún Ailinne: A Summary Excavation Report. *Emania* 7:10-21.

——— 2004. Iron Age Ireland. In *Ancient Europe: Encyclopedia of the Barbarian World 8000 B.C.-A.D. 1000,* ed. P. Bogucki and P. J. Crabtree, pp. 232-39. New York: Scribner's.

Wainwright, F. T. 1963. *The Souterrains of Southern Pictland.* London: Routledge and Kegan Paul.

Wainwright, G. 1979. *Gussage All Saints: An Iron Age Settlement in Dorset.* Department of Environment Archaeological Reports No. 10. London: Stationery Office.

Wait, Gerald A. 1985. *Ritual and Religion in Iron Age Britain.* Oxford: BAR.

Wakeman, W. F. 1883. Untitled Paper on the Excavation of the Crannog at Lisnacrogher, near Broughshane, Co. Antrim. *Journal of the Royal Society of Antiquaries of Ireland* 4:375-406.

——— 1884. On the Trouvaille, of Which the Exhibits Formed a Portion, from the Crannog at Lisnacroghera, near Broughshane, Co. Antrim. *Journal of the Royal Society of Antiquaries of Ireland* 16:375-406.

——— 1889. On the Crannog and Antiquities of Lisnacroghera, near Broughshane, Co. Antrim (second notice). *Journal of the Royal Society of Antiquaries of Ireland* 19:96-106.

——— 1891. On the Crannog and Antiquities of Lisnacroghera, near Broughshane, Co. Antrim (third and fourth notice). *Journal of the Royal Society of Antiquaries of Ireland* 21:542-45, 673-75.

Warner, Richard B. 1976. Some Observations on the Context and Importation of Exotic Material in Ireland from the First Century B.C. to the Second Century A.D. *Proceedings of the Royal Irish Academy* 76C:267-92.

——— 1986. Preliminary Schedule of Sites and Stray Finds in the Navan Complex. *Emania* 1:5-9.

——— 1988. The Archaeology of Early Historic Irish Kingship. In *Power and Politics in Early Medieval Britain and Ireland,* ed. Stephen T. Driscoll and Margaret R. Nieke, pp. 47-68. Edinburgh: Edinburgh University Press.

———1991. Cultural Intrusions in the Early Iron Age: Some Notes. *Emania* 9:44-52.

——— 1994a. On Crannogs and Kings (Part 1). *Ulster Journal of Archaeology* 57:61-69.

——— 1994b. The 'Ernean' House. *Emania* 12:21-27.

——— 1994c. The Navan Complex: A New Schedule of Sites and Finds. *Emania* 12:39-44.

——— 1995. Tuathal Techtmar: A Myth or Ancient

Literary Evidence for a Roman Invasion? *Emania* 13:23-32.

——— 2000. Keeping Out the Otherworld: The Internal Ditch at Navan and Other Iron Age "Hengiform" Enclosures. *Emania* 18:39-44.

Warner, Richard B., and I. G. Meighan 1981. Dating Irish Glass Beads by Chemical Analysis. In *Irish Antiquity*, ed. Donnchadh Ó Corráin, pp. 52-66. Dublin: Four Courts Press.

Warner, Richard B., J. P. Mallory, and M. G. L. Baillie 1990. Irish Early Iron Age Sites: A Provisional Map of Absolute Dated Sites. *Emania* 7:46-50.

Waterman, D. M. 1963. A Neolithic and Dark Age Site at Langford Lodge, Co. Antrim. *Ulster Journal of Archaeology* 26:43-54.

——— 1997. *Excavations at Navan Fort 1961-71*. Belfast: Stationery Office.

Watkins, Calvert 2000. *The American Heritage Dictionary of Indo-European Roots*, 2nd ed. Boston, MA: Houghton Mifflin.

Webster, G. 1965. Further Investigations of the Site of the Roman Fort at Waddon Hill, Stoke Abbott, 1960-62. *Proceedings of the Dorset Natural History and Archaeological Society* 86:135-49.

Webster, Jane 1995. Sanctuaries and Sacred Places. In *The Celtic World*, ed. Miranda J. Green, pp. 445-64. New York: Routledge.

Weir, David A. 1989. A Radiocarbon Date from the Navan Fort Ditch. *Emania* 6:34-35.

Wells, Peter S. 2001. *Beyond Celts, Germans and Scythians*. London: Duckworth.

Werner, J. 1961. Bemerkungen zu nordischem Trachtzubehör und zu Fernhandelsbeziehungen der Spätlatenezeit im Salzburger Land. *Mittelungen Gesellschaft für Salzburger Landeskunde* 101:143-60.

Wheeler, R. E. M. 1931. Prehistoric Scarborough. In *The History of Scarborough*, ed. A. Rowntree, pp. 11-33. London: Dent.

Whittaker, John C. 1994. *Flintknapping: Making and Understanding Stone Tools*. Austin, TX: University of Texas Press.

Wild, J. P. 1970. Button-and-Loop Fasteners in the Roman Provinces. *Britannia* 1:137-55.

Wilde, W. R. 1862. *A Descriptive Catalogue of the Antiquities of Gold in the Museum of the Royal Irish Academy*. Dublin: Hodges, Smith.

Williams, B. B. 1986. Excavations at Altanagh, Co. Tyrone. *Ulster Journal of Archaeology* 49:33-88.

Willmot, G. F. 1938. Three Burial Sites at Carbury, Co. Kildare. *Journal of the Royal Society of Antiquaries of Ireland* 68:130-42.

Woodman, Peter C. 1967. A Flint Hoard from Killybeg. *Ulster Journal of Archaeology* 30:8-14.

——— 1987. The Impact of Resource Availability on Lithic Industrial Traditions in Prehistoric Ireland. In *Mesolithic Northwest Europe: Recent Trends*, ed. P. Rowley-Conwy, Marek Zvelebil, and H. P. Blankholm, pp. 138-46. Sheffield: Dept. Archaeology and Prehistory, Sheffield University.

——— 1988. The Archaeological Importance of Flint Sources in Munster. *Journal of the Cork Historical and Archaeological Society* 93:66-72.

——— 2004. Mount Sandel. In *Ancient Europe 8000 B.C. - 1000 A.D.: Encyclopedia of the Barbarian World*, ed. P. I. Bogucki and P. J. Crabtree, pp. 151-53. New York: Scribner's.

Woodman, Peter, and Máiréad Scannell 1993. A Context for the Lough Gur Lithics. In *Past Perceptions: The Prehistoric Archaeology of South-West Ireland*, ed. Elizabeth Shee Twohig and Margaret Ronayne, pp. 53-173. Cork: Cork University Press.

Wood-Martin, W. G. 1886. *Lake Dwellings of Ireland*. Dublin: Hodges, Figgis.

Zeder, M. A., and B. C. Hesse 2000. The Initial Domestication of Goats (*Capra hircus*) in the Zagros Mountains 10,000 Years Ago. *Science* 287(5461): 2,254-57.

Contributors

Douglas V. Campana is Research Associate, Anthropology Department, New York University, New York, NY.

Pam J. Crabtree is Associate Professor of Anthropology, Center for the Study of Human Origins, New York University, New York, NY.

Genevieve Fisher is Registrar, Peabody Museum of Archaeology and Ethnology, Harvard University, Cambridge, MA.

Elizabeth G. Hamilton is a Research Assistant, University of Pennsylvania Museum of Archaeology and Anthropology, Philadelphia, PA.

Ronald Hicks is Professor of Anthropology, Ball State University, Muncie, IN.

Susan A. Johnston is an Associate Professorial Lecturer at George Washington University.

Katherine Moreau is an Independent Researcher, New York, NY.

Bernard Wailes is Professor Emeritus of Anthropology at the University of Pennsylvania and Curator Emeritus of the European Section of the University of Pennsylvania Museum of Archaeology and Anthropology.

Index

Ailbe 184, 186-89
Aillenn xxv, 184-86
animal bones. *See* faunal remains
antler 43, 83, 130, 159
artifacts
    discarded 41-42, 45, 172
    missing 39, 41-45, 93, 115, 130, 157, 171-72
assembly sites xxv, 186-87, 189-95, 199-200, 204
astronomy 191

bank. *See* enclosure
beads
    amber 38, 116-19, 135, 137, 139-41, 178
    glass xxvi, xxviii, 9, 38, 44, 111-12, 115-23,
        140, 178, 181, 195, 202
    modern 138, 172-73
    stone 11, 35-36, 38, 39, 73, 74-76, 134-35,
        137-42, 177
Beltane xxix
Blue 10-12, 19-20, 32-33, 36
bone, worked/boneworking xxviii, 43, 125-31, 141,
    167, 191, 205
    needle 94, 125, 131, 167, 205
    pin 58, 83, 127, 131, 167
botanical remains 41, 155-56, 191
    seasonality 156
Brigit 185, 189-92, 194, 204
Bronze Age
    artifacts xxvii, 38-39, 177-78
    features 11-12, 38
Carbury Hill 183, 186, 189, 193

Carman 184-87, 189-91, 194, 206
Cashel 88-89, 188, 195, 199
ceramics 75, 79-80
    Bronze Age 162
    Neolithic 35, 36, 38, 46, 73-74, 77-81, 83, 177,
        201, 210
chert
    cores 38, 61-62, 64
    flakes 48, 63-66
    natural fragments 45
    projectile points 52-54
chevaux-de-frise 4, 27-28
chronology
    Iron Age 178
    Neolithic 177
    radiocarbon age-determinations xxiv, 29, 123,
        178-80, 182
    thermoluminescence 42, 177-78
clay
    balls 135-37
    pin 83
copper alloy
    bracelets 101, 105
    casting jets 109-10, 122, 205
    fastener 110-11
    fibulae 101
    ingots 109-10, 205
    metallographic analysis 148-52
    pins 101-6
    spiral rings 101, 106-8
    tracer 108-9, 122, 205

cresset lamp 171-73
Crimson xxviii, 17, 19-20, 22-24, 31-33, 37, 47, 69, 83, 140-41, 158-59, 163
Cruachain xxi, xxv, 68, 195, 202. *See also* Rathcroghan
cupmarked stone 82, 133, 177, 201
Curragh, The 183-84, 187-89, 191-94

Dindshenchas 184-90, 193-94
ditch. *See* enclosure
Dun 17, 19-25, 141, 143

Emain Macha xxi, xxv, 68, 184-85, 187-89, 191, 194, 202. S*ee also* Navan Fort
embankment, Dún Ailinne xxviii, 1, 4, 11, 17, 69, 172, 183, 187
enclosure
    bank xxv, 1, 3, 181-82, 187-88, 196, 198, 200, 203, 207
    ditch xxv, 1, 3, 67, 182, 187, 196-98, 200-201, 203, 207
Eochaid xxii, 186-87, 189, 193

faunal remains 21, 32, 67, 125, 157-59, 161-62, 168-69
    bone working 125, 129, 131, 167-68
    butchery 131, 157-58, 165-67, 169
    cattle 36, 125, 128-29, 131, 141, 159-69, 189
    dairying 167-68
    dog 159-60, 167, 169
    horse 126, 128, 130-31, 159, 164-67
    pig 36, 125, 129, 159-60, 163, 165-67, 169
    sheep 159, 161, 163-65, 167
feature
    feature 42 (Mauve) xxviii, 11, 16-20, 22-25, 198, 207, 209
    feature 60 (Rose) 13
    feature 281 (Tan) 11, 13
    feature 293 (Tan) 11
    feature 512 (White) 13
    feature 513 (Rose) 14-15
    feature 514 (Rose) 14, 180
    feature 515 (Mauve) 180
    feature 516 (Mauve) 180
    feature 2302 (White) 13, 209
    feature 2506 (Tan) 11, 35
    feature 2780 (Khaki) 12
    feature 2935 21
    numbering of 31-44
    summary of 31-44
"Félire nÓengusso" 202
festivals 185, 189-92, 194
figure-of-eight structures 195, 197-99
    Navan Fort xxix, 197
    Rose xxvii, 197-98, 207, 209
Fionn Mac Cumhail 133, 184, 186
Flame xxviii, 17, 19-23, 25, 32, 37, 40, 44, 46-48, 69, 73-74, 76, 82, 89-90, 92, 94-95, 101, 103-4, 115, 134-36, 138, 141, 145, 149-50, 152, 154, 157, 159, 161, 164, 168-69, 203, 206, 209
flint
    cores 61-62, 64, 68-69
    flakes xxvii, 4, 9, 35, 38, 48, 63-69
    hollow scrapers 45, 48, 54, 56-58, 61, 67-69
    implements 42, 45, 48-49, 53-57, 59-69
    natural fragments 42, 45
    projectile points 11, 38, 53-54, 61
    raw material 66-67
    round scrapers 45, 48, 54-55, 57, 59, 68
    straight scrapers 48, 54, 56, 68
floral remains 155-56
folklore 133, 183, 189
food vessel xxvii, 12, 24, 38, 50-51, 71, 81-83, 112-13, 116, 133, 177, 179, 181, 202

geophysical survey 4-5, 197
glass 39, 41-42, 44, 115-17, 171, 174, 210
    bracelets xxi, 44, 115, 117, 120, 122-23, 178, 195
    toggles 40, 94, 115-17, 120-23, 142, 178, 205
    working 117, 121-22, 142, 205-6
gold strip 102, 113
Goloring 200
Grey 17, 31

"Hail Brigit" 202, 204
Harry 6, 17, 19, 22-23, 31, 73, 207
Henge xxix, 1, 3, 27, 68, 181, 184, 186-89, 192-93, 196, 199
Hill of Allen (Almu) 133, 183-84, 186, 189, 193-94

Imbolc 190-92
inner roadway 13, 28-30, 210
iron
    artifact counts 39
    binding strips 87-88, 90-91
    blades 86-89, 91-92, 96-98, 102, 177, 205

finger ring 86-88, 92, 97
metallographic analysis 153-55
needles 86-88, 93-94, 96, 205
preservation xx, 87-88, 94, 96-97
spearhead 87-90, 153-55, 177
sword xxviii, 41, 87-90, 178, 181, 200, 203
tools 39-40, 96-97, 205

Jade 11, 19-20, 22-23, 31, 39, 145, 159, 207

Khaki 11-12, 36, 47

Lemon 16
Linkardstown
    Vessel 11, 73-74, 76, 80, 82, 177, 201
    burial xxvii, 34-35, 37, 71, 76, 80, 82, 135, 137, 139-40, 197
lignite xx, 39, 134-35
    bracelet 134-35
    pendant 134-35
low mound (Dún Ailinne) 1, 4, 6, 11, 17, 19-25, 39, 73, 83, 101, 115, 134, 181
Lower Emerald xxviii, 11, 17, 19-24, 73, 101, 141, 151, 159, 181
Lugh 185-86, 190, 193
Lughnasa 185-86, 188-94

Macha xxi, xxv, 68, 184-89, 191, 194-95, 202
magnetometer survey xxvi, 4
manufacturing xxviii, xxix, 24, 40, 62, 78, 94, 97, 101, 110, 16, 122-23, 142, 205-6
    bone waste 129, 205
    glass waste 121-22
Mauve
    entrance xxvii, 21-25, 203
    features 16, 18, 22-24, 31
    palisade xxvii-viii, 14, 19-24, 88, 142, 197, 203, 207, 209
    phase xxvii-viii, 6, 11, 16-17, 19, 24-25, 37, 40, 46, 86, 95, 101, 133, 136, 141, 145, 151, 154, 178, 181, 193, 206-7
    reconstruction 19, 200
    timber circle 18, 20, 24, 200, 203, 207
Medb 185-86, 191
Medieval artifacts 32, 37, 171-73
modern objects 41, 42, 171-73
    beads 119, 173
    coins 172
myth 183-85, 187, 193

Naas 184-86, 189
Navan Fort, Co. Armagh xix, xxv, 102, 140-41, 160, 185, 204. *See also* Emain Macha
Neolithic
    artifacts xix-xx, xxvii, 9, 11, 13, 35-38, 68, 73, 201
    features xxviii, 12-13, 31, 34-35, 46, 66, 76, 201
    site parallels 68-69, 80, 137, 199-200
Niamh 11, 19-20, 22-23, 159, 207

O'Donovan, John xxv, xxviii, 2, 4
oenach (*pl.* oinage, óenaige) 186-90, 193-94, 199, 206
outer roadway 28-30, 182, 210

palisades xxvii-xxviii, 13-15, 17, 20-21, 23, 25, 27, 198, 203, 207-8
phase, definition of 6
plant remains. *See* botanical remains
post-holes 11, 13-18, 21-24, 28, 31-34, 36-39, 42, 46, 69, 73, 81, 104, 158, 181, 206-9
pre-Niamh 11, 19-20, 22-23

quartz
    flakes 63-66
    implements 48-49, 54, 59
    natural fragments 45

radiocarbon dating xxix, 89, 182, 190, 196
    age-determinations 11, 12, 22, 29, 76, 83, 123, 179
    samples xxvii, 178
Raffin Fort 195, 199
Ráith na Ríg 3, 28, 160, 167, 169, 197
Rathcroghan, Co. Roscommon xxi, xxix, 3-4, 25, 173, 196-98. *See also* Cruachain
resistivity survey xxvi, 4
ritual
    economic 191, 194, 204-6
    landscape 188-89
    political 25, 204-6
    religious xxix, 184, 191, 202-4, 206
Rose
    annex 14-15, 112
    entrance xxvii, 11, 13-16, 30, 210
    features 13-17, 31, 39
    palisade xxvii, 11, 13-17, 22, 197, 208-9
    phase xxvii, 24-25, 30, 37, 40, 46-47, 86, 92, 95, 101, 115, 135-36, 143, 145, 169, 181, 193,

198, 200, 203-4, 207
reconstruction 14, 16-17
royal sites xix, xxv, xxix, 3, 25, 68-69, 80, 91, 102,
    122, 160, 168-69, 173, 181-82, 184-89, 193-200,
    202-5, 209. *See also* individual names
        characteristics 188, 196-97, 199, 203
        chronology 122, 182, 196

Samhain xxix, 185, 190-92
site entrance
    causeway 28-29
    construction 13
    excavation 6-7, 27-29
    original 4, 16, 27-28
    survey 28
slag
    analysis 145-47
    distribution 145
spearhead 87-90, 153-55, 177
spindle whorls
    bone 125, 131, 167, 205
    stone 141-42, 205
stake-holes 6-7, 9, 13-16, 21, 29, 33, 35, 69, 104,
    206, 209
        Harry 19-20, 22, 31, 39, 207
        Jade 20, 22, 31, 39, 207
        Niamh 20, 22, 207
stone
    axes xxvii, 36, 38-39, 45, 57, 69-71, 82, 177

miscellaneous objects 133-35, 143
whetstone 142
summit, excavation of xxvii, 4-9, 15, 21, 29
sword, possible uses 41, 89, 200, 203

Tan
    features 11, 31, 35-36
    phase xxvii, 37, 46, 73, 136
Tara, Co. Meath xix, xxi, xxv, xxix, 3-4, 25, 28, 68,
    80, 120, 121-22, 159-160, 165, 167, 169, 173,
    184-85, 188, 190, 195-98, 204, 206
temples, Iron Age 200, 203
timber structures
    Mauve xxix, 6, 22-23, 31, 39-40, 47, 88-89, 95,
        104, 115, 134, 143, 145, 169, 200
    Rose xxix, 22, 31, 39-40, 47, 92, 95, 115, 145,
        169, 181, 200
    White xxix, 22, 31, 40, 169

Uaininn 31
Uisneach 93, 193, 199
Upper Emerald xxviii, 17, 19-24, 40, 101, 134-36,
    142, 151

whetstone 127, 142
White
    palisade 12-13, 22, 197
    phase xxvii, 13, 22, 24, 31, 37, 86, 203, 209